The discovery and conquest of the Molucco and Philippine Islands. Containing, their history, ancient and modern, ... Written in Spanish by Bartholomew Leonardo de Argensola, ... Now translated into English: and illustrated ...

Bartolomé Leonardo y Argensola

Eighteenth Century
Collections Online
Print Editions

Gale ECCO Print Editions

Relive history with *Eighteenth Century Collections Online*, now available in print for the independent historian and collector. This series includes the most significant English-language and foreign-language works printed in Great Britain during the eighteenth century, and is organized in seven different subject areas including literature and language; medicine, science, and technology; and religion and philosophy. The collection also includes thousands of important works from the Americas.

The eighteenth century has been called "The Age of Enlightenment." It was a period of rapid advance in print culture and publishing, in world exploration, and in the rapid growth of science and technology – all of which had a profound impact on the political and cultural landscape. At the end of the century the American Revolution, French Revolution and Industrial Revolution, perhaps three of the most significant events in modern history, set in motion developments that eventually dominated world political, economic, and social life.

In a groundbreaking effort, Gale initiated a revolution of its own: digitization of epic proportions to preserve these invaluable works in the largest online archive of its kind. Contributions from major world libraries constitute over 175,000 original printed works. Scanned images of the actual pages, rather than transcriptions, recreate the works *as they first appeared.*

Now for the first time, these high-quality digital scans of original works are available via print-on-demand, making them readily accessible to libraries, students, independent scholars, and readers of all ages.

For our initial release we have created seven robust collections to form one the world's most comprehensive catalogs of 18ᵗʰ century works.

Initial Gale ECCO Print Editions collections include:

History and Geography
Rich in titles on English life and social history, this collection spans the world as it was known to eighteenth-century historians and explorers. Titles include a wealth of travel accounts and diaries, histories of nations from throughout the world, and maps and charts of a world that was still being discovered. Students of the War of American Independence will find fascinating accounts from the British side of conflict.

Social Science

Delve into what it was like to live during the eighteenth century by reading the first-hand accounts of everyday people, including city dwellers and farmers, businessmen and bankers, artisans and merchants, artists and their patrons, politicians and their constituents. Original texts make the American, French, and Industrial revolutions vividly contemporary.

Medicine, Science and Technology

Medical theory and practice of the 1700s developed rapidly, as is evidenced by the extensive collection, which includes descriptions of diseases, their conditions, and treatments. Books on science and technology, agriculture, military technology, natural philosophy, even cookbooks, are all contained here.

Literature and Language

Western literary study flows out of eighteenth-century works by Alexander Pope, Daniel Defoe, Henry Fielding, Frances Burney, Denis Diderot, Johann Gottfried Herder, Johann Wolfgang von Goethe, and others. Experience the birth of the modern novel, or compare the development of language using dictionaries and grammar discourses.

Religion and Philosophy

The Age of Enlightenment profoundly enriched religious and philosophical understanding and continues to influence present-day thinking. Works collected here include masterpieces by David Hume, Immanuel Kant, and Jean-Jacques Rousseau, as well as religious sermons and moral debates on the issues of the day, such as the slave trade. The Age of Reason saw conflict between Protestantism and Catholicism transformed into one between faith and logic -- a debate that continues in the twenty-first century.

Law and Reference

This collection reveals the history of English common law and Empire law in a vastly changing world of British expansion. Dominating the legal field is the *Commentaries of the Law of England* by Sir William Blackstone, which first appeared in 1765. Reference works such as almanacs and catalogues continue to educate us by revealing the day-to-day workings of society.

Fine Arts

The eighteenth-century fascination with Greek and Roman antiquity followed the systematic excavation of the ruins at Pompeii and Herculaneum in southern Italy; and after 1750 a neoclassical style dominated all artistic fields. The titles here trace developments in mostly English-language works on painting, sculpture, architecture, music, theater, and other disciplines. Instructional works on musical instruments, catalogs of art objects, comic operas, and more are also included.

The BiblioLife Network

This project was made possible in part by the BiblioLife Network (BLN), a project aimed at addressing some of the huge challenges facing book preservationists around the world. The BLN includes libraries, library networks, archives, subject matter experts, online communities and library service providers. We believe every book ever published should be available as a high-quality print reproduction; printed on-demand anywhere in the world. This insures the ongoing accessibility of the content and helps generate sustainable revenue for the libraries and organizations that work to preserve these important materials.

The following book is in the "public domain" and represents an authentic reproduction of the text as printed by the original publisher. While we have attempted to accurately maintain the integrity of the original work, there are sometimes problems with the original work or the micro-film from which the books were digitized. This can result in minor errors in reproduction. Possible imperfections include missing and blurred pages, poor pictures, markings and other reproduction issues beyond our control. Because this work is culturally important, we have made it available as part of our commitment to protecting, preserving, and promoting the world's literature.

GUIDE TO FOLD-OUTS MAPS and OVERSIZED IMAGES

The book you are reading was digitized from microfilm captured over the past thirty to forty years. Years after the creation of the original microfilm, the book was converted to digital files and made available in an online database.

In an online database, page images do not need to conform to the size restrictions found in a printed book. When converting these images back into a printed bound book, the page sizes are standardized in ways that maintain the detail of the original. For large images, such as fold-out maps, the original page image is split into two or more pages

Guidelines used to determine how to split the page image follows:

• Some images are split vertically; large images require vertical and horizontal splits.
• For horizontal splits, the content is split left to right.
• For vertical splits, the content is split from top to bottom.
• For both vertical and horizontal splits, the image is processed from top left to bottom right.

THE
DISCOVERY
AND
CONQUEST

OF THE

MOLUCCO and PHILIPPINE Iſlands.

CONTAINING,

Their Hiſtory, Ancient and Modern, Natural and Political: Their Deſcription, Pro- duct, Religion, Government, Laws, Languages, Cuſtoms, Manners, Habits, Shape, and Inclina- tions of the Natives. With an Account of many other adjacent Iſlands, and ſeveral remarkable Voyages through the *Streights* of *Magellan,* and in other Parts.

Written in Spaniſh *by* Bartholomew Leonardo de Argenſola, *Chaplain to the Empreſs, and Rector of* Villahermoſa.

Now Tranſlated into Engliſh: *And Illuſtrated with a Map and ſeveral Cuts.*

LONDON, Printed in the Year, 1708.

THE
PREFACE.

*O*UR *Author,* Bartholomew Leonardo de Argensola, *was a Learned Clergyman, and as such employ'd by the President and Council of the Indies to Write this History. He calls it,* The Conquest of the Molucco *Islands, without Enlarging any further in his Title, tho' at the same time his Work contains their first Discovery, their Description, the Manners, Customs, Religion, Habit, and Political and Natural History, with all the Wars, and o-ther Remarkable Accidents in those Parts, since they were first known to* Europeans, *till their Reduction under the Crown of* Spain. *In Speaking of them he Occasionally runs out to give the same Account of the* Philippine *Islands, and of several others in those Eastern Seas. This is frequent in* Spanish *Books, wherein we generally find much more than the Titles promise, contrary to what is Practis'd with us, who strive to fill up a Title Page with abundance of Inviting Heads, the least part whereof is Treated of in the Body of the Work, or at best so Superficially, that scarce any more can be made of them there, than was in the Frontispiece.*

For the Compiling of this Work the Author, being Employ'd by the Au-thority abovemention'd, had the Command of all Authentick Manuscript Relations, which were either in the Kings Custody, or in Private Hands; besides the Testimony of such Persons then Living, as had been Eye-Witnesses to any part of what he delivers. His Design was only to Write the Conquest of those Islands, by King Philip *the Third of* Spain; *but considering how few were acquainted with them, and that of Consequence most Readers would be at a loss to know where, or what these* Moluccos *were, he Judiciously Re-solv'd to bring down his History from its proper Source. To this End he begins with the Antient, and Fabulous Original of their Kings; then comes to the Discovery of them by* Europeans, *and proceeds to the Wars between them, and with the Natives, for the Possession of those so much coveted Do-minions.*

His

His Description of them is very Exact; That of the Cloves, their principal Commodity, no less Curious; and that of the other Product and Animals, Inferior to neither. The Wars carrying him over from one Place to another; he gives a short Account of the Islands Papúas, and that of Celebes. The Spaniards, to avoid passing through the Portuguese Sea, attempted to settle Trade at the Moluccos, by the way of the Streights of Magellan, which gives occasion to Argensola to entertain us with a particular Account of the Spanish Fleet sent into the said Streight, under the Admiral Sarmiento, which has been hitherto very Imperfectly Deliver'd in English, tho' very Remarkable, and full of Surprizing Accidents. In short, not to stretch out this Preface, with the Subject of the Work, we shall find in it a brief Description of the Island Sumatra; of the vast Empire of China; of all the Philippine Islands, and those of Ceylon, Banda, Java, and many others of less Note. Nor does he omit to speak of the Dutch Voyages; and Undertakings of Sir Francis Drake, and other English Adventurers; and Embellishes the whole with such variety of pleasing Incidents, that few Books of Travels afford so much Profitable Entertainment, with such good Authority.

No Author ever had a better Reputation, among all that Understand, and have had the good Fortune to Meet with him; for being so Valuable, he is extraordinary Scarce, rare to be met with in Spain, and consequently much more in England. This may perhaps be the main Reason why he has not yet been Translated, and being so Valuable, he cannot miss of that Reception which he has found in the Original. But it is not intended to prepossess the Reader, who is left to make his own Judgment, and therefore a long Preface is designedly avoided, that he may the sooner enter upon so Useful and Diverting a Work. It is not improper, nevertheless, to Advise the Reader not to take notice of some Reflections in Point of Religion, and in other Cases, considering the Book was Writ by a Spaniard, and that it was not proper to Omit, or Alter any thing, where a Fair, and Entire Translation is promised. Besides, That these are very few, and inconsiderable, and consequently not worth observing, as indeed the generality of Judicious Readers will be sufficiently satisfy'd, and this Caution is given for their Sake, whom perhaps Passion, or overmuch Zeal may move to condemn a Work on such an Occasion, when they can find no other matter to Carp at.

THE

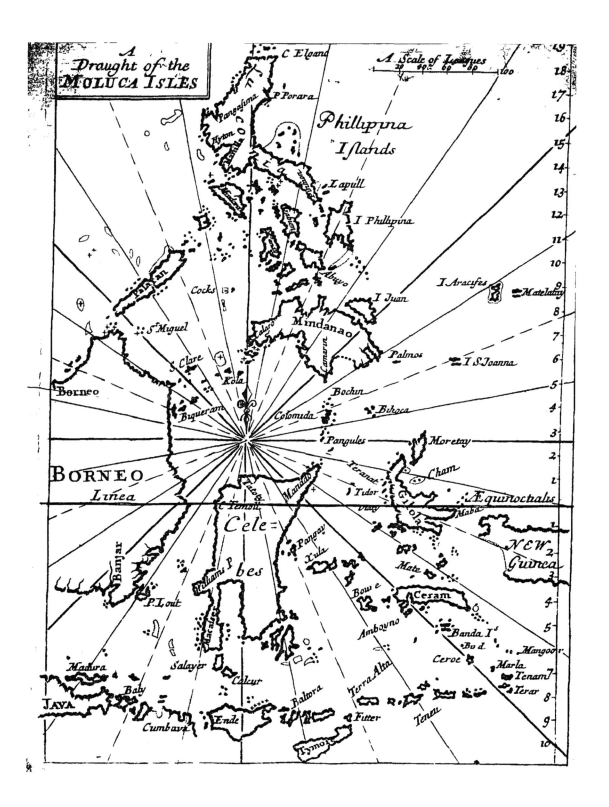

THE
HISTORY
OF THE
DISCOVERY and CONQUEST
OF THE
Molucco and *Philippine* Iſlands, &c.

BOOK I.

I Write the Conqueſt of the *Molucco* Iſlands by King *Philip* the III. of *Spain*, and the reducing of their Kings to their former Subjection, to his Predeceſſors, by Don *Pedro de Acunha*, Governour of the *Philippine* Iſlands, and Admiral of the *Spaniſh* Fleet; a Victory worthy the Foreſight of ſuch a Godly Monarch, the Application of thoſe worthy Stateſmen that compoſe his ſupreme Council, and the Valour of our Nation; not ſo much on account of the Wealth, and Fertility of thoſe Countries, as for that it took from the Northern Nations all occaſion of Sailing in our Seas, and Debauching the new Converted *Aſiaticks*, and the Inhabitants of our Colonies Trading among them. The Celerity with which the Expedition was concluded, does not in the leaſt diminiſh the Glory of the Event; which, for that very Reaſon, might rather deſerve a place in a more ample Relation. I am ſenſible of the Dangers I expoſe my ſelf to; but am no leſs ſatisfy'd, that I ſhall find ſome to ſtand by me. The moſt famous Painters, and Carvers, have generally a great value for Heads, Arms, and other Limbs, which have been drawn to perfection from the Life, by which they compoſe all the Parts, when they deſign ſome excellent Piece. The ignorant in thoſe Arts have no Eſteem for ſuch Fragments, being only taken with the entire Statue, or Picture, conſiſting of all its Limbs, without examining the Defects there may be in each of them. The Relation I undertake to write of theſe Iſlands will find the ſame Eſteem, and be expos'd to no leſs Contempt; for the Judicious, who under-

B   ſtand ftand how Hiftory is Compil'd, will value this part drawn to the Life, whereas thofe, who, as they fay themfelves, Read only to divert the Time, will make little account of it, as being more fond of fome Romance, full of Monfterous Events; or of fome bulkey Work, bearing the Title of a Hiftory, treating of numerous Armies, and mighty Slaughters, and beftowing the Succefs, not where Providence gave, but where they would have it. This is the Reafon why many Things, worthy to be known and preferv'd, remain bury'd in Oblivion; becaufe being left for General Hiftories, there are only flight Sketches of them Drawn at the Time when they hapned, by thofe who had a fhare in them, fo that when thefe Manufcripts are to be made ufe of, either they are not to be found, or elfe they reduce the Writer to a neceffity of fubfcribing to whatfoever either Self-Love, or any other Paffion dictated to the Authors of fuch Memoirs, without any poffibility of examining into the Truth. To obviate this Inconveniency, in a matter of fuch moment as that of *Ternate*, the Capital of the *Molucco* Iflands, I was Commanded to write an Account of it, at a time when they were ftill living who acted in and directed it. And I have fuch full Information of all that is requifite for this purpofe, that I hope Truth will make amends for my want of Ability. This is as much as I have thought fit to Advertife the Reader, without entering upon the Advantage he will reap by perufing this Relation; becaufe, if he is well affected, all I can fay for it will be fuperfluous; and if otherwife inclin'd, tho' I endeavour to fet him right, he will never conceive it.

Kings of the Moluccos.　Among the fourteen moft potent Princes, who Lord it over the *Archipelago* of the *Molucco* Iflands, under the Title of Kings, thofe of *Ternate* and *Tydore* boaft of a Divine Original; fuch Liberty to be vain do Men take upon them, or fo much do they afcribe to obfcure Antiquity. There is an ancient Tradition among thofe People, look'd upon as Sacred, That they were once Govern'd by a moft Ancient Prince, called *Bicocigara*, who failing along the Coaft of *Bachian*, perceiv'd that among fome craggy Rocks there were grown up abundance of *Rotas*, fo they call a fort of folid Canes, which, when fmall, they make ufe of inftead of Ropes. He lik'd them, and

A Fable of their Original.　order'd they fhould be cut down, and brought into his Veffel. His Subjects going to fulfil his Orders, and having fearch'd all the place, return'd to their Mafter, defiring he would look again, leaft his Eyes deceiv'd him, for they could meet with no fuch Canes. *Bicocigara*, who faw them diftinctly from his Boat, was pofitive with his incredulous People, and order'd them again to be brought; but to decide the matter, went himfelf Afhore, where immediatly they appear'd to them all. He commanded them to be cut down, and as they went about it, Blood ran from the Canes that were cut. Being aftonifh'd at that Prodigy, he difcover'd clofe to the Roots of them four Eggs, which look'd like a Snakes Eggs, and at the fame time heard a Voice, proceeding from the hollow of the Canes cut down, which faid, *Keep thofe Eggs; for from them fhall come four excellent Governours.* He took up thofe fatal Eggs, with Religious Refpect, and carry'd them home, where they were kept in the beft place of his Houfe. In a fhort time, from the four Yolks proceeded four Rational Chickens, being three Men, and one Woman, who afterwards Reign'd, the firft of them in *Bachian*, the fecond in *Butsn*, and the third over the Iflands call'd

Papuas,

Papuas, lying Eaſt from the *Moluccos*. The Woman was Marry'd to Prince *Loloda*, who gave Name to the Country of *Batochina*, not far from the great *Boconora*. This Fable has gain'd ſuch Reputation, that they honour *Bicocigara* as a Hero, worſhip the Rocks, and adore the Eggs. The truth of it is, that the cunning Man, by this prodigious Superſtition, Sanctify'd his own Race, and gain'd Kingdoms, and Reſpect for his four Children. So *Greece* feign'd, or beleiv'd, that *Leda* Conceiving of the Adulterous Swan brought forth the Eggs, from which came *Caſtor*, *Pollux*, and *Helena*. Fortune, when ſhe raiſes Men to a high pitch, perſwades thoſe ſhe deſigns to Crown, to lay the Foundation of their Majeſty on Fables, reſembling true Miſteries, ſo to perſwade the Multitude that they are ſomewhat Divine, and to diſtinguiſh the Royal Race by a peculiarity even in the Univerſal Law of being Born into the World. Of this Race thirteen Idolatrous Kings ſucceeded one another in *Tydore*, down to Sultan *Tydore Bongue*, the firſt that receiv'd the *Mahometan* Alcoran, tho' intermix'd with Idolatry, which laſted above Eighty Years, and being confounded among the Precepts of that abominable Sect, bred Diviſions, and Diſtractions among the People. Afterwards, when the Commander *Brito* arriv'd in that Iſland, as we ſhall ſoon ſee, he found a *Caciz*, or Prieſt, taught them the new Superſtition, and that many oppos'd him, on account of the old Fable of the Eggs, which the *Perſian Morabout* could never Decry ; ſo great is the power of Error tranſmitted from our Fore-Fathers.

King *Tydore Bongue*'s Succeſſor, was his Son *Cachil Boleyſe*, no leſs Superſtitious than the Father, but in another way. He pretending to the Spirit of Prophecy, gain'd ſuch Reputation, by the Experience and Foreſight of his Riper Years, that he came to be Honour'd by his Subjects as a Prophet ; or by the leaſt Credulous, as a Perſon of ſingular Prudence, ſo that all Men gave Ear to him, as to an Oracle. Puffed up with this Vanity, he pretended to Fore-tell future Events ; which when no particular Perſons, or ſet Times are appointed, is a ſafe way of Predicting, without Danger of being found Falſe ; either becauſe in proceſs of Time ſomething Accidentally happens, that may be adapted to the Prophecy, or in regard, that is always expected which will never come to paſs. For this Reaſon, as in moſt Countries there are ſome current Notions of future Expectations, conceiv'd upon trivial Occaſions, rather than any Obſervation of the Stars ; therefore *Boleyſe* us'd to tell thoſe about him, That the time would come, when Iron Men ſhould arrive at *Ternate*, from the remoteſt parts of the World, and ſettle in its Territory ; by whoſe Power the Glory, and Dominion of the *Molucco* Iſlands ſhould be far extended.

A falſe Propheſie.

In the Reign of King *John* the firſt, of *Portugal*, his Son, Prince *Henry*, having employ'd ſeveral Perſons on Diſcoveries, *John Gonzales*, and *Triſtan Vaz* found the Iſland of *Madera*, in the Year 1419, and others ſoon after thoſe of the *Azores*, and *Cabo Verde*, and ran along the Coaſt of *Guinea* and *Africk*. Afterwards, in the Reigns of King *Edward*, and *Alonſo* the V. thoſe Diſcoveries were continu'd, till under King *John* the II. they proceeded as far as the Cape of *Good Hope*, and a Hundred Leagues beyond it, along the Coaſt, call'd *Rio del Infante*. The honour of this Diſcovery is due to that famous Seaman *Bartholomew Diaz*, if we may believe the Manuſcript Memoirs of *Duarte Reſende*, for the Hiſtorian

Firſt Diſcoveries.

Barros

Barros. This rais'd Emulation in the *Spanish* Nation, already engag'd in such Voyages, as having Discover'd the Western Islands, call'd *Antilles,* or *Caribbee* Islands. This Discovery occasion'd a Controversy about the Right to them, *Portugal* pretending to, and *Spain* defending its Possession. After much Contention, the Difference was adjusted by *Ruy de Sousa,* and *Don John* his Son, and *Arias de Almada,* Commission'd by *Portugal,* who in the Year 1404. agreed with the *Spanish* Embassador, That, since this inferior Globe, consisting of Earth and Water, answers to the Degrees into which the Celestial Sphere is divided, it should be equally parted between the two Kings, by a Meridian Line drawn through the North and South Poles, and compassing the Land and Sea, so as to cut them into two halves. It was appointed, That the Share to the Eastward should belong to the Crown of *Portugal,* and the other to the Westward, to that of *Castile;* and that it should be so mark'd down on the Sea Charts; the Line passing through a fixt Point on the Earth, which was to be the Boundary of both Nations. This was by mutual Consent settled 360 Leagues West from *Cabo Verde,* and so the Line, or Meridian, fell upon the Country we call *Brazil,* about the most Westerly part of the Mouth of the River *Marañhao,* which disembogues there to the Northward. This Line cuts through that Country, and to the Southward runs off beyond the River of *Plate,* from whence the *Spaniards* begin to reckon their Degrees of Longitude Westward, and the *Portuguese* Eastward, 180 belonging to each of them, for as much as the whole Circumference of the Earth contains three hundred and sixty Degrees.

Vasco de Gama discovers India. *Vasco de Gama,* employ'd by King *Emanuel* of *Portugal,* to Discover and Conquer *India,* prosecuted this Enterprize, look'd upon by *Ptolomy,* as impracticable, he travers'd the main Ocean, within the *Portuguese* Division, where he Discover'd, and since the *Portuguese* Commanders have Conquer'd so many Kingdoms, Nations, and Islands, so distinct in Customs, Manners, Laws, Languages, and Colours. They returning home admir'd what they had seen, and lay'd it down in Maps, but stretching out the Longitude, that is the Distance from West to East, beyond what it really was; thus Craftily providing for the Controversy which might arise upon this Occasion, as it soon happen'd, through the Falshood of the Sea Charts.

Portugueses Pretentions to the Moluccos. By virtue of this practice, and by the *Pope's* subsequent Authorizing of it, the *Portugueses* pretend that the *Molucco* Islands, and those of *Banda,* and *Amboyna,* are within their Bounds, as they were adjudg'd, and settled by experienc'd Sailers, calculating the Extent of that Meridian, and they even stretch it 15 Degrees further. *Resende* complains, That *Magalhaens,* whom the *English* call *Magellan,* magnify'd the Opinion conceiv'd of the Eastern Seas, when in the Year 1519 he went away Disgusted into *Spain.* *Magellan* grew up in the service of Queen *Ellenor,* then serv'd King *Emanuel,* and went over into *India* with that *Alonso de Albuquerque,* of whose Bravery, and Conduct, we have written Histories, besides what Fame, and Tradition have deliver'd. This Man, not satisfy'd with the first Conquests, sent *Antony de Abreu, Francis Serrano,* and *Ferdinand de Nagalhaens* from *Malaca,* with three Ships, to Discover the *Molucco* Islands. All these three Commanders steer'd several Courses. We shall
soon

foon speak of *Magellan* again. *Antony de Abreu* arriv'd at *Banda*, and returning towards *Malaca*, richly Laden with Spice of that Country, *Serrano* was parted from him in a Storm, and Shipwrack'd on the Islands of *Lucopino*, signifying Islands of *Tortoises*, so call'd from the Plenty and Bigness of those Creatures.

There the Tempest left the *Portuguefes*, only their Lives and Arms sav'd, for their *Junck*, which is a sort of light Veffel, was Stav'd. The *Lucopine* Islands were Horrid, by reason of their want of Water, and being Defert; for their Rocks lying under Water, and the many Sea Robbers that frequent them, and always keep Sentinels posted to discover any Sailing by, that they may fall upon, and plunder them. Had not Hunger and Thirst threatned the *Portugufes* with speedy Death, they had reason to expect it at the Hands of those Pyrats; but that which had been the Destruction of others, at this time prov'd their Safety. Those Miscreants had obferv'd the Shipwreck, and Rowing up in a Veffel call'd a *Caracoa*, as it were to a certain Booty, drew near to those who had so narrowly escap'd perishing in the Sea; but the *Malaca* Pilots, and Mariners were not ignorant of their design. They acquainted their Captain with the Danger, defiring him to take such Measures as might be for his own, and their Safety. *Serrano*, like a Man of Valour and Difcretion, having view'd the Shore, conceal'd his Men in a hidden Place. The Pyrates landed to purfue them; but as fcon as ever they were at some diftance from the Shore, the Strangers rufh'd out, and poffefs'd themfelves of the *Caracoa*. The Barbarians thus furpris'd, reflecting on their Mifmanagement, and perceiving they were loft Men, gave over the thoughts of Robbing, and had recourfe to Intreaties, throwing down their Bows and Arrows, and begging they would not leave them in that Ifland, but rather take pity, and pardon what they had done; and promifing, if he would carry them off, to conduct him to another place, where Strangers were well receiv'd, and there was Trade. *Serrano* granted their Requeft, and admitted them, and having repair'd the fhatter'd *Junck*, and Embarking together, they directed their Courfe to the Ifland of *Amboyna*, where they were well receiv'd by the People of *Rucutelo*, who were ancient Enemies to thofe of *Veranula*, a Neighboring City of *Batochina*, with whom thofe of *Rucutelo* coming to a Battle, they obtain'd the Victory, through the Affiftance of the New-comers. The Fame of this Succefs flew over to the *Molucco* Iflands, at the Time when *Boleyfe* Reign'd in *Ternate*, and *Almanzor* in *Tydore*, who were both not long before Idolaters, and then *Mahometans*. Thefe two were at Variance about the Limits of their Dominions, and underftanding that the *Portugufes* were at *Amboyna* each of them defiring to Strengthen himfelf againft his Enemy, fent Imbaffadors, and Ships, to invite, and bring over to them thofe Forreign Soldiers; thinking it alfo convenient upon other accounts, to enter into Alliance with thofe People, whofe great Actions were then fo frefh in the Mouths of all Men. *Boleyfe* was quicker than *Almanzor*, and fent ten Snips for *Serrano*, with a Thoufand well Arm'd Soldiers for their Defence, the whole under the Command of his Kinfman *Cachil Coliba*. The *Tydore* Embaffadors return'd from *Rucutelo* difappointed. It is but a fhort Cut between *Amboyna*, and *Ternate*, and therefore *Boylefe*'s Ships foon return d with the *Portugufes*. That king went out attended by his

Subjects,

Marginal notes: Serrano caft on the Iflands of Lucupine. His Efcape. Arrives at Amboyna.

Subjects, to receive the new Guests, all of them concluding, That they went to see the fulfilling of their so long expected Prophecy. *Serrano* Landed in bright white Armour, and his Companions in the same manner. When the King saw them, he embrac'd every Man, with a Countenance full of Pleasure and Admiration, shedding Tears, and lifting up his Hands to Heaven, bless'd God, and gave hearty Thanks, for that he had granted him to see that which had been Predicted so many Years before *These*, said he, *my Friends, are the Warriers you have so long wish'd for, on account of my Prophecy. Honour them, and let us all vie in Entertaining them; since the Grandeur of our Country depends on their Arms* The *Portuguese*, well pleas'd to be thought worthy of a Prophecy, the Belief whereof was a Politick Invention, conducing to their Reputation, made no less Courteous Returns, expressing their singular Affection. They settled Amity, and Trade in the *Moluccos*; whence they spread it to the adjacent, and remoter Islands, which it will be now requisite breifly to Describe, for the better Understanding of this History.

Archipelago described. The Eastern *Archipelago*, not to speak of the Division of those Oriental Parts into Northern, and Southern, Contains so many Islands, that the certain Number of them is not yet known. Hence Modern Authors distribute it into five Divisions, being so many *Archipelagos*, under the names of *Molucco, Moro, Papuas, Celebes*, and *Amboyna*. The Name of the First, in their Language, is *Moloc*, signifying, the Head, because it is the Chief of all about it Others will have it to be *Malucco*, which, in *Arabick*, imports, the Kingdom, as the Principal of them. It Contains five most Remarkable Islands, all of them under the same Meridian, one in sight of another, their whole Extent being 25 Leagues, the Equinoctial crossing them, so that the most Northern of them has but half a Degree of Latitude that way, and the most Southern, one Degree on the other side. Near to them, on the East, is the Island *Gilolo*, by the *Portuguese* call'd *Batochina de Moro*, and by the *Moluccos, Alemaera*. Among all the others lying about them, call'd also *Moluccos*, as we say the *Canaries*, the *Terceras*, or the *Oreades*, these are the most Remarkable, for their great Plenty of Spice. The Names of them, beginning with the Northermost, are, *Ternate, Tydore, Motiel, Machian*, and *Bachian*; by the ancient Heathens call'd, *Cape, Duco, Montil, Mara*, and *Seque*. This last, which is *Bachian*, is divided into many Islands, seperated from one another by little Channels, Navigable only in small Vessels; for which reason, as also because it is under one Soveraign, it has but one Name, and all the *Molucco* Islands are Subject to three Kings They are divided by small Arms of the Sea, and some Desert little Islands, as also by their Antient Enmity. The Coast both near the Shore, and farther off at Sea, full of Dangerous Shoals; among which there are some Inlets, where the Ships Ride in Safety. The Soil of them all is generally Dry and Spungy, sucking up all the Water, tho' it Rains never so much, and in many Places the Brooks that run down from the Mountains do not reach the Sea. According to that grave Historian *John de Barros*, these Islands afford an ill Prospect, and are no way pleasant to behold; because the Sun being always so near them, sometimes passing over towards the Northern, and some times towards the Southern Solstice, the natural Damp of the Earth fills them so full of Trees, and

Plants,

Plants, that it thickens the Air, and hinders the Sight; for by reason of the Earthly Vapours, the Trees are never naked of Leaves, but before one falls another has sprung out; and the same is among Herbs Others affirm, they are Pleasant to look to, but not Healthy, especially for Strangers, who are all subject to the Disease call'd *Berbei*, which is common in that Country. This Malady swells the Body, and disables the Limbs, but is cur'd with Cloves, the Wine of the *Philippine* Islands, drank with Ginger, and the use of a certain Herb, known to the Natives; and the *Dutch* do it with the juyce of Lemmons, a Remedy found by their own Apprehension, and Experience.

Providence has stor'd these Spice-Islands with *Bananas, Coco-Nuts, Oranges, Lemmons, Lignum-Aloes, Sanders, Cinamon, Mace, Mastick-Trees,* but above all, with abundance of *Cloves,* and other Plants; all of them valuable for their Fruit, or delightful for their Ornaments: They have neither *Wheat* nor *Rice*; but Nature gave them Industry, and Matter to supply this Defect. They beat a sort of Tree, like the *Wild-Palm,* with Mallets made of strong Canes; and those dry Trunks, so batter'd, yield an extraordinary white Flower, coming from the bruized Pith; which they mould up in square *Pipkins,* and this is the *Sagu,* or *Landan,* so made into square Loaves, like the *Castile Sope.* This Plant is about Fifteen Foot high, and from the Top of it sprout out some Branches, like those which produce the *Tamarinds.* These bear a Fruit like the *Cypress-Nuts,* in which there are certain fine Hairs, which if they touch a Man's Flesh, burn it. From the tender Branches of the same Plant cut, flows the Liquor which serves them for Drink, putting the Ends of the said Branches so cut into narrow Mouth'd Vessels, which are fill'd in a Night, and the Liquor so gather'd, is like Milk Whipped, and Frothy, which they call *Tuac.* When Drank new, it is Sweet and very Fat'ning; boil'd like new Wine it tastes like Wine, and after grows sharp as Vinegar. The same Advantage they reap from two other Plants call'd *Nipo,* and *Coco*; the last of them yields also *Oyl, Boards,* and *Timber* to build Houses. They also Drink another pleasant Liquor, which Nature has shut up in the Hollow of the Canes they call *Bambooes,* so large that the Knots are a Yard asunder. They abound in Flesh; but the People are more affected to Fish; notwithstanding *Hugo,* the *Dutchman,* says they want both. Providence afforded them no Mines, either of *Gold,* or *Silver*; whether it was a Punishment, or Mercy we do not decide. Neither have they found any, of other less precious Metals; but not far from them is *Lambuco,* an Island abounding in Iron and Steel; whence, and from the Mines of *Sula* and *Butva,* the People of the *Maluccos* bring them, to make their *Caampilanes,* which are sharp heavy *Cymiters,* and their *Crises,* being small *Daggers.* The *Portugueses* and *Dutch* have now furnish'd those Islands with small Fire-Arms, and Cannon of all sorts known among us.

Product of the Moluccos.

Sagu.

Ternate is the Capital City, and Court of that King, near to which a dreadful burning Mountain Flames out, about the Equinoxes, because at those Times the Winds blow; which kindle that natural Fire, on the Matter that has fed it so many Ages. The Top of the Mountain, which exhales it, is cold, and not cover'd with Ashes, but with a sort of light cloddy Earth, little different from the *Pomice-Stone* burnt in our Fiery Mountains.

A burning Mountain in Ternate.

Descending

Descending thence to the Foot of the Hill, which stretches out like a Piramid, down to the Plain; it is all uncooth, being thick with Trees, whose Verdure is spar'd by the Flames, and the very Fire, Waters and Moisiens them with Brooks, which it draws together in the Hollow of the Mountain, and forces it to Sweat, and pour out.

People of Ternate. The Natives Differ from one another, as it were through a Miraculous Bounty of Nature; for it has made the Women Fair and Beautiful, and the Men, of a darker Colour than a Quince; their Hair lank, and many anoint it with sweet Oyls. Their Eyes are large, the Eyebrows long, which, and their Eye-lashes, they colour Black Of Body they are Strong, much addicted to War, and sloathful for all other Employments. They are long Liv'd; grow grey earlie, and are as Active by Sea as by Land, Officious, and Courteous to Strangers; but when they grow Familiar, Importunate, and Troublesome in their Requests; in their Dealings, all bent upon Interest; Jealous, Fraudulent, and False. They are Poor, and therefore Proud; and to name many Vices in one, Ungrateful.

Religion, Manners, Laws. The *Chinese* possess'd themselves of these Islands, when they subdu'd all those Eastern Parts; and after them the *Javeneses,* and the *Malayes,* and lastly the *Persians,* and *Arabs*; which last, together with their Trade, Introduc'd the *Mahometan* Superstition among the Worship of their Gods, from whom some Families boasted they were descended. Their Laws are Barbarous: They have no limited Number of Wives. The King's chief Wife, call'd in their Language *Putriz,* enables and gives the Right of Succession to which her Sons are preferr'd, tho' younger than those by other Mothers. *Theft* is not pardon'd, tho' never so inconsiderable; but *Adultery* easily. When the Dawn appears, Officers appointed by Law for that purpose, beat a sort of broad, flat Tabors about the Streets, to awake Marry'd People, who they think deserves this Care from the Government, on account of Procreation. Most Crimes are punish'd with Death; in other Respects they Obey the Will, or Tyranny of the Conqueror.

Their Habit. The Men, on their Heads, wear *Turkish* Turbants of several Colours, with abundance of Feathers on them. The King's ends above like a Miter, and serves instead of a Crown. For their other Garb they all wear Wastecoats, which they call *Cheninas,* and Blew, Crimson, Green, and Purple Breeches. Of the same they make their Cloaks, or Mantles, which are short, Soldier-like, thrown over, or knotted on the Shoulder, after the Ancient *Roman* manner, known by the written Descriptions, Statues, and other Monuments of those Times. The Women are Proud of their Hair; sometimes they spread, and sometimes they plat it, sticking abundance of Flowers among the Ribbons, which hold it together; so that in their Dress, they are not encumber'd with loose Viels, Plumes, or Feathers. All that variety adorns them without Art; they wear *Bracelets, Pendants,* and *Necklaces* of *Diamonds* and *Rubies,* and great Strings of *Pearls,* which are not forbid even the meanest, no more than Silks, wherein the Women particularly are Clad after the *Persian* and *Turkish* Fashion; and all this costly Attire is the Product of the Neighbouring Lands and Seas. Both Men and Women in their Habit show their natural Haughtiness.

Language. The variety of Languages among them is great, for sometimes one Town does not understand the People of the next; the *Malaye* Tongue is most us'd,

the Melancholy Tree

The Habit of ỹ Molucco Islands.

us'd, as eafieft to pronounce. This Diverfity of Languages fhows, that thofe Iflands were Peopled by feveral Nations. In thofe Parts all-Antiquity, and the Art of Navigation are afcrib'd to the *Chinefes*. Some affirm, That the People of the *Molucco* Iflands are Defcended from the *Jaos*, who fettled there, being invited by the Fragrancy of the Spice. They loaded their Veffels with Cloves, till then unknown, and holding on that Trade, carry'd it to the Gulphs of *Arabia*, and *Perfia*. They Sail'd about all thofe Countries, tranfporting Silks, and Porcelance, the Product, and Manufacture of *China*. The Cloves were by the *Perfians*, and *Arabs* tranfmitted to the *Greeks*, and *Romans*. Some *Roman* Emperors had a defign of Conquering the Eaft, till they fhould come to the Spicy Countries; fo covetous were they of that Commodity; and believing they all came from *China*, call'd all thofe People *Chinefes*. The *Spaniards* formerly brought them among other Goods from the *Red-Sea*. The Kings of *Egypt* for fome time poffefs'd themfelves of all the Spice, which they Tranfmitted from the Hands of the *Afiaticks* into *Europe*. This the *Romans* continu'd, when they reduc'd *Egypt* into the Form of a Province. Long after, the *Genoefes*, Transferring the Trade to *Theodofia*, now *Caffa*, handed them about to all Parts; and there the *Venetians*, and other Trading Nations, had their Confuls, and Factors. They afterwards were convey'd over the *Cafpian* Sea and *Trabifond*; but this Trade fell with the Eaftern Empire; and then the *Turks* carry'd them in Caravans of Camels, and Dromedaries to *Berytus*, *Aleppo*, *Damafcus*, and feveral Ports on the *Mediterranean*. The Sultans of *Egypt* brought them back to the *Red-Sea*, and thence to *Alexandria*, down the *Nile*. The *Portuguefes* having Conquer'd the *Eaft-Indies*, took them from *Egypt*, and brought them in their Fleets by the Cape of *Good Hope*, finking and taking all Ships that attempted to carry any to *Grand Cayro*. For that purpofe they kept Squadrons on the Coafts of *Arabia* and *Perfia*, and at Cape *Guardafu*. By this means the Trade of *Egypt* was fupprefs'd, and all the Spice brought on the Kings account to *India*, and thence taking a prodigious compafs, to *Lisbon*. He who is Mafter at Sea will be poffefs'd of this Wealth; by which, and other Commodities, we fee that is made good, which fome write *Themiftocles* was wont to fay, *That he has all things who has the Sea.*

The Kings, *Boleyfe*, of *Ternate*, and *Almanzor*, of *Tydore*, contended about Entertaining *Serrano*, and each of them courted him to build a Fort in his Ifland. It is well worth Obfervation, To fee how eagerly thefe Kings fought after, and begg'd for that which they were foon after to be averfe to. They writ about it to the King of *Portugal*; but *Antony de Miranda* coming to the *Moluccos*, befides a wooden Fort, or Houfe he built at *Talangame*, erected another at *Machian*, an Ifland belonging to the two Kings, by which means he fatisfy'd the Requeft of both. Soon after *Cachil Laudin*, King of *Bachian*, made Application to *Don Triftan de Menefes*, on the fame account. *Don Triftan* was come to the *Moluccos* to Load Spice, and with a defign to carry away *Francis Serrano*, and to induce *Boleyfe* to confent to it, he perfwaded him, it was requifite that *Serrano* fhould go to *Portugal*, to prevail upon King *Emanuel* to order the Fort he defir'd, to be built upon *Ternate*, and not elfewhere. *Boleyfe* approv'd of his defign, and to that end, fent *Cachilato*, as his Embaffador, with

How Cloves were brought into Europe.

C ·   *Serrano.*

Serrano. Don *Triftan* fet out, and his Ships being difpers'd in a Storm, was oblig'd to return to the *Moluccos,* and to Winter in the Wooden Houfe above mention'd, but as foon as the *Monfon,* blew, he put to Sea again, and touching at *Bachian* was inform'd, That they had kill'd fome *Portu-guefes,* of *Simon Correa*'s Veffel in that Ifland. This troubled him, but he diffembled it, and proceeding on his Voyage, return'd to *Malaca,* by the way of *Amboyna.*

Brito *at the* Mo-lucco's. *Antony de Brito,* appointed by the Governour of *India* to fucceed *Serrano* in that Poft, Sail'd from Cape *Sincapura,* through the Streights of *Sabam,* with 300 Men, and fome experienc'd Commanders. He touch'd at *Tuban,* a City in the Ifland of *Jaua,* and went over to another, call'd *Agazim,* a Mart in thofe Parts, oppofite to the Ifland *Madura.* Its nearnefs inviting him, he fent a Roving Veffel thither to get fome Information what Courfe he was to Steer. Seventeen Men there were in the Veffel Landed on the Coaft, and went up along the fide of a River, cover'd with beautiful Trees, whofe Fruit deceiv'd the Sailers; for they attracted with the pleafant fight, and unexpected fatisfaction, forgot to fecure their Veffel. The Natives obferving the Opportunity, firft took the Veffel, and then all the Men, whofe Ranfom prov'd afterwards difficult, tho' the Lord of the City, fa-vour'd it. *Brito* fail'd directly for the *Moluccos,* and touching at *Bachian,* fent *Simon de Abreu* in all hafte to burn a Village, and kill all the Inhabi-tants, in Revenge for *Simon Correa*'s Companions flain there; that King *Laudin* might underftand, they fhould not efcape unpunifh'd, who wrong'd the *Portuguefe,* and that fince his Ifland was the firft that took up Arms *King of* Ternate *Dies.* againft them, it fhould alfo be the firft that felt their Vengeance. He exe-cuted his feverity without any Lofs, tho' that King did not forget the Obli-gation he laid on him. *Brito* went on to *Tydore,* and was Inform'd by *Al-manzor* of the Diforders there were at *Ternate,* becaufe *Boleyfe* was dead, and it was fuppos'd he had been Poyfon'd. He being near his Death or-der'd, That during the Minority of his eldeft Son *Cachil Bohat,* or *Boyano,* the Queen his Wife, who was Daughter to the King of *Tydore,* fhould Govern; and that *Cachil Daroes,* Natural Son to the faid *Boleyfe,* fhould Act jointly with her. The Queen who was Crafty, fufpecting that her Father *Almanzor* might under that colour aim at fome Advantage, to the Detriment of her Son, call'd her Subjects together and told them, That it was enough for her to take care of her Sons Education; and therefore fhe laid the greateft ftrefs of Government on *Cachil Daroes.*

A Fort Built at Ternate. The King, and the Governour *Daroes,* expected the Commander *Antony Brito,* as the Kingdoms, and the young Kings Protector. They went out to meet him in a Fleet of *Carcoas,* with the Noife of that Barbarous Mufick of Brafs Bafons, and Tabors. He Landed, fhewing State, and appearing wor-thy of that Applaufe; vifited the Queen, the King, and his Brothers; and after the Ceremony of Condoling the Death of *Boleyfe,* ordering Affairs in Conjunction with *Daroes,* he approv'd of that Form of Government, and upon all occafions Defended his Province againft that of *Tydore.* To do this with the greateft Security, he pitch'd upon a proper fpot of Ground, according to the Rules of Fortification, which were not then very perfect, no more than Military Difcipline. The Foundation being dug, *Brito,* in the prefence of the King, and all the People, laid the firft Stone of the new Fort, with his own Hand. This happen'd on Midfummer Day, and there-fore

fore he gave the Fort the Name of *St. John Baptist*; and tho' it was built for the Defence of *Ternate*, yet in *Brito's* mind it was Dedicated to the service of the Gospel, and its Ministers. He us'd endeavours to send away the *Caciz* he found there spreading of *Mahomet's* false Doctrine, as an Obstacle to the True; but the War which is there always settled and natural against *Tydore*, obstructed these Designs; tho' at the same time the Troubles of those two Revengeful Nations increas'd the Revenues of *Portugal*, by contributing of their Spice; and the desire of Superiority brought them into Subjection. However, in *Portugal Brito* had a Successor appointed him, and he was inform'd, That the other was already sailing for the *Moluccos*; and there was need enough of them both, and of doubling their Forces; because *Spain* still insisted upon taking those Countries as its Right, and *Brito* began to be hated, on account of his offering Violence to the Royal Family.

At the same time *Magellan* having Sail'd 600 Leagues towards *Malaca*, was in certain Islands, whence he corresponded with *Serrano*; who having thriv'd so well in *Ternate*, with *Boleyfe*, sent his Friend word what Kindness, and Wealth he had receiv'd from him; advising him to return to his Company. *Magellan* consenting, resolv'd to go to the *Moluccos*; but in case his Services were not Rewarded in *Portugal*, as he expected, he would take the way directly for *Ternate*, under whose King *Serrano* grew so Rich in Nine Years. He consider'd, that since the *Moluccos* were 600 Leagues East from *Malaca*, which make 30 Degrees, little more or less, they were out of the *Portuguese* Limits, according to the antient Sea Chart. Returning to *Portugal*, he found no Favour, but thought himself wrong'd, and resenting it, went away into *Castile*, carrying with him a Planisphere, drawn by *Peter Reynel*; by which, and the Correspondence he had held with *Serrano*, he perswaded the Emperor, *Charles* V. that the *Molucco* Islands belong'd to him. It is reported, That he Confirm'd his Opinion with Writings, and the Authority of *Ruy Falepio*, a *Portuguese* Judiciary Astrologer, and much more with *Serrano's*. *Magellan goes over to Spain.*

Hereupon the Emperor gave him the Command of a Squadron, with which he sail'd from *Sanlucar*, on the 21*st.* of *September*, 1519. He stay'd four days at the *Canaries*, where a Caravel overtook him, with private Intelligence, that his Captains went with a Design not to Obey him; particularly *John Cartagena*, who had the same Commission as *Magellan*. He bravely seem'd to take no notice, and sailing away with a fair Wind, being pass'd *Rio de Janeyro*, in the Province of *Santa Cruz*, commonly call'd *Brazil*, the Sea growing very cold, and much more the *River of Plate*, which is in 35 Degrees of South Latitude, the Captains question'd him about the Voyage, since they could not find the Cape, or Streight, they went in search of. He answer'd, as to Men that were entirely Subordinate to his Direction and Authority, *That they must go on, for he knew what he was about, and the Coasts of* Norway *and* Ireland *were in a greater Latitude, and yet Ships sail'd along them.* These Contests lasted almost all the Voyage, and increas'd with the cold and dreadful Winds, and the hideous sight of the Mountains of Snow and Ice, grown old, which they met in the Latitude of 52 and 53 Degrees. They magnify'd these Difficulties, alledging, That it requir'd six, or seven Months to come from *Castile*, *Sets out on his Discovery.*

cross

crofs the Line, and run all along the Coaft of *Brazil*, through fuch diverfity of Climates, in each of which the Weather vary'd. That this was throwing away Men and Ships, which were more valuable than all the Cloves in the *Molucco* Iflands.

The Aftrologer, *Ruy Faleyro*, being Diftracted, was left in the Mad-Houfe at *Sevil*; and in his Place went *Andrew de San Martin*, to whom *Magellan* gave Ear, as to what he faid of the Weather; but not in other Cafes, as fome lay to his Charge, and with fuch Moderation and Integrity, as becomes Chriftian Piety. Nor is it to be believ'd, That *Magellan* fhould confult fuch a Deceitful a Science as Judiciary Aftrology, upon fuch difficult Points, or fhould prefer it before Aftronomy, amidft fuch dreadful Dangers. The Hardfhips became intollerable; and Difcord fo far prevail'd with the Captains, *John de Cartagena*, *Gafpar Quefada*, and *Lewis de Mendoza*, that they refolved either to Kill, or Secure *Magellan* This Confpiracy coming to his Ears, as he lay at the Mouth of the River of St. *Julian*, having contriv'd what was to be done, as *John de Barros* writes, he caus'd *Lewis de Mendoza* to be Stab'd, which was done by *Gonzalo de Efpinofa*. Next *Gafpar de Quefada* was Quarter'd Alive; and a Servant of his, who was concern'd, had his Pardon *Cartagena* he condemned to a lingering Death, leaving him in that Defert Country, with a Clergy Man, guilty of the fame Crime, which was High Treafon againft their King. So fay the *Portuguefe* Hiftories; but the *Spanifh* inform us, That they were privately proceeded againft, and the Judgment was Read to them. This done he made fome Speeches to Juftify the Fact, and Comfort his Companions. *Cartagena*, and the Clergy-Man, who were left with fome Provifions, got away a few days after, in one of the Ships of the fame Squadron, which return'd to *Spain*. *Magellan* overcoming incredible Difficulties, found the Streight, and Paffage, which makes the Communication between the two Seas, and preferves his Name to this Day. He there took Giants above fifteen Spans high, who wanting raw Flefh, which they us'd to feed on, foon Dy'd; then he paffed the Streight fuccefsfully. But tho' he got under the Equinoctial, either by reafon of the Currents, or the Faultinefs of the Sea Charts, he Sail'd round about, and almoft in fight of the *Molucco* Iflands, yet could never come at them. He Touch'd at others, where he was oblig'd to Fight; and went on to thofe of *Zebu*, or the *Manilas*. At this fame time his Friend *Serrano* was failing for *India*, and tho' it happen'd in feveral Places, yet they both Dy'd on the fame Day, and much after the fame Manner.

It would be fuperfluous to dilate upon the Story of *Magellan*, his tedious Navigation, and the many Difficulties he met with, before and after he pafs'd through his Streight into the *Pacifick*, or *South-Sea*; his Arrival at the Ifland of *Zebu*, and perfwading the Idolatrous King to embrace the Chriftian Faith, and the Battles he fought on his account, with his Enemies; for befides that thefe things are Related by very good Authors who Treat of the Difcovery of the *Molucco* Iflands, which was the main Object of his defperate Undertaking, we muft be brief in repeating them, to fhow how eager feveral Princes, and Nations were for thefe Iflands, and the Notion they had of what great Confequence they would be to them.

The King of *Zebu* was Baptiz'd, rather to make his Advantage of the

He difcovers the Streight of his Name.

Spanish Arms, than out of any Zeal or that he knew the Faith he Embrac'd. He took the Name of *Ferdinand* in Baptifm, to flatter his Godfather, who was *Ferdinand Magalhaens*, himfelf. After obtaining feveral Victories by his Affiftance, thinking he could fhake off the fecond Yoke he expected thofe Strangers might lay on him, he turn'd againft them. He contriv'd an Entertainment, in Honour of *Magellan* and Thirty five *Spaniards* being at it, he fell upon them at a time appointed, with a Multitude of Barbarians, and confounding the Feaft, murder'd his Guefts, who handled their Arms to defend themfelves, which only ferv'd to render their Deaths more Honourable. The reft of the *Spaniards*, who efcap'd becaufe they were at Sea, for their better Government under that Misfortune, prefently chofe *Barbofa*, a Kinfman of *Magalhaens*, for their General, and *Lewis Alfonfo*, a *Portuguefe* to be Captain of the Ship, call'd the Victory. The perfidious King, thinking to conceal his Treachery and Apoftacy, as if it were poffible to keep it fecret, fent to invite *Barbofa*, faying he would deliver him the Jewel he had promis'd for the King of *Spain*. *John Serrano*, thinking it a Rafhnefs, to truft a Man again, whofe Hands were ftill Bloody with the late Execution, diffwaded *Barbofa* from accepting of the Invitation; but was not regarded. *Barbofa* went with the other Guefts, and *Serrano* himfelf, who, to fhow it was not Fear that mov'd him to give fuch Advice, was the firft that got into the Boat. They were conducted into a Wood of *Palm-Trees*, where the King expected them, with a fmall Retinue, the Tables being fpread in the Shade, amidft the Mufick of Bag-Pipes. When they were feated, and began to Eat, a great number of Archers that lay in Ambufh, rufh'd out, and fhot our Men. They faved *Serrano*, whom they lov'd, not out of Kindnefs, for they fhow'd him bound to thofe that were at Sea, demanding for his Ranfom, two Brafs Guns, and then he told them, the Slaughter that had been made. Our Men, not trufting to them, any longer, fet Sail, and did not only fee the *Indians* carry *Serrano* back to their Town, but foon after heard mighty Shouts in it; and it was afterwards known that they gave them when they killed *Serrano*, and ran to throw down a great Crofs, fet up before the New-Church, which they could not perform. The *Spaniards* wanting Men, burnt the Ships, call'd the *Conception*, and chofe *John Caravallo* for their General, and *Gonzalo Gomez de Efpinofa*, Captain of the Ship the *Victory*. They came to *Borneo*, on the Coaft whereof they found thofe Peoples Fleet of *Carcoas*, Painted, and the Prows of them like Serpents Heads gilt.

He is Murder'd with others.

The Soldiers appear'd well Arm'd, who having fpy'd our Ship, acquainted their King with it. He order'd 2000 of his Guard to go out, and receive them, before they reach'd the City. Thefe Men came brandifhing their Bows and poifon'd Arrows, Trunks, Cymitars, and Sheilds, and wore Breaft-plates made of *Tortois* Shells, and encompafs'd an Arm'd *Elephant*, on whofe Back there was a wooden Caftle. When the *Spaniards* came up the Elephant ftoop'd down, and fix arm'd Men coming out of the Caftle, put *Gonzalo Gomez de Efpinofa*, who was then General, into it. Thus attended, he went to Vifit the King, in whofe Prefence his Secretary fpoke to him through a Trunk, and *Efpinofa* gave him an Account of the King of *Zebu*'s Perfidioufnefs. All condol'd the Accident, and our Men taking Leave Sail'd away for the *Molucco* Iflands, being reliev'd with what they wanted, and furnifh'd with able Pilots. Not

Soldiers of Borneo, and Reception of Spaniards.

Spaniards
at Tydore.
Not far from *Borneo*, they met 150 Sail, whereof they took two *Junks*, in which they found an Hundred Men, five Women, a Son of the King of *Luzon*, and an Infant two Months Old. This they thought would be a ſufficient Ranſom to recover their Companions; ſo they let go the Prince upon his Parole, he promiſing to reſtore them the Captive *Spaniards* They had ſome Storms; but arriv'd at *Tydore*, on the 8th of *November* 1521, When *Almanzor* heard the ſalute of the Canon, he ſent to enquire what People they were, and preſently after he came to our Ships in a little Boat. His Shirt appear'd woven with Gold and Silk, a white Cloth which trail'd being girt over it. About his Head a fine Veil of ſeveral Colours, made like a *Perſian* Miter: Being Aboard the Commodore, the Relations of that Voyage ſay, he ſtopp'd his Noſe with his Fingers, either at the Smell of our Meat, or of the Ship. *Mahometaniſm* was newly come into his Iſland, and moſt of his Subjects, eſpecially thoſe Inhabiting the Mountains, ador'd Idols. He bid our Men wellcome, gave them good Words, and afterwads was as kind in his Actions; and being inform'd of their paſt Sufferings, gave them leave to load Cloves. They preſented him with a Chair of Crimſon Velvet, a Robe of Yellow Velvet, a great Looſe Coat of falſe Cloth of Gold, a piece of Yellow Damaſk, four Yards of Scarlet Cloth; Handkercheifs, and Towles, wrought with Silk, and Gold; Drinking-Glaſſes, Glaſs Beads, Looking-Glaſſes, Knives, Scizers, and Combs They gave his Son another parcel of Gifts, and a Cap, and did the like by his *Cachiles* and *Sangiacks*. When they aſk'd the Kings leave in the Emperors Name to Trade, he granted it, adding they ſhould kill any that offer'd to hinder them. He ſeriouſly view'd his Majeſty's Picture and Arms on the Standard, and deſired to ſee our Coin. And pretending to be an Aſtrologer, or Soothſayer, or as others ſay, having Dreamt, or Gueſs'd it, or
Ally with
that King.
being told it by *Chineſe* Prieſts, he ſaid, *He knew the Chriſtians were to come to his Lands for Spice; and deſired that they would not leave him.* They treated about an Alliance, and when they were agreed, two *Tydores* brought ſomething in their Hands to the Ships, which they afterwards underſtood was the *Alcoran*, tho' at firſt they did not, becauſe cover'd with Silks, and Strings. *Almanzor* lay'd his Hands on it, and then on his Head, and Breaſt; and this was the Ceremony of his Swearing Friendſhip, and Fealty to the Crown of *Caſtile*, and that he would allow them Cloves, and all Commerce for ever. Then the General *Eſpinoſa*, in the Emperor's Name, before an Image of the bleſſed Virgin, ſwore to protect them both in Peace and War, and preſented King *Almanzor* with Thirty *Indians* he had taken Priſoners. Soon after, as ſome Authors affirm, *Corala*, Prince of *Ternate*, Nephew to *Almanzor*, came to *Tydore* to ſwear Fealty in like manner, as did *Luzuf.* King of *Grlolo*, of whom it is Written, That he had Six Hundred Sons, and that *Almanzor* had Two Hundred Wives. Theſe Kings Writ to the Emperor; ratifying their Fealty, and *Sebaſtian del Cano* ſail'd away in the Ship, the *Victory*, by the way the *Portugueſes* uſe, with the Letters and Inſtruments; the General *Eſpinoſa* returning towards *Panama*, for *Caſtilla del Oro* on the Continent of *America*, to paſs thence to *Spain*.

At this time the new Governor, *Don Garcia Henriquez*, was under Sail, to ſucceed *Antony Brito*, and being come to *Banda*, waited for the *Monſon* to carry him to *Ternate*. *Monſon* is the Name by which the *Portugueſe* call the Wind, which blows ſix Months to carry them to *India*, and then ſix Months again to bring them back. There he furniſhed himſelf with all Neceſſaries for the Fort built by *Brito*. He had need ſo to do, for he received Advice, That *Spaniſh* Ships were ſailing thro' the Bays, and openeſt Parts of the *Archipelago*. He ſent to diſcover them, by the Induſtry of his Soldiers, and being receiv'd at *Ternate*, view'd the Fort, and obſerv'd the poſture of the Government. He propoſed a Peace with *Cachil Almanzor*, King of *Tydore*. We ſhall have frequent Occaſion to repeat theſe Words *Cachil* and *Sangiack*. *Cachil* is perhaps deriv'd from *Katil*, which in *Arabick* is the ſame as among us, a Valiant Soldier. In the *Molucco* Iſlands they Honour their Nobility with this Title, which is ſomething more than *Don* in *Spain*. The Title of *Sangiack*, which anſwers to that of Duke, or Earl, might come from *Senchaq*; which in the *Turkiſh* Language, imports a Commander: To conclude this Peace, he thought it convenient to ſecure the Royal Family; which he accordingly executed, and though he colour'd it with fair Pretexts, they plainly perceived this was an Introduction towards Oppreſſing them, and ſhow'd a miſtruſt. We may ſafely affirm, This was the firſt Diſtaſte which, as being a notorious Wrong, diſturb'd that Nation, and from that time they grew Cold, and Jealous, thinking themſelves oblig'd to ſeek Revenge; and this Action was the occaſion of all the enſuing Slaughters, as we often ſee a great Fire riſe from one ſmall Spark.

Cachil Daroes endeavour'd to obſtruct this Peace, as Tutor, and Governor, fearing the Trade of Cloves would be transferr'd to *Tydore*, to the Deſtruction of the Infant King's Dominions. But notwithſtanding this Oppoſition, the Peace was concluded, upon certain Conditions, as, That the King of *Tydore* ſhould deliver a Ship he had taken, the *Canon*, and ſome runaway *Portugueſe*. *Almanzor*, who ſtood in need of a Peace, and the Friendſhip of the *Portugueſe*, to gain the Affection of *Cachil Daroes*, propos'd to Marry him to one of his Daughters. *Don Garcia* believing that this Union among them would produce that of their Forces, and leſs Submiſſion to the *Portugueſe*'s Dominion, to obſtruct this dangerous Alliance, ſent to the King of *Tydore* to borrow the Canon. That King excus'd himſelf, alledging, that he had lent it a few days before, to the King of *Bachian*. *Cachil Daroes* complying with him, agreed to all the Articles. *Don Garcia* being diſſatisfy'd, waited an opportunity to break all that Contrivance, and be Reveng'd. *Almanzor* fell Sick, and deſir'd *Don Garcia* to ſend him a Phyſician; who ſent an Apothecary, and he either not underſtanding Phyſick, or, as was believ'd, by order of *Don Garcia*, kill'd the Patient. Manifeſt tokens of Poyſon afterwards appear'd. The Funeral was order'd, and at the ſame time the Commander, *Don Garcia*, appear'd in the Morning, in a parcel of *Carcoas*, before *Tydore*. He ſent *Baldaya*, the Clerk of the Fort, to demand the Canon, threatning War, in caſe of denial. The Regents excuſing themſelves at that time, with juſt Reaſons, and particularly the Funeral Solemnity, when they were in the Height of the Ceremony of Burying their King, they heard the Shouts of *Don Garcia*'s Men giving the Aſſault. The *Portugueſe* enter'd the City, firing the Houſes, plundering and killing, which oblig'd the *Tydores* to abandon their

King's

King's Body, and fly to the Mountains. During their Abfence, *Don Garcia* feized the Canon, and carry'd it away to *Ternate*. Thofe who had fled return'd, with fome Apprehenfion, and found the City ruin'd hideous, and almoft reduc'd to Afhes, but recovering from their Fright, they proclaim'd *Cachil Raxamira*, the Son of *Almanzor*, King. They committed the Education of him to *Cachil Rade*, his Kinfman, the War being declared between *Ternate* and the New King of *Tydore*, who was feafonably fupported by the *Spaniards* that came to his Country.

Spanifh Ship firft round the World. The Ship *Victory* returning into *Spain*, with the Letters from the King of the *Molucco* Iflands, which the Emperor receiv'd, he was more fully convinc'd, that thefe Iflands were within his Limits. Their Wealth, and his Right to them were fo lively reprefented to him, that he order'd another Squadron of four Ships, two Galloons, and an Advice Boat to be made ready at *Corunna*, to be Commanded by the Commendary *Fray Garcia de Loayfa*, a Gentleman of *Bifcay*, and under him, as Vice-Admiral, *Sebaftian del Cano*, and the Captains *Don Rodrigo de Acunna*, *James de Vera*, &c. They Sail'd on the Eve of St. *James* the Apoftle, 1525, touch'd at *Gomera*, and running along the Coaft of *Guinea*, could not make Cape St. *Auguftine* for want of Wind. By reafon of this Calm, all agreeing to it, he alter'd his Courfe to the Cape of *Good Hope*. A *Portuguefe* Ship guided them to

Another Squadron paffes Magllans Sreights. the Ifland of St. *Matthew*, which is Defert, and full of lofty Orange Trees, where they faw Hens, the Track of wild Boars, and fome *Portuguefe* Words carv'd on Trees, which fhew'd they had pafs'd that way. The Ships leaving them, they pafs'd Cape St. *Auguftine*, making for the Streights of *Magellan*. In this Courfe they endur'd Storms, and Err'd in their Accounts. *Sebaftian del Cano* ftruck on a Shoal, and was reliev'd. The Galloons and Advice Boat made *New Spain*. The Admiral, by the Advice of *Cano*, pafs'd the Equinoctial, upon information, That in 12 Degrees of South Latitude, he would find certain Iflands that were rich in Gold and Silver. All the Men fickn'd, the Admiral, and *Cano* dy'd, with fome others. The remains of the Squadron chooling *Toribio de Salazar* for their Commander, return'd under the Line; but he dy'd at the Iflands *de las Velas*, now call'd *Ladrones*, or of *Thieves*. After fome Strife, *Martin Iniguez*, and *Ferdinand de Buftamante* fucceeded him, and agree'd to Command by turns. Thus divided they came in fight of *Mindanao*, and thence to the *Molucco* Iflands, took in fome Refrefhment at *Cope*, a Town of the Ifland *Moratay*, whence they went on to *Camafo*, of *Morotoja*, whofe *Sangiack* is Subject to the King of *Tydore*.

War betwixt Spaniards and Portuguefes. They proceeded through the Gulph of *Camafo*, where they were Inform'd by the Ship of *Don George de Menefes*, who had been forc'd thither by the Currents, that the *Portuguefes* held the Fort of *Ternate*, and *Don Garcia* made War on *Tydore*. *Iniguez*, and *Buftamante* offer'd them the Affiftance of *Spain*, by which, coming fo opportunely, they gain'd the Affections of them all, and furnifhed themfelves with Neceffaries. *Don Garcia* being already provided againft the new Enemy, gather'd fome *Carcoas*, and tho' he could not perfwade *Daroes*, the Tutor, to go along with him, oppos'd the *Spaniards*. Firft the *Portuguefe* fent an Admonition, wherein he offer'd them Peace, and Entertainment, as Subjects to the Emperor, who was fo near Ally'd to the King of *Portugal*; protefting, That the *Molucco*

Iflands

Iflands were within his Limits. This avail'd nothing, and *Dai oes* Embarking in 12 *Carcoas*, with *Emanuel Falcao*, fent that Proteftation in Writing, and in cafe it was Rejected, to declare War. The *Spanifh* Comman- Portuguefe
der receiv'd the Lawyer that was to make the Proteftation, with much Ci- *and* Spa-
vility and Refpect, and anfwer'd, That the *Molucco* Iflands belong'd to the nifh *War*.
Crown of *Caftile*, and therefore he, in the Emperors Name, required *Don*
Garcia not to break the Peace eftablifh'd between their Kings. After all
they were oblig'd to have recourfe to Arms. *Iniguez* Landed on *Tydoi e*
ftrengthen'd the Works, and furnifh'd them with Canon. The *Portuguefe*
follow'd, and both fides Firing, there was a great Slaughter; but thofe of
Ternite retir'd fo diforderly, that the *Tydoi es* remain'd Victors However
neither the Proteftations, nor the War ceas'd, the *Spaniards* urging *Ma-*
gellan's Difcovery, and the *Portuguefe*, *Seri ano*'s, and *Bi ito*'s. The *Tydoi es*
and *Spaniards* took fome *Carcoas* belonging to *Gilolo*, in which they kill'd
a *Portuguefe*, and fome *Ternates*, as alfo a *Champan* Laden with Provifions
for *Talangame*.

In the *Philippine* Iflands they give the Name of *Carcoas* to a fort of Carcoas,
Veffels that ufe Oars, open, and bigger than our Barks, and are Steer'd by *what* fort
two Rudders, the one ahead, and the other aftern. The *Ternates* call'd *of Veffels,*
them *Janguas*, which differ from the *Carcoas* only in having two Half- *and others.*
Moons of Wood, Painted, or Guilt, rifing above the Keel at the Head and
Poop. About 100 Men Row in each of them, to the found of a Tabor,
and a Bell. They carry twenty Soldiers, and fix Mufketiers. The reft are
employ'd about four or five little Brafs Guns. Both the Men that Row, and
the Soldiers are Arm'd with *Campilancs*, that is *Cymiters*, and *Shields*, and
abundance of *Calabays*, and *Sagus*, being long Canes burnt in the Fire, to
harden them; which they throw, without tacking, as the *Moors* do their
Darts. Their way of Fighting is to come within Gun-fhot, and as foon
as they have Fir'd, both fides fly with all fpeed, till they have Loaded a-
gain, and then return to the fame Poft. They fet three Men to each Gun,
the one Levels, the other Charges, and the third Fires it. This is the way
among the Iflanders; for when they have to do with *Europeans*, our Example has Improv'd them in the Art of War. But in their *Carcoas* they
are always expos'd to be kill'd by our Cannon, becaufe they have no Fights
to cover them; and the fame is in the *Champanes*, which differ but little
from the others.

The Victory we have fpoken of Encourag'd the *Tydores*, and with the D. George
Affiftance of the *Spaniards*, they Arm'd, and falling upon *Gaca*, a Town of de Mene-
Ternate, Plunder'd and Burnt it; but at their Return, they met with *Mar-* fes *at* Ter-
tin Correa, whom they Fought, plying their *Carcoas*, the Succefs remaining nate.
doubtful. Whilft this War was at the hotteft, *Don George de Menefes*
came from the *Papuas* to *Ternate*, to whom *Don Garcia* prefently refign'd
the Poft, tho' the Hoftilities continu'd, with Burning and Slaughter on both
fides, which it was expected would be greater when the *Portuguefe* Succours came from *Malaca*, and the *Caftilian* from *Spain*. The new *Portuguefe*
Commander in Chief, and *Martin Inniguez* came to a Conference, and with
much Courtefy, and defire of Peace, concluded a Truce, which lafted not
long, tho' not on account of the main caufe.

There were many Battles between the *Spanifh* and *Portuguefe* Nations,
                                D   from

from *Gilolo* and other adjacent Islands, about the Possession of the *Moluccos*, and they were under several Commanders, the Event whereof we shall see in its Place. Therefore, and because others have Treated of them Copeously, they shall be now pass'd by, that we may return to the Actions of those Kings, which ought to be distinctly deliver'd now at the Beginning, for the better Understanding of the Causes why they came to be Lost.

King of Tydore makes Peace.

　　The King of *Tydore* was less Supported by *Spain* than he had been before, and was therefore oblig'd to sue for Peace, laying some Burden of Tribute, on his own Revenue proceeding from the Cloves. He also promis'd never to admit of any *Spanish* Succours; besides some other Conditions, which put an end to the Wars for a time.

Daroes, and the Queen govern in Ternate.

　　We have already observ'd, That *Cachil Boleyfe*, King of *Ternate*, left three lawful Sons, viz. *Cachil Bayano*, *Cachil Dayalo*, and *Cachil Tabarija*. The Eldest of them was not above six Years of Age; besides whom there were seven Bastards, the Eldest of them, *Cachil Daroes*, was Governor of the Kingdom, in Conjunction with the Queen. When *Brito*, in the Year 1521, Built the Fort, to secure the Subjection of the Island, tho' he had another Pretence for it, he took the Infant King, and the Queen his Mother, into it. She generously resenting this Violence, as not able to endure, that they should oppose the course of her Government, which she manag'd, together with her Step-Son, loudly Complain'd, and Threatned, as a Queen, and as a Mother. She wanted no Conveniencies for the Education of the Children; but there being Wrong disguiz'd among all that seeming Kindness, neither her Family, nor the Nurse, nor the Perswasions of Great Persons, could appease her Anger. The Natives observ'd the Difference of the *Portuguese* Domination, and that since their building of that Fort, they us'd intolerable Rigor, and consequently began to grow cold in their Affection,

Portuguese Insolent.

and to flacken in their Respect, especially when they perceiv'd that *Brito's* Successor continu'd to keep the Royal Family under Oppression. The young King was bred up in the Fort, till he was of Age to enter upon the Government of his Kingdom; and being 18 years old, soon dy'd, not without the usual suspition of Poison, but it was affirm'd to be given by private order of *Cachil Daroes*. O the wonderful Effects of the Desire of Rule !

　　Sultan *Bayano* being Dead, order was taken that the People should immediatly Swear *Cachil Dayalo*; but *Don George* found also means to get him into the Fort; the Mother demanding him, as fearing his Death, by the example of the Elder. *Don George* condescended, not so much in compliance to her Fears, as to oblige *Cachil Daroes*, with whose Government he was well satisfy'd; and it was he that had interven'd in, and advis'd

They Insult the Natives.

that way of Breeding the Princes. Soon after there happen'd an Accident, which broke off their good Intelligence; for *Daroes* grew jealous of the Commander in chiefs Behaviour, observing him much to favour *Cachil Bayaco*, a Man of note, whose Friendship he was suspicious of, and he with reason fear'd, that the Commander would in time value *Bayaco* more than him. This well grounded Fear grew up in his Breast, till it turn'd to down right Hatred, and he contriv'd to kill *Don George*. The Design could not be carry'd on so private, as to be conceal'd from him, and he to disappoint it, retir'd into the Fort. *Daroes* puffed up with the Applause of the People, sent immediatly to require him to deliver up *Bayaco*, to try

him

him upon some Complaints he had against him, being his Judge, as Governour, and oblig'd to do Justice. *Don George* was desirous to save *Cachil Bayaco*, and to that purpose assembled the *Alcayde*, and other Officers. Some said he ought to deliver him, others advis'd to appease *Daroes* by fair means. *Bayaco*, who hated him so mortally, that he woul'd chuse any sort of Death, rather than fall into his Hands, being lock'd up in a Room of the Fort, understood that his Case was doubtful, for they Consulted without any great Privacy. This made him Resolve what to do, and going to a high Window, he threw himself out with such Fury, that he beat himself to Pieces. *Don George* was troubl'd at the Accident, and thought himself oblig'd to Revenge it; which he began upon finding a Sow kill'd, either to spight him, or because the Neighbours were *Mahometans*, and had done it as she graz'd, or went about the Courts of the Fort. This was a rediculous Occasion, but of Moment enough among those People; Enquiry was made who had kill'd her, and it appear'd, or *Don George* would have it, that the Fault belong'd to *Cachil Baydua*, a near Kinsman to *Cachil Daroes*, very Learned, and Zealous in the Law of *Mahomet*, as also a *Caciz*, or Priest, and of great Authority in the Kingdom. He was seiz'd by *Don George*, and carry'd into the Fort, without regard to the publick Peace. *Daroes*, in a great Consternation, went with the chief Men of the Kingdom, to desire he would release that Sacred Person. Whilst they were discoursing this Point, *Peter Fernandez*, a mean Fellow, Servant to the Commander in Chief, by his Masters Order, or of his own Accord, in the Presence of them all, went up to *Cachil Baydua*, and rubb'd his Mouth, and Face with a fat Collop of the same Sow, neither the Opposition he made, nor his Complaints to God, and the Commander in Chief availing him; but on the contrary, the *Portuguefes* laugh'd out aloud, approving the Action by their Applause. *Daroes* on his part, cast himself on the Ground, and Weeping, prevail'd to have *Baydua* restor'd to him, whom, *Don George* being fatisfy'd, or appeas'd, and taking Security, sent to his House. *Daroes* attended him, and all the Prime Men; and *Baydua*, by Reason it is an Abomination among them to touch Swines-Flesh, presently used their Purifications, and the more to express his Concern, voluntarily left the Island for some Years, and travel'd about all the others in the Neighbourhood, preaching, and magnifying the Affront offer'd to one of *Mahomets* Priests, thus stirring up the Natives, and perswading them to Unite in Defence of their Honour.

Rudeness.

This Accident, which as a Disgrace to their Religion, exasperated the People, was seconded by another much worse, which quite render'd the *Portuguefes* Odious. The contrary Winds kept back the Trading Galeon, that us'd to carry the Soldiers Pay, and their Wants increasing, they began to seek Relief, breaking into the Natives Shops, and Store-Houses, and taking away their Provisions, without Paying for them. *Daroes*, offended at it, order'd, That no Provisions should be brought into the City to sell, and that the Shops which dealt in them, should be shut up. This was accordingly done, and reduc'd those in the Fort to such Distress, that the Soldiers mutinying, rail'd at their own Commander, and the Governor of *India*, demanding Relief with their Arms in their Hands. *Don George* being hard press'd, and blaming the Avarice of his Country Men, sent some

Portuguefes become odious for Rapine, &c.

Carcoas

Carcoas with Soldiers, under the Command of *Gomez Arriz*, to barter, Goods in the adjacent iflands for Provifions. They Landed on an Ifland near by, where, being defperate with Hunger, they Plunder'd the Town of *Tabona*, the Inhabitants whereof, no longer able to endure fuch Affronts, and Robberies, running to Arms, fell upon them, and kill'd the greateft Number, and moft of the reft being Wounded, were Difarm'd. They embark'd for *Ternate*, where their Wounds and Nakednefs fpoke what had befallen them, as much as their Words. *Don George*, who, befides his being naturally Paffionate, was now quite enrag'd, threatned *Daroes*, That if he did not deliver up the principal Actors in this Mifchief, he would feek his Revenge other ways. He was obey'd, and tho' *Cachil Daroes* knew that all the Fault belong'd to the *Portuguefes*, yet he deliver'd up the Governor of *Tabona*, and two other Chief Men of the Place, to *Don George*, thinking he would be fatisfy'd with keeping them Prifoners for

Barbarous Cruelty.

fome Days. As foon as they were brought before him, he order'd the Hands of the two to be cut off, and that they fhould be then fet at liberty. The Governors Punifhment was anfwerable to the Cruelty of him that was his Judge; they ty'd his Hands behind his Back, and expofing him on the Shore, fet two fierce Woolf-Dogs upon him, he having no way to withftand their Fury, made feveral vain attempts to flip afide from them, and endeavour'd to defend himfelf with what little Power was left him in thofe Limbs that were not Bound. The Multitude with Horror beheld the Spectacle, touch'd with Compaffion, and admiring the Inhumanity of the Punifhment. The wretched Man attempted to Fly, but perceiving that the arm'd Soldiers, had fhut up every way, on the Land fide, he caft himfelf into the Sea, the only Refuge accidentally left him, to feek fome uncertain Hope of Safety. However the Dogs being already blooded, left him not; but barking and howling, bit and tore him, tho' he ftill fwam with his Legs. At laft, being defperate, and almoft in the laft Agony, he took a horrid Refolution and fell upon thofe fierce Creatures with his Teeth; fuch was the Effect of Pain and Defpair. Thus the unhappy Man took hold of one of the Dogs by the Ear, and holding faft, funk with him to the Bottom. The like Barbarity had never before been feen in any of thofe Countries, to which the *Portuguefes* Traded; and by it they loft the Reputation they had before gain'd, to their great Applaufe, that they inflicted Punifhments, as it were by Compulfion, and Oblig'd to it, and that with Mildnefs, and Compaffion, to fhew their Generofity.

Confpiracy to deftroy the Portuguefes.

This Action brought them into general Hatred, and all the People of the *Molucca* Iflands being exited by *Cachil Daroes*, contriv'd to kill *Don George*, with all the *Portuguefes* and *Spaniards*, and fo deliver themfelves from their Yoke. *Daroes* undertook to Unite all the Kings of thofe Iflands in a League againft the Chriftians; fent away trufty Perfons to ftir up the Confederates; and particularly to *Cachil Catabruno*, Governor of *Gilolo*, during that Kings Minority, advifing him, at a Time appointed, to rife in Arms againft the *Spaniards* inhabiting his Dominions, and then to kill the Infant King, and Ufurp the Crown; for the compaffing whereof he promis'd his Affiftance, for they fhould both make that their common Caufe, becaufe he defign'd the fame Slaughter upon the *Portuguefes*, and upon the Infant King *Sultan Dayalo*, whom he would Succeed in the Throne, and never fubmit

to

to any *Spanish* Tyranny. At this time the Voice of the Gospel refounded in the Ears of the Barbarous Nations of the *Archipelago*, by the Preaching of the Religious Men of the Orders of St. *Augustin*, St. *Dominick*, and St. *Francis*, and of Father *Francis Naverius*, a *Jesuit*, and his Companions; Churches were built, and therefore God, who was taught by them, would not suffer the Ministers of the Gospel to be extirpated. *Don George* was inform'd of the Conspiracy, and the Preparations that were making to put it in Execution, which he kept to himself. *Daroes*, the better to diffemble it, never abfented himfelf, but reforted to the Fort, and paid Vifits to the Governour; fometimes when fent for by him, and others, of his own Accord. He fent one Day defiring he would come to him, and bring *Cachil Tamarano*, Admiral of the Ifland, and *Cachil Boio*, the chief Juftice of the Kingdom, to treat about fome important Affairs. *Cachil Daroes* knowing nothing of *Don George*'s Defign, took thofe two *Cachils* with him, and went away to the Fort. *Don George* receiv'd them courteoufly, and with a chearful Countenance; but being come into a Room where all Things were prepar'd for the Purpofe, they were feiz'd and put to the Rack, on which they difcover'd the Confpiracy. Immediately he pafs'd Sentence upon them in Form, and at the fame time caus'd a Scaffold to be erected, adjoyning to the Fort, on the Outfide, where the People were already gather'd in a Crowd. Then *Cachil Daroes* being brought out, and plac'd high on the Scaffold, a Cryer proclaim'd his Crimes, and the Penalty he was condemn'd to. His Head was cut off, and his Companions put to a lefs honourable Death; but what that was, no Hiftory or Relations inform us. *Doroes and others put to Death.*

The Queen and all the Natives, were fo terrify'd by this Action, that they fled out of the City, to a craggy ftrong Mountain at the Town of *Toruto*: Thence the Queen fent to demand her Son, whom the Governour kept as a Prifoner; but he not anfwering her Letter, fhe was fo offended at, and jealous of his Silence, that fhe caus'd Proclamation to be made, forbidding all the People of the Ifland, upon Pain of Death, to fell any Provifions, or other Neceffaries, to the *Portuguefes*. Her Orders were readily obey'd, and the *Portuguefes* prefs'd by Hunger, found it a more powerful Enemy, than thofe they had wrong'd. Their Skins began to fhrivel, they grew Lank and Weak, and muft have perifh'd, had not *Gonzalo Pereyra* arriv'd then with the Trading Galeon. *Gonzalo Pereyra* came from *Malaca* to fucceed *Don George de Menefes* in the Poft of *Ternate*; and improving the Opportunity, touch'd at *Borneo*, where he vifited the King, with whom, the *Spaniards* not obftructing, he fettled perpetual Peace and Amity; thence he fet out immediately for *Ternate*, where he arriv'd in Safety. He prefently took Poffeffion of the Fort, and paid the weak Soldiers. The Queen fent to vifit him, and to complain of *Don George*, and demand her Son *Cachil Dayalo*, which was her greateft Concern. *Gonzalo Pereyra* anfwer'd her generoufly, promis'd to do her Juftice; and to begin, fecur'd *Don George* in the Principal Tower, to appeafe the Queen, engaging his Word, That he would reftore her Son, as foon as the Fort was in a good Pofture. He fent to intreat her to return to the City, and former Amity; that Juftice might be peaceably adminifter'd. She feeing fome Effects of his Promife, in the Imprifonment of *Natives fly, and ftreighten the Portuguefes.*

New Governour.

her

her Enemy, and the Expectation of Releasing the King her Son, turn'd
past Sorrow into Joy, return'd to Court, and *Gonzalo Pereyra* reform'd
Abuses, repair'd the Fort, and built Bastions of Square Stone, which till
then had been unhew'd, the Queen furnishing Workmen and Materials.
Still *Cachil Dayalo* was detain'd in the Fort, without being restor'd to
his Liberty; and the Queen and People help'd to build the Fort, as the
sure Means of obtaining their King's Liberty. *Gonzalo Pereyra*, when he
thought it a proper Time, resolv'd to execute some Orders he had brought
from *Goa*, which were the same that had before endanger'd the Distur-
bance of those Kingdoms.

Some Governours, says the *Portuguese* Historian, *Couto*, only study to
enrich themselves, impoverishing the Provinces, and their King; for no
Prince can be rich, if his Grandeur depends upon poor Subjects. The Governour now perceiving that all Things were quiet, and he had little or
no Dependance on those People, made Proclamation, that none should buy
Cloves in those Islands, but the King, his Master's Factors. At the same
Time he order'd, that his Officers should enter the Houses of marry'd Men,
which are the Richest, and take away all their Cloves; and this not only
among the Natives, but in the Habitations, and Colonies of the *Portugue-*
ses, paying for it after the Country Rate; and that they should break all
their Weights, Scales and Measures, and other Implements of this Sort,
all which he caus'd to be publickly burnt. The Island was again in an
Uproar, and the *Portugueses* were for quitting it, because it was to no
Purpose to live there, if they were depriv'd of that Trade. Most of the
Portugueses repair'd to the House of *Ferdinand Lopez*, a Priest, who was
the Bishop's Vicar in the Fort, and ought to have given them an Example
of Modesty There one *Vincent Fonseca*, a seditious Fellow, heading the
Mutiniers, they resolv'd to require the Governour to permit them to live
in their former Liberty; and in case he should not Consent, they would
depart the Fort, and the Country, and go over to the *Spaniards*, or else to
the *Mahometans*, and Idolaters Towns. Some there were, who boggled
at the Crime of abandoning the Service of their King, together with the
Fort; and voted it would be less Harm to procure the Governour's Death,
by Means of the Natives. Whilst they were thus unresolv'd, the Governour sent to seize *Vincent de Fonseca*, for some disrespectful Words he had
spoken upon this Occasion, to another Soldier who was viewing the
Guards. The Multitude, who had already given themselves up to the
Direction of *Fonseca*, were as much concern'd at his Imprisonment, as if
every one of them had been put into Irons: and as generally in such Mu-
tinies, they are not without some specious Pretence, tho' it be but super-
ficial, many of the Seditious, being incens'd, and resolute, repair'd to the
Queen's Palace, where they were easily admitted, and some of them to
more Privacy with certain Counsellors of her's. There they represented
the Hardship of depriving them of the Trade of Clove, without any De-
merit on their Side. *But*, said they, *they may as well deprive us of this*
common Air, of this Light, and of the Benefit of our Senses. Our Kings
give no such Orders, but they proceed from the Avarice of the Governours
and Commanders, who tyrannize over us, and this Man more than all his
Predecessors, being come to destroy, that which he was sent to preserve.

He

Fresh Up-
roars
caus'd by
the Gover-
nour.

Portugue-
ses mutiny.

He has no Design to restore your Majesty your Son, but on the contrary we are satisfy'd he contrives to destroy both the Son and the Mother. Her he will secure, as soon as he has brought his Works to perfection, that he may not be again kept from Provisions. If you will stand up for your Country, and kill the Commander, we shall not obstruct it, but on the contrary shall be as vigorous to act against him, as we are ready to promise it.

The Queen and her Councellors were well pleas'd, hoping by that means to get rid of Tyrants, as they call'd them, and therefore would not let slip so favourable an opportunity to compass their Ends. The Queen assembled the prime Men of the Island; represented to them the Condition it was in; put them in mind, how King *Boleyfe* her Husband, protected the *Portugueses,* who came thither in Distress; how they had sworn Amity, and solemnly given their Hands upon it; the Honour and Kindness he show'd them; and that for their sakes he forfeited the good will of the Neighbouring Princes, that after he had receiv'd them, he maintain'd Wars, and sustain'd losses, even to the hazard of his life, to protect them; that he treated them as affectionately as if they had been his own Children; and how they, in return for his Entertainment and Favours, *as soon as the Breath was out of his Body, presum'd,* said she, *to lay violent Hands on me; from whose Tyranny and Oppression I escaped, by absconding long among the Rocks, and Brambles. My Children, they snatch'd from their Nurses Breasts, to confine them in Prison, in their own Kingdom, and among their Subjects When* Cachil Bayano *came to age to govern, they poyson'd him. They now design after the same manner to destroy his Brother, a lawful King, as if he were some run-away Slave. See what regard a parcel of intruding Strangers have for your Fortunes, your Houses, your Daughters, and your Wives, in your own Country, and in my Presence. Any one of these things ought to be a sufficient motive to cast off the Yoke we laid upon our Necks through our own Credulity. What then will not they all together oblige us to do? But besides all this, what ought we not to do, seeing our Religion affronted? Our Temples polluted? Our Priests trampled on? And all our selves in general despis'd? Can you have a greater Testimony of the justice of your Cause, than to see the* Portugueses *themselves on your side? Do not let slip this Opportunity, my Friends, stand by them, since they promise to assist us Deliver by their means your King, your Country, and your Religion; that all these may be afterwards rescu'd from them, and we may exclude such ungrateful Guests.*

The Queen stirs up her People.

These and other Exhortations made by the Queen, as *Maseus* writes in his *Latin* History, were receiv'd with Abundance of Tears, and they all engag'd to put their helping hands to the execution of what had been concerted, and fixt the day and hour. Great Dissimulation was us'd, and the Queen forwarded the work of the Fort with much application, without sparing any Cost, giving out, so as it might come to the Governour's Ears, That the King her Sons Liberty depended on the finishing of the Fort. This was the effect of Motherly Affection. The appointed Day being come, the Natives appear'd in Arms, just during the scorching Heat of the Noon-day; Some hid themselves in a Mosque, behind the Fort; others in a Wood, not far off, all of them ready to assault it, upon a Signal given, they being to enter at a Breach, which was not yet made up. Some

Conspiracy against the Governour.

of

of the Arm'd Islanders slily mixt themselves among the Masons, and Labourers, and among the King's Servants, who were going and coming with kind Messages between the Son and the Mother, and by this means convey'd him his Arms, and being us'd to talk to him freely at other times, they had then the Opportunity of acquainting him with the Design, and advising to be in a readiness to fall on boldly in due time   Thence they *His Death.* went to the Governour's Apartment, where he was taking his Afternoons Nap in all possible Security, his whole Family being asleep.   The *Ternates* burst the Doors open with their Shoulders, and rush'd upon the Governour, whom the noise had awak'd.   He defended himself with his Sword and Buckler for a considerable space ; but his Enemies being numerous, and all pressing forwards, they cut him in pieces.   A Woman-slave of his hearing the Hubbub, shreek'd out, which with the other Noise brought the Islanders out of the Mosque, without expecting the Signal.   They laid hold of a *Portuguese* they met, but he broke loose, and escap'd their Fury by flight   The Slave continu'd crying out, *Moors, Moors.*   With this the Governour's Servants came running arm'd, and going up to the chief Tower, where their Master was wont to divert himself, found all the Murderers there, whom they laid hold of, and cast down headlong, and then shut the Gates of the Fort   Then they rang the Bell, the sound whereof, and their not hearing the Signal, discourag'd the *Ternates* who lay in Ambush, so that they slunk away into the City.

Fonseca made Governour. The *Portugues* Conspirators went slily dissembling into the Fort, and finding the Governour dead, requir'd the rest in his place to admit of the *Alcayde*, or Constable of the Fort, because the King of *Portugal* had so order'd.   They refus'd him, and particularly the Vicar, who took upon him to head them all, and prevail'd so far that they chose *Vincent de Fonseca* for their Governour, who immediately took Possession of the Fort, and beginning to go on in the Tyrannical Design of *Gonzalo Pereyra*, left the Trade of Clove as it was before, but secur'd King *Dayalo*.   No notice was taken of the Governour's Death, as being executed by the consent of them all.   The Queen insisted to demand her Son, since she had furnish'd all Necessaries for that Work ; *Vincent Fonseca* refer'd the Answer to the Marry'd Men.   All those Nations are of opinion that the discreetest among them are the Marry'd Men, both on account of their Age, and as more faithful Councellors, because they have a greater interest in the publick Good, and therefore it is usual to refer to them all Debates and Answers in matters of Difficulty.   They all voted, That the Queen should not have her Son deliver'd to her, because it was convenient to keep him as an Hostage, fearing the second part of what had been concerted, and that their Friendships would last no longer than till it could be executed.   But to palliate the true cause of detaining him, they answered, That they must first acquaint the Governour of *India*.   In the mean while the Mother did not cease to weep, and to intreat.   She fed upon these Hopes, grounded on the Hatred the *Portugueses* still retain'd for *Pereyra*, and on the Generosity she had us'd in restoring the Trade of Clove, and other means.   The most prevalent of these seem'd to be the gaining the affections of the Marry'd Portugueses, to whom that Affair was referred, and under-hand of *Vincent Fonseca* himself, by rich Presents, and extraordinary Gifts.   But she was

soon

soon undeceived, for *Fonseca* offered her such Reasons or Excuses, as proved his Tyrannical Design; alledging, that having already sent to consult the Governour of *India* about the King's Liberty, it was not in his power to come to any Resolution in that affair, till the Answer came from *Goa*, for they would cut off his Head, should he go about to act of himself. The Queen perceiving that neither Gifts, nor Intreaties would prevail to get her Son, she resolv'd to use Force.

She stir'd up all the Neighbouring Kingdoms against the *Portuguese*; and order'd the Provisions to be all remov'd, that none might come to the Fort, either by Sea or Land. Those within began to feel the want of all Necessaries, to such a degree, that they su'd to the Queen for Peace, which was concluded, and they gave up her Son, which was the only thing she aim'd at, without regarding the inconveniency of losing the Fort. The Queen having obtain'd the King's Liberty, granted the *Portuguese* all the Conditions they demanded, and was so throughly appeas'd that the Christians continu'd their Settlements and Colonies, and Trade, and Provisions were restor'd. The Queen put the Government into the hands of her Son, who at first shew'd some Severity and Harshness towards the prime Men, and discover'd some Weaknesses, which till then his Confinement had either conceal'd, or supprefs'd. These things render'd him so odious, that the case was alter'd, and they would have been glad he had been Prisoner again. The Mother could not curb his ill Inclination, for the extravagant Youth's deprav'd Nature would not allow of it. *The Queen recovers her Son by force.*

At this time three mean Fellows of the *Portuguese* Colony, went to those of the Natives to rob; besides which they ravish'd some Women. The Islanders would not bear with that Insolence; but those who had been wrong'd in revenge kill'd the Offenders. *Vincent de Fonseca* hearing of it, magnify'd the Heinousness of the Fact, without mentioning his Countrymens Guilt, and order'd strict Enquiry to be made after the Slayers. What Care ought Princes to take to secure the Affection of their Subjects. The King was so hated, that certain Natives went to the Governour, and being conducted into a private part of the Fort, because they were Men of Quality, they assur'd him that the King had been the Occasion of the killing of those *Portuguese*, grounding the Accusation on their own Surmises, and aggravating the Offence with other Circumstances, in such manner, that had *Fonseca* lov'd the King, he could not but have believ'd them. He presently contriv'd to seize him; but being impatient, and despairing of securing him by Art, had recourse to Force. The King did the like, tho' sensible how little Affistance he could expect from his People, however he arm'd a few Vessels, and falling upon some Christian Towns, took several Prisoners. The Governour on the other Hand, without sparing *Ternate*, attacked what Towns he could, so that Cruelty and Rapine were again in use, even to affaulting of Cities, the very Sufferers approving of it, and pleas'd with their Losses, that so they might be reveng'd of their King. He fearing that the Hatred they bore him, might occasion his being seiz'd and deliver'd up to *Fonseca*, went over to *Tydore*, where that King for the present entertain'd and affisted him, as a Friend and Relation. The Governour sent with speed to call the King's younger Brother, named *Sultan Tabarija*, who was fled with some Malecontents, and with the content of *Portuguese Robbers kill'd.*

King of Ternate flies.

Sultan Ta-barija mad King.

all the reſt of the People, who were before no leſs diſſatisfy'd, proclaim'd him King, with all the Forms and Ceremonies us'd in that caſe. Many approv'd of it, yet ſome were ſcandaliz'd. The ſame Diviſion reign'd among the *Portugueſes*, remembring the unjuſt Election of *Vincent de Fonſeca*, and that he was the firſt and main inſtrument of the Death of *Gonzalo Pereyra*. *Fonſeca* himſelf was not at Peace with his own Conſcience; but ſo full of Apprehenſions and Dread, that he was never unarm'd, diſconſolate, melancholy, and attended by all thoſe ill Symptoms, the Memory of Guilt produces in the Mind; and he could wiſh he were diſcharg'd of the Burden he had taken upon him. The new King *Tabarija* began his Reign ſhewing Kindneſs to all Men, and cheriſhing the *Portugueſes*, which offended his abſent Brother; and adminiſter'd occaſion to irritate the Kings of *Tydore* and *Ternate* againſt him ſo haſtily, that he immediately broke the Peace, and declar'd himſelf their Enemy.

Triſtan de Atayde Governour of Ternate.

At this time *Triſtan de Atayde* came to *Ternate*, whoſe Preſence brought all Things into better Form. He appeas'd the Queen, and commending *Tabarija*'s Government, gain'd his Affection. Trade went on without any Obſtruction. *Vincent de Fonſeca* imbark'd for *India*, and was ſeiz'd by the Viceroy of *Goa*, for the heinous Crimes he had committed in the *Molucco* Iſlands, whence a full Account of them was ſent with him; yet he was not puniſh'd, but liv'd quietly for the future. *Ternate* flouriſh'd under this mild Government; the King, his Subjects, and the *Portugueſe* Officers being united; but all thoſe Garriſons ſo remote from the Head, being Receptacles of ſeditious Perſons, who are contriving Innovations to diſturb the Peace, and thrive by Diſcord, there wanted not ſome Promoters of ſuch Changes, who perverted *Triſtan de Atayde*, and diveſted him of his former Mildneſs. About the beginning of his Government two Carcoas of Barbarians plunder'd and almoſt deſtroy'd the City *Momoya*, the Inhabitants whereof were Idolaters, in the Iſland *Moro*. The Lord of it a powerful *Sangiack*, and good Moral Man, tho' a Heathen, made his Eſcape. *Gonzalo Velloſo*, a *Portugueſe*, was then not far from his City, following his Trade, and going thither, upon his paying a Viſit to the *Sangiack*, he told him the Havock that had been made, complaining of the dangerous Neighbourhood of the other Iſlanders, and asking his Advice, how he might be reveng'd and ſecur'd for the future. *Velloſo*, God directing his Tongue, told him, That the ſureſt way was to ſue for Peace to the Commander in chief of the *Moluccos*, and entertain Amity with the *Portugueſes*, for if his Enemies once ſaw he was ſupported by their Power, no King nor *Sangiack* would dare to offend him. He aſſur'd him that the King of *Portugal* ſent them for that End, being oblig'd to put down Tyranny and Oppreſſion; but that for the obtaining that benefit more fully, it was requiſite he ſhould become a Chriſtian; for by that means he would ſave his Soul, and ſecure his Eſcape, which was the leaſt important of the

A Sangi-ack con-verted.

two. *Velloſo* ſaid ſo much to this Point, and the Spirit which directed, ſuggeſted ſuch important Truths, that the *Sangiack* at firſt admiring them, approv'd and ſubmitted to them, and grew very earneſt to be admitted to Baptiſm. He deſir'd *Gonzalo Velloſo* to be aſſiſting to him, and gathering ſome of his Family and Friends, they ſet out for *Ternate*, the *Sangiack* himſelf ſtaying behind for their Anſwer. The Heathens came with *Vello-*

ſo

fo to *Ternate*, where they were generoufly received, and entertain'd by *Triftan de Ataide*. Having heard what they came about, he put them all into the Chriftian Habit, appointing Clergy-men to inftruct and Cate-chize them. Being thus prepar'd, they receiv'd Baptifm with extraordi-nary fatisfaction, the Commander in chief being their God-father. Then he commended the *Sangiack*'s Refolution, fhewing how advantageous it would be to him to become a Son of the Church, and reject the abominable and foul Ceremonies of Idolatry, in which he had liv'd. He fent him word, to appoint the Day and Place for being Baptiz'd, and he would fee all perform'd as he fhould direct, for which Reafon he left it to his Choice. The Meffengers returning to *Momoya*, were not only proud of having em-brac'd the Chriftian Faith, but of the good Ufage they receiv'd from the Governour and other Chriftians, telling the *Sangrack* all that had happen'd, and the Anfwer they brought him. The *Sangrack* led by his own inclina-tion, and encourag'd by their Account, imbark'd in fome *Garoa* with the greateft Splendor of Mufick and Gayety he was able. Being come in Sight of *Ternate*, *Triftan de Ataide* went out to meet him with no lefs Pomp. He lodg'd and entertain'd him accordingly, and order'd a learned and Re-ligious Man to Catechize and inftruct him. Some Days after when the Cathecumens were fitted for it, they receiv'd Baptifm, with publick Re-joyceings, and greater Solemnity than had ever been feen in *Ternate*. There was not a Chriftian but what brought Palm-Branches and Flowers from that natural Garden of the Ifland; befides Mufick, Dancing Firing of great Guns, and even the very Barbarians rejoyc'd. The *Sangiack* in Baptifm took the Name of *Don John*; he ftay'd fome Days rejoycing and Feafting with the *Portuguefes*, and then return'd home, taking along with him the Prieft that inftructed him, call'd *Simon Vaz*, to improve him in the Know-ledge of the Faith. That Prieft liv'd with him fome Years in his City, leading an Exemplar Life, and exercifing himfelf in Works of Office and pure Charity, by which means he converted great Numbers of Hea-thens, and particularly the Inhabitants of *Momoya*. But he being alone, and the Number of thofe God was pleafed for his Glory to bring to him in-creafing very faft, he fent to *Triftan de Atayde* for another Prieft to affift him in that Function, and he accordingly fent F. *Francis Alvarez*. They both in a fhort time converted the Infidels of that Part, throwing down all the *Pagodes*, fo they call'd their Idols, cleanfing thofe Places, and con-verting the Houfes of Abomination and Darknefs into Churches the li-ving God. *Triftan de Atayde* fo far favour'd the new *Don John*, as to fend along with him fome *Portuguefe* Soldiers to defend his Perfon and Fort, and this Prince maintain'd very friendly Correfpondence with him. His End we fhall foon fee and admire in the Sequel of this Hiftory.

The People of *Ternate* at the fame time took another Courfe, for they hating *Sultan Tabarija*, and defiring his Death, talk'd with the Govern-our in private, and gave him to underftand that his Life was in Danger, for *Tabarija* contriv'd to kill him, as had been done by *Gonzalo Pereyra*, that fo ne might feize the Fort, turning out the *Portuguefes*. The Go-vernour hearing his Life, and the Fort were both in Jeopardy, and calling to mind the yet frefh Example of his Predeceffor, eafily believ'd the Defign, but cunning'y diffembled. He contriv'd that fome *Portuguefes* on account

Portu-guefes fet re the King.

of real or pretended Differences fhould have Recourfe to the King's Favour, as fometimes they us'd to do, and fhould prevail upon him to come to the Fort to fpeak for them. He was apply'd to by fome, and like an innocent Man fufpecting nothing, went to the Fort to intercede for them. He was immediately feiz'd and loaded with Irons, and being brought to Trial, the fame Perfons that contriv'd his Imprifonment, appear'd as Witneffes a-gainft him. After a tedious Examination, or fhow of it, the Refult was, that he fhould be fent to *India* to juftifie himfelf. He imbark'd with a fafe Confcience, and his Caufe being examin'd before the Viceroy *Antony Bar-reto* at *Goa*, he was clear'd, and confeffing the Holy Spirit had taken that method to draw him to Salvation, was Baptiz'd in that City with great Satisfaction, by the Name of *Don Emanuel*. In his Return homewards, expecting the *Monfon* at *Malaca* to put to Sea, he dy'd with extraordinary Tokens of a fincere Chriftian; and having no lawful Heir, appointed King *John* the Third of *Portugal* to fucceed him in all his Kingdoms. The Will was afterwards carry'd to *Ternate*, where the great Ones and Commonalty accepted of it, owning King *John* for their Soveraign. This was per-form'd with Acclamations in the Streets and publick Places, as alfo in the Courts of Judicature, taking Poffeffion with the Royal Standard of *Portu-gal* difplay'd, and all other ufual Solemnities and Ceremonies. In the Year 1549, *Jordan de Freytas* carry'd the publick Inftruments of the Pof-feffion to *Lisbon*.

His Con-verfion and Death.

To return to the Courfe of the Hiftory when *Triftan de Atayde* had Im-bark'd King *Tabarija* for *India*, he fought out for a Baftard Brother of his call'd *Aerio*, born of a *Javanefe* Mother. The Lad was then ten years of Age, bred by his Mother in a retir'd manner, at a Pleafure-Houfe en-compafs'd with perpetual Greens, the natural Difpofition being improv'd by Art, which fo far prevail'd that the Flower fo wonderful for its Fra-gancy and manner of growing call'd *Trifte*, or melancholy, found only in *Malabar* and *Malaca*, abounded in this Ladies Gardens. She ador'd the Sun, and brought up her Child in that Folly, that he might forget the Rudiments he learnt at *Goa*, when in the Colledge of the *Jefuits*. The Idolaters believe, or feign, that a moft beautiful Daughter of *Parizataco*, a *Satrapa*, or Nobleman, fell in love with the Sun, and that he after com-plying with, and obliging her, fetled his Affections on another, and the firft not able to endure that another fhould be preferr'd before her, kill'd her felf. From her Afhes, for in thofe parts they ftill retain the Cuftom of burning dead Bodies, fprung that *Melancholy Tree*, fay they, whofe Bloffoms or Flowers ftill preferving the Memory of their Original, have fuch a Hatred for the Sun, that they cannot bear his Light. This Plant is call'd in the *Canarine* Tongue *Parizataco*, from the *Indian* Womans Fa-ther, who was Metamorphos'd like *Daphne*, tho' on another Account. The *Malayes* call it *Singadi*; the *Arabs*, *Guart*; the *Perfians* and *Turks*, *Gul*; the *Decanines*, *Pul*; and the *Portuguefe*, *Arvore Trifte*; that is, the Me-lancholy Tree. It fhoots out abundance of flender Branches, regularly di-vided by Knots, from each of which two Leaves fprout, oppofite to one another, like thofe of the Plum-Tree, but foft like Sage, and cover'd with a white Down. From each Leaf fprouts a Nib, or Nipple, whence five Heads fhoot out fmall at the end, each of them adorn'd with four fmaller

The Me-lancholy Tree, and Flower.

round

round Leaves; from each little Head proceed five Flowers, the fifth in the midst of the other four; among them the white Flowers visibly grow out, being bigger than Orange Flowers, and so fast after Night fall, that the Motion of them is perceptible. This Fruitfulness lasts all the Night, till the Appearing of the Sun renders it barren, and causes all the Flowers and Leaves to drop off, the Boughs remaining wither'd. On a sudden all that Fragrancy ceases, which enrich'd the Air with all the sweet Odours of *Asia*, included in this alone; till the Sun leaving the Horizon again, the Plant again flourishes in its beloved Darkness, as if it then retriev'd the Wrong it receiv'd from the Light. The *Asiaticks* are excessively fond of Perfumes, which is an Argument of their Lasciviousness. Great Taxes are laid in several Provinces, on all sweet Scents.

The *Portuguefes* came arm'd to that House, where the aforesaid Princess bred her Son, and demanded him in the Name of *Triftan de Atayde*; she would willingly have hid him, but could not, and therefore began to excuse her self, and beg they would leave him. It avail'd nothing, for the Messengers had Orders not to return without him, and to gain her Consent, swore they would carry him to reign in the stead of *Tabarija*, and that as soon as he came to the Fort, he should be received as King, both by the *Ternates* and *Portuguefes*. Some Relations tell us, that then the Mother, shedding Abundance of Tears, streightly embracing the Prince, cry'd out, saying, *Were I assur'd that you took him away to reign peaceably, without any Oppofition, or Apprehenfion, well belov'd and obey'd by his Subjects, and in fettled Profperity, undisturb'd by any Frights; yet would I rather fee him grow up and continue in a private Life, without burdening himself with any publick Concern, than that he should reign to pleafe your Humour; this was my Intention in retiring with him, and I would gladly conceal him from all humane Converfation. If fo, what can I think of what you now promife me? Will it be reafonable, that I deliver you my Son to receive the Crown, and that you at the fame time defign him for Imprifonment and Fetters, from which nothing shall, or can poffibly deliver him but Poifon and falfe Accufations, which have brought his Brothers and Parents to their End? What Security have I from Fortune, that she will in this Child be reconciled to that Family, which she has condemned to immortal Enmity with the* Europeans, *in Requital for having friendly entertain'd them; and decreed that, inftead of the Protection it hop'd to find in your Arms, you should lay on it an intollerable Joke? Leave us then, both Mother and Son, to employ our felves about the Works of Nature, fince cofily Experience has fo fully undeceived us as to the Effects of Fortune. Permit us to divert the Thoughts of them, with the Quiet, and Improvements of these Gardens. Let us be allow'd to want that which fo many feek after.* James de Couto, in his *Decades* relates this Fact, and the Mother's Lamentation, and Words. The *Portuguefes*, no longer able to give Ear to thofe difmal Reflections, which did not favour of a barbarous Woman, ran up to her, and forc'd away her Son, whom she ftruggled to defend. He, says the fame Author, obferving his Mother's Tears, and the Reafons she alledg'd for not parting with him, and having fome anticipated Notion of the Sweetnefs of Reigning, which he had not yet tafted, ftood gazing on her and them, full of Confufion. The Rudenefs, and Infolence

c f

Portuguefes fent to fetch Aerio.

His Mother's Speech to keep him.

of the Soldiers put an End to all ; for tho' they had no such Orders from their Commander, being deaf to, and weary of hearing the Complaints of a Disconsolate Woman ; they at the same time seiz'd the Son, and laying hold of the Mother, cast her headlong out at the Window : The new King was carry'd to the Fort, and at the same time that the Subjects swore Fidelity to him, they with general Lamentation celebrated his Mother's Obsequies, which were perform'd with greater Solemnity, than even those of the Principal Queens. This Inhumanity exceeding even the *Canibals*, and consequently unworthy the pretended *Portuguese* Bravery ; being bruited Abroad in the Neighbouring Provinces, produc'd that just Hatred which was of Force to unite ; and actually drew into a Confederacy all the Kings of the *Archipelago*, against the *Portuguese*. They assembled in Council, and in the Meeting concerted their Design, declaring that the Oppression they were under, was intollerable, the *Portuguese* making and deposing Kings to their own Humour and Fancy, insulting those Crowns which had given them the Power they had abus'd, contrary to all Laws of Humanity, without allowing the Natives so much as a Vote in Elections. Having agreed upon the Enterprize, they provided all Things for the Execution, whilst the appointed Time came, which they diligently made as short as might be, and expected with Dissimulation.

The *Spanish* and *Portuguese* Fleets at this Time continu'd their Voyages to the *Archipelago*, their several known Ways ; the *Spaniards* from *New Spain* to the *Phillippine* Islands, the *Portuguese* along the Coasts of *Africk*, and so to *Malaca*. Both Sides exercised their Power, and carry'd on their Trade with Ambition, and, as some say, with Cruelty; but the most bloody Theatre of continual Tragedies, was *Ternate* and all the *Molucco's*. There both Nations of *Castile* and *Portugal* decided their Quarrel by the Sword, whilst their Kings in *Europe* only contended by Dint of Cunning, and Cosmography. At this time the Matter was not so plain, as when the Cosmographers and Commissioners on both Sides, lay'd down the Meridian, whereby to assign each of them one half of the World to their King. For the Admiral *Christopher Columbus* returning from his first Discovery of the *West-Indies*, in the Y ar, 1493. Pope *Alexander* the VIth. granted the Investiture of them, for the Crown of *Castile*, to their Catholick Majesties, King *Ferdinand*, and Queen *Isabel*, or *Elizabeth* ; and to obviate the Differences that might arise between the two Crowns, to the obstructing the Propagation of the Gospel, by the same Apostolical Authority, which in that spiritual Capacity is not limited to any part of the Globe, he divided it betwixt those two Crowns, ordering a Line to be drawn along the Heavens to cut both the Poles, distant on the Earth one hundred Leagues from the Islands of the *Azores* and *Cabo Verde*. By Vertue of this Division, the Emperor pretended that the *Molucco* Islands were within his Limits, ever since *Gonzalo Gomez de Espinosa*, his Commander in chief, *Sebastian del Cano*, and his Companions, who went with *Magellan*, took Possession of them for his Crown. Pretending at the same Time, that they were the first Christians that arriv'd at the *Moluccos*, and that then he was own'd as Sovereign by *Sultan Corali*, King of *Ternate*, who reign'd before *Sultan Bongue* ; by *Sultan Almanzor*, King of *Tydore*, by *Luzuf*, King of *Gilolo*, and other Princes, who all swore

Fealty

The Portuguese murder her.

Confederacy against them.

Difference about the Moluccos, between Spain and Portugal.

Fealty by their Idols, and the *Alcoran*; and that *Gonzalo Gomez* admitted them, and fwore to the Obfervance of what had been agreed on, in his King's Name, before an Image of the Bleffed Virgin. He urg'd, that by *Argments for Spain.* Mathematical Demonftration, and the Judgment of Men learned in that Faculty, it appear'd, that the *Moluccos* were within the Limits of *Caftile*, as were all others, as far as *Malaca*, and even beyond it. That it was no eafy Undertaking for *Portugal* to go about to difprove the Writings of fo many Cofmographers, and fuch able Mariners; and particularly the Opinion of *Magellan*, who was himfelf a *Portuguefe*. And that in Cafe he might be thought partial, becaufe of his being difoblig'd in *Portugal*, that Exception did not lie againft *Francis Serrano*, who was alfo a *Portuguefe*, and had been favour'd and cherifh'd. That to fay the Sea Charts had been malicioufly contriv'd, was a groundlefs Objection, and not probable. Befides that, in Relation to the Article of Poffeffion, on which the Controverfy depended, it was only requifite to ftand by what was writ by, and receiv'd among Cofmographers.

In Anfwer to this, King *John* of *Portugal*, deny'd the Fact of the Dif-covery, as to its Precedency; for *Serrano's* was in the Year 1511, and *Portuguefe Anfwer.* that of *Magellans* Companions nine Years later, in 1520. He declar'd the Globes, Aftrolabes, and Sea Charts to be partial, and that in Cafe they were rectify'd, drawing the aforefaid Meridian, according to Rules of Aftrology, his Limits would not only comprehend the *Moluccos*, but reach far beyond the *Philippine* Iflands. He offer'd King *Tabarija's* laft Will on his Behalf; and faid, that if the Line were fairly drawn, obferving Eclip-fes, as had been done fometimes, the Truth of his Affertion would ap-pear. To this they added, the Papers of the Geographer and Aftrologer, *Andrew de S. Martin*, by which it appear'd, that he failing with *Magel-lan*, his before unattempted Voyage, had obferved feveral Eclipfes, and Oppofitions. Among the reft, on the 17th of *December*, 1519. He in the River call'd *Rio de Janeyro*, took an Obfervation of a Conjunction of *Jupiter* and the *Moon*; on the firft of *February* 1520, another of the *Moon* and *Venus*; foon after another of the *Sun* and *Moon*, after paffing the Streights, another Oppofition of the *Sun* and *Moon*, and others at other times; all which, tho' calculated by him to the Meridian of *Sevil*, avail'd nothing to his Defign, which was to prove that the *Molucco* Iflands did not belong to *Portugal*; for which Reafon he found Fault with *John de Monteregio's* Tables and Almanacks. All thefe Papers were preferv'd by *Edward Refende* Factor at the *Moluccos*, a learned and curious Man. They faid, that fince there was, then a Treaty about the Poffeffion of thofe Iflands; in a Cafe of that Confequence it was not proper, to avoid al-ledging, and examining the Grounds of their Property, to prevent the De-cifion of the Sword, which was the Court where that Controverfy was pleaded; and when once it comes to that pafs, there was no Poffibility of ftanding to fpeculative Writing, which not being made good by Experi-ence, muft at leaft be look'd upon as uncertain.

The Poffeffion of the *Molucco* Iflands was of great Confequence to the King of *Portugal*, for carrying on the Trade of Spice, and being inform'd of the War ftill maintain'd between his Subjects and the Emperor's, in thofe Parts, he daily us'd frefh Endeavours to bring that Bufinefs to fome Conclufion, that fo the War might ceafe. The Emperor had not fo much

much Intelligence of what his Commanders did in *Asia* ; becaufe the *Portuguefe* fuffer'd no Ships, but their own to pafs by the Cape of *Good Hope* ; and the way of *New-Spain*, that Voyage was not much frequented, and therefore not fo well known ; and befides all this he then flood in need of a great Sum of Money. In the Year 1525, there was a Treaty at *Segovia*, by his Majefties Order, for compofing of this Difference, and in 1526 it was held at *Sevil*, where the *Portuguefe* Embaffador; and the Licenciate *Azevedo* of that Kings Council, were met by the Bifhops of *Ofma*, Prefident of the Council of the *Indies*, Doctor *Lawrence Galindez*, of the fame Council, and *Don Garcia de Padilla*, firft Commendary of *Calatrava*, on the Emperor's fide, as Commiffioners, and Plenipotentaries, befides the Lord-High-Chancellor, and the Popes *Nuncio, Mercurio Gatnara*. After many Meetings, and much Strife, to which there were alfo Civilians, Geographers, and Mariners admitted ; all which only puzzled the Caufe, whence enfu'd Law Suits, Arbitrations, and other Fruitlefs Negociations in *Spain*, and Wars in *Afia* between the Ships of both Crowns: After all this there was a Ceffation, and Quietnefs, the Emperor Mortgaging thofe controverted Iflands to the King of *Portugal*, for 350000 Ducats. This was concluded at *Zaragoza*, on the 22d of *Auguft* 1529, as his Imperial Majefly was going over to be Crown'd in *Italy*. The Line of Divifion was again examin'd, and what Parts of the Earth it is to run through ; the Times of Payment were fix'd, with other Conditions, and Salvos of the Right on both fides, that fo neither Oblivion, nor the Kindred between the two Kings might confound it.

By Relations Written in thofe Days it appears, that the Emperor confulting *Peter Ruyz de Villegas*, a grave and learned Gentleman, about this Mortgage; his Anfwer was condemning it, and declaring, That his Majefty had better to have Mortgaged any other of his Kingdoms, than that of the *Moluccos, Trapobana*, or *Malaca*, or any other in the Eaft ; all which, in his Opinion, belong'd to his Majefty ; and he grounded his Opinion on Time's cafting Treaties into Oblivion, and the great uncertainty of State Affairs. Many others advifed the Emperor to repay that great Sum to the King of *Portugal*; and what is yet more, the Reprefentatives in the *Cortes* of *Caftile*, propos'd that the Emperor fhould make over to them the *Molucco* Iflands for fix Years, by way of Farm, and they would pay King *John* the Mortgage Money, and bring the Trade of Spice to *Coruna*, and after the fix Years his Majefty fhould carry on that Trade. The Emperor hearing of this Innovation, order'd a ftop to it, and that no further Progrefs fhould be made in fitting out the Fleet defign'd for the *Moluccos*, under *Simon de Alcazova*, and forwarded by the Bifhop of *Ciudad Rodrigo*.

Orders, and Letters Patents, were drawn and fealed, for both Nations to forbear Hoftilities, but the Emperor's Subjects never receiv'd Commands from him to withdraw their Forces for any other Enterprize, nor did they know what had been agreed on in *Spain*, any other way than by the Account they had from the *Portuguefes* who had receiv'd Orders from their King, to conclude a Peace, and to Ship off the *Spaniards* by the way of *India* for *Spain*. This Agreement put an End to all Judicial, and Military Contention. Since then the Viciffitude of Times has invefted all the Right, and Title in our King. So that, according to grave Civilians, he

might,

might, as they fay, invert the Titles, or poffefs by them all, without confounding the Right; Heaven having defign'd him to be Sovereign of fuch a vaft Monarchy, and given him that Hereditary Zeal, which makes him offer his whole Power to oppofe Hereticks and Sectaries, and to fpread the Faith, and its perfect Politicks among fuch Multitudes of Souls as have received it, in fo many barbarous Provinces. For this fame Reafon it will be fuperfluous to examine any further into the Limits affign'd by that Law, which could never be fettled.

This Accommodation being concluded, the *Portuguefe* Fleets, without any Oppofition from thofe of *Caftile*, peaceably poffefs'd themfelves of the Iflands of *Ternate*, *Tydore*, *Bachian*, and the others about them. From the firft of thefe, as their Head in Spirituals, our Priefts went Abroad to preach the Word of Truth, which was receiv'd by feveral Kings and Nations, leaving but inconfiderable Remains of Idolatry, and other Sects. Whole Cities, whofe Soveraigns chofe to continue in their Darknefs, not regarding their Prince's Example, which ufes to have the Force of a Law, threw down their Idols, and confecrated Profanenefs, dedicating their Temples to the True God. The Kings of *Portugal* built Garrifons, and Factories for the Chriftians to inhabit; fending their Commanders and Officers, who curbed the Kings, and the *Sangiacks* their Subjects. Some Governours there were, who befides the Care they took of propagating the Gofpel, and maintaining Peace in thofe Parts, endeavour'd by endearing Means to attract the Barbarians to love our Habits, to affect our Ways of Entertainment, and the *European* Affability and Converfation, and gently inclin'd them to our Cuftoms and Manners, which in fome Places made them look upon that as a Sort of Equality, when it was no better than Servitude. The powerful Union of Juftice and Religion was however the moft prevalent; but the Commanders and Governours being defective in the firft of thefe Virtues, on which inward Felicity and Government depend; the Subjects loft the fecond, and return'd to their former Blindnefs, as appears by what has been already faid, and more fully by what is to follow, fince we are now come to the Election of *Sultan Aerio*, in whofe Days *Ternate* was utterly loft, and could never be recovered either by Force or Art, till the Reign of our Sovereign Lord the King; a juft Reward of his Piety and Zeal. The lawful Queen, by thofe People call'd *Putiiz*, was as much concern'd for *Aerio*'s Mother's Death, as for any of her own Sons. She was prefent at her Funeral, and lamenting immoderately, curs'd the Domination of the *Portuguefes*, calling it Tyranny. All the Machinations of thofe who ftudy'd Revenge were known to her, and fhe forwarded them with her Advice; for as they faid, nothing now remain'd of the former Moderation of the Governours fent thither out of *Europe*, nor of that Regard and Refpect they ufed to have for them.

Portuguefes Poffeffion of the Moluccos.

Converf.-ons.

The End of the Firft Book.

F

·THE
HISTORY
OF THE
DISCOVERY and CONQUEST
OF THE
Molucco and *Philippine* Iflands, *&c.*

BOOK. II.

THE Alliance concluded betwixt the Kings of the *Archipelago*, and particularly *Vaygamano*, *Vaigeo*, *Quibibio*, and *Mincimbio*, reigning in the Iflands *Papuas*, was follow'd by fuch an Accident, that tho' the Minds of the Confederates had not been already fo well difpos'd, nor the Blood of thofe Innocent Kings fo newly fpilt, it would have confummated the Hatred they had conceived againft the *Portuguefe* Nation. All the Ports of the *Molucco* Iflands were fo well fecur'd, and the Paffage for Provifions fo wholly ftopp'd up, that *Triftan de Atayde* defpairing of Relief, fent Captain *Pinto* to *Mindanao*, and the Neighbouring Iflands, to furnifh fuch things as were abfolutly neceffary for the Support of Life, there being nothing to be had within his Liberties. *Pinto* failing in a good Ship, arriv'd at *Mindanao*, vifited the King, by whom he was well receiv'd ; and he having feen his Credentials, and confulted the *Sangiacks* of his Council, eftablifh'd Peace and Amity with him. He fold the Commodities he carry'd at his own Rates, and buying and barterring, loaded with Provifions to his own Content ; thence he went over to the Ifland *Serrago*, where he was no lefs fuccefsful with the King. In this Ifland, that their Friendfhip might laft for ever, they concluded the Peace with a barbarous Ceremony, which when practis'd in thofe Parts, they never break the Articles. The Parties being met, certain Officers appointed for that Purpofe, draw a Quantity of Blood from their Arms, and each drinks the other's, as a Gage of Affection, believing they convey it into their Souls, by that horrid Draught. This Contract fo ratify'd, produc'd fuch Confidence, that their Ships repair'd to our Ports,

Pinto fent for Relief.

Barbarous Cuftome.

Ports, and ours to theirs, with all possible Security, without any Let or Prohibition. *Pinto* perceiving what a Multitude of the Natives resorted to his Ship, resolved to make a Prey of them; and the last Day, Forty of them coming Aboard to Trade, he perswaded them to go down into the Hold, on Pretence of showing them its Bulk and Conveniencies, and as *Villany of* soon as they were down, shut the Hatches upon them, this he practised se- Pinto. veral times, till at last, tho' he observ'd them close, one of them forcing his Way out, leap'd into the Sea, and swam ashore. He went directly to the King, whom he acquainted with the villanous Practice: The King justly enrag'd, to see Friendship so newly contracted, and confirm'd by the the most sacred of Tyes, in his Opinion, so perfidiously violated by the *Portuguefes*, thinking Religion affronted, immediately order'd all the Ships that were afloat to be brought together, and such as were finish'd in the Docks, to be launch'd; all which being well equipp'd, stor'd with Guns, and full of those furious Barbarians, encompass'd the *Portuguese* Ship, attacking her on all Sides. *Pinto* was beginning to weigh his Anchors, having seen the Ships in Motion, and the Men hasting Aboard; he defended himself with only 25 Soldiers, who had scarce time to handle their Arms; for the Natives of *Seriago* began already to Board, and those who were Prisoners under Deck had prevaild, but that the Mariners loos'd their Sails. At this time there fell a dreadful Storm of Rain, with such amazing Thunder and Lightning, as if the Heavens had been rent asunder. The *Seriagos* quitted the *Portuguese* Ship, endeavouring to recover the Shore in their own Vessels, with their Sails rent, the Hulls shatter'd, and the Rigging disabled; and to get off the better, they threw over-board their Cannon and Arms, being in danger of sinking. This Tempest lasted two Days, during which Time, *Pinto's* Ship could not escape, his Men and he being so far spent, that they had neither Strength nor Courage to stand by their Tackle; they let the Ship drive with the Sea, and threw over-board their Provisions, Merchandize, Guns, Arms, Cloaths, and all they could come at; and being convinc'd of the Justice of the Judgment, for having broken their Faith, and solemn Engagement they had made, arriv'd at *Ternate* astonish'd, dumb, and out of Countenance, thinking they were still in the Storm. Such are the Effects of a guilty Conscience, which presently provokes God's Wrath.

All the Kings of the adjacent Islands were soon acquainted with the *Leagues* Perfidiousness of those few *Portuguefes*, that they had transgress'd the sa- *against the* cred Laws of Hospitality, and always made a mischievous Use of Benefits; *Portugue-* whereupon they immediately concluded their League, to be exercised like *fes.* desperate Men. They presently made Proclamation, forbidding, under most severe Penalties, the conveying of any Provisions to the *Portuguefes*, either by Sea or Land, that so they might be reduc'd to quit all those Provinces, and fly into *India*, and since they could not batter the Fort, for Want of great Guns, they should starve it out; enjoyning all Persons of all Ages, and both Sexes, to be vigilant in observing this fatal Decree, that so the Trading Galeon might not afford them the Comfort of hoping for Relief. Then considering that the main Motive of their exercising such Tyranny, was the Spice of Cloves, wherewith *Ternate*, and all the *Molluccos* abound, the Natives resolv'd to set Fire to all the Trees, endeavouring

that

that the Conflagration fhould be fo Univerfal, as that the *Moluccos* might ever after remain barren. They well knew that this was contriving their own Ruin; but they look'd upon it as a pleafing and advantageous Deftruction, fo they might but be reveng'd of their Enemies.

Reflection.   The Crop of Cloves makes the Wealth of the *Molucco* Kings, much more than the Taxes their Subjects pay; and tho' Rage, and Defpair put Fire into their Hands, to burn their Country, it might happen, as fometimes Miftakes prove advantageous, that what they defign'd to render their Fields Barren, might make them more Fruitful. It is well known that courfe Afhes mix'd, and fcatter'd on the Face of the Earth often Fertilize it. Nothing is more frequent in *Europe* than to burn the Stubble, and Straw upon barren Lands, becaufe, either the burnt Earth gathers fome unknown Strength, and produces good Pafture, or elfe the Fire confumes its Ranknefs, and exhales the fuperfluous Moifture. Perhaps the intenfe Heat opens feveral Paffages, and dilates the clofe Pores, and hidden Veins, thro' which the Nourifhment flows, and thence the Earth receives it in all Parts, to make it capable of a new Product; or elfe it hardens, and clofes the Veins which were open'd, that fo the thin Waters, or the continual Intenfenefs of the Sun, or the piercing Cold of the North-Eaft Wind, which is chilling, may do it no Harm. Befides, Nature having chofen that only Part of the World to produce this fort of Fruit, in which there has never been obferv'd any Failure, or Intermiffion, it cou'd not be believing that a Momentary Violence fhould utterly caufe it to ceafe. However the Defign of thofe People was not to renew thofe Spicy Groves, but entirely to deftroy them. This fhows how mifchievoufly they were bent againft themfelves, and againft all Nations. It will be therefore convenient in this Place to treat of the Cloves at large.

Account of Cloves.   The firft that made any Account of it, were the *Chinefes*, who attracted by the Scent, began to load their *Junks* with it for the Gulphs of *Perfia* and *Arabia*. *Pliny* was acquainted with, and defines it, faying, It is a long Pepper; and calls it *Garyophillum*. The *Perfians* gave it fince the Name of *Calafur*, it does not belong to us to decide which of thefe Words was derived from the other. The *Spaniards* formerly call'd it *Girofe*, and afterwards *Clavos*, becaufe they are like Nails, which bear the fame Name. The Head of the Clove, having four fmall Teeth that crofs it, refembles a Star. The Natives of the *Moluccos* call the Tree *Siger*, the Leaf *Varaqua*, and the Fruit *Chamque*. The Plant is not unlike our Bay-Tree, but bears a greater Head. When it begins to bloffom, it fpreads a moft delicious Fragrancy, and on the very Top like the Myrtle, from one fingle Stock produces an infinite Number of Clufters, like thofe of *Elder*, or the *Honey-Suckle*. At firft coming out they are White, as they grow up Green, and the third Seafon, when Ripe, makes them Red; this Variety of Colours, by inward Virtue, fhowing the feveral Terms that bring it to Perfection. Thofe that remain on the Clufters, which they call *Mother Cloves*, continue there a year, growing larger and ftronger. They either threfh the Branches to gather them, or elfe fhake them with Cords they have made faft above, drawing from below, after the Ground about is clean'd; but it is naturally clear from Weeds, for this Sovereign Tree fuffers no fort of Herb to grow about it. It draws all the moifture fo powerfully to it felf, that all

Roots

Roots about are deſtroy'd, or ſtarv'd. It bears at eight Years ſtanding, and laſts an hundred. Some ſay it would hold longer, were it not ſtrip'd with ſuch Violence, which it avenges by growing Barren; but they are miſtaken, for in the Iſlands of *Bachian*, they lop the Branches, that they may produce more Cloves, and the low Branches bear leaſt. From theſe they gather the Cloves with their Hands, and they only bear when the *Monſon* blows. They yield their Fruit from *September* to *February* every two Years. Others ſay once in three; becauſe when they gather the Clove, beſides that the Plant is much impair'd, they break off thoſe Buds, which produce the Bloſſoms of the Cloves; but then they afford certain hopes of another Crop. The Truth of it is, that Nature allows them a Year's reſpit, during which they reſt like the Olive-Trees in *Europe*. They are gathered when Ripe, and their Ripeneſs appears by being Red. Being ſpread in the Sun, in three Days they dry up, and contract a blackiſh Aſh-colour. *Avicen*, by his leave, was deceiv'd, when he ſaid that the Gum of *Miſtake of Avicen.* the Clove Tree is anſwerable in its Virtue to Turpentine; for Experience has prov'd the contrary. Beſides, that Trees exceſſive hot or cold, yeild no Gum, but only thoſe which are temperate between both. Sea-Water Feeds, and Freſh does them Harm. A certain Hiſtorian Writes, that they yield Fruit twice a Year; if by it he means the middle Crop, which is very ſmall, we grant it; but if he ſpeaks of the moſt Fruitful, as the Triennial, which with general Amazement produces enough to ſerve all Nations, the Belief of his Aſſertion will remain in the Author himſelf. Theſe Plants make amends for their delay in the Abundance of their Product; which is ſuch, that after enriching all Nations with it, the K. of *Spain's* Revenue out of it, Yearly amounts to two Millions of pieces of Eight, little over or under. It is generally reckon'd that only the five *Molucco* Iſlands produce all the Clove, becauſe of the prodigious Quantity they yield. They always amount to Four Thouſand *Bars*, each Bar of *Ternate* being four hundred Weight, and three quarters, and this for that Iſland; but the third of the whole taken for the King amounts to ſix thouſand *Bars*, and every common Bar is better than five hundred Weight of ours. Perhaps the Word *Bar* might come from the *Greek Baros*, ſignifying a Load. The Cloves grow alſo in the ſmall Iſlands of *Ires* and *Meytarana*, about *Ternate*; thoſe of *Pulo* and *Cavali* near *Tydore*, and in *Gilolo*, *Sabugo* and *Gamoconora*, Towns of *Ratachina*; as alſo in the Iſlands of *Amboyna* and *Veranula*, more in this laſt than in all the others, but they are weak, and ſmaller. The Clove Trees grow up without any Help of Art, like all Trees coming from Rocks, and they made the only Woods in theſe Iſlands, which ſucking in all the moiſture Heaven affords, it is a wonder to ſee any other Plant near. When they have a mind to Tranſplant a Clove Tree, they ſet it where many Weeds grow, that it may thrive the ſooner, by the help of the Moiſture, and Virtue it ſucks from them, and as the Tree thrives thoſe Plants periſh. For the ſame reaſon Cloves are ill Neighbours to full Veſſels. The Ring Doves, whereof there are great numbers in *Gilolo*, eat many of thoſe Cloves which grow Old upon the Tree, then flying they purge in the Air with the Motion, and from their Excrements dropping on the Ground Clove Trees grow up. Heaven has given them ſo plentfully only to theſe Iſlands, abſtractly from all the World beſide; being at firſt not valu'd, or

known

known by the Natives. This is what they would have deſtroy'd by Fire, that it might be totally annihilated, becauſe the Flames gather more Strength among combuſtible Matter, than other Violences, to which ſublunary things are ſubject.

Since we are now upon the Deſcription of the *Moluccos*, and in regard that thoſe delightful Provinces are ſo remote from us, we will go on with what is remarkable in them, to ſhow the deſperate Fury of thoſe People, who had condemn'd them to the Flames. All the five *Molucco* Iſlands are almoſt round, and of the ſame Shape. The compaſs of the biggeſt is not ſeven Leagues. They have all Crags, of a wonderful Height, cover'd with an odoriferous Fragrancy of wild Cloves; and about them ſeveral Cities, Towns and Forts. Their exact Roundneſs is the Reaſon they have no good Harbours for both the *Monſons* of Norweſt and South. Only *Ternate* forms the Port they call *Talangame*, and a League from it, that of *Toloco*, where Ships ride ſafe, and with their Boats cloſe to the Shore. The Forts were not erected in either of them, becauſe they ſhould not be remote from the King's Court. Both theſe Ports look to the Eaſtward, and have ridges of Rocks that break off the Sea, and ſecure the Veſſels. That of *Ternate*, oppoſite to the Fort admits of Caravels, at high Water and ſpring-Tides, which being unloaded ride where they will. This Ridge of Rocks is of a ſort of Stone, that turns into Coral, which when old hardens, and ſhooting out many Branches, knits together, and turns again into Stone, whereof excellent Lime is made. It is ſo contriv'd that thoſe who come to it by Sea, think they ſee noble Structures erected for the Defence of the Harbour. The Mountain, which riſes in the midſt of *Ternate*, two Leagues in Height, and cover'd with Palm, and other rare Trees, has on the Top of it a Mouth or Cave, that ſeems to reach down to the very Center. A Man can hardly be ſeen from the one ſide to the other. Within it is a Square Spot, like a Threſhing-Floor, made of Stones and looſe Earth. Some curious Perſons have view'd it, and among them one *Gabriel Rebelo* Factor, and Alcayde of the Fort; who having ſounded it, tying together ſeveral long Fiſhing-Lines, found it was 500 Fath. deep. At the Bottom guſhes out a beautiful Spring, tho' no Man has dar'd to Taſt of it, or try whether it is Sweet or Sower. The looſe Floor ſhakes with the Fire in the Bowels of the Mountain, whereof the firſt Account was given by *Anthony Galvam*, who Obſerv'd it in the Year 1538, when he was Commander in Chief over theſe Iſlands. He went up to ſee that Wonder in Nature, at a ſate Time, for he could not have done it in *April*, or *September*, when the Sun moves from one Hemiſphere to the other, and croſſes the Equinoctial, which cuts half a Degree of *Ternate*, becauſe of the Winds then kindling the Flames. Had *Pliny*, when he went out of Curioſity to ſee the Burning of Mount *Veſuvius*, in *Italy*, taken another opportunity, he had not been Burnt to Death, as his Nephew writ to *Cornelius Tacitus*. It ſtinks, and caſts out Smoke, Sulphur, and Red-Stones, as it were out of the Mouth of a Canon, ſhewing the Mountain to be hollow at the Foundation. It cauſes Earthquakes, and Noiſe; and the Flames, and burnt Stones, have reach'd to the City, and Fort, and even to the Iſlands of the *Meros* and *Cafues*, twenty Leagues from *Ternate*. The Smoke is of ſeveral Colours, becauſe the Moiſture and Corruption of the Earth exhales it thick, and diverſify'd,

which

(marginal notes:)
Moluccos deſcrib'd.

Burning Mountain.

which is help'd by the ill Quality of the Air, and that, with the falling of the Excrements the Fire casts out upon the Springs, corrupts the Waters, and destroys Health. Going up this Mountain two thirds of the Height, it is all Green and Fruitful; but the Top is excessive Cold, without any sort of Fowl, or Birds, but abundance of Flyes. Thence is descry'd a spacious Sea, and an infinite Number of Islands; because the Purity of the Air, free from Exhalations, as is said of the Top of Mount *Olympus*, represents curious Objects to the Sight, and favours it without any Let, the greater part of the Year. Where the Thickness of the Trees Terminates, a Spring of fresh Water gushes out, so very cold that there is no Drinking of it, but by Sips. At the Top, some distance from the Mouth, which casts out the Flames, they at this time tore away a piece of the Mountain, whence for two Days abundance of Water flow'd; great pieces of Rocks roul'd down the side of the Hill, to the Sea, forming Concavities, and bearing down Trees, and Ruins. The same Mountain, on the Top, has a spacious sweet Pool, encompass'd with Trees, wherein there are blew, and gold-Colour Alligators, above a Fadom long, who, as soon as they hear People stirring, plunge down to the Bottom.

These Islands know no Difference of Summer and Winter; nor is there *Seasons.* any settled Rainy Season, but it generally Rains more with the North-East, than with the South Wind. The *Molucco* Islands breed Snakes above 30 *Snakes.* Foot long, and proportionably thick; but they are neither Quick of Motion, nor Venomous. Those who have seen them affirm, That when they want Sustenance, they chew a certain Herb Nature has shown them, and climbing the Trees by the Sea-side, cast into it what they have chew'd; many Fishes come to Eate it, and being made Drunk, lye helpless upon the Water, then the Snakes launch out upon them, and satisfy their Hunger, till they are full of those stupify'd Fishes. The Crocodils on the Land are *Crocodils.* the fiercest of Monsters; the Ancients write almost the contrary of those of the *Nile.* These in the Sea are so Timorous, that they suffer themselves to be bound under Water. A Crocodile has been taken that had four Eyes, and a very little Heart. Here are also found certain Insects, which they *Insect.* call *Cuzos*, living on Trees, on whose Fruit they feed: They are like Rabbits, their Hair thick, harsh, and curl'd, of a brightish Brown; their Eyes round and sprightly; their Feet small; and a very long Tail, by which they hang, the better to reach the Fruit; and they stink like Foxes.

In the Desert Parts there are Wild-Fowl; some of the Tame are the same we have in *Europe*. The Parots, in their Tongue call'd *Noies*, of se- *Parots.* veral Colours intermixt, Cry excessively, but Talk well. An Islander affirms, That at this time, when the People were Conspiring, a Parrot in the Air cry'd, *I Dye, I Die*; and beating his Wings, fell down Dead. A Relation tells us of another, that came from *Amboyna*, on the Mast of a small Vessel, when they went to take him, he cry'd out, *Sebastian, Sebastian,* who was his Master, and came to his assistance. There are great flocks of *Brids and* black Geese, with Parrots Feet; Martins, Swallows, Feldefares, Thrushes, *Fishes.* and Sparrow-Hawks. The variety of Fish is infinite, the Sea-Cow, like that of *Brazil*; a sort of Crab, one part whereof Eaten, kills in 24 Hours; this is on the Sea-shore, under certain Trees, whose shade suffers no Grass or Herb to grow; those who Sleep in it Sicken, and it dries and parches up the

the very Ground. There is another fort of Crabs, not unlike Lobſters, but with leſs Claws; they have ſtrong white Teeth, with which they break the Shels, to eat the Almonds; they breed among Rocks, are taken at Night with Light; their Body, Claws, and all the Fleſh, is like that of a Lobſter. Near the Tail they have a Bag, full of a certain Subſtance delicious to the Taſt, for which they are as much valu'd as Pullets.

Strange Sticks.

All over the *Moluccos* there grows a ſort of reddiſh Sticks, which burn in the Fire, raiſe a Flame, and are like a burning Cole, without waſting: They look to be of a Stony Nature, moulder away betwixt the Fingers, and are eaſily broken by the Teeth. Not far from the Fort of *Ternate*, is to

Tree of Butter-Flies.

be ſeen the Plant call'd *Catopa*, from which there drop Leaves leſs than the common ſort; the Stem whereof, on a ſudden, is form'd into the Head of a Worm, or Butter-Fly; the Body and Fibers coming from it, make Feet, and the Leafy Part, Wings; ſo that it ſoon becoms a perfect Butter-Fly, and at the ſame time a Leaf. This Tree buds out every Year, like a Cheſtnut-Tree, and from the Buds proceed theſe Worms, which run upon Threads faſtened to the Leaves. Nature was profuſe with thoſe People; eſpecially as to the Cloves, which I diſtinguiſh from the Long-Peper *Pliny* perhaps ſpoke of, when he nam'd the *Garyophillum*. But ſince the Profit of that ſo highly valu'd Product, was to occaſion ſuch bloody Wars, ſuch incredible Voiages, from all Parts of the World, that the real Dangers, are even beyond human Belief; it may well be controverted, whether it were

A good Remark.

moſt for the publick Tranquility, that this Spice ſhould be known, or ever conceal'd; for its Plenty and Virtue, which awaken'd the Avarice of the remoteſt Nations, has glutted thoſe Seas with the Wracks of Ships, and Fleets, and call'd thither Armies of Rebels, making their paſſage through Streights before unknown, in the Sight of Mountains cover'd with blew Ice and Snow, as never reach'd by the Suns bright Beams; and yet they venture at all, not out of any Zeal of promoting Religion, or Civility, but only to load with that Spice, which has occaſion'd Diſobedience and Superſtition. This is the precious Commodity, which gives Power and Wealth to thoſe Kings, and cauſes their Wars. A Wonder of Nature, which plainly ſhows it has created nothing ſo harmleſs, but what is abus'd by human Malice This is the true Fruit of Diſcord, rather than the fabulous Apple of the three Godeſſes, ſince for it there has been, and ſtill is, more Fighting, than for the Mines of Gold. Had this happen'd in the Days of the *Greek*, or *Latin* Poets, how much more would thay have ſpoken of our *Moluccos*, than they did of the Iſlands *Gorgones* in the *Ethiopick* Ocean? Let us ſtop a little to reflect on the Dangers Mortals expoſe themſelves to, rather, perhaps, to pleaſe their wanton Appetites, than to confirm their Health.

The Confederates ruces.

The People of *Ternate, Tydore, Bachian,* and all the Neighbouring Princes, being impatient to put in Execution their deſperate Deſign, choſe the King of *Tydore* for their Head, to joyn with him of *Ternate,* that had been expell'd on account of the Death of *Gonzalo Pereyra.* Among the Relations uſually collected by the Chriſtian Curioſity of the Religious Men of the Society, we find that theſe Kings met in the little Iſland, which divides *Ternate* from *Tydore,* before they went each of them to his proper Poſt for performing what was ſtipulated in the Confederacy, and there the King of

Tydore,

Tydore, as Chief of the League, spoke to them in this Manner. *I cannot mention the Occasion of this our Union, without shedding Tears, for the Joy of the Success, which we look upon as present, produces the same Effects it would do, were we already Victorious. Our Forces are assembled to deliver us from the* Spanish *Yoke, punishing those Men with the Hazard of our Total Ruin, whom neither our Benefits could oblige, nor our Threats correct. They are the great Robbers of the World, who usurp it, by shrowding their Avarice under specious and godly Pretences. In vain have we endeavour'd to moderate their Pride by Means of our Modesty and Submission. If they meet with Wealthy Enemies, the* Portugeses *show themselves Covetous, if with Needy, they are Ambitious; this is the only Nation that equally seeks after others Wealth and Miseries. They rob, kill, and subdue, taking away our Dominions under false Titles, and think they have no settled Peace, till they have reduc'd the Provinces into Desarts. We possess the most fruitful Islands in* Asia, *only to purchase Servitude and base Subjection with their Product, converting this blessed Bounty of Heaven into Tribute paid to the Ambition of Intruding Tyrants. Experience has show'd us, how odious our Valour has been to the Christian Commanders, whom, for the same Reason, we must never hope to find more modest, or less our Enemies. Assure your selves then, and remember, both Kings and Subjects, both you who seek Glory, and you who provide for your Safety, that neither of these is to be had without Liberty, nor this without War; nor is the War to be maintain'd without Courage and Unanimity. The Power of the* Portugeses *is increas'd, and on it their Reputation depends. Having then discover'd the Mystery, and Cause of this Tyranny, who is there that will not prepare to try the utmost of Fortune, to purchase the greatest of human Felicities, which is Liberty. Other Nations, which when they hear of our Resolution, will call it Despair and Savageness; if they weigh it with the Occasion, will rather Commend than go about to find Excuses for us. Besides, every Man knows what is fit for his Religion, his Honour and his Country, better than those who judge of these Things at a Distance. In short, What is Life worth without Liberty?*

King of Tydore's Speech.

Those incensed Kings made suitable Returns to these Words, and having taken proper Measures to commence and carry on the War, went away in their Vessels, without losing Time, or admitting of Delay; as well knowing the many Dangers a great Undertaking is expos'd to, which depends on Secrecy, and is imparted to many.

On the Day appointed, all the Natives departed the City of *Ternate,* with their Families, not in good Order, as in Transmigrations, but raging, in Confusion, and loaded with their Children, and a few Necessaries, having before sent away their Effects to other Islands. To convince the *Portugeses* of their Design, and that the People of *Ternate* abandon'd the Country, they set Fire to the City in several Places, the Flames began to take hold and spread, till they met, and of many small ones became one general Conflagration, with hideous Noise and Cries; for not only the Houses were Burnt, which had for so many Ages belong'd to their Forefather, and Ancestors, but all that attracts the Affection to our Native Country, the Temples, all their worldly Treasure, and the Bounty of Nature; for the open Country began now to feel the Desolation, the Caves,

Ternate City abandon'd and burnt.

G   Lakes,

Lakes and Springs, the Rocks, and the very Sea it self fhin'd, boil'd up and crack'd, and the Fire receiv'd into the fubterraneous Caverns, lying in the hollow Mountains, pierc'd into the deepeft Receffes, roaring and overturning Stones and Trees. In the mean while, the People travell'd towards the Defarts, looking back to view the Effects of their Revenge.

Resolution of the People.

Triftan de Atayde, amaz'd to behold that dreadful Practice, having arm'd fome Soldiers, fent Meffages to the Queen and Governours, to propofe fome Accommodation, and appeafe that inhumane Rage. He promis'd to make Satisfaction, and that all Things fhould be fet right, but it avail'd nothing; for they rather grew more furious, and would not hearken to any Propofal, or admit of Treaty, that might make them flacken in their Refolution. Being come to thofe Places which Nature has made ftrong among the Rocks, they arm'd, and in Parties fell upon the Chriftians, lying in wait for them when they went out for Wood or Water, and killing or wounding them by Surprize. The Edict was put in Execution throughout all the Iflands at the fame Time, deftroying all the *Portuguefes* that were in them. In the City *Momoya*, they kill'd eight that were with F.

Portuguefes flaughter'd.

Francis Alvarez, but he fled to a Ship, after receiving feveral Wounds. In the Ifland of *Chion*, the Head of *Moratay*; they alfo flew the Prieft, *Simon Vaz*; an Infidel rufhing into his Chamber, broke in Pieces the Picture of the Bleffed Virgin, he found there painted on a Board; but Heaven fuffer'd him not to go unpunifh'd, for his Hands drop'd off on the Spot, and he dy'd a few Days after. It was further obferv'd, that within a Year there was not one left alive of all his Race, which was deftroy'd in War, and by other Misfortunes and Calamities; as the laft of them was fifhing, a Needle Fifh fprung out of the Water, and ftruck him with the Snout in the Eye, whereof he dyed. The whole Town perifh'd miferably within a few Years. *Triftan de Atayde* foon receiv'd the News of this Slaughter of the *Portuguefes*, and fo fucceffively of the others, throughout all the Iflands. He encourag'd his Men, and labour'd to hide his Concern for being fhut up among fo many Enemies; he regulated the Diftribution of Provifions; fent out feveral Spies, to get Information of the Enemies Motions and Defigns; and order'd the Guard upon King *Aario*, who was in the Fort, to be always watchful, for the more Security, leaving only the Nurfes, and other Women that attended him. Then he again employ'd other Perfons to propofe a Peace to the Queen, and the King of *Tydore*, with ample Commiffion to offer advantageous Conditions, which were to be immediately perform'd; but all prov'd ineffectual, for an Accident which foon happen'd confirm'd the Enemies Obftinacy.

King of Tydore poifon'd.

Catabruno, Governour of *Gilolo*, and Tutor to the Infant King, finding his Ufurpation eftablifh'd by Time, and a good Difpofition in the Minds of his Accomplices, poifon'd the King; and poffeffing himfelf of the Palace and Forts, afcended the Throne, making the Subjects fwear Allegiance to him. Tho' no Man in all thofe Eaftern Parts expected any other Event, yet was it look'd upon as moft certain, that *Triftan de Atayde* was confenting to the Poifoning, and his Ufurpation; befides other Circumftances produc'd to prove his Guilt, it was notorious, that *Atayde* fent *Catabruno* a Robe of blew Velvet, which he wore the Day he rebell'd, and was fworn King. God fo order'd it, that as foon as he

was

was poffeſs'd of the Kingdom, he broke his Faith with *Triſtan de Atayde*, and confederated with the other United Princes, proving the greateſt Enemy the *Portugueſes* had, for he fitted out numerous Fleets wherewith he warr'd on all the Chriſtians of thoſe Iſlands, threatning and tormenting them that they might renounce their Faith.

At this time the Governour of *India*, tho' there were ſome Troubles at *Goa*, and in other Places, ſent Succours to *Ternate*, becauſe it was towards the End of Summer, and one muſt of Neceſſity go to ſucceed the Governour. *Antony Galvam* was the Man appointed, who laid out above 10000 Ducats of his own towards reſtoring the Places that had been burnt, by which it may be truly ſaid, he redeem'd the *Moluccos*. He was deſirous, not only to People, but even to enlarge *Ternate*, and to this Purpoſe he treated with ſome poor marry'd Men, and needy Families, to go over with him and their Wives and Children to thoſe Iſlands; the ſame he did with Men and Women, who were lewd Livers, that they might mend their Lives in another Country, and embrace the legal State of Matrimony; to which End, he lent them Money, and provided Neceſſaries for their Voyage. In the mean while, the Tyrant *Catabruno*, aſſembled his Forces, and mov'd againſt the City *Momoya*, where the *Sangiack* of it liv'd, who had been before an ignorant Idolater, but then a Chriſtian Prince. He finding himſelf inferiour in Power, retired into a Fort, with his Wife, Children and Family. Some *Portugueſes* ſent him by *Triſtan de Atayde*, not daring to truſt themſelves ſhut up there with him, withdrew into the Mountains, where they were ſoon kill'd, purſuant to the Edict of the League. *Catabruno* enter'd the City, without any Oppoſition, where he exercis'd his Cruelty, becauſe the wretched Inhabitants would not quit it; and many new converted Chriſtians recanted for Fear, or thro' the Violence of Torments. Being Maſter of the City, he laid Seige to the Fort, giving it ſeveral furious Aſſaults, which *Don John* withſtood, making a reſolute Defence, and in ſome Sallies return'd Victorious; yet his Example prevail'd not on his People, as it uſually does where it meets with generous Souls; ſo that this Prince ſoon diſcover'd how faint-hearted moſt of them were, he ſuſpected that ſervile Fear would degenerate to ſuch Baſeneſs, that they would deliver him up to his Enemy, and therefore like a brave Man, he preſently bent his Thoughts to ſecure the Salvation of his Soul. He knew *Catabruno* valu'd himſelf upon his Zeal for the Law of *Mahomet*, and therefore ſpar'd the Lives of all Chriſtians that Apoſtatiz'd, putting to Death ſuch as prov'd ſtanch and conſtant; he fear'd his Wife and Children, being puſilanimous, would fail in the Confeſſion of their Faith, and being fill'd with this Spirit, drew his Cimiter, ran to them, and ſhedding Tears, which were not the Effect of Cowardice, ſlew them one after another, firſt telling them his Reaſons for ſo doing, and that tho' in the Eyes of the World he might appear inhumane, yet conſidering the Salvation of their Souls, what he did was a Religious Magnanimity, and therefore they ought rather to thank him for it. This was a miſtaken Notion, and to go through ſtitch with it, he would, ſtill perſiſting in the ſame Error, have kill'd himſelf, but that he was hinder'd by his own Servants, who to purchaſe the Tyrant's Pardon, deliver'd up to him that Chriſtian Prince, who had been ſo ill advis'd by his Zeal. Being brought

Galvam ſent to govern the Moluccos.

Momoya taken.

Amazing Action of an Indian Convert.

G 2 before

before *Catabruno*, who was inform'd how cruelly he had slain his Wife and Children, he ask'd him, Why he had undertaken so barbarous and inhumane an Action? *Don John* answer'd him with great Courage and Undauntedness. *At that Time, and in my Thoughts, I had more regard to the Salvation of their Souls, than to the preserving of their Lives I mistrusted the Sex, their Age, and your Torments, and would not hazard their persisting in the true Faith. Souls are Immortal, and I took nothing from my Children that they can feel the want of, or which Time, or your Sword would not have depriv'd them of, the latter we should all have been thankful to, as the Instrument of the Divine Will. But I much more dreaded your Pardon and Mercy, by which you might have perverted their Minds, with those Soothings which please frail Mortality. I being more resolute, tho' expos'd to all your Fury, am so far from fearing the Effects, either of your Torments or Intreaties, that I shall look upon you as God's Executioner, and were it his Will, that you should take away my Life, I should receive a greater Benefit from your Sword, than from your Mercy.* *Catabruno*, enrag'd at his Answer, order'd him to be kill'd; but the Tyrant's own Friends, who lov'd *Don John*, the *Sangiack*, carry'd him out of the Room, and contriv'd he should have his Liberty, and be restor'd. Their Intreaties prevail'd on *Catabruno*, and he liv'd many Years after in his own Dominions, with a Christian Constancy, confessing his indiscreet Zeal, which had caused his own Sword to deprive him of Wife and Children. A Mind truly worthy the best Part of *Europe*, and not to be the Product of the most remote barbarous Nations; and highly commendable, had it been directed by more solid Rules, to curb that Fierceness, so opposite to all natural and divine Laws, which looks upon such horrid Murders, as a Piece of Piety.

Tristan de Atayde was troubl'd at these Misfortunes, which were almost under his Eyes; tho' he wanted nor for others nearer, for the People of *Ternate* being now Masters of the Island, burnt all the new and old Towns, belonging either to themselves, or the Christians, and amongst others, those of *Trutupalate, Calamata*, and *Isico*, yet they met with brave Opposition in them all, and they cost much Blood. Twice our Men went out to Fight the *Tydore* Fleet, which came within sight of the Fort, and tho' they both times retir'd Shatter'd, and well Beaten, the Barbarians had not much cause to Boast of their Victory, for Abundance of them were kill'd, and scarce any went off unhurt. The Confederates fitted out other numerous Fleets, wherewith they much Streightened the Christians in the Fort, till *Antony Galvam* arriv'd, who was at this time Sailing. But Relief came before, *Don Stephen de Gama*, sending a Galeon laden with Provisions and Ammunition to *Ternate*, under the Command of *Simon Sodre*. The Galeon arriv'd safe, and with it the Support of those Disconsolate People. They took Heart, and ventur'd to go abroad, spreading themselves about the Island, and going into the Woods, met with ruin'd Buildings, the remains whereof still smoked, and when it was Dark, they observ'd the high Flames on the Mountains. However they made Incursions upon the Barbarians, and throughout all the Islands there were hourly Engagements, either with the Christian Inhabitants, or the Soldiers of the Forts; and at Sea they heard the Martial Musick, which Sounded whilst they Sail'd, or Fought Manfully, and at that time was dreadful.

In·

His Words.

Several Actions.

In the mean while Captain *Alvarado*, a *Spanish* Gentleman, sent by *Ferdinand Cortes* to *Ternate*, that the Valour he had shown in those Parts, serving God and his King, might not lie idle, discover'd the Islands of the *Papuas*, and fought those Barbarians with Resolution, tho' the *Portuguese* Histories assign the Honour of this Discovery to *Don George de Meneses* who arriv'd at them in the Year 1526, as we have seen. The great Commander *Alvarado* also Discover'd other Islands, call'd *Gelles*, in one Degree of North Latitude, and East from *Ternate*, 125 Leagues from *Batochina*. The Natives of those Islands are like those of the *Moluccos* in Colour, Habit, and Customs, differing only in Language, which is peculiar to themselves.

Antony Galvam sail'd from *Malaca* with the proper *Monson*, with the Men, and all Necessaries to fight, and settle Colonies. When he was past the Island *Borneo*, and the ridges of Rocks which lie under Water, in sight of that Coast, as F. *Marta*, the Jesuit, writes to the Governor *Gomez Perez*, and appears by his Papers, in Sight of *Malaca* he Discover'd a great Fleet of *Carcoas*, and other *Chinese* Ships, with Sails made of Canes, and Palm-Tree Leaves wove together. He was soon satisfy'd, that they were the Auxiliaries which had joyn'd the *Janguas* of *Tydore* and *Catabruno*, who, with the expell'd King of *Ternate*, were Cruzing to meet the *Portugueses*, or *Spaniards*, that shou'd come into their Seas. *Galvam* order'd his Men to be in a Readiness, to clear his Guns, and prepare all Things, doing the Duty of a Commander, and of a Soldier. The Enemy drew up in three Lines, each of its particular Nation, as if the *Portugueses* had many Ships. He was himself in the Trading Galeon, and with it a Pink, and another small Vessel, wherein, among the Marry'd Men, and Families unfit for that Service, there were some few that could take up Arms. The Infidels drew near, but without Artillery, the *Gilolo* Archers let fly a great number of Arrows upon our Men, and then one Line shearing off, the other discharg'd, the Air resounding, being peirc'd by the Darts, and *Calabays*, or Staves hardned at the Fire. *Galvam* not regarding the Danger, tho' at first he defended himself with Fights and Planks; when he thought they had spent most of those flying-Weapons, among which they fir'd some Muskets, he began to play his great Guns, tearing their Vessels, and destroying the Men. He Sunk a considerable number, and Took several, because they fought disorderly, relying, as it were a Land-fight, on the Multitude of their Soldiers, as ours did on their Valour, and Experience. But *Galvam*, whose Business it was to get to *Ternate*, held on his Voyage, and arriv'd there as he desir'd. His Men landed in that dismal Solitude, among Smoke and Ruins. The Joy of those who were in the Fort, and the extraordinary Relief, coming quite unhop'd for, were an Encouragement to them all. The Clergy came out to receive him, the Soldiers shouting amidst the Divine Hymns, confounding the Procession, and their Satisfaction. It was a Pleasure to behold, and they gazed on him as a Deliverer sent from Heaven. *Tristan de Atayde* resign'd his Post, and *Antony Galvam* took Possession, enquir'd into the Nature of the Confederacy, and the Fame of his Arrival being spread Abroad, Things began to mend. To this Purpose he arrested *Tristan de Atayde*, and afterwards sent him to *Goa*. He had before sent Messengers to the Queen, to acquaint her with his Arrival,

Spaniards at the Papuas.

Galvam Fights at Sea.

Arrives at Ternate.

rival, and the End of it, which was to serve her, and retrieve all the Mischiefs an inordinate Desire of Revenge had occasion'd. In the mean while he began to repair the City, the Colonies, Churches, Keys, and Houses, distributing those Families he had brought with him. Nor did he neglect Husbandry, but planted Vines brought from *Portugal*, which he soon saw grown up into substantial Vinyards He deliver'd to the Clergy the new Constitutions drawn up by Cardinal *Henry*, afterwards the last K. of the House of *Portugal*. He offer'd Peace to all that would comply, sent Religious Men to inculcate to those who liv'd like Outlaws, the Love of their Country, its re-establishment, and how dishonourable it was to them to make choice of a Life like that of wild Beasts, only for a cruel Satisfaction.

Strength of the Natives. The Queen, who not to speak of her natural Fierceness, expected to see her Son restor'd, and set at Liberty, and to drive away the *Portugueses*, would not give Ear to any Accommodation. The greatest Burden of the War lay then upon *Tydore*, where the Confederate Kings, with the deposed *Dayalo*, a most Fierce Man, gather'd above Fifty Thousand Fighting Men; but they had not yet enclosed that City with a Wall and Ditch, being satisfy'd with having built a Fort upon high Rocks, whence they spread abroad to pick up the Fishermen, and other *Portugueses* that went out from *Ternate* to get Provisions, and thence they infested that dangerous Coast. *Galvam* fearing lest the Prolonging of the War should reduce him to the former difficulties, sent other Messengers to treat of Peace, and perswade those obstinate Kings, to Publish an Oblivion of all past Wrongs, without taking Notice of the late engagement, offering them mighty Presents, to purchase Commerce at the Price of them. They being puffed up with some good Success, and their mighty Power; would not hearken to any Proposals Peace; but on the contrary, as *Maffæus* Writes, they return'd an Answer very abusive to the *Portugueses*. *Galvam* imploring the Assistance of Heaven, so managed the Affair, that it was look'd upon as amazing, even by such as view Things impartially. Nor would it be credible, unless confirm'd by other Enterprizes of his suitable to this. He had only four Tall *Galvam sails over to Attack them.* Ships, and a few smaller Vessels in the Port; these he speedily form'd into a Squadron, putting in 400 Men, 170 of them *Portugueses*, the rest to make up the Number, Slaves, and the common sort of *Ternate*. He left *Tristan de Atayde* with some Men to defend the Fort, and secure *Sultan Aerio*, and sail'd away himself for *Tydore*, without meeting any Enemy, the reason of it not known, and lay by in a safe Place, about a Musket-shot from that Island Being come to an Anchor, he took a full View of the Multitude that guarded the Shores, considering the Nature of the Country, and Situation of the City. Having called a Council of War, he resolv'd to Storm the Fort on the high Rock, then little regarded, the Confederates thinking themselves safe. He made a Speech to them in plain Terms, without any Rhetorical Ornaments. *These are the same People*, said he, *we have so newly Vanquish'd, to restore whom to the Liberty they desire, would be a matter of small moment, did they when possess'd of it allow the Freedom of preaching the Gospel. This is the Cause we are imbark'd in. Who then can doubt of Victory, or not wish to Die for the obtaining of it? As these Enemies are the same we Defeated, so are we the same Victors, so that I need not have Recourse to Foreign Examples, to encourage you. Their Disobedience and Restlessness is of a long standing, it will be but reasonable that our Arms*

cd

add one Victorious Day to so many Turbulent Years, that so we may lay the Ax to the Root of Rebellion. They call us Tyrants; that does not at all trouble me; because after the Victory, we shall have the Opportunity of dispelling that Slander by our Moderation.

They would not suffer *Galvam* to put an end to his Speech, all of them *The manner of the* pressing earnestly to Fight, and he resolving to make himself Master *Attack.* of the Rock, as he had contriv'd, pick'd out 120 *Portuguese*, and made out 300 from among the Rest, leaving the Remainder to secure the Ships, and keep the Enemy in Play, if they should attack them; making show of a greater Number, by appearing in several Places, and shouting, by which such as fear are easily impos'd upon. In the mean while, *Galvam* having taken a Native of *Tydore*, and oblig'd him to serve for a Guide, set out at the fourth Watch in the Night with his Men, through by-ways remote from the City, over-grown with Brambles, and scarce practicable, and with the greatest silence he could came to the Top of the Mountain. The *Portuguese* had march'd the greatest Part of the Way by the first Dawn of Day, and resting them a little from the Fatigue, descry'd the Enemy's shining Helmets and their Feathers on them. *Galvam* then beginning, all the rest raised the Cry, *To Arms, to Arms.* The Confederates, with Horrid Shouts, which resounded on the Rocks, and in the Woods, made ready for their Defence, notwithstanding the surprize; but soon perceived they should fall a Prey to our Men. The Fight began, and King *Dayalo*, enrag'd for that he had been depos'd, appear'd the foremost with some Troops, to secure the Passes, and advanced to meet the *Portuguese* in a Plain. They avoided him not, and both Parties mixing, much Blood was spilt. *Dayalo* was visible by his bright Helmet, adorn'd with Variety of standing high Fea- *King of* thers, and his Body cover'd with a Steel Coat of Mail, brandishing with *Ternate* both Hands a Lance, as like a small Yard of a Ship, and charging with *Kill'd.* desperate Fury; but happ'ning to rush in among our Pikes and Musketiers, unadvisedly, he receiv'd several Wounds on all Sides, and fell down raging. He was wonderful strong, and started up immediately; concealing his Wounds and Pain, and beginning a fresh Charge in the first Ranks, for fear of discouraging his Men. He Fought a considerable Time; but not being Dress'd, and the Action causing the Blood to run the faster, his Eye sight fail'd him, and he dropt a second Time, saying to his Guards, *Move hence as fast as you can, and carry me carefully that the Dogs,* so he call'd the *Portuguese, may not have the Satisfaction of cutting my Body in Pieces.* His Soldiers did so, not without great Danger; and he soon after he had been carry'd off, gave up his haughty Soul. His Forces daunted by this Accident, turn'd their Backs, hiding themselves among the Rocks and Bram- *The Indi-* bles, throwing down their Arms, and getting off through almost inacessi- *ans routed* ble Ways. Others return'd to the City, and meeting some Troops that march'd to their Assistance, made them return another Way. The *Portuguese* follow'd the Chace, killing such as fled, and *Galvam* came to the Fort, with the Loss of only one Slave. This Victory, which happen'd on the Feast of St. *Thomas*, the Apostle, in the Year 1537, humbled the Pride of the Confederates, was ascrib'd to the Intercession of that Apostle, and they observ'd a solemn Thanksgiving. The Fort was fired with good Advice, for the Citizens and Traders, seeing the Flames so near, abandon'd

their

their Houses, and departed the City with the flying Multitude. *Galvam*. was now coming down from the Hill, having drawn together his Men, and form'd them into small Bodies, with sound of Trumpets and Singing, to make his Victorious Entry into that City, now void of Defendants, and full of Wealth. Considering that the Avarice of the Victorious Soldiers spur'd them on to take Possession of that inestimable Booty, for all the Merchants had brought their Effects to *Tydore*, as the safest Place. *Galvam* order'd to set Fire to the Houses, all which were consum'd with their harmless Treasure, in Sight of those who had hop'd to be Masters of it, only the Provisions being providentially sav'd.

Tydore burnt.

Of the People of *Tydore* as many were taken as did not in Time save themselves by Flight, as also a Junk in the Port, and several other small Vessels. The Enemies afterwards perish'd in other smaller Actions. The daunted King, hasted Home to secure their own Lands, dissolving the Confederacy, and being sufficiently warn'd, gave Ear to, and embrac'd Proposals of Peace ; taking leave of him of *Tydore*, and agreeing with *Galvam*, whose Vertue and Discretion gain'd so much upon *Cachil Rade*, that King's Brother, that he came to a Conference with him and concluded a Peace upon certain Conditions. The King of *Tydore* oblig'd himself to restore *Galvam* the Cannon ; not to assist the Enemies of *Portugal* ; not to permit the Clove to be dispos'd of into any other Hands than the *Portuguese* Officers ; and to sell it as was usual at *Ternate*. *Galvam* went over next to subdue *Gilolo*, and the other Kings, all which he compass'd successfully. The Queen also submitted, either on Account of the King of *Tydore's* Falshood, or that, as she said, she grew weary of the War, or else because the depos'd King was kill'd. *Catabruno* was appeas'd by *Galvam's* good Behaviour, and accepted of Conditions, among which the chiefest was, that *Galvam* should set *Sultan Aerio* at Liberty. Thus the Confederacy was dissolv'd, and the *Maluccos* laying down Arms, submitted again. Provisions were furnish'd as before, and the Crops, and Trade of Spice were restor'd.

Peace concluded.

Sultan Aerio attended by the Christians and Gentiles, Dancing, and making other demonstrations of Joy, went from the Fort to his Palace, where he remain'd with his Guard, and Family. Before he Marry'd, tho' he never wanted for Concubines, he in Person took a Progress to the principal places in his Dominions of *Ternate*, *Moutil*, and *Machian*. Those in the Fort attended and assisted him, together with the *Sangiacks*, who went all about that *Archipelago*, first on that side they call *Del Moro*, that is towards *Batochina*, and is distant from the *Moluccos* 60 Leagues Northward, beginning at the Isles of *Doe*, two Leagues to the Point of *Bicoe*. All these are Inhabited by Wild People.

Sultan Aerio King of Ternate.

Batochina is 250 Leagues in Compass, and Subject to two Kings, which are those of *Gylolo*, and *Lolada*. This last is Ancienter than all those of the *Moluccos*, or in those Seas, and formerly was the most Powerful, but now the Weakest. The Inhabitants of the North part of *Batochina* are Savage, without any King, Laws, or Towns, living in Deserts. Those on the East-side have populous Towns, on the Sea Shore, and tho' they speak several Languages, yet they understand one another. This Coast they call'd *Morotia*, that is, *Land Moor*. The other Islands opposite are call'd *Morotay*,

Batochina, that is Gilolo described.

that

that is, *Sea-Moor*, and all thofe Ifles breed deceitful, brutal and daftardly
Men Only the City *Moncoya* is Warlike. It ever wanted Laws, Weights,
Meafures, Coin, Gold, Silver, and all other Metals, and a King; but it
is overftock'd with Provifions, Arms, Idols, and Devils fpeaking in them.
The Women Till the Land. Each of thefe Towns is Govern'd by a Magi-
ftrate chofen by the People ; they pay him no Taxes, but have Regard to
his Defcent. The *Molucco* Kings conquer'd them, and every one kept what
he could get ; the better part belongs to him of *Ternate*, and lefs to the
King of *Tydore*, whofe Dominions were enlarg'd by the Power of Spain.
They went on to eftablifh their Poffeffions among the *Papuas*, or *Papous*,
Eaft from the *Moluccos*, being Iflands little reforted to, becaufe many of
them are all encompafs'd with Flats and Shoals. The Natives of them are
Black, like the *Cafres* ; they wear their Hair wound about in large curl'd
Locks, their Vifages lean and ugly. The Name of *Papuas* in their Lan- Papuas, or
guage fignifies Blacks, being a ftern People, enur'd to Labour, and fit for Papous.
any piece of Treachery. All their Iflands are fubject to Kings, and abound
in Gold, which they do not Tranfport, becaufe no Man lays up any more
of it than is us'd in their Ornaments. Among thefe Black-men there are
fome as White and fair as the *Germans*; if thefe go out in the Sun, they
are ftruck blind, tho they do not look at it. Thofe in *Spain* are call'd
Albinos; yet fome of them are ftrong, and can behold any Object. Among
thefe *Papuas* there are many deaf. As to the Extent of this Country, if we
may believe the Accounts of *Spanifh* Pilots, who have fail'd that way,
thefe Iflands run along a vaft Continent, which terminates at the Streights
of *Magellan*. Thefe Kings entertain Friendfhip with *Ternate*, whither
they fent Embaffadors, and as much as was here fubject to the *Moluccos*,
had no Share in the defperate Fury of the League. So did thofe of *Cele-*
bes to the Weftward, being many notable Iflands, the great Ifland *Celebes*
it felf, as alfo *Mindanas* ; fo thofe of *Bifaya*, abounding in Iron ; *Maf-*
caga, and *Masbate*, which have much Gold, as well as *Mindanas* ; that
of *Sologo*, and others producing Provifions, Spice, Sanders, Eaglewood,
Cinnamon, Camphire, Tortofhell, Ginger, and Long Pepper. Some of Other
thefe Iflands are fubject to the King of *Borneo*, others to thofe of *Tydore* Iffands.
and *Bachian*, but the moft to him of *Ternate*. The People are generally
treacherous ; many of them go naked, painting their Bodies in Falcage,
and other Figures ; their Hair long, hanging on their Backs, or elfe knotted, and cut fhort over the Forehead, like our Peafants ; their Faces large;
their Teeth well fhap'd and black; and their Ears bor'd. The Natives of
Celebes are filthy, and vile in their Behaviour ; the Æquinoctia paffes Celebes.
over their Ifland, which is full of little Towns ; a whole Race living in
every Houfe. On their Walls they hang the Hair of thofe they have kill'd
in War; and the greateft number of them is moft Honourable. There are
among them feveral forts of Monftrous Productions. One of thefe is a
Tree bearing a vaft Head, the fhade whereof kills any Man that lyes down
under it on the Weft-fide, unlefs he immediately lye down on the Eaft-
fide ; the fame fhade at only a Yard diftance being an Antidote againft its
oppofite Malignity. In thefe Towns there are horrid Stews of Sodomy;
tho there are no fuch at *Ternate* ; but they have gone as far as *Amboyna*,
which lyes South of it. Among the *Moluccos* there are many Iflands fub-

H   iect

ject to their own Chiefs, full of excellent Waters, and delightful Banks·
Formerly they were free, afterwards conquer'd by the Kings of *Ternate*
and *Tydore* , against whom they also rebell'd, and submitted to the Queen
of *Japara*, and many Christian Towns were subject to the *Portuguese*.
They yield above 2000 Hundred Weight of Cloves Yearly ; which the
Jaos are Masters of, none being to obstruct them , they go over and Barter, and carry it away in their Junks   We speak elsewhere of their Fertility. Our Relations tell us, they produce a fort of Reeds, or Canes, a-
bove fifty fathom long, and no thicker than a mans little finger. South
from *Ambeyna* lye the Islands of *Banda* : and about 300 Leagues to the
Eastward;some affirm,there is one which is all over an entire Mine of Gold,
and the Natives not above a Yard high. If this be so, and these the true
Pigmies, who will look upon the Battels mention'd in *Homer's* 3d *Iliad*,
betwixt them and the Cranes, as Fabulous   Those scatter'd Dominions
were again united and submitted to *Sultan Aerio*, whose Marriage Solemnities, Building of Masques, Publick Festivals, and other Works of
Peace, we must pass over in silence, as not proper for our purpose, they
being only a pleasing fort of Digressions.

Mezquita
Governs
at Ter-
nate. The Kings of *Portugal* sent several Commanders in Chief to *Ternate*,
and last in the Year 1570, *James Lopez de Mezquita*, who had command-
ed on the *Molucco* Seas, took Possession of the Fort.   In his Time *Sultan
Aerio*, a courteous and affable Man, continu'd in Subjection to *Portugal*,
valuing himself upon being true to his Word in all his Actions.   Nevertheless, there wanted not some ill-meaning Persons, who mislik'd his Government, and pretended that he did not exercise his Power legally. They
said, he had given way to those Vices, into which luxurious Princes are
wont to fall ; those being generally the Fruits of a long Peace. They fancy'd, he retain'd the Memory of past Tragedies , and particularly his Mother's inhuman End, and therefore persecuted our Religion ; tho at the
Pretences
to destroy
King Ae-
rio. same Time the Memories of those Days do not charge him with any Temporal Disobedience, or want of Fidelity ; but they rather compar'd him to
Massinissa, King of *Numidia* , and say the *Portuguefes* ought to have respected him, as the *Romans* did the other. The Commander hearing of those
Abuses, and fearing greater might ensue, some Religious Men encreasing
his Jealousie, he endeavour'd to redress them by Friendly Admonitions,
and other Contrivances. Those Methods had no effect on him, for he anfwer'd, he was in his own Dominions, where, without offence to the
Portuguese Soveraignty, he might live as he pleas'd. *Mezquita* resolving
to try harsher means, since the others did not at all move the King, nor
make him uneasie, as relying on his Innocency ; began to deprive him of
his Revenue,and the Income of the Spice : threatning also, that he would,
in all other Respects, execute the last Will made by his Brother *Tabarija*,
wherein he appointed the King of *Portugal* for his Heir ; or at least would
treat him so like an inferior Person, that he should scarce be able to assume
the Name of King , for such is the Punishment they are lyable to, who do
not observe that Decorum which was inviolable in their Ancestors.

Cachil Babu, Son to *Sultan Aerio*, taking a Progress about this Time,
through his Father's Island , a Subject came to complain to him against
certain *Portuguefes*, who had taken away his Daughter ; for which fault
he

he order'd them all to be kill'd, as it they had been acceffary to the ravi-
fhing of the Maid. He had no Directions, nor fo much as the confent of
King *Aerio* for this exorbitant Command, which took no effect. On the
contrary he afterwards fo generoufly refented *it*, that he order'd the Prince
to be feiz'd, and would have punifh'd him feverely, had he not been hin-
dred by thofe the wrong was offer'd to. This plain Demonftration was
not fufficient to divert the *Portuguefe* Commander from imputing the Sons *The Por-*
Fault to the Father, contrary to all Reafon and Likelihood. All difcreet *tuguefes*
Methods us'd by well-meaning Perfons to reconcile them two, failing, *feize and*
James Lopez by his King's Authority, which generally is moft unreafona- *fend him*
ble, the farther it is from the Prince, from whom it is deriv'd, prefum'd *to Goa.*
to imprifon the *Sultan*, being dragg'd away from a Pleafure-Houfe,
where he was paffing the Heat of the Day, among his Women. His Subjects lov'd him, and their Refentment for this wrong was proportionable
to their Affection; nor did the *Portuguefes* approve of the Fact. The
Commander perceiving that all Men were againft him, and that after all
Enquiries and Examinations, the King's Caufe ftill appear'd the better,
and his Fidelity was more vifibly made out, he gave him his Liberty, to
the great Satisfaction of his Kingdoms, which were attentive to the Event;
but upon Condition he fhould go to *Goa* to clear himfelf, where he expected they would cut off his Head, upon the Informations he would fend a-
gainft him. The King fet out, and before he came to *Malaga*, the Vice- *The Vice-*
roy writ to him, begging he would return to his Kingdom, for he was *roy ac-*
fully convinc'd of his Innocence, and promis'd to punifh the Caufer of *quits him.*
thofe Troubles; but at that Time, for fome Confiderations, was fatisfy'd
with reproving him. The K. returning to *Ternate*, the Commander was fent
Prifoner to *Goa*, and had been more feverely punifh'd; but that Fortune preferv'd him, to be an Inftrument of the lofs which has lafted till our Days.

Within a Year after his Imprifonment he was reftor'd to his Command
in *Ternate*, where he again practic'd againft that King; for there are fome
Difpofitions which never part with the Jealoufies they have once conceiv'd. *Pretended*
Ternate was as it were the Metropolis in Religious matters, and King *Ae-* *Reconcili-*
rio had never offer'd any Affront to us either in Spirituals or Temporals, *ation.*
for which Reafon there never wanted fome grave Perfons in his Court.
Thefe Zealoufly reconcil'd them two, and that perfectly, as to outward
Appearance, and that their renew'd Amity might be lafting, the King affur'd the Commander upon Oath, according to his Sect, that he would
never privately harbour the leaft Jealoufie of him; but before he admitted
of any, would difcover it to him, that fo he might either receive, or make
Satisfaction; to the end no Accidents might revive any Miftrufts. The
Commander made the King the fame folemn Promife, both of them being *Falfhood of*
thus pacify'd, and in the Opinion of all thofe who mediated betwixt them, *Mezquita.*
fo Friendly, that none could imagine fuch perfect Amity could ever be dif-
folv'd. But there being nothing lefs permanent among Men than Recon-
ciliations, the *Portuguefe* Commander reaffuming the Hatred which never
was extinct, or perhaps fo much as lay'd afide, refolv'd to deftroy *Sultan*
Aerio, when only five Days were elaps'd fince the Re-eftablifhment of their
Friendfhip fworn to on both fides. This could not be kept fo private, as
not to come to the *Sultan*'s Ears, but the Confideration that he was a King,

his

his own Sincerity, and the fresh Reconciliation, made him think he was secure. But if the Nature of Man be such as not to forgive when it has done a Wrong, what can be less secure than injur'd Innocence? The Commander feigns himself Sick, and sends to desire the King, that since he is not able to wait on him in his Palace, he will be pleas'd to honour him with a Visit in the Fort, there to confer with his Highness about some important Affairs which concern the King of *Portugal*, his Master, and are not fit to be communicated to any other. All the Answer the King return'd, was to go himself to Visit the Sick Man, tho' he had Information better ground-ed than on bear Surmises, that *Martin Antonio Pimentel*, the Commanders Nephew, had Orders to murder him, as soon as ever he came into the Fort.

Aerio's Innocent Bravery. He could not prevail upon himself to believe a Treacherous Design; so far does Innocence prevail over a generous Soul. But when he saw that at the Gate, they stopp'd his Guards, the *Sangiacks* and *Cachiles*, that attended him, he then began to be convinc'd of the Villany, yet went on without being disorder'd, and showing an undaunted Countenance. And tho' he could not forbear dropping some Tears, when he took leave of his Sons, however he presently compos'd his Countenance, so that he was not at all dismay'd, tho' in the Commanders Nephew's Looks he saw visible Tokens of his Unkles Commission. He would have complain'd to the Commander of the Disrespect of those who stopp'd his Attendance, but they would not suffer him to go on. The Mask being now laid aside, and the true Design ap-pearing, in Violence he call'd out to the *Sangiacks*, but the Gate was shut against him and them. *Pimentel* came up to him with a Naked Ponyard, and begg'd his Pardon like an Executioner. The King, without showing any Surprize, or Disorder, Bid him consider what he was going to do; for there were many left to revenge his Death, besides his Sons and Sub-jects, all the Kings of the *Archipelago*, as well the Sovereigns who were in Alliance, as those who ow'd Fealty to the Crown of *Portugal*. *This In-stance, said he, will make them dread every Capricious Humour of a Com-mander in chief If still that Jealousie survies, which has so often been prov'd groundless, I will deliver my self up to the King of* Portugal, *and if my Death be of such Consequence to you, yet respite the Execution but a little, for at my Age, Time will soon perform what your Swords are to do.* They

He is mur-der'd now began to fall upon him, and he seeing a Brass Cannon, on which were the Arms of *Portugal*, clasping his Arms about it, said, *Christians, at least show some Respect to these Arms, for you kill a King that has paid the greatest Deference to your Crown.* This last Testimony of his Innocence was of no Force to appease those Murderers; though formerly in *Rome*, the embracing the Statues of the Emperors was sufficient to deliver Slaves from being punish'd by their Masters. It may be a Question whether his Soul was sav'd; for there are those who affirm, he intreated the Murderer to permit him to be Baptiz'd; who answering, It was then too late, with-out granting his Request, or any Respite, ran furiously upon that Antient Prince, who made no Resistance, and stabb'd him in several Places. They carry'd the Body into a Vault. The King's Kindred and Servants heard the Noise, and suspecting the worst, went away in great Disorder, to the City, where there was already a confused Rumour of what had happen'd, and being Distracted, ran shrieking about the Streets, where nothing was
to

to be heard but Weeping, Threats, Complaints and Diforder.

The Principal Queen, with the Kings other Wives, and Slaves, his Sons, and Brothers, laying a fide all State' came out of the Palace, already furrounded by the Multitude, in Confufion and Difpair, and being follow'd by moft of the *Portuguefes*, who no lefs abhorr'd the Fact, ran to the Fort, crying out to let them fee their King, as ftill doubting of what they heard. The Commander appear'd in Armour on the Wall, and faid, *They fhould fee him immediatly*, and then came up a Soldier, bringing the Kings Head with the Royal Turbant on it. After him came others, wth his Arms, Legs, and Body cut into fmall pieces, all which they hung upon the Battlements in the fight of his People. Afterwards they Salted them, *as if* the perpetuating of the Wrong had been requifite. This was what moft provok'd the injur'd People, who no longer able to behold fo inhumane a Spectacle, and being befide themfelves, and fearing more Mifchief, return'd with their Family. The Sons out of Refpect to their Fathers Body, went away from *Ternate* to feveral Iflands, tho' in Reality they departed to excite others by their Prefence, reprefenting the Hideoufnefs, and Horror of the Fact; and to difpofe their Revenge. For the prefent they were fatisfie with fending to complain of the Commander in Chief.

Their Embaffador arriv'd at *Goa* clad in White, which is the Mourning of the *Molucco* Iflands, and upon the Faith of his Credentials, acquainted the Viceroy with the whole matter; proving the Innocency of the Murder'd *Sultan*; reprefenting the Wrong done to, and the Sorrow of his Family, and Kingdoms, who fo paffionately Lov'd him; and befeeching him, in the name of them all, to Right them againft the Man, who with the Power and Authority of the *Portuguefe* Arms, had Violated the publick Faith and the Laws of Nature. The Viceroy gave him a favourable hearing, tho' by that Time the matter was otherwife reprefented at *Goa*, at leaft among the *Portuguefe* Nation. They faid, That King *Aerio* going to vifit the Commander in Chief, *Martin Antonio Pimentel* went in with him, and they contended in Words upon fome Point, when the *Portuguefe* anfwering him angrily, they fell to their Weapons, and the King was kill'd in the Quarrel. They added, That he was Advis'd fo to do, by fome of our Religious Men, who were offended at the Perfecution of the Chriftians, and the Obftructing of the King of *Portugal*'s Service. *Pimentel* made his Defence with the Original Letters, of thofe who perfwaded him to commit the Fact, and who afterwards fav'd him. However the Viceroy did not Reject the Plaintifs; but promis'd to Right them; and to ffew that he defign'd them farther fatisfaction than a bare Promife, he fent away the neceffary Supplies for the Security of the Fort of *Ternate*, and *Nunno Pereyra de la Cerda*, a Gentleman of Courage, and the neceffary Sagacity to fucceed the other in a Poft where all things were in Confufion He alfo writ to King *Sebaftian* of *Portugal*, acquainting him with the Death of King *Aerio*; how Cruelly and Unjuftly he had been kill'd; what a Revolution there was caufe to fear it might produce; whom he had fent to fucceed *Mezquita*; the Orders he had to Secure him, as alfo *Pimentel*, if he could find him.

Nunno Pereyra arriv'd at *Malaco* with the *Molucco* Embaffador, whence, at the proper Seafon, they Sail'd to *Ternate*, where as foon as they Landed, order was taken for Correcting the Infolency of thofe in the Garrifons, who

rob'd

robb'd, and obſtructed Trade When he had ſettled theſe Affairs, he ſeiz'd the late Commander in Chief, *James Lopez*, but did not punniſh him there, in the ſight of thoſe who had been wrong'd, which would have appeas'd them. The new Commander ſollicited the Kings Sons to return to *Ternate*, and endeavour'd to give them, and the Kingdom Satisfaction. He eaſily convinc'd them, that the Publick was no way guilty of their Fathers Death, but only the Commander *Mezquita*, who ſhould be ſeverely puniſh'd. That

He fawns. he deliver'd them the Kings Body, to be Bury'd with due Honour. That they ſhould ſettle the Succeſſion, offering it to *Cachil Guarate*, *Aerio*'s Eldeſt Son. He told them, the King of *Portugal* did not ſend his Commanders to be Enemies, but Protectors of the Royal Family and State of *Ternate*, and therefore they ſhould make uſe of his Arms, as their own. They return'd apparent Thanks for what *Pereyna* did, and being indifferently ſatisfy'd with his Promiſes, took the Kings Body. A few Months after, on the Day appointed for the Barbarous Obſequies, Embaſſadors from the neighbouring Kings, and Kingdoms landed at the City, who all repair'd to the Palace, clad in White, with the dead Kings Sons, and Brothers, the *Sangiacks* and

Revenge vow'd Soldiers, and the Chiefeſt of them, going into the Room where the Coffin was before the Mourners, who are Officers of the Grave, began their Lamentations and Cryes, they all ſwore upon the dead Body, to take a Revenge ſuitable to the Wrong; but becauſe this Reſolution requir'd a more deliberate Preparation, they ſuſpended it for a Year. It is reported, that Heaven anticipated them within that time, puniſhing *Pimentel*, ſtriking him to the Heart with the Diſeaſe call'd *Berber*, whereof he dy'd ſwelling up, and raving.

Aſſembly of the Indians to conſent. The Funeral Rites being perform'd, the Prince took leave of *Nunno Pereyra*, to go over to the Iſland *Ires*, where they have a moſt ſtately Country-Houſe, and the principal Moſque. There they all met on pretence of Diverting themſelves after their Sorrow, tho' it was now almoſt two Years ſince the occaſion of it happened. The *Cachilas* and *Sangiacks* repair'd thither under the ſame Colour, and without looſing any Time, they propoſed the Uniting the Forces of their Kingdoms, and ſhaking off the *Portugueſe* Yoke. *What ſhall we,* ſaid they, *value the* Portugueſes, *if once we come to be ſenſible of our own Strength? What can we Fear, or not Dare to attempt? The* Portugueſes *value him who Robs moſt, and is guilty of the greateſt Crimes and Enormities. The forcing away of our Product, then one lewd Pleaſures, and our Wrongs, are Occaſion for them to make War, ours are our Country, and the Defence of our Parents, our Wives, our Children, and our Liberty. It is neceſſary to expedite the Execution, becauſe a Secret is not laſting among many, and in Affairs of this Nature, there is more Danger in Conſulting, than even in Execution. We have been already too long in Confuſion, without a Head.* No Man contradicted, but neither *Cachil Guarate*, the Eldeſt of the Brothers, nor the Second, durſt take upon them ſo difficult an Enterprize. *Cachile Babre*, the Third, undertook it, with the uſual Ingagement, either to Conquer, or to Dye They preſently lifted him up, with general Applauſe, and his Election being made publick, the Kingdom eaſily ſubmitted to him through the deſire of Revenge, tho' according to the Cuſtom of the *Molucco* Iſlands, as ſoon as the King has any Son born, they ſwear him his Succeſſor, in his turn, and there was then no need of any other Oath, yet they again fwore to *Cochil Babu.* This done, they went out to their Mofque, in Proceffion, to offer Sacrifice. A Boy went foremoft with a naked Sword on his Shoulder, and with the other Hand *Sacrifice.* leading a Kid, which was to be the Victim, with the little Horns Gilt. The *Alcoran* forbids Sacrifising, but thefe Iflanders receive the Rites of *Mahometanifm* fo confus'd with them they alfo retain thofe of their ancient Idolatry, and intermix the Ceremonies. He that conducts the Sacrifize, is, according to their Cuftom, follow'd by part of the Kings Soldiers, with their Pikes advanc'd, and after them goes one holding up on high a fmall Gold Veffel, or Pan, with burning Coals in it, the Frankincenfe they throw in Smoking. Next to him was the new King, over whofe Head they always carry an Umbrello, made of Feathers of feveral Colours, in fhape of a large Semicircle. The King was encompafs'd by thofe Soldiers, that are given him by his Subjects by way of Acknowledgement, like the *Turkifh Janizaries.* In this Order they came to the Mofcue, at whofe Gates, whenfoever they are to enter, they find Kettles and Pots full of Water, to wafh their Hands and Feet before they go in. As foon as the King was upon the Threfhold the Mufick-play'd, and they fpread Milk-white Carpets, as is the Cuftome: Kneeling on them, they mutter out their vain Prayers, bowing their Heads down to the Ground. In the midft of the Mofque ftands a Pulpit, cover'd with white Cloth. Inftead of a Bell, there hangs up the holy great flat Drum, which they beat with Sticks; tho each Mofque has a great Bell, without a Clapper, which they ftrike with a Stone, or piece of Iron, when requifite. All that hear it, of what Condition foever, repair to the Temple, with Pikes, Shields, Cymitars, and Muskets. The profane Sacrifice being ended, they conducted the new King to the Harbour; he went into his *Carcoa,* with his Family, and the other *Sangiacks,* and great Men, into many others. The King's is fo contriv'd, that there 's a *The King's* Gang-way all round it, made of Canes. There are two Slaves to each Oar; *Carcoa.* others do the Service of the Veffel, and near every one lies a Number of Arrows Inftead of Oars they ufe a fort of great Paddles, like Spoons, with which they alfo lade out the Water the Veffel takes in. On the upper part they make Mufick with their Tabors, and Sounding-Bafons of Metal, according to which they Row fafter or flower, as we Dance to our Mufick. In the fame Place there are feven Brafs Guns; a confiderable number of Pikes advanc'd, longer than ours, and a Bed adorn'd with Quilts interwoven with Gold, and by it hung the King's Helmet, Breaft, and Back Plates. He fat, or lay on that rich Bed, the Servants of his Bed-Chamber Fanning him with a large Wing, made of various colour'd Feathers of the Birds that fly about his Iflands, thus he Coafted about, the Sea and Shore refounding with Guns, Shouts, and Barbarous Inftruments.

At the fame time that they feem'd to be wholly taken up with Sports *War Pro-* and Diverfion, in the Ifland *Ires,* they Vow'd an irreconciliable Enmity *claim'd.* to the *Portuguefe* Nation, with the fame Solemnity as they had fworn Allegiance to their King; and this Secret having been inviolably obferv'd, when the new K. thought convenient he caufed it to be Publifh'd throughout all his Dominions, which confifts of feventy two Iflands in that *Archipelago,* betwixt thofe of *Mindanao,* on the North; *Bima* and *Coica* on the
Coaft

Dominions of Ternate. South; and the Continent of the *Papuas*, or *Papous*, otherwiſe call'd *New Guinea* on the Eaſt: The Inhabitants whereof pay him their Tribute in Gold, Amber, and Birds of Paradiſe, all which Provinces have been Uſurped from other Kings, on whoſe Ruins his Pride is ſwollen ſo high, that he ſtiles himſelf in his own Language, Emperor of the *Archipelago*. In moſt of them there were at that Time ſome Chriſtian Towns, Churches, and Preachers, and the Goſpel was receiv'd in the eight principal Nations. Idolater and Mahometan Embaſſadours came from them all to acknowledge, and ſwear Fealty to *Cachil Rahu*. In this great Aſſembly the Deſire of Revenge was made the Cauſe of Religion, and in it began the longeſt Perſecution the true Faith has undergone in our Days. It will be therefore requiſite, diſtinctly to deſcribe the remote, and neighbouring Countries and Nations that carry'd it on; and the Strength, and ſtanding Forces, they have ready at all times upon any Occaſion.

Forces of the Kings of Ternate and Provinces. The ſixteen greater Towns of *Ternate* furniſh their K. with 3000 Arm'd Men; the Iſland of *Montil*, diſtant from it ſix Leagues South, 200; that of *Machian*, eight Leagues diſtant, 1500; that of *Caroa* four Leagues from *Mechian*, the ſame way, 300, thoſe of *Gazea*, twelve Leagues from *Caroa*, 300, thoſe of *Xula*, fifty Leagues from *Ternate*, 4000; thoſe of *Burro*, ſeventy Leagues diſtant, 4000; thoſe of *Veranula* eighty Leagues from *Amboina*, and are the ſame Number of Leagues in compaſs 50000; thoſe of *Ruaro*, and *Manipa*, lying betwixt thoſe of *Veranula* and *Burro*, 3000; thoſe of *Na*, *Nolo*, and *New Guinea*, which are many, and very populous, fifty Leagues Eaſt from *Ternate*, ſend no certain, but numerous Forces; that of *Ies*, where the King then was, 400, and pays Tribute in Amber, and Birds of Paradiſe. Thoſe of *Meaos* and *Taſure*, on the North, 400. Thoſe of *Doe*, diſtant thirty Leagues ſome way, 900. Thoſe of *Rao* and *Saquita*, ſeventy Leagues North, 1000. The great *Batochina*, or *Gilolo*, four Leagues from *Ternate*, 10000. The large Iſland *Matheo*, contains ſeveral Kingdoms, thirty Leagues to the Weſtward, each of them ſubject to its own King, and all of them to him of *Ternate*; ſend him Arm'd Troops. *Totole* and *Bool* 6000 Men; *Guaydnda* 7000; *Gorontano* and *Iliboto*, 1000; *Tomine*, 12000; *Manado*, 2000; *Dondo*, 700; *Labague*, 1000; *Pulo*, and *Jaqua*, 10000; *Gaſe*, *Tobuquo*, and *Butu* are all ſubject to him, and the number of their ſupplies is uncertain; but *Sanguien* and its King, 40 Leagues from *Ternate*, ſerve him with 3000 Men. This was the ſtanding Force, which without adding to it the uncertain number, nor the multitude of ſlaves, amounts to 120300 Men. This particular *F. Martin* ſent to the Governor *Gamez Perez*, and the original was deliver'd to me. Since then, that Kings Power is increaſed, and becauſe more Formidable, by reaſon of his Alliances with ſeveral Princes, entering Amity with ſome, and Oppreſſing others, and practiſing the Rules of Tyranny among them all, as Artfully as was formerly done by *Greece*, *Rome*, and *Carthage*. Of their Game, Fiſh, Rice, Sagu, and other Stores of Fruit and Spice, and the Royal Mines, we ſhall ſpeak when the Subject in Hand requires it; and ſo of their Weapons, of which laſt it is to be obſerv'd once for all, that thoſe they Dart, are all poiſon'd, and the Fire-Arms differ not from ours.

For managing of this great Defign, the King privately fent about his Brothers, and *Sangiacks* ; but fo great an Army could not be contracted from fuch diftant Parts, without being heard of by the Chriftians, and particularly *Nunno Perey ra*. He fufpecting that the Defire of Revenge ftill prevail'd in the injur'd Parties, and that the firft Effects of it would fall upon his Fort, tho' the *Sultan's* Murderer was not then in it, ftrengthned it proportionably to the Siege he expected Prudence fupplies the Place of Prophefy The Fort was not then erected, which is fince to be feen in *Ternate*, on a high Ground of difficult Afcent, next the Sea, and the Back of it defended by a Lake, next the Mountain ; being three Miles diftant from the firft Fort : It was afterwards built to defend themfelves againft great Fleets ; not fatisfy'd with that they had before on the Plain, next the Sea, made of dry Stones, without Mortar ; which being fince improv'd in all Refpects, is now built with Lime, the Walls a Yard and half thick, and Fifteen in Height ; Forty in Length next the Sea, with a round Tower at each Angle, like the ancient *Spanifh* Fortreffes. *Nunno Pereyra* endeavour'd with all poffible Diligence, to fhut up in it the greateft Number he could of all the Chriftian Families, and to be in a Readinefs to ftand the Siege, which foon enfu'd. He fent Advice to *India* and *Portugal* of the Intelligence he had receiv'd, demanding Succours, as in a certain Danger ; but it could never have come in Time ; for fome Part of thofe Forces being affembled in the Ifland *Ires*, the Reft ftaying on *Botochina*, in that Part which is properly call'd *Gilolo*, and is remote from the *Portuguefes*, they there began to perfecute Chriftianity by publick Decree

Pereyra prepares his Defence.

The Portuguefe Fort

The Apprehenfion of thefe Mifchiefs, had much perplex'd all the Governours of thofe Provinces, becaufe it was daily confirm'd by vifible Proofs of an open Infurrection *James Lopez de Marquita* was already kept Prifoner in the Fort of *Benaftarim* at *Goa*, thofe confin'd, and the Viceroy expected Orders from *Spain* to difpofe of him, and the Forces ; becaufe it was fear'd the King of *Ternate* might make ufe of the great Supplies which cou'd be fent him from *China* ; efpecially if that were certain which was then difcourfed in *Spain*. It was reported, That the Council of State, obferving that the *Philippine* Iflands were rather an Expence, than an Advantage to the Crown, being many, and hard to be maintain'd, had propos'd to King *Philip*, to quit them, and withdraw the Court of Juftice, and the Garrifons that defend them. They added the Example of the *Chinefes*, who abandon'd them, tho' they are fuch near Neighbours, and can relieve them with as much Eafe, as if they were joyning to their Continent. That as *Spain* governs them, the Lofs they occafion is confiderable, without any Hopes that it can ever be alter'd for the better ; a vaft Quantity of Silver being fent thither from *New Spain*, both for the ufual Expences, and to buy Commodities ; that fo all that Treafure is convey'd by the Hands of the *Chinefes* into the Heart of thofe Dominions, render'd intractable by the Severity of their Laws, by which they are trench'd in, as it were with Fortification, againft all Commerce with Strangers. They alledg'd that a Monarchy difpers'd, and divided by fo many Seas, and different Climates, could fcarce be united ; nor could humane Wifdom, by fettled Correfpondence, tye together Provinces fo remov'd from one another by Nature. That thefe Arguments are not the Ofspring of Wit, but of Experience, and Truths obvious to the Senfes That all fuch as might be urg'd againft them, were only grounded upon Honour, and full of a generous Sound, but difficult in the Execution ; and therefore the beft Expedient, was for the King to ftrengthen himfelf in *Europe*, where his Forces can be ready to meet all Dangers, without being expos'd to the Hazards of the Sea, and the Dominions of others. Each of thefe Arguments was fo fully reprefented by the Officers of the Revenue, that the Propofal was thought worthy to be debated and confider'd ; and had God permitted the King to exclude the *Philippine* Iflands his Monarchy, leaving them expos'd to the firft that would take Poffeffion, the *Moluccos* had fo far been ftrengthen'd, as to become unconquerable.

Project of abandoning the Philippine Iflands.

Reafons for it.

The fame Thing has been propos'd at other Times, and in the Days of King *Philip* the IIId. who fticking to his Father's Anfwer, has always rejected that

I   mifchievous

King Philip
rejects it.

mifchievous Advice. That moft prudent Monarch anfwer'd, That the _Philippines_ fhould be maintain'd, in the fame Manner they were, and the Court fhould be invefted with more Authority, that Juftice might prevail, for he laid the Strefs of Government, on its being upright, and impartially adminifter'd That in the fame manner the Troops fhould be kept up there, and maintain'd out of the Revenues of _New-Spain_, or any other of his Kingdoms, fince all the Treafures difcover'd, or ftill hid in the Bowels of the Mines, ought to be apply'd to the Pro-

His Reafons

pagation of the Gofpel. For what would the Enemies of _Chrift_ fay, if they perceived that the _Philippine_ Iflands were left deftitute of the true Light, and its Minifters to propagate it, becaufe they did not produce rich Metals, and other Wealth, like the Reft of the fruitful Iflands in _Afia_ and _America_? That all the Power of Kings, ought to be fubfervient to this Sovereign End, as becomes Sons of the Church, and Promoters of the Apoftolical preaching, which is continu'd by Succeffion. That fince he had refufed to mitigate the leaft Point of his Severity towards his Northern Subjects, or to grant them Liberty of Confcience; why fhould he remit any thing among Heathens, and _Mahometans_, which were the Harveft God had affign'd him, to enrich the Church with thofe Children, fo remote? Thus the Project was put down, and this has always been the glorious Refolution, when miftaken Zeal, or worldly Interefts have propos'd the quitting of thofe Dominions. This feems to have been a peculiar Providence of Heaven, which knew how foon they were all like to belong to the fame Mafter, and that the Right and Conquefts fhould be all United in his Perfon, the one being the Means to recover the other, as has been feen in our Days

Product of
Afie

King _Philip_ was govern'd by this Religious Motive, but there were others urg'd by fuch as were acquainted with the Riches of _Afia_, which are chiefly Diamonds, Rubies, large and Seed Pearl, Amber-Greece, Musk, Civet, Camphir of _Borneo_ and _China_, Vermillion, Coral, Quick-Silver, Copper, fine Muflins, and Calicoes of _Cambaya_ and _Bengala_, Carpets, Coverlets, and fine Quilts. _Perfian_ Silks, Brocard, Ivory, Rheubarb, Cardamome, _Caffia Fiftula_, Frankincenfe, Benjamin, Wax, ChinaWare, Lake for dying, and Phfiyck, Cloves, Mace, Gold, Silver, Medicinal Plants, Aloes, Eagle Wood, Calamba, Ebony, and very many more rare Trees, Drugs, Spices, and Ornaments. All this they faid, _Venice_ loft, when the Trade was remov'd to

Arguments
againft
quitting
the Philippines.

Portugal; and this fame ftir'd up the Sultan of _Egypt_, as well knowing therein confifted all fubftantial Wealth, to enter into a Confederacy with all the Kings of _India_, who were already alarm'd by the _Portuguefe_ Fleets, fo that they at the common charge fitted out a Navy of Galleys, and other Veffels, in the Port of _Suez_ furnifh'd it with Cannon, and put aboard 3000 _Mamelucks_, befides a great Number of _Venetian_ and _Genoefe_ Renegadoes With this Power the Sultan enter'd _India_, in the Year 1508, and tho' the King of _Cambaya_ affifted him, he was vanquifh'd by the _Portuguefes_ in the Port of _Chaul_ They urg'd, That at prefent thefe Riches are ftill more valuable, and that if the Trade of them were once brought into the Way of the _Philippine_ Iflands, it would fave all the Dangers met with, by the way of _Amboyna_, _Banda_, _Borneo_, and the many Shoals about them, as alfo the many Storms thofe narrow Seas are fubject to. For the Clove particularly was brought by the _Portuguefes_, in their Trading Galeon, which goes from _Goa_ to the _Moluccos_, to pay their Garrifons. In this Ship they every year carry'd away to _Malaca_ and _Goa_, 24000 _Quintals_, or Hundred Weight of Cloves, little more or lefs. At thofe Ports it was dealt to _Perfians_, _Turks_, _Chinefes_, and _Africans_, fo that fcarce the third Part came to _Europe_. The King of _Achem_, in _Sumatra_, fecur'd another Part, whence it was fent to _Alexandria_ All thefe Commodities, when they come to _Malaca_, pay eight _per Cent._ The Spice that comes into _Spain_ is diftributed into all the Kingdoms of _Europe_; and it might be eafily contriv'd, fay thefe People, to bring the greateft Part to _Spain_ from the _Philippine_ Iflands; which would be one of the nobleft Projects, that will be thought of for the improving of the Revenue, confidering what a great Price Clove bears in _Spain_, and how cheap it is in the _Molucco_ This was the Opinion when thofe Iflands belong'd to another Mafter, and it was no eafie Matter to divert the Trade of Spice, and other Goods, from the ufual _India_ Voyage. Befides the Religious Men of the Orders of St.

Auguftin

Augustin and St. *Dominick*, had already propagated the Faith in those and other Islands, whence that which flourish'd, and advanc'd in *Ternate* and *Tydore* was Fed

Cachil Babu sail'd with his Brothers, and a great Number of Vessels from *Ires* for *Ternate*, with much Joy, and forebodings of Victory, greater Forces continually joyning him, through the earnest Desire they had all of delivering those Parts from the *Portuguese* Domination As soon as ever they arriv'd at *Ternate*, they landed, and immediately invested the Fort, which they call'd the *Seat of Servitude* They assaulted the Houses of the *Portuguese*, and that so suddenly, that though they had Notice before, and lived in Fear, they scarce stood upon their Defence. Rage and Success made a more than Barbarous Havock They set Fire to the Houses with Fury, and popular Tumult, so that whatsoever was not within a Wall and Ditch, perish'd that Day. Those in the Fort attempted to succour their People; but greater Numbers of *Ternates* coming on, kill'd some of those, who had sally'd out, not only with Darts of solid Canes, which they cast most dexteriously, with Arrows, Cymiters and Shields, which they us'd when Idolaters; but with Muskets and other Fire Arms. The rest of the *Portuguese* routed, fled to their Fort; for those who had gain'd Reputation by so many brave Exploits, were that Day depriv'd of their Courage, by the Injustice of the Action they had been concern'd in. They sent again to *Goa* to desire Relief, and to represent the Distress, not only of the Fort of *Ternate*, but of all the others the King of *Portugal* held in those Eastern Parts; for they had cast off Subjection to him in most of them. They forgot not to mention the persecution of the Religion, and the scarcity of Arms and Provisions, of both which the *Ternates* had depriv'd them. These News were flown into *India* and *Spain* by other Ways; and all the while the Siege lasted *Goa* sent Succours to the *Moluccos*, in their trading Galeons; but the vast Distance, the many Shoals, and the violent Storms those Seas are subject to, occasion'd the Loss of those Ships, or put them by their intended Voyage.

The Commanders in those Eastern Ports, who follow'd the Example of those of *Ternate* were not Idle; for the *Portuguese*, tho' the reducing of those Rebels succeeded not at that Time, did not miss of obtaining other Victories, which should we relate them here, would make this look more like a History of all *India* than of one small part of it, besides that the *Portuguese* Nation has not wanted Learned Authors, who have transmitted them to us, where they may be seen at large The *Spaniards* have also done the like, in a much more loftier Stile than mine We must therefore circumscribe our selves, and return to the *Moluccos*, where the Besieged, as it were forsaken, and abandon'd by all the Earth, endure the Hardships and Perils of Places so streightned

Thus all their Hopes, under Heaven, depended on their own Valour, and the inviolable Friendship of the King of *Tydore*, so implacable an Enemy to him of *Ternate*, that neither the Neighbourhood of the Kingdoms, divided only by an Arm of the Sea, a League and half over, in the midst whereof is a small Desart Island, which almost joyns them, nor the ancient and reiterated Alliances, do in the least abate of their Hatred, which seems to be fatal, and consequently unavoidable betwixt those two Kings and Nations

However, the *Ternates* being always intent upon War, and thinking no Practice unlawful, that may secure their Success, they ply'd their Weapons on one Hand, and on the Other, carry'd on their Intrigues, for a Pacification with the King of *Tydore* not so much out of any Desire of coming to a Conclusion with him, as to the End that being amaz'd with the Hopes of Peace, he might grow slack in Relieving and Assisting the Besieged They offer'd to restore him some Places, taken from him during the late Wars; and to give him those and others, as a Portion with a Daughter to the King of *Ternate*, besides other Advantages, of which Accommodation the King of *Bachian* was the chief Manager. To these fair Offers, they added Threats, and both the Kings and their Nations agreeing in Religion, and it being easy to cover any Occasion of War under fair Pretences; it happen'd that the *Tydores*, at least while this Politick Game was playing, did not afford their Succours with the same Zeal as they had done at first, and that

King,

Portuguese Fort besieg'd

Desolation.

Tydore and Ternate mortal Enemies.

Practice of Babu with Tydore.

Policy of the K. of Tydore

King, who till then had been a conftant Friend, upon another Confideration, deferr'd his coming to a Refolution. He waited, as well as the Befieged, the Arrival of the *Portuguefe* Succours, and feveral of his *Carcoas* often touch'd at the
Iflands of *Borneo*, to enquire what Ship pafs'd that Way from *India*. They examin'd every Veffel they met, and every flight Intelligence puff'd them up, or
quite caft them down. In fhort, both Parties protracted the Time, with fo little
Regard to any other Principles, that all their Courage and Fidelity, depended on
it alone.

This is fo certain, that the King of *Tydore* being juft at the Point of accepting
the Wife, and Lands offer'd him by the Enemy, fell off upon the News brought
him, that a Galleon was feen failing for the *Molucco* Iflands, and he rejected all
the Propofals. It was afterwards known to be bound for the *Philippine* Iflands,
and belong'd neither to the *Portuguefe* nor *Spaniards*; but to *Venetian* Merchants, who traded between *Manila* and *China*, with feveral Commodities of
their own Country, and other Parts of the *Levant*, fo that the King of *Tydore*,
and the Befieged themfelves began to make frefh Reparations, like Men that fhar-
pen their Weapons, and fit their Armour.

Sallies, and the Length of the Siege.

Thefe Succours encourag'd them to feveral bold Attempts. The Befieged made
a Salley, to nail up the Enemies Cannon, and tho' few in Number, feveral Times
affaulted their Camp, ftill returning Victorious, without any confiderable Lofs.
They difmounted all their Cannon from the Walls, their Works nothing availing
them, becaufe they were not made according to Art. The Siege lafted five Years,
the *Portuguefes* fuftaining it with notable Refolution, and the *Indians* preffing with
no lefs Obftinacy; nor would the Hunger, Thurft, Nakednefs, and the Hardfhips of the Seafons have been tollerable, had not they been common to both Parties. Extream Want, was the Occafion of feveral fignal Exploits of that Valour,
wherewith they defended their Lives, and the Fort. This produc'd Rage and
Admiration in the Enemy; and an affectionate Compaffion in the Women of the
Ifland; among whom they found Advice, Secrecy, Intelligence and known Favour. So great is the Power of Perfecuted Virtue, that it prevails, even upon
thofe Enemies, who harbour the Memory of a Wrong, to convert it, firft into a
Defire of forgetting it, and without long Interpofition of Time, produces a Zeal
to fupport that Valour they firft hated.

The End of the Second Book.

THE
HISTORY
OF THE
DISCOVERY and CONQUEST
OF THE
Molucco and *Philippine* Iſlands, *&c.*

BOOK. III.

BOTH Sides now took the Breathing of a ſhort Ceſſation; ad- *Ceſſation* vantagious to *Ternate* for the Liberty of Trade, and to the *Por-* *of Arms.* *tugu
eſes*, becauſe it gain'd Time to their Hope of Relief, which they concluded muſt be near at Hand, by Reaſon it had been long expected. They were not diſcouraged by Events, thoſe having prov'd alternatively Succeſsful and Unfortunate, and Victory was toſs'd to and fro ; beſides that the Interruption of Commerce had knit ſome the cloſer together in Friendſhip. I could mention ſeveral Inſtances of this Sort, contain'd in Letters, and other *Spaniſh* and *Portugueſe* Re-lations, ſent by Religious Men from the *Moluccos*, to the Governours of the *Philippine* Iſlands, whoſe Papers have, upon this Occaſion, been lay'd before me, for my better Information, for which Reaſon we may make Uſe of ſome of them, without departing from the main Subject. The graveſt of the *Greek* and *Latin* Hiſtorians ſometimes intermix private Adventures, as it were ſhort Epiſodes to divert the Reader. The Example of great Maſters is a ſufficient Authority for Learners, for which Reaſon I may well be allow'd this Freedom.

One *Duarte*, a brave Enſign, had contracted ſtrict Friendſhip with *Cachil* *A Love* *Tuduria*, which was no way obſtructed by the Difficulties of the Seige, nor *Story.* ſo much as interrupted. *Duarte* was wont in the dead of the Night, to go ſafely into the City in the Habit of the Country, and by the Help of the Language, being Maſter of it, where he was privately admitted into his Friend's Houſe, and well receiv'd there on another Account by *Tuduria*, his

K

his

his only Daughter, who, being prevail'd on by the Love she bore *Duarte*, imbrac'd the Christian Religion. The Father was not unacquainted with their Love, but he also knew that it was attended by Modesty in *Tudurisa*, and true Courtesy in *Duarte*. Returning to the Fort, he used to be taken in the same dangerous way, by those Persons who had let him down with a Rope. He brought with him some Intelligence and Provisions; but he came not so entire himself, for the *Indian* Woman, who was to be his Wife, had robb'd him of his Heart. *Nuno Pereyra* going the Rounds miss'd the Ensign at his Post, and enquiring into it, understood the Cause of his Absence; in Respect to which, considering the mighty Power it often has over great Souls, he conniv'd at the Breach of Martial Discipline, assigning that to the Passion, without reproving the Lover. Whether he follow'd the Example we read of *Quintus Fabius Maximus*, in the like Case, or on Account that Experience shows, there is Nothing can hold a Lover so fast as the Presence of the lov'd Object; *Pereyra* enjoining all Persons to keep the Secret, contriv'd, without offending *Tudura*, that his Daughter should come privately into the Fort, which she consented to, without many Perswasions. Having so done, the Commander in Chief, calling his Ensign, said to him, *I am inform'd, that at certain Times, and that when the Danger is greatest, you forsake us; but that it is not for want of Affection, or not knowing the Duty of your Post; tho' ne were not confin'd to these narrow Walls, I would not punish your Failure, because Mildness has ever been more efficacious for correcting of Generous Souls, than Rigour. It will not be convenient for the Future, that we be left without you, and in Fear for what may befall you: Here is your Wife,* and then she appear'd, *brought hither without any Force, or Opposition from her Father. Take her to you lovingly, and do not suffer the Honour of* Portugal, *depending on these few Men, to want the Bravery of so able an Officer.* Duarte was amaz'd, generously out of Countenance, full of Love, and knew not what to say; but was excus'd by his Friends, and even by *Nunno Pereyra*.

Hopes and Despair of the Besieged. It was now the Year 1575, when the Besieged began to conceive some Hopes of their Deliverance; because the *Sangiacks* and *Cachils* of the King of *Ternate*'s Race were divided into Factions, and there wanted not some among them, who endeavour'd to draw the *Portugueses* over to their Party. These Misunderstandings made them act less vigorously; and did not they look on theirs as the Common Cause, the Design had succeeded. The *Portugueses* in this Condition, despairing of all Relief, the Natives of *Ternate* on the other Side of the Island, next those of the *Meaos*, discover'd a Galeon coming from *Malaca*, having coasted about *Borneo*, they concluded it was that which brought the Succours from *Portugal*, and being assur'd it was so, they became unanimous again, and press'd on the Seige; but Force little prevailing against the Resolution of the Besieged, *Cachil Tulo*, by Permission, propos'd some Terms, which

Proposals of Accommodation, and Reasons for it. the Commander in Chief had long listen'd to from the Wall. One Day making several Overtures, *Tulo* told him, That the King, his Brother, was willing to put an End to that tedious Seige, upon any Conditions. That to this Effect he had concluded a Peace with the King of *Tydore*, that he might not relieve them for the Future. That the King of *Bachian* had

joyn'd

joyn'd him for the same Purpose; to the End, that since they were all convinc'd that was their common Cause, they might with their joynt Power make their utmost Efforts. That the Cessation which had lasted till then, tho' advantages to the King, as encouraging the Trade with the *Javanese*, and *Rumes*, who came to Load Clove, must of Necessity cease. He ask'd how long they would expose their Lives to the utmost Dangers, only to gain an empty Name of *Loyal Subjects*, which, perhaps, would never be known to him that was to reward it. He bid them consider the Villany of his Father, King *Aerio's* Death, and that by their Obstinate holding out they made the Murderers Cause more Criminal. That they thus show'd they approv'd of anothers Treachery, whose Punishment they would compass by other Means That they ought to be very thankfull, that the King would not involve them in the Guilt of that Wretch, who contrary to his solemn Oath, to the Laws of Friendship, and the Honour of the *Portuguese* Nation, or rather to Nature it self, had Murder'd that King, who most inviolably observ'd the Faith he had engag'd to him. Besides, that they were sensible how little Comfort uncertain Hopes could afford amidst real Wants; and how impracticable it was for Relief to come from so great a distance, through such boisterous Seas, causing so many Shipwrecks, and which seem'd to have conspir'd against those who had oppress'd and injur'd *Ternate.*

He concluded his Discourse requiring the Commander in Chief, to deliver up the Fort, or expect the utmost Rigour; for if he once refus'd the Terms offer'd, and provok'd them, they would spare neither Sex, nor Age. The Besieg'd were not free from Jealousie, that there was Fraud in these Offers; yet, perceiving that the Succours never came from *India*, either because retarded by the *African* War, in which King *Sebastian* had engag'd himself, *The Besieged Surrender.* or by the Difficulties of that dangerous Voyage; and believing that the two Kings of *Tydore* and *Ternate* were reconcil'd, as *Tulo* told them, thinking he of *Tydore*, without whose support they could not subsist, had forsaken their Friendship, the Proposals were accepted by unanimous Consent, after *Nuno Pereyra* had return'd a resolute Answer, suitable to that Part of *Cachil Tulo's* Words, which contain'd any Threats, signifying to him, how little they mov'd himself, or his Men; and that he would hearken to no Conditions to the disservice of his God, or his King, or to disparage the Bravery of his Soldiers, which had been so often try'd to the cost of the Natives of *Ternate*; nevertheless upon some other Considerations, he would surrender the Fort, provided that all the *Portugueses* might march out in a *The Capitulation.* Body, Colours Flying, with their Wives, Children, Slaves, and all their *tulation.* Goods, having first Hostages given them to their content, that no Harm, or Injury should be done them. That the King should secure them their Passage to *Amboyna*, and find them Vessels; and that such as should happen to be left in his Dominions for want of them, should have no Ransome demanded of them, either then, or at the time of their departure. That the Fort and Guns should be deliver'd to King *Babu*, upon express Condition, that he should hold it for the King of *Portugal*, and in his Name, to whom he should restore it, whensoever he effectually punish'd the Murder of King ..... The King easily Granted, and Swore to perform all those Conditions, being eager to possess himself of the Fort, before the Succours arriv'd, *The Port* which days now near at hand. On the Day appointed, which was Saint *Deliver'd.* Stephen's,

Stephen's, the *Ternates* took up all the advantageous Posts to view the *Portugueses*, who march'd out as if they had been Conquerors; and no sooner were they out of the Fort, than the Natives running in, possess'd themselves of the Guns, with loud Laughter and Shouts, Scoffing at those that left it; for the third Day after the Galeon arriv'd, well Mann'd, and furnish'd with Guns, and all Necessaries, and *James de Azambuja* in it, as Commander in Chief. They had thoughts of Recovering the Fort, but it was too late, because the Enemy was possess'd of all Things, without any Opposition. *Pereyra* then perceiv'd how great an Obstacle Precipitation is to the chusing of the safest Advice, and how infallibly it is follow'd by fruitless Repentance; since had he delay'd but never so little longer, tho' it were only to weigh the Enemies Proposals, who ought never to be suppos'd Sincere, he might have sav'd himself and Destroy'd them. For this Reason, tho' he wanted not an honourable Excuse, he resolv'd not to return to *Goa*, having private Intelligence that the Viceroy would not fail to secure him, in Order to cut off his Head *Azambuja* protected him in his Galeon, and he went over with many others to *Amboyna*. The rest spread themselves throughout the Neighbouring Islands, in Vessels they begg'd. Some return'd to *Malaca*, and only sixteen *Portuguese* Families remain'd in *Ternate* for want of Shipping; who at first submitted to the change of their Fortune; but could not afterwards comply with the Dif-

Portugue-
les *settle*
at Tydore.

ference there is betwixt Domination and Servitude. The King of *Tydore* a most trusty Friend to the *Spaniards* in their greatest Affliction, offer'd them his Islands, Houses, and Trade of Spice. He sent them a good Number of *Carcoas*, which carry'd them over to his Dominions, and soon after assign'd them a convenient Place to build their Houses and Churches. This Colony was increased, and the Number of its Inhabitants augmented by *Sancho de Vasconselos*, who sent others from *Malaca*, being Commander in Chief of *Goa*, and afterwards of *Amboyna*, in the Year 1578. At last he came thither himself, and erected a Fort, a quarter of a League from the City of *Tydore*, which gives its Name to the Island.

Tydore
describ'd.

Tydore, in the Language of those Parts, which was formerly spoken, signifies, Fertility and Beauty. *Europeans* generally give it this Name; but its King, as appears by his *Arabick* and *Persian* Subscriptions, Writes *Tudura*, and not *Tydore*. It is not inferior to *Ternate* for Fruitfulness, and Delight, but far exceeds it in Magnitude and Populousness; and yields the same Aromatick Product. Curious Persons have there try'd to improve the Clove, watering and pruning the Tree at proper Seasons, and it appears to embrace the Helps of Art, by growing bigger, more active in its Vertue, and the Scent stronger. The white Sanders here come to more Perfection, than in any other of the Eastern Parts. In this, as well as the other *Molucco* Islands are found those Birds, they, in their Language, call

Birds of
Paradice.

Manucodiatas, signifying Birds of Paradise, from a Fable, credited by those superstitious People, that they came down from Heaven. The Fort here was afterwards enlarg'd by *Nuno Pereyra*, not far from the Port, and then by *James de Azambuja*. The latter did not only contribute with his In-

Fort of
Tydore.

dustry, but with his Labour, carrying the Materials himself, when it was requisite to set the Soldiers an Example, and forward the Work; which the King often view'd, and was well pleas'd to see the Fortifications. He

difcours'd

difcours'd familiarly with the Officers, advis'd with them in his Wars, and comforted the Chriftians, and they far'd beft, for from that Time forward, there being none in *Ternate*, and that Fort in the Hands of the Natives, the Heathens and *Mahometans* feem'd to be Superior and Conquerors throughout all thofe Provinces. They ftrengthen'd themfelves with Works and other Preparations, erected Forts on high Places, and bending their Minds againft the Chriftians, put many to cruel Martyrdoms; that *Perfecu-* fo the Foundation of our Faith may be in all Parts cemented with the Blood of the Faithful. They difmember'd the Bodies, and burnt the Legs *Perfecu-* and Arms in the fight of the ftill Living Trunks. They impal'd the *tion.* Women, tore out their Bowels, and they furving themfelves, beheld their ftill moving Flefh in the Hands of their Executioners. Children were pull'd Piecemeal before their Mothers Eyes, and Infants ftill in Embrio were rent from their Wombs. It has been made out, that above 60000 Chriftians fell by the Sword in only the King of *Ternate's* Dominions. This is afferted in the Annual Relations of the Fathers of the Society, who preach'd in thofe Parts. They give an Account of this difmal Perfecution, with all the Circumftances of the Cruelties; as how the perfecuted Perfons fled to the Mountains, feeking for Compaffion among the wild Beafts, others caft themfelves into the Sea, where they perifh'd, either devour'd by its Monfters, or fwallow'd by the Waves themfelves, not being able to reach the other Iflands. A confiderable Number of thefe religious Fugitives, as they fwam met a *Portuguefe* Ship, coming to the Relief of thofe at *Amboyna*, and with difmal Voices cry'd out, *Help, Relieve us, for we are Chriftans.* They carefully took them up in their Boats, and having view'd them at Leafure, found that none of them were above 12 Years of Age. Yet at this fame Time, when cruelty advanc'd God's Glory, Providence feem'd to act Counter in the very Cities, and Deferts. Idolaters and *Mahometans* were converted, and our Religious Men preach'd and catechis'd, without any Fear of Punifhment, which they rather coveted, and thought themfelves unworthy of it; encouraging one another with the Examples the Tyrant made, for feveral Purpofes. But all thofe People looking upon it as their Duty to feek Revenge, their Cruelty gaining Applaufe under that Name, and *Europe* being involv'd in Difmal Troubles, they met with no Oppofition in the Execution of their Vengeance, and the Calamity ran fo high, that in the fpace of thirty Years, they either quite obliterated, or much obfcured the Name of Chriftianity in thofe Eaftern Parts, deftroy'd our Churches, and, like thofe who prepare to hunt wild Beafts, arm'd themfelves againft the Faithful who liv'd in more fecurity among thofe favage Creatures, or in Deferts never penetrated by Men, feeding on Herbs, and gaining Time, by that lawful Retreat for the fake of the Gofpel, for the Wrath of Heav'n, whofe Executioners thofe Men were, to pafs over. Above 36 Towns, of each 800 Inhabitants in *Gilolo* and *Celebes*, a fpacious *Many Apo-* and populous Country, and in thofe of the two Kings of *Sian* and *Sanguil*, *ftatize.* who profefs'd Chriftianity, with moft of their Subjects, in the Kingdom of *Cauripana*; in that of *Bachian*, whofe King and his People were Sons of the Church; in the Iflands of *Amboyna*, where Forty Towns worfhipped CHRIST, in the Bofom of his Faith, and in thofe of *Tydore*, which were

not

not without this Light ; in all thofe Places they fell off from Chriftianity, and were utterly loft ; firft through the Infolency of the *Portuguefe* Commanders, and laftly on Account of the Death of *Sultan Aerio* ; who, as was prov'd, had given no real, nor fo much as a likely Token of Falfhood, for which they might be provok'd to deftroy him. However the Chriftians dy'd with fuch Refolution, that the Perfecuters took not away any Life but what became a frefh Example of Magnanimity, and perhaps Providence might permit that Accident of *Aerio*, with a Defign to advance the Churches Glory.

Auguftin Nune*z* fent to Command at Amboyna. *Sultan Babu* making his prefent Victory an Inftrument to obtain others, Ship'd his Men, in Order to befiege *Tydore* and *Bachian* ; and tho' he met with a vigorous Defence in both Places, and the *Portuguefe* Auxiliaries made fome Amends for his Superiority of Power, yet they fubmitted to the Tyrant. This Revenge made him ftick at no Cruelty. In *November*, this fame Year, a Galeon came to *Malaca* from India, to carry Succours for the *Moluccos*, commanded by Captain *Auguftin Nunez*, the Eldeft and Braveft Commander in thofe Days, as he made it appear in the Expedition of *Chaul*, when it was befieged by *Niza Moluco*, when *Don Luys de Atayde* was Viceroy of *India*, in the year 1578. The Galeon was ftor'd with all Neceffaries, and in it *James*

James Lopez de Mezquita* fent Prifoner to Ternate. *Lopez de Mezquita*, the Murderer of *Aerio*, defign'd for Punifhment, in Satisfaction for the Wrong done. He was fo ftrong, and fierce, that to fecure him, he was fetter'd with a great Chain, the End whereof was made faft to a heavy Piece of Brafs Cannon. *Auguftin Nunez* had Orders to convey him to the new King of *Ternate*, to be deliver'd to him bolted, like a Criminal, that he might pafs fuch a fentence of Death on him as he thought fit, which fhould be executed in his Prefence, purfuant to the Orders fent by the King of *Portugal*. They put him on double Fetters, Manacles, and Chains, and kept him in the Steeridge. *Auguftin Nunez* went to fucceed *Sancho de Vafconcelos*, in the Fort of *Amboyna* ; but a ftorm rifing, he was forc'd into the Port of *Japara*, of *Sunda*, in the greater *Java*. The Galeon wanting water, and Refrefhment, he there fent for it ; which the Native *Javanefes* brought him in 40 Veffels. Among them came 150 Soldiers in the Habit of Peafants, and Fifhermen ; who making many words as is ufual among Buyers and Sellers, drew the Ponyards they brought conceal'd, and furprizing the *Portuguefes*, fell on with fuch Fury and Cruelty, that they

The Murderer kill'd kill'd them all. Among them dy'd *James Lopez de Mezquita*, but fighting with extraordinary Bravery, tho' held by his Chain, hinder'd by his Fetters, and other heavy Encumbrances, and reftrain'd by the Cannon, to which his Chain was made faft. However he got a Sword and a Buckler wherewith he cut down ten *Javanefes*, revenging on them the Death of the *Portuguefes*, and they on him, that of King *Aerio* of *Ternate*, which had occafion'd fo much Slaughter. Seventy three Chriftians were kill'd and above the fame Number of *Javanefes*, and their Veffels had been taken, but that others came to their Affiftance from the Shore in the Heat of the Action, in which there were Men with Fire-Locks and Lances, fix Yards and a Quarter long, the Points of them poifon'd. The Galeon was taken without any Succour, nor was the Cannon of any Ufe.

It is but reafonable that fo manly and honourable a Death fhould, as is ufual,

ufual, render all this Gentlemans Life honourable ; and that his Fetters, and *His Vindi-*
Sufferings joyn'd to it, excite Compaffion and Affection in the minds of the *cation.*
Readers, fo to blot out the Hatred they have conceiv'd againft him on Account of *Sultan Aerio's* Death. It is to be obferv'd, for his Iuftification that
it does not appear, nor is it reported, he was incens'd to perform that Act
through Intereft, Ambition, or any other private Motives ; but was mov'd
to it by Informations which perfwaded him it was convenient, for the
Eftablifhing and Advancement of Religion, and the publick Peace. Very
brave men muft alfo be allow'd fome Exceffes of Fierceneʃs, which proceed
from an extraordinary Force in the irafcible Part of the mind, and wherein
Valour is fubdu'd. When thefe Perfons find themfelves encompaʃs'd by
great Numbers, and ftreightned by wrongful Violence ; if they are not to be
daunted and overcome, it comes to paʃs that Patience often provok'd turns
that Courage into Fury and Rage, which caufes them to make mighty Slaughters, and Examples of Cruelty ; led to it not only by Paffion, but alfo by
Judgment and Thought, which directs them to caufe themfelves to be dreaded even to Aftonifhment, to fave themfelves and their People from other
great Cruelties which ufually mean Souls attempt and practice upon thofe
they ftand much in Fear of. Let this Reflection ferve for a general Excufe
to other Offences of this fort mention'd, or blam'd in our Hiftory.

This Accident, in as much as related to the Death of *James Lopez de* *Peter Lo-*
Mezquita, was forgot, or at leaft not known for many Years, for in 1603 *pez de Sou-*
the King of *Ternate* demanded Juftice of our King, againft that Man not *fa fent to*
knowing that God had fummon'd him before a more upright Tribunal. *Moluccos.*
The News being brought to *Malaca*, the Commander *Arias de Saldana* im-
mediately fent away another Galeon, he call'd *S. Peter* and *S. Paul*, for the
Moluccos under command of *Peter Lopez de Soufa*, and a Galley with 150
Soldiers to relieve *Sancho de Vafconcelos* at *Amboyna*, where he wanted
Provifions, and was ftreightned. They faild in May 1579, to touch at
Borneo, there to take in all Neceffaries for the Defign. He arriv'd on
that Ifland in *June*, and found it in an Uproar, occafion'd by the *Spaniards* *Spaniards*
who came thither with Doctor *Sandi*, Governour of the *Philippine* Iflands *at Borneo.*
in 30 rowing Veffels. He took the City, and put the King to flight, who
was a Lover of the *Portuguefes*, and from that time *Manila* began to be
look'd upon as a place of Arms, for the recovering of the *Molucco Iflands*;
and if *Sandi* had then employ'd thofe, he carry'd to this other Expedition
againft them, he would have found the Tyrant leʃs fettled, and confequently
his Revenge more eafy. *Vafconcelos* died at *Amboyna*, and *James de Azam-*
buja fucceeded him, fo that nothing came now from *India* but fair Promifes. In the *Philippine* Iflands they had no Orders at that Time to intermed-
dle in thofe Wars, becaufe they then belong'd to another Sovereign, and
therefore they were only Lookers on to thofe Martyrdoms, and Revolutions
and employ'd themfelves as they us'd in *Camboxa*, *Mindanao*, *Japan* and
China, and then particularly in *Borneo*, without regarding thofe other Succeʃses.

Borneo lies between *Malaca* and the *Moluccos*, and according to the Opi- *Borneo de-*
nion of *Gerard Mercator*, is that which *Ptolomy* calls, the Ifland of Good *fcrib'd.*
Fortune. A Point of it lies under the Equinoctial, and the greater Part
ftretches out to 6 Degrees of North Latitude, taking up the two firft Paral-
lels. Thus it appears to be above 400 Leagues in Compafs. It abounds
in

in Provisions, and all other Neceffaries for the Support of humane Life And produces abundance of Camphire, Agarick Diamonds, vaft Numbers of Horfes, fmaller than the *Spanifh* ; but it has not fuch plenty of Sheep, or Kine There is a general Refort of Trade in all its Populous Cities and Ports.   The Capital is *Borneo*, which gives Name to the Ifland, built on a Spacious Lake the Sea Forms, like *Venice*, and faid to contain 23000 Houfes.   The King is a *Mahometan* , no man fpeaks to him but by the Interpofition of an Interpreter.   The Natives worfhip Idols. They are White, good Natur'd and fharp Witted. They have no certain Fa-fhion of Cloaths.   Many of them wear Cotton Shirts, and others of white common fingle Tabby, with red Lifts.

King of Borneo's Brothers at Manila.   S.relela, Brother to this King, came to *Manila*, where Doctor *Sand* being then Governour, he laid before him his Pretenfions, and fome Means he had for bringing his Defigns to bear ; but he put the main Strefs upon his having a greater Party there, than the King his Brother.   He promifed which would be no difficult Matter, in Regard of the Hatred the People bore the King, that he would make the Kingdom Tributary to the Kings of *Spain*.   The Governour having taken fufficient Precautions, condefcended to his Requeft, and arming as many *Spaniards*, and *Philippines* as he thought convenient, with all Neceffaries for a great Enterprize, fhip'd them, and arriv'd happily at *Borneo*.   He attack'd it in feveral Places; the

Spaniards overthrow that King.   beft of the People immediately declar'd for the Brother.   The King think-ing himfelf weakeft at Sea, referv'd his Forces for the Land, and being de-ceiv'd in his Expectation, was forc'd to fly, his Army being routed, with-out any Remains to attend him in the Deferts, and Retreats of the Moun-tains, where he liv'd miferably.   *Sirelela* afcended the Throne ; the Victo-rious *Spaniards* return'd to the *Philippine* Iflands loaded with Booty ; and among other Things, if we may believe Relations, brought 600 Pieces of Artillery.   However the depos'd King, a few Months after, got to a Head

He is re-ftored.   again. No Man ought to Defpair in Adverfity, for Fortune is nothing but the Will of God.   Thus the King, with the Affiftance of the *Portuguefes*, recover'd his Throne, cafting down his Brother, and defeating him, till he was utterly deftroy'd.   Hatred is frequently no lefs intenfe than Love among thofe whom Nature has moft clofly link'd   In the *Molucco* Iflands the War did not ceafe, nor the general Malice againft Chriftians.

A Prodigy.   The News of what had happened there was not known in *Europe*, where, and in *Africk* greater Dangers were apprehended; of the Event whereof Providence thought fit to inform our free Wills, by ftupendious Prodigies. On the 15th of *June* 1580, about the declining of the Day, there appear'd to certain Sailers a Large Crucifix in the Body of the Sun the Foot of the Crofs ftanding on Mount *Calvary*, as we fee in common Pictures; on the Right Side of it a Figure clad in White, and another on the left in a deep Red.   The Crucifix afcended upwards, and was ftill feen to mount till the Sun Setting, the Day fhut in.   This was feen by all thofe who came in a Caravel, from the Ifland of St. *Michael* ten Leagues before they came to that of St. *George*, the Bifhop whereof refiding in that of *Angli*, fent the Affidavit of it to King *Philip* the Second, which was receiv'd and much talk'd of by the Judge *Freytas*, a grave Perfon.   All the Men of the Cara-vel fign'd it, as Eye-Witneffes, who affir , That being touch'd with it,

the)

they confeſs'd their Sins at the Sight of the Prodigy, begging Mercy with Sighs and Tears. Our Underſtandings ought to ſtand amaz'd, and praiſe, him that produces both what is Natural, and Miraculous, and who by ſo many Warnings ſhows us, that he has reſerv'd Times, and Moments in his own Hand

King *Sebaſtian*, at that Time had other Conqueſts in View. The Loſs or the Recovery of *Ternate* and the neighbouring *Moluccos* concern'd him alone, but he referr'd that to the Governour of *India*; whilſt he himſelf, ſolicited by the *Xerif Muley Mahomet*, whom he deſign'd to ſet upon the Throne of *Morocco*, tho' with a good Deſign, joyn'd the *African* Army, with another of Catholicks, conſiſting of the *Portugueſe* Gentry, of *Spaniards*, *Italians*, and *Germans*. And, if we may believe thoſe who committed that Expedition to writing, he went over into *Africk*, contrary to all the known Rules and Maxims of Martial Prudence, which Proportions the the Strength to the Undertaking, to aſcertain the Succeſs and forecaſts, in Caſe Things proſper, to ſecure and preſerve them. This he did upon the Aſſurances the *Xerif* gave him, that as ſoon as ever the *Portugueſe* Forces appear'd, the People would ſubmit to him. But God permitted that moſt Chriſtian Prince to be kill'd, the *Xerif* periſhing with him; and their Armies to be routed, *Muley Moluc* the third Perſon remaining Victorious, tho' he alſo dy'd in the ſame Battel, and was bury'd in triumphant Manner. The Prodigies, and Fears of the wiſer ſort were verify'd in the King of *Portugal*, and particularly that which happen'd before his Birth. It is certainly reported, that the Princeſs *Joanna* his Mother, one Night ſaw a great Number of *Moors* come into her Chamber, in the Palace at *Lisbon*, clad in ſeveral Colours; ſhe believ'd or fancy'd they might be thoſe they call *Monetios*, who are ſuch as do the Duty of Guards in the Royal Apartment. Some went out to enquire, and found them all ſtill, as huſht as at other Times. The Princeſs ſeeing the imaginary *Moors* come in again, ſwoon'd away in her Ladies Arms. Afterwards at the proper Time, ſhe was deliver'd of King *Sebaſtian*, whoſe ſingular Virtues, ſupported by the Loyalty of his Subjects, might have ſhin'd as bright as his natural Magnanimity, had not that haſten'd his End. That was mourn'd for and lamented by all Chriſtendom, and brought Trouble to all its Princes, who began ſeriouſly to diſcourſe about the Succeſſor to the Crown of *Portugal*. There they preſently ſwore *Henry*, the Prince Cardinal, Unkle to the late King, then Eighty Years of Age, and the laſt Lawful Male of that Royal Houſe, which began in another of his Name. *Antony*, Prior of *Crato*, Son to Prince *Lewis*, pretended to ſucceed him, and tho' declar'd illegitimate, there was a Party that follow'd him. This Revolution, and the Hurry in ſuch difficult Exigences, were the Occaſion, that Care was not taken to ſupply other Places, much nearer than *Ternate*. Beſides that diſmal Accounts brought 5000 Leagues, tho' they were repreſented by *Demoſthenes*, would come cold from his Mouth and ſcarce move the beſt diſpos'd Prince, when never ſo much at Leaſure; and King *Henry*, had no Power, but only his Zeal for Religion, to oppoſe the Tyranny practis'd in the *Archipelago* of the *Moluccos*. The Cardinal King thought all his Forces little enough, and neceſſary conſidering the extraordinary Jealouſie he had conceiv'd, upon our King *Philip*'s declaring himſelf a Pretender to thoſe Kingdoms, and having order'd a conſiderable

King Sebaſtian prepares for the War in Africk.

Is Kill'd there.

Prodigy.

Henry the Cardinal King.

L   Army

Army to make up to the Frontiers, which he had drawn together during the said Cardinal's Life. The Generals were the Duke of *Alva*, and the Marquess *de Santa Cruz*, the first at Land, the other at Sea, and in the mean while the ablest Divines and Civilians of *Europe*, in all the Schools, and Parliaments writ concerning his Right.

First English Voyage to the Moluccos.

The Year before, being 1579, about the Beginning of it, Q. *Elizabeth* of *England*, seeing the Princes of *Europe*, particularly those in the Western Parts, make Warlike Preparations, as being divided in Opinions; form Leagues, and direct all their Designs towards the Kingdom of *Portugal*, she to make some Diversion with Security, had on a sudden fitted out four Ships, of eighteen Brass Guns each, and in them two hundred Men, and ten young Gentlemen, who besides employing their Valour, on such Occasions as it should offer, were to be very intent upon the Business of Navigation for greater Ends. She appointed *Francis Drake* of the County of *Devon* their Commander in Chief, who at his own, or at the Charge of *John Hawkins*, from whom he stole a great Quantity of Gold and Silver at *S. John de Ulva*, in the Year 1566, added some more Ships. He set sail from the Port of *Plymouth*, for the South Sea, and to find out that Streight of *Magellan*, scarce believed by the Vulgar, and declar'd by several Cosmographers. He promis'd to sail as much as might be to the Northward, and to take rich Prizes, infesting all those remote Seas, and to return Victorious into *England*, through the same Streight. This presumptuous Hope he grounded on his own Valour, on the Negligence of the *Spaniards*, who are intrusted with the Places of Strength, on our want of Ships; and above all on that Opportunity, or Season so full of sundry and extraordinary Commotions. He touch'd on the Coast of *Africk*, and refitted all his Ships at Cape *Bojador*. The *Moors* took two of his Men, and a *Portuguese* Ship pay'd for it, he robbing her at *Cabo Blanco* of an hundred Quintals, or hundred Weight of Bisket, besides much Fish, and many Arms. He touch'd at the Islands of *Cabo Verde*, where he took another small *Portuguese* Vessel, richly Laden with Wine, Cloth, Holland, and several other Commodities, with *Sylva*, the Pilot in it, who was well acquainted with those Seas, and better on the Coast of *Brazil*. But six or seven Days after the Vessel sunk, and not a Man was sav'd except only the said Pilot. *Drake* went on to the River of *Plate*, and Winter'd for some Months in *S. Julians* Bay, which is not well shelter'd, but expos'd to excessive cold Winds, in 50 Degrees of South Latitude, where he lost some Men.

Sir Francis Drake his Voyage.

One *Thomas Haughton* rais'd a Mutiny there, in order to Debauch the Squadron, *Drake* laid hold of him, and struck off his Head. Here they saw eight *Indian* Giants to whom the tallest *Englishman* look'd like a Dwarf. They show'd their Bows and Arrows, and an *Englishman*, who valu'd himself upon his Dexterity at those Weapons, breaking the Peace establish'd with those People, let fly an Arrow at one of them, which pierced him through, and he dropt; the others in Revenge discharged theirs, and kill'd two of the *English*. The rest then assail'd the *Indians*, but they fled so swiftly that they seem'd not, to those *English* who saw and writ this, to set their Feet on the Ground. They departed thence, as soon as the North Winds they had expected began to blow, and holding on their Course to the Southward, in fifteen Days came to the Mouth of the Streight.

Giants.

From

From thence to the fecond Narrowing they fpent five Days, by reafon of the Currents and Shoals; at a fmall diftance from them they found no Bottom. They met with fome Calms and Storms, and being come into the South-Sea had one which lafted forty Days, and in it loft fome Ships. The Vice-Admiral return'd through the fame Streight into *England*, where the Queen order'd him to be Hang'd for having forfaken his Admiral, but he was repriev'd till *Drakes* Return, and then Pardon'd, at his Requeft. He went on with only his own and fome other Ships, but wanted not Men, Provifions, nor Ammunition, he took fome belonging to private Perfons, and the Kings, loaded with the Plate they were bringing for *Spain*, a Robbery of great Confequence, not fo much for the Quantity of the Treafure, as for the Ufe it is apply'd to in our Monarchy, which is the Advancement of the Catholick Church, and which thereby ceas'd, and deplorable for the unjuft Abufes it was to be apply'd to in Scifmatical Kingdoms. Having wander'd, Steering various Courfes, in which his Pilots made their Obfervations by Sounding and their Charts, he touch'd at fix Iflands, to fome whereof he gave Names, in Imitation of the fabulous Heroes, and even of true Catholicks, who affign fuch Names according to their particular Devotion. One he call'd *S. Bartholomew*, another *S. James*, and a third, which he thought larger and more fruitful, *New Albion*, from the Ancient Name of *England, this is California*. There he ftay'd a Month and a half, refitting his Ships, and failing thence to thofe call'd *de los Ladrones*, or of Thieves, in nine Degrees of North Latitude, kill'd 20 *Indians*, becaufe they attack'd him with 100 *Canoas*. Twenty Days after, he came to an Anchor at the *Molucco* Iflands, having before touch'd at others, without any Action worth remembering. His Cruelties, and Robberies might well gain him the Title of the greateft of Pyrates, in thofe remoteft Parts, as he had it in *Europe*. He came to *Ternate*, but fucceeded not at firft, that People being War-like, and at that time Arm'd by their own Malice, and an implacable King. He attempted to barter for Clove, without his Leave, was inform'd how feverely he handled fuch as Tranfgrefs'd, and flighting the Advice, the King came to hear of it, and order'd him to be Kill'd. It came very near the Execution; but *Drake*, whofe Genious well experienced in Frauds was no Stranger to Diffimulation, retir'd to his Ships, to make his Efcape by Flight. Thence he contriv'd to appeafe the King, which was no difficult Matter, by means of fome Prefents he fent him. With them he purchas'd the good Will, and an Audience of that cunning Tyrant, and going afhore feveral Times to vifit him, agreed he fhould enter into Amity with the Queen, and Nation of *England*, and that Factories fhould be fettled out of Hand. The King confented, and *Drake* promis'd him the Protection and Arms of *England*; and taking with him, among other Gifts, a rich Ring the King gave him for the Queen, he fail'd homewards, with a great quantity of Clove. He met a *Portuguefe* Ship croffing the fmall Channel of *Tydore*, but either durft not, or thought not fit to attack her, whether it was for being Inferior in Strength, or out of a Defire of fecuring the new acquir'd Wealth. Scarce was he got clear of *Ternate*, before the Winds began to tofs him, in that Sea full of Flats, whence they forc'd him, in order to deliver him quite up to Tempefts. He was oblig'd to lighten his Ships, and among other Things of Value, threw over-Board a Cannon, of an ex-

Drake takes the Kings Plate.

He gives Names to Iflands.

Arrives at the Moluccos.

Is in a Storm.

traordinary

traordinary Bigness, which the King of *Ternate*, hearing afterwards of the Storm, caused to be taken out of the deep Sea. Then he built a House before his Palace, on the Roof whereof he planted it openly, and pointing over, either on Account of its Magnitude, or by way of Oftentation, and in Memory of the first *Englishman*, that came into his Kingdoms, from whom and the Sea he had taken that new offensive Booty. *Drake* went on to the greater *Java*, where he laid in Provisions of *Cazabi*, *Plantans*, and *Ficul*, in exchange for Cloth. Next he put into another Island, in four Degrees of North Latitude, where he stay'd six Weeks. There he left a Woman, and two Men, all Blacks, that belong'd to him, giving them Fire, Rice, and some Grain, that they might People the Place. An Heroick Foundation of a Colony. Then he continu'd his Voyage, turning in and out to several Places, with unexpected Dammage to all those he touch'd at.

Reflection of the Spanish *Author*. It is to be obferv'd, that it being pofitively believed in *Spain* and the *Indies*, that none had ever pafs'd the Streights of *Magellan*, since the first Difcoverer, except *F. Garcia de Loayfa*, and one of the Ships fent by *Don Gutierre de Vargas*, Bishop of *Palencia*, to the Spice-Islands, it was look'd upon as incredible, that any Pyrates were come into the South-Sea, especially through the Streight, and to the Islands of *Ternate*, and that *Archipelago*. This Man was the first that open'd the Passage to the Sectaries *Hugonots*, *Lutherans*, and *Calvinists*, who afterwards pierc'd into those Seas, with Ship Loads of perverted Texts, Heretical Bibles, and other Books of unfound Doctrine; but the Divine Providence has given Proofs, that it is fo much Offended at this Hellish Innovation, tho' it permits Idolatry, and *Mahometanifm*, that it has not fuffer'd those Souls which through its profound Judgments, lie involv'd in the Shades and Darkness of Ignorance, to imbibe that Poyfon, till it fent them the Gofpel in its Purity. It has Oppos'd those new Apoftacies making ufe of, as Inftruments of *Spanish* Religious Men, giving Strength to our King, who protects them, his main Defign being the Support of Religion. This Truth plainly appears in the many Victories the Church has obtain'd through his Officers, and the Armies maintain'd in the remoteft Parts of the Monarchy, for the Propagation of the Faith preach'd to the moft diftant *Indians*.

Reafon for this Digreffion. But the better to demonftrate this true Forecaft and Care, I think it a neceffary Digreffion, fo far from being fuperfluous, to relate the Preparations made by the Viceroy *Don Francifco de Toledo*, directing his Actions to this End, as became a Minifter who follow'd his Princes Defigns, in Order to fecure himfelf againft *Drake*'s furprizing Celerity and Boldnefs; for as much of this as concerns the *Molucco* Iflands, obliges us to write it, and we will flightly run over all the particular Paffages.

Preparations of the Viceroy. The Viceroy of *Peru* was of Opinion, That in Order to fecure the *Indies*, their Peace and Religion, and for the removing, at firft, of all Obftacles to its Exaltation, and making Examples for a Warning, it was of the greateft Confequence to erect Forts, as divine and humane politick Precautions, and to Arm againft that Pyrate, fo to give a Check to the Northern Parts by his Punifhment. To this Purpofe, and in Order to his Deftruction, a more exact Obfervation was to be taken of the Paffes into the South-Sea, and more particularly of the Way he was to take, to return into his own Country. He was egg'd on by Fear, or the Lofs of Repu-

tation

tation, becaufe fome Englifh Ships, Part of *Drake*'s Squadron, ran along the Coafts of *Chile* and *Arica*, obliging the People to Arm ; it being apprehended that *Drake* had erected Forts to fecure the Paffage, for carrying on the Trade of Spice and Jewels, and the bringing in of perverfing Minifters with their poifonous Doctrines. For this Effect, he pitch'd upon *Peter Sarmiento de Gamboa*, a Gentleman of *Galicia*, who had twice already engag'd with that Pyrate. The firft in the Port of *Callao* near *Lima*, where he took from him a *Spanifh* Ship, laden with Commodities of *Spain* ; the feconda few Days after, purfuing him as far as *Panama*. The Viceroy refolv'd he fhould go to difcover the Streights of *Magellan*, an Enterprize look'd upon as impracticable by the South Sea, by Reafon of the many Mouths and Channels which obftruct the Accefs to it, where many Difcoverers fent by the Governours of *Peru* and *Chile* have been loft. Others have attempted it, entering from the North Sea, and mifs'd of the Streight ; fome were caft away, or beaten back by Storm, and all generally defpair'd of finding it. But now that Terror being remov'd, they can take a fix'd Latitude, fettle a Rumb, and fteer a fafe Courfe to the Streight, fo to fecure the Paffage before an Enemy poffeffes himfelf of it. The Viceroy made Choice of two Ships, which he took Care to fee well rigg'd, arm'd and provided. *Sarmiento* call'd the Bigger, *Our Lady of Hope*, which was Commodore ; the other being fubordinate, had the Name of *S Francis*. Two Hundred Seamen and Soldiers were put into them, with virtuous and learned Religious Men, fit for that Employ. Captain *John de Villalobos* was appointed Vice-Admiral. *Ferdinand Lamero* Head Pilot, and under him *Ferdinand Alonfo* and *Antony Pablo*, all of them very able Pilots in both Seas. Thefe took an Oath of Fidelity, and the Viceroy gave the Admiral particular Inftructions, the Purport whereof was, That they fhould purfue the Pyrate, fight him till taken or kill'd, and recover the great Booty he had taken upon the King's Lands and Ships, whatfoever the Hazard might be, fince they had fufficient Men, Arms and Ammunition to overcome the Enemy. That they fhould fail into 50 or 54 Degrees of South Latitude, as might be moft Advantageous, about the Mouth of the Streights of *Magellan*. That both Ships fhould have Lights out at Night, that fo they might not lofe Sight of one another in the Dark, but always keep together. He charg'd them to be unanimous in their Confultations, particularly the two Commanders ; which Direction was not fo well obferv'd, as it ought to have been, thro' the Vice-Admiral's Fault. They were commanded to lay down the Ports, and Seas in exact Draughts. To take Poffeffion of any Country they landed on for his Majefty. When they met with any Towns of *Indians*, to mollify and endear them by difcreet Courtefy, and gain their Affections with fuch Gifts, as fhould for that Purpofe be deliver'd to the Commodore, being Siffars, Combs, Knives, Fifhing-Hooks, Buttons of feveral Colours, Looking-Glaffes, Hawks-Bells, Glafs-Beads, *&c*. To carry with them fome *Indians* to ferve for Interpreters ; and fo provided difcreetly for all other material Points Then to encourage them he made a Speech, intermixing it with Hopes and Exhortations. The Commodore having conferr'd with his Vice-Admiral and Pilots, concerning the Defign of their Voyage ; they agreed, That if any Strefs of Weather fhould happen to part the one

Difficultie of the Streight of Magellan.

Sarmiento fent after Drake with two Ships.

His Inftructions.

one Ship from the other, they fhould carefully feek one another out, or make the Mouth of the Streight in the South-Sea to the Weftward, there to wait for one another   The next Day being *Sunday*, the 11th of *October*, 1579. when they had all confefs'd and receiv'd the Holy Euchariſt, they embark'd in order to introduce the Faith into thofe Nations void of all Worfhip.   On Board the *Capitana*, or greater Ship, the General, or Commodore *Sarmiento*, *F. Antony de Guadramiro*, of the Order of *S. Francis*, and Vicar-General of this Expedition ; the Enfign *John Gutierrez de Guevara*, *Antony Pablos*, and *Ferdinand Alonfo*, Pilots, with 54 Soldiers. In the other Ship, with *John de Villalobos*, *F. Chriſtopher de Merida*, of the faid Order of *S. Francis*, *Ferdinand Lamero*, chief Pilot of that Ship, with whom, and the Seamen and Soldiers, they made 54 ; and the whole Number in both Veffels as was faid above.

His Strength.

They fail'd from the Port of *Callao*, belonging to the City of *Lima*, and that Night came to an Anchor at the Ifland, two Leagues from *Callao*, in 12 Degrees and a half of South Latitude. On the firſt of *November* they pafs'd in Sight of thofe they call Unfortunate, in 25 Degrees, 20 Minutes, which were accidentally difcover'd by the Pilot *John Fernandez*, being bound for *Chile* the fecond Time, immediately after *Magellan*'s Difcovery, fince the Year 1520.   They are now call'd, the Iflands of *S. Felix*, and *S. Ambos*.   Here *Sarmiento* obferv'd the Difference, betwixt this Courfe, which he calls the True one, and the Imaginary.   This he noted down with extraordinary Curiofity, employing all the Care and Art of his Pilots, and his own, which was not inferior to theirs, nor to others in any Martial Knowledge, as will appear by his Treatifes, if publifh'd, of Navigation, cafting great Guns and Bullets, Fortification, and Knowledge in Aftronomy, for failing in all Seas.   They never quitted the Lead, the Aftrolabe, and the Charts, either in the Deep, in Ports, Bays, or among Mountains, and Currents, which produc'd a very ample Relation he fent to King *Philip*, whence we took this Abridgement.   There he fets down the Points in the Heaven anfwering to the Earth, the Dangers, Iflands, Promontories and Gulphs, Geographically and Corographically.   He lays down the Rumbs that are to be follow'd, and, thofe to be avoided ; and thus diftinctly leads us into and thro' the Streight, giving vifible Signs, and alfo invifible of the Winds for all Ports.   At the firſt unknown Land where he anchor'd, they found the Latitude to be 49 Degrees and a half South.   They faw no People, but Tokens of them, as the Prints of Mens Feet, Darts, Oars, and little Nets.   They climb'd up vaſt high Mountains, above two Leagues in the Afcent, over Stones, fome of them fo fharp, that they cut their Shoes.   Others, to avoid them, made their Way on the Boughs of Trees.   From the Top they difcover'd great Channels, Inlets, Rivers and Harbours, and all the Land as far as their Sight could reach, feem'd to them cut and rent afunder.   They judg'd it to be an *Archipelago*.   It is to be obferv'd, that our Difcoverers give the Name of *Archipelagos*, to Seas in the New Word, which are ſtrew'd thick with Iflands, as it were great Stones, like the *Archipelago* of *Greece*, fo well known to all Nations in the *Egean* Sea, which contains the *Cyclades*, tho' the Name is not ancient.   They perceiv'd the Channel to run on, Wide, Spacious, Open and Clean ; and were fatisfi'd that *Drake* came out that

His Voyage

His Care and Capacity.

Land at the Mouth of the Streights.

Way

Way into the South Sea. They found the Latitude by three *Aftrolabes* to be 50 Degrees. The Harbour they call'd of, *Our Lady of the Rofary*, and the Ifland of the moft Holy Trinity.

The next *Sunday*, *Sarmiento* order'd all the Men to land, in order to take Poffeffion, and perform'd all that is contain'd in the Authentick In-ftrument of what happen'd that Day, the exprefs Words whereof are thus,

Sarmiento takes Poffeffion of the Land.

The Form of it.

' In the Name of the moft Holy Trinity, Father, Son, and Holy Ghoft,
' three Perfons, and one only God, who is the Beginning, Maker and
' Creator of all Things; without whom nothing that is Good can
' be done, began, or preferv'd. And in regard that a good Beginning
' muft be in God, and through God, and in him it is requifite to begin,
' to his Honour and Glory, and in his moft Holy Name, Be it known to
' all thofe who fhall fee this Inftrument, that this Day, being *Sunday* the
' 22d of *November*, 1579. this Royal Navy of the Mighty Renowned
' Lord, King *Philip* of *Spain*, and its other Dominions, my Sovereign,
' being arriv'd in this Country by Order of the moft Excellent Lord,
' *Don Francifco de Toledo*, Viceroy, Governour, and Captain General of
' *Peru*, to difcover the Streight of *Magellan*, under the Command of
' the General *Peter Sarmiento*, the Land by him nam'd, *Our Lady of the
' Rofary*, and the Bay of, *The moft Holy Trinity*. The faid Lord General
' having landed with moft of the Sea and Landmen belonging to his Na-
' vy, and the Religious Men, he brought afhore a Crofs, which he de-
' voutly worfhipp'd, with all his Men. The Religious Men fang the
' Hymn *Te Deum laudamus*, and he with a loud Voice, faid, That in the
' Name of his Majefty *Philip* the Second, our Lord, King of *Caftile* and
' *Aragon*, and their Dependencies, whom our Lord God long preferve,
' with the Addition of greater Kingdoms and Dominions, for the Glory
' of God, and Good and Profperity of his Subjects; and in the Name of
' the moft Potent Kings his Heirs and Succeffors for the Time being; he,
' as his Commander in chief, and Admiral of this fame Navy, and by
' Virtue of the Order and Inftructions given him in his Majefty's Royal
' Name, by the faid Lord Viceroy of *Peru*, took, did take, feiz'd, and
' did feize the Poffeffion of this Land on which he is now afhore, and
' which he has difcover'd for evermore, in the faid Royal Name, and of
' the faid Crown of *Caftile* and *Leon*, as has been faid, as being his own,
' and really belonging to him, by Virtue of the Donation and Gift the
' Holy Father *Alexander* the Sixth, Pope of *Rome*, pafs'd *Motu proprio*,
' in Favour of their Catholick Majefties *Ferdinand* the Fifth, and *Ifabel*
' his Wife, King and Queen of *Caftile* and *Leon* of glorious Memory,
' and to their Heirs and Succeffors, of the one half of the World, being
' 180 Degrees of Longitude, as is more fully contain'd in the faid Bull,
' dated at *Rome*, on the 4th of *May*, 1493. By Virtue whereof, thefe
' faid Lands fall, lye, and are included within the Limits and Meridian of
' the faid Partition of 180 Degrees of Longitude, belonging to the faid
' Royal Crown of *Caftile* and *Leon*. And as fuch he takes, and did take
' Poffeffion of thefe faid Lands, and their Territories, Seas, Rivers,
' Creeks, Ports, Bays, Gulphs, *Archipelagos*, and of this faid Harbour
' of the *Rofary*, where at prefent this Navy is at Anchor. And he fub-
' jects,

‘ jects, and did subject them to the Power, Possession and Dominion of the
‘ said Royal Crown, as has been said, as being their own Property.   And
‘ in Token of Possession, or as it were, drawing the Sword he had by his
‘ Side, with it he cut Trees, Branches, and Grafs, and remov’d Stones,
‘ and walk’d over the Fields and Shores, without any Opposition; requir-
‘ ring such as were present to be Witnesses thereof, and me the under-
‘ written Notary, to give him a Testimonial thereof in publick Form.
‘ And immediately, taking up a great Crofs, and the Men belonging to
‘ the Navy being drawn up in martial Manner, with Muskets and other
‘ Arms, they carry’d the Crofs in Proceffion, the Religious Men, *F An-*
‘ *tony de Guadramiro,* the Vicar and his Companion, singing the Litany,
‘ and all the others answering.   And the said Proceffion being ended, the
‘ said Lord General planted the Crofs on a hard Rock, and rais’d a heap of
‘ Stones at the Foot of the Crofs, in Token, and as a Memorial of Pof-
‘ feffion of all the Lands and Seas, difcover’d, adjacent, and contiguous.
‘ And he gave the Name of *Our Lady of the Rofary* to this Port, as has
‘ been faid.   And as foon as the Crofs was fet up, they worfhipp’d it a
‘ fecond Time; and they all pray’d, befeeching and intreating our Lord
‘ *JESUS CHRIST,* would be pleas’d that what they did might be for
‘ his Glory, and to the End that our Holy Catholick Faith might be ex-
‘ alted and dilated, and the Holy Gofpel preach’d and fpread abroad
‘ among thefe barbarous Nations, which have hitherto been remote from
‘ the true Knowledge and Doctrine ; that it may defend and deliver them
‘ from the Frauds and Dangers of the Devil, and from the Blindnefs they
‘ are in, that their Souls may be fav’d.   And then the Religious Men
‘ fung in Honour of the Crofs, the Hymn *Vexilla Regis.*   Next the Father
‘ Vicar faid Mafs on an Altar there erected, being the firft that was
‘ ever faid in that Country, to the Honour and Glory of our Almighty
‘ Lord God, and for the Extirpation of the Devil and all Idolatry.   And
‘ he preach’d to that Purpofe, and fome confefs’d and communicated. And
‘ as foon as the Mafs was faid, the General, for a more abfolute Token
‘ and Memorial of Poffeffion, caus’d a large Tree to be trimm’d, and on
‘ it caus’d a very high Crofs to be made, and on it plac’d the moft Holy
‘ Name of our Lord *JESUS CHRIST. J. N. R. I.*   And under
‘ it, *Philippus Secundus Rex Hifpaniarum.*   Of all which, I *John de Ef-*
‘ *quivel,* Royal Secretary to this Navy and Admiral Ship, do give Affida-
‘ *v* t and true Teftimony, that it was fo done as is faid.   Then follows
‘ *Efquivel’s* Subfcription.

Sarmiento *gives Names to Places.*   Four Days after, *Sarmiento,* in the Vice-Admiral’s Boat, with the Pilots, *Pablos* and *Lamero,* and ten Sailors and Soldiers, with Muskets,
Bucklers and Swords, and four Days Provifion, fet out of this Port to
difcover the Channels they faw, that they might not endanger the Ships.
Going out by the Ridges of Rocks, he run along the Gulph, clofe to
the Shore, all which he obferv’d, and founded the Harbours, giving Names
to them and the Mountains, according to their Shapes, fuch as *Sugar-
Loaves, Pitchers, Guinea Peppers,* and the like.   He obferv’d the Trees,
the Plants and the Birds.   At one Place on the Shore he found feveral
Tracts of People, and two Poniards or fuch Weapons made of Bone, with
a Crofs on the Handles, near a fmall Stream of frefh Water, whofe
Sands

Sands are Red, and therefore he call'd it the *Red-River*, which falls into a Harbour, and that also took the same Name   They saw abundance of Fish, and among the Shells thrown up by the Sea, vast Quantities of Oysters and Mussels, and in those that were left upon the Rocks above the Water, great and small Pearls, some Grey, others White.   This Sort of Fish, at certain Times, the Shells being first open, gape with their Mouths, and receive the pure and substantial Dew, which, as it were, impregnates them with Pearls, which are in Colour answerable to the Nature of the Dew.   If they receive it pure, they produce them white ; if disturb'd, they are of a Dark, or other Muddy Colours. *Sarmiento* describes the Vexation that tormented him and his Men ; for being eager to satisfy their Hunger with Oysters and Mussels, and they being unfit to Eat, because of the Hardness of those Pearls they found in them, they threw them away, cursing the Inventors of putting a Value on those Productions, or Hornynesses of Fishes, which Nature had trebly hid in the Waters of the Sea, in Shells, and in the Fish it self.   They said, that true Wealth consisted in tame Cattle, Fruit, and Corn brought up by Tillage, as they had in *Spain* ; for that precious Obstacle to feeding, then not valu'd, depriving them of the Sustenance of the Shell-Fish, and being forc'd to live ten Days on the Provision they brought for four, the Fast made them all Philosophers.   From this Red Harbour, he was obliged to return to the Ships left in that of the *Rosary*, no Day passing without violent Storms; when they had run backward, and forward, above 70 Leagues, landing on Islands, and taking Possession of them.   They were Fruitful and Habitable, but till then Untill'd and Desart. From a very high Hill, he discover'd the main Chanel, which runs out into the great Ocean, and so many other Channels and small Islands, that they could not be reckon'd up in a long Time. Whilst he staid, he founded Harbours, Deeps, Channels, Creeks, Inlets, Flats, Roads and Bays, making Draughts of, and giving them Names. He settled the Latitude, and certain Course to be steer'd, in the Presence, and with the Opinion of the Pilots, Seamen, and Soldiers, in order to reconcile those disagreeing Persons by examining all that were present.

Pearls despis'd for Hunger

Here the Vice-Admiral began to caivl, saying, They were imbay'd, and that it was impossible to hold on their Voyage that Way ; and would have quitted his Admiral, as he did afterwards.   From *Red-Port* they held on their Course, trying those in other Islands. *Sarmiento* came to a Bay, which he call'd *S. Francis*'s, where, as they were taking their Station, a Soldier fired a Piece at some Birds, and in Answer to the Gun, certain *Indians*, near a Mountain, on the other Side of the Bay, gave horrid Shouts. By the first Noise, the *Spaniards* thought it had been made by Sea-Wolves, till they discover'd the naked Red Bodies.   They afterwards found the Reason of that Colour, for they daub'd themselves from the Head to the Feet with a glutinous Red-Earth. *Sarmiento* took some of his Company into a Boat, and coming to a Thicket, found them in the closest of the Trees, without any other Cloathing but that Clay as Red as Blood.   Only one old Man, who talk'd to, and commanded, and was obey'd by them, appear'd cover'd with a Cloak of the Skins of Sea Wolves.   Fifteen Youths came out upon the open Shore, near the Sea-and drawing near, with peaceable Demonstrations, very earnestly pointed,

Vice-Admiral disagrees with Sarmiento.

Painted Indians.

M   lifting

lifting up their Hands towards the Place where the Ships remain'd. The *Spaniards* did the same. The *Indians* came close, and *Sarmiento* giving them two Towels and a Night-cap, 'or he had nothing else then, and the Pilots some o her Trifles, they were well pleas'd. They gave them Wine, which they tasted and then threw away. They eat of the Bisket, but all this did not satisfy them; for which Reason, and because they were on an open Shore, in Danger of losing the Boat, they return'd to their Station, making Signs to the *Indians* to go to the Boat. They did so, and *Sarmiento* posted two Sentinels for the more Security, then forcibly seiz'd one of the *Indians* for an Interpreter, put him into his Boat, embrac'd him lovingly, cloath'd and fed him. This Place he call'd, *The Point of People*, as being the first where he found any. Thence he proceeded to Three small Islands, lying in a Triangle, and lay there. They went on, taking Draughts of the Lands, and being before a very craggy Country, the *Indian* who had never ceas'd shedding Tears, throwing off a Shirt they had put him on, leap'd over-board, and swam away. They held on their Way, quite weary of seeing so many Islands, containing strange Productions of Nature, but without any Inhabitants. Only in one of them, which they call'd, *The Cleft Rock*, near a deep Cave, they found much Tract of Men's Feet, and the whole Skeleton of a Man or Woman. They went on thence with Storms through incredible Solitudes, which it would be too much to describe, tho' our Design were to treat only of this Voyage. At another Land, where they arriv'd full of Uncertainty, as it were by Accident, in the Bay they call'd, *Our Lady of Guadalupe*, thinking to discover whether one Channel ran to the East, and another to the North; they saw a

A Piragua. *Piragua*, being a Vessel made of Planks put together, without any Sides, and sometimes of Rushes, and of *Calabashes*, and properly a Float, coming along on the Water, and in it five *Indians*, who getting to the Shore, left the *Piragua*, and ran up a Mountain in a Consternation. The Pilot went into the *Piragua*, with four Soldiers, and the Boat proceeded further.

A Cottage Coming to another Point, where they thought there were more People,
and what they only found a low round Cottage, made of Poles, and cover'd with
in it. broad Barks of Trees, and the Skins of Sea-Wolves. In it were little Baskets, Shell-Fish, small Nets, and Bones for Sticking of Fish, like Harping Irons, and Scrips full of that Red Earth wherewith they dye their Bodies, instead of Cloaths. This is all the Gayity and Habit they use, instead of the Gold and Silks worn in the Courts of Princes. *Sarmiento* left the *Piragua*, and return'd to the Ships with only the Boat, because his Provisions were spent. In this small Vessel, and a Brigantine, he found newly built by his Company, whilst they were viewing those most desart Islands, with the Advice of the Vice-Admiral, he went from the *Red Harbour*, and finding no other safe for the Ships, return'd to the same. Then in the Boat call'd *Nuestra Senora de Guia*, or *Our Lady of the Guide*, he went away to make Tryal of the Mouth which appear'd to the East-

Snow of ward under a mighty long Ridge of Snowy Mountains, so various, that
several they saw some Tops cover'd with white, others with blew, and others
Colours. with black Snow. *Sarmiento* calls that the Continent. There is no Number of the Islands he took Possession of, and those he discover'd, being inaccessible in other *Archipelagos*, from the Top of a Mountain rising above
those

thofe about it, and cover'd with blew Snow, which he compares to the Colour of the *Turky* Stones. This Height he call'd *Anno Nuevo*, that is, *New Year*, becaufe he found it on the firft Day of the Year, 1580. He left no Saints Name, or the Refemblance of any natural Thing, but what he apply'd to diftinguifh thofe Iflands he touch'd at, erecting Croffes on them all, and writing as he did in the firft. He faw Men, only in thefe here mention'd.

He ran again in his Boat through thofe Seas, where Nature feem'd to fet up new Iflands every Day ; and Anchor'd in a Harbour, where, among other Precautions for Navigation, he drew a Meridian Line on the Earth, and mark'd the Magnetick Needles, refrefhing them by touching again, becaufe they had receiv'd fome Damage by the Storms and Damps. How weak a Guide have Men for mighty Enterprizes! He profecuted his Difcovery of little Iflands, and taking Poffeffion ; and obferv'd an Eclipfe for the Benefit of Navigation, in the Port of *Mifericordia,* or *Mercy,* as he nam'd it. The Vice-Admiral not coming to him, he fuppos'd he was return'd to *Lima,* however he waited for him ten Days, and five more in another newly difcover'd, and call'd, *Nueftra Senora de la Candelaria,* or *Our Lady of Candlemas,* three Leagues from the other. This Time having been agreed upon between them to expect one another, which when expir'd, each was to make the beft of his Way into *Spain* ; *Sarmiento* being pofitive, contrary to the Opinion of the Pilots, that there was the Streight of *Magellan.* Sarmiento's *Induftry.*

On St. *Agnes's* Day he Anchor'd at the Ifland which forms that Harbour, for which Reafon he gave it that Saint's Name. From the Ridge of a Hill, which hangs bending like a Bow over a River, he perceiv'd five Native *Indians,* who with Cries and Signs defired him to come to them ; the *Spaniards* anfwering them in the fame Manner, the *Indians* held up a white Scarf, and our Men another. When they were come down to the Shore, they feem'd to requeft they would draw near. *Sarmiento* fent them his Enfign, and the Pilot *Ferdinand Alonfo,* with only four Men, that they might not fear ; however they durft not come near the Boat. One of our Men went afhore, and yet they would not truft him, yet drawing nearer becaufe he was alone, he gave them *Chaquiras,* that is, Glafs-Beads, Hawks-Bells, Combs, Ear-Rings, and Hempen-Cloth. Obferve what mighty Defigns were couch'd under thofe Childifh Gifts. Then the Enfign and Pilot came afhore, cherifhing and giving them other Toys, and fhow'd them what every Thing was for, by applying it to the Ufe before them. This pleas'd them extreamly, as did fome little Linnen Flags, or Bannors, our Men carry'd, made of narrow Slips of *French* Linnen, Canvas, and *Silefia* Cloth. This made *Sarmiento* judge that they had before feen *Europeans,* and they, without being ask'd, fignify'd by intelligible Tokens, that two Ships like ours had pafs'd that Way, or were ftill thereabouts, pointing to the South Eaft, and in them bearded Men, clad and arm'd after the fame Manner. This was the firft Intelligence they found of the *Englifh* Ships under *Drake.* The *Indians* with fmiling Countenances promis'd to come again. They went up the Land, and our Men aboard the Ship, which not being far off, *Sarmiento* came afhore to take Poffeffion, with the ufual Religious and Civil Ceremony. Indians by Signs fhow *that* Drake *pafs'd that Way.*

The next Day the Enfign and *Ferdinand Alonfo* were with fix Soldiers by Break of Day in the Harbour, carrying a confiderable Quantity of Toys, to

gain

Spaniards catch three Indians.   gain the Affections of the Natives, who came also; but would not draw near our Men. They made the same Signs they had the Day before. The *Spaniards* to be better inform'd of what Course the *English* Steer'd, ran at the *Indians,* and took three of them, every two Soldiers holding one of them, and tho' they gave our Men many Blows and Bangs, struggling to get loose, they could not prevail, and yet were very strong. The *Spaniards* put up all that they might get them to the Ship, where *Sarmiento* receiv'd, and treated them Courteously. They Eat and Drank, and Kindness so far prevail'd, that they laid aside all Fear, and Laugh'd. Being show'd the narrow Slips of Linnen, they pointed with their Hands to a Bay, where the Ships had Anchor'd, with the bearded People, who had Arrows, and Partesans. One of them show'd two, and another one Wound they had receiv'd fighting against the Men of that Fleet.

Vice-Admiral returns to Chile.   The Vice-Admiral was now gone back to *Chile,* and among other Accidents which happen'd in his Return, he was wont to tell, that being come to the Island *Mocha,* he sent his Boat thither to ask some supply of Provisions, and understanding how Friendly they behav'd themselves towards *Drake,* and that the Hatred those People bear the *Spaniards* might be an Obstacle to him, his Messengers, by Order, conceal'd their being such, pretending they were *Lutherans.* The Islanders gave Credit to the Fiction, being desirous *He deceives the Indians.* to gain Friends, for preserving of their Liberty. Accordingly they sent them Flesh, Bread, and Fruit, with a Letter, in answer to theirs, the Superscription thereof in *English* run thus, *To the very Magnificent Lords, the Luthe-rans, in the South Sea.* Our Men answer'd, That since they had supplied them with such plenty of Provisions, they desir'd they would come and partake. About 30 of the Prime *Caciques* accepted of the Invitation, and came very Joyfully, in a *Canoe,* to our Ship. No sooner were they Aboard, than the Vice-Admiral, not regarding their Complaints, gave order to loose the Sails, which were ready, and carry'd them away Prisoners to *Chile.* Some things that befell him, might justify his deserting his Superior, but they must be left to those who write a particular History of those Actions.

Sormiento press'd to go back   To return to *Sarmiento.* In the aforesaid Port of *Candelaria,* or *Candle-mass,* the Pilots press'd him hard, with Intreaties and Protestations, to do as his Vice-Admiral had done, representing how much his Men were harrass'd, and his Ship disabled, and that he had done more than all the Discoverers before him. That they wanted Anchors, Cables, and Rigging; that the Winds oppos'd him, without which it was impossible to proceed. This was a Dangerous Tryal, because amidst the Complaints, and almost Threats of the Pilots, there was a mixture of Flattery, commending him, for that no other Discoverer had ventur'd so far, so that *Sarmiento* was no *He is resolute, and goes on.* less mov'd by their Praises than by their Anger. However he bore up against both, and severely check'd the Pilots: Who knows but he might conceal the same Fears they urg'd? And in short, he appear'd so Resolute against all they could say, that he brought them to his Beck. He sail'd thence, keeping the Channel, and about a League to the South-East, the *Indians* show'd him the way the Bearded Men took, of whom, after killing many, they, as was afterwards known, sav'd one *Catherine,* and a Boy, both *English,* who *Account of Drake's Passage.* still liv'd among those wild Beasts, which they were more like than Rational Creatures. Somewhat farther in another Island, which the *Indians* said was call'd *Puchachailgua,* full of extraordinary high grey Rocks, the

bearded

bearded Men again fought the Natives without Succefs. They went on to another Ifland Nam'd *Capitlotlgua*, on the Coaft call'd *Cayrayxaxnilgua*. *Sarmiento* did not change the Ancient Names of Countries, when he could learn them. They were fufficiently difmay'd in the next they came at, thinking they were Imbay'd ; but prefently after they took Heart again, at the Sight of the Channel, which begins at the Mouth call'd *Xaultegua*, and it widen'd, bringing them out to a moft fpacious Sea, full of thoufands of Iflands. Paffing by, in Sight of one of them, they perceiv'd high Smokes; and the Captive *Indians* began to Weep, and they faw it was for Fear of the Natives, expreffing that they were Giants, and fought defperately. Our Men encourag'd them, giving them to underftand that they fhould be able to deal with thofe People. They went afhore on that Country, which is call'd *Tinquichifgua*. *Sarmiento* alter'd it, in Honour of the Crofs he erected there, calling it, the Ifland of the Crofs. There he faw Abundance of Whales, Wolves, and other Sea-Monfters, and great Clods of Snow, on the Waves. He made ready his Cannon, and fmall Arms, providing againft both Pirates and Natives, for he expected to find the *Englifh* poffef-fed of the Land. From that Time he ftood upon his Guard, and no Man quitted his Arms. They went on to a third Ifland, which is the biggeft, heard Humane Voices, and faw fome *Piraguas*, with the People that cry'd out, who were croffing from one Ifland to another. Our Men drew near in the Boat to take a View, and all of them put into a clean Harbour, whence they difcover'd a Town, not Barbarous, but Decent and Lofty, like ours in *Europe*, and abundance of People, who having funk the *Piraguas*, and ftanding on the Mountains, with their Arms in their Hands, call'd to our Men from a Wood, to Land, as ours did them to draw near the Sea. Among the Trees appear'd many more of thofe Iflanders, with Bows and Arrows, as if they intended to fall on. This made our Men difcharge fome Muskets at them, the Noife whereof fo terrify'd the *Indian* Women, that they fet up hideous Shrieks, and therefore the *Spaniards* forbore Firing, for fear of lofing all hopes of gaining their Affections. By this time the Ship which had been Cruizing up and down, came into the Harbour. *Sarmiento* made a Gun ready, and the Boat came Aboard, Towing a Pira-gua after it. Having writ the Inftrument of Poffeffion, tho' he had not inquir'd into the Government of the Inhabitants of that great Town, he Landed on the Shore, whence is difcover'd a vaft high Mountain, all white with aged Snow, and encompafs'd with Rocks. Ancient Relations call'd it *Orlanro's* Bell, he being one of *Magellan's* Companions. He Sail'd on to 54 Degrees Latitude, at the Point he call'd of *S. Ifidorus*. Near to it the Natives call'd out to him, and coming up to our Men, Embrac'd them fa-miliarly. *Sarmiento*, befides Hawks-Bels, and other Toys, fent them Bisket and Flefh from the Ships. They fat down to Converfe, by Signs, with the Enfign, the Pilot, and Eight other Chriftians, fignifying, that they were pleas'd with their Friendfhip, and thofe rich Gifts ; and gave fuch confufe Tokens of the *Englifh* having pafs'd that way, as the others had done. Then they return'd to their Huts, and the Admiral having taken Poffeffion, and found the Latitude to be 53 Degrees, and 40 Minutes, advanc'd in fight of the Coaft, which eight Leagues from thence lies flat with the Sea, and forms a Shore of white Sand. Before he came to it he Difcover'd a pro-digious high burning Mountain, cover'd with Snow ; where the Fire and the

Several Iflands.

Populous Iflands.

Tractable Indians.

the Snow seem, out of natural Courtesy, to Respect one another, and to
conf . within themselves their Force, and Effects; for neither is the one
Quench'd, nor the other Melted by their near Neighbourhood. The Channel carry'd him to the Point he call'd of *S. Anne*, in 53 Degrees and a half
of Latitude. He took possession, and rais'd a heap of Stones, at the Foot of
a Cross, and left a Letter written with Charcole-Dust, which he thought
incorruptible, in the Shards of an Earthen Vessel, well Pitch'd, among those
Stones. In it he declared to all Nations, That those Lands and Seas belong'd to the King of *Spain*, and by what Title he held them. In the same
Letter, he left Orders for his Vice-Admiral, to return to *Peru*, and give
the Viceroy an Account of all that happen'd, till they discover'd the Streight.

Indian Pre- The Ship steer'd off with the Ebb, and the *Indians* when it was gone came
sents. down with their Wives and Children, and a Present of great pieces of Sea
Wolves, stinking Meat, Sea Foul, call'd *Minnes*, which are White and
Yellowish, *Murtina*, a fort of Fruit like Cherries, and bits of Flint, bor'd
through and Painted, in a small Box of Gold and Silver. Being ask'd,
what that was for, and they answering, *To strike Fire*, one of them took
some Feathers he brought, and with them lighted it, as if it were Tinder.
A little before, when our Men made a Fire to melt the Pitch, for securing
the Vessel the Letter was in, which was left stopp'd at the Foot of the
Cross, the Flame spread upon the Mountain, and rais'd a Smoke. The *Indians* believing they were Fires made by those so much dreaded Enemies of
theirs, went away and could not be stopp'd by any means; nor was their
Fear groundless, for they answer'd immediatly in the opposite Island, with
great Smokes. The River which falls into the Sea at the Point *Sarmiento*
call'd *S. John's*; and the Streight dividing these Islands, which is the very Old one of *Magellan*, look'd and fought after with so much Danger, he
nam'd of *The Mother of God*, changing its first Appellation, that through
this Devotion she may obtain of her Son the Salvation of those numberless
Provinces, extending the Voice of his Gospel to them, that it might reach
the Ears of so many Souls, most of which are Ignorant of their own Immortality, without knowing any more than common Nature has taught them.

Possession *Sarmiento* was so well pleas'd with having thus express'd his Devotion,
taken. that when he return'd to *Spain*, he intreated the King, to direct that Streight
to be generally so call'd, and his Majesties Orders. The Possession of this
so remarkable Place was taken with extraordinary Joy, inserting in the
Instrument the Clause of Pope *Alexander* the 6th's Bull, the Title that gives
the Kings of *Castile*, and the Limits assigned by the Line he drew through
both the Poles of the World, as Gods Vicar. *F. Guadramiro* said Mass,
and they all heard it devoutly, considering it was the first offer'd up in
that Place by Man to his Creator. It was intended as a Thanksgiving, and
they all took Courage to undertake any difficult Enterprize. They saw the
Track of Tigers, and Lions, and also White and Grey Parrots, with Red
Heads; and they heard the sweet Notes of Goldfinches, and other Birds.
Holding on their Course along the Channel, with excessive hot Weather,
they came into a Bay, that was cover'd with white Weeds, and Anchor'd
at the Point, on which a Company of Giants immediatly appear'd, who
call'd out to them, lifting up their Hands Unarm'd, our Men imitated
their Actions, which denoted Peace on both sides. They being come to
the *Boat*, which was Guarded by ten Musketeers, the Ensign leap'd Ashore,

with

with four others. The Giants made Signs to him to lay down his Leading-Staff, and then they withdrew, to the place where they had hid their Bows and Arrows. The Ensign did as they directed, and then shew'd them the Toys and Gifts he defign'd for them. This withheld them, but still they were jealous, wherefore our Men suppofing their jealoufy proceeded from what they had suffer'd before, and gueffing they had receiv'd fome dammage from the *Englifh* Pyrate, to be the better enform'd of it, ten of our Men fell upon one of the Giants, whom they took; but had enough to do to fecure him. The others running to their Arms, return'd fo quick upon the *Spaniards*, that they had fcarce time to get into their Boat. They fhot their Arrows, which flying thick, and our Men taking care to avoid them, they dropt two Muskets. The Steward of the Ship was fhot in the Eye with an Arrow. The *Indian* they took, was a Giant even among the other Giants, and the Relation fays, he look'd to them like one of the *Cyclops*. Other Relations affure us, each of thefe Giants is above three Yards high, and they are proportionably fpread and brawny. Being brought into the Ship, he was extraordinary melancholy, and tho' they offer'd him the beft they had to Eat, he would take nothing all that Day. They fet Sail, crofling Channels, and paffing by Iflands, in moft of which they faluted them with Smokes. In the narroweft Part, which they call'd of *Our Lady of Grace*, through which they muft pafs of Neceffity, and is in 53 Degrees and a half Latitude, *Sarmiento* was of Opinion, Forts might be erected on the two Capes to fecure the Paffage. They made hafte thro' it, and again faw the Natives on another Point of Land, calling out, and fhaking their Cloaks, or Woolly Blankets. *Sarmiento* went to them with eighteen Soldiers, Only four *Indians* appear'd with Bows and Arrows, and making Signs of Peace with their Hands, faid, *Xiftote*, which, as was afterwards known, fignifies Brothers. They pofted themfelves on a rifing Ground, and when the *Spaniards* were landed, made Signs to them for one of our Men to come to them. One went unarm'd, with fome Gifts, as Glafs-Beads, Hawks-Bels and Combs, which they receiv'd pointing to him to go down again. He did fo, and the Enfign went up in his ftead, obliging them with other Prefents. They accepted of them, and yet neither they, nor any Courtefie could difpel their Jealoufie. *Sarmiento* left them, to avoid provoking them, and going up the Mountain another way, to view the Ridge, Plains, and Channels, the four Archers appear'd before him, and without any Provocation receiv'd, but on the contrary after receiving the aforefaid Gifts, they furioufly affaulted our Men, wounding the General with two Arrows in the Side, and betwixt his Eyes; and another Soldier had an Eye put out. The reft of the *Spaniards* covering themfelves with their Bucklers ran at them, but the Giants fled up the Country fo fwiftly, that a Mufket Ball would fcare over-take them. This Action feems to verifie the Cowardice the Authors of Fabulous Books, commonly call'd *Romances*, afcribe to their Giants. *Sarmiento* view'd the Land, call'd it *Nueftra Senora del Valle*, or *Our Lady of the Vale*, difcovering betwixt two fpacious Ridges, fome delightful Plains, numerous Towns, lofty Buildings, Towers and Pinacles, and to his Thought fumptuous Temples of fo Majeftick an Appearance, that he fcarce believ'd his own Eyes, and judg'd it an imaginary City.

A Giant Taken.

Other Indians.

The End of the Third Book.

THE
HISTORY
OF THE
DISCOVERY and CONQUEST
OF THE
Molucco and *Philippine* Iſlands, &c.

BOOK. IV.

Reaſons for Di-greſſions.

THESE Endeavours us'd by *Spain* to ſhut out the Monſters of Hereſy, diſpell'd the Dread ſpread abroad by *Drake*, and his Example in the North and South Seas. And ſince his coming to *Ternate*, oblig'd us to write all theſe Particulars, we could not, once they began to have any Place in this Relation, forbear making it perfect by delivering the Succeſs of them. A compleat Hiſtory is the Witneſs of Times, the Light of Truth, the Life of Memory, and in fine the Miſtreſs of Life. Therefore, to perform the Duty incumbent on it from ſuch important Employments, it is not to ſpare any notable Digreſſions; eſpecially when they deviate but little from the main Subject, and have ſome Connexion with it. This here is due to a moſt prudent Action of King *Philip* IId. and his Miniſters; and ſhows his Catholick Indignation againſt Sectaries, and his Zeal for preſerving the Faithful of his *Indies* untainted, and improving the Diſpoſition in the Souls of Idolaters, towards drawing them to the Faith. It demonſtrates how he compaſs'd the whole World by Means of his Commanders, that he might introduce the ſaid Faith in all Corners thereof; to the Reputation of his Watchulneſs in the Service of this Miſtical Empire, which is now Militant, in order to its being Triumphant. For this Reaſon it is abſolutely Neceſſary, not to conceal *Sarmiento*'s Reſolution, nor to leave him in thoſe remote Seas, till we have brought him back to *Spain*, and then we will return to the *Molucco* Iſlands, which were in the mean while buſy about their own Deſtruction.

Sarmiento

Sarmiento did not go up to the great City he uncover'd at a Distance, because he would not depart from his Ship, to which he return'd, leaving us still desirous to be throughly satisfi'd of so strange a Thing. By the Way he found two extraordinary long Cloaks, or Barbarian Blankets, made of Sheep-Skins with the Wooll on, and a pair of Shoes made of raw Hides to bind about the Feet, which the *Indians* could not carry off, thro' the fearful Precipitation of their Flight. They continu'd their Discovery, and the Wind oblig'd them to strike over to the Southern Coast, five Leagues distant from *Our Lady of the Vale* ; and tho' the cold Winds blew, they found this Country more Temperate than the others. It is inhabited by proper People, has wild and tame Cattel, and Game, as was declar'd by *Philip*, so they call'd an *Indian* they brought over, in Honour to King *Philip*. It produces Cotton, a certain Sign of its being Temperate ; and Cinnamon, by them call'd *Cabea*. The Air is very serene, and the Stars appear bright, so that they are plainly to be observ'd, lay'd down, and describ'd. *Sarmiento* says it is useful in those Parts to observe the *Crozier*, which is 30 Degrees above the *Antartick* Pole, and that he made use of it, for taking of Latitudes, as we do in our Hemisphere of the *North Star*, tho' with another Sort of Computation. And in Regard that the *Crozier* does not serve all the Year, he sought out another *Polar Star*, nearer to the *Pole*, of a shorter Computation, but general and perpetual ; and he us'd such Industry, that he discover'd, and ascertain'd it by Observations, and Experiments of several clear Nights. He settled the Stars in the *Crozier*, and two other *Croziers*, and two other *Polar Stars*, which take a very small Compass, thus he did for the common Benefit of curious Sailors. Notwithstanding all these Tokens, and the Incouragement of humane Curiosity, no Man has ever gone to those Towns, which had such promising Signs of Civility ; tho' those rude Giants did not seem to confirm those Appearances of a well-settled Country. *Sarmiento* ran along the Streight, never ceasing to sound, and lay it down till he came to a Cape, he call'd, *Of the Holy Ghost*, from which to that of the Virgin *Mary*, there are 110 Leagues from the South to the North Sea. Here they began to order their Course with due Difference. They saw Whales, and on the Shores, Thickets of several unknown Plants. They ran thro' Storms and Dangers, surprizing even to such experienced Sailors as they were. They all vow'd Offerings to Churches, Alms, and Pilgrimages to Places of Devotion in *Spain*, with other solemn Engagements, on which fearful Mortals in Danger, devoutly ground and encourage their Hopes. The Tempest ceas'd, and on the 25th of *March*, about Midnight, *Sarmiento* saw a low white Rainbow, opposite to the Moon, which was moving against it ; and it was occasion'd by Repercussion of her Rays, which fell by Refraction on the opposite Clouds. He says, That neither he nor any other Person, ever saw, heard, or read of the like; but by his good Leave, in *Albericus Vespusius*'s Epitome of Voyages, we read that the same happen'd in the Year 1501, in that same Place, where both of them taking the Sun's Altitude, they found him in 23 Degrees large, which is as good as 15 Leagues. This Day they were within the Tropick of *Capricorn*. Proceeding forward, they lost their Reckoning, and the Hopes of recovering it, for Want of Mathematical Instruments; but on the first of *April*,

South Coast.

Observations for Sailors.

Sarmiento comes into the North Sea.

1580, at Night, they discover'd, and observ'd the *Polar-Star* of the Triangle in 21 Degrees ; and on the 10th of the same Month, they saw the Island of the *Ascension*, at eight Leagues Distance. They anchor'd there, found Water, and saw several Crosses, erected by some *Portuguese*, who in their Way to *India*, were cast away there by a Storm, and the Living, out of Devotion, set them up on the Graves of those that dy'd. On one of them they found a Board nail'd, with this Inscription, Don John de Castel Rodrigo, *Commodore, arriv'd here with five India Ships, on the* 13th of *May*, 1576. Near to it, *Sarmiento* set up another, as a Memorial, that the first Ship coming from *Peru*, touch'd there, having pass'd thro' the Streight from the South to the North-Sea, on the King's Account, with the Occasion of his Voyage. This Island abounds in Sharks, which are Sea-Monsters, Fish, and a Sort of such greedy and troublesome Fowl, that
they make at whatsoever they see. They took the Ensigns Hat off his Head, to snatch away a Letter he had stuck in it. He sav'd his Hat, by clapping up his Hand immediately, but lost the Letter, which they pull'd away by Force ; and afterwards they saw a Fray in the Air, the others endeavouring to take it from that Harpy, which first snatch'd it away. This Island lies in 7 Degrees and a half of South Latitude, and it is very observeable, that tho' the *Spaniards* were very attentive to their Compass, and took so many Precautions for their Security, yet such was the Force of the several Currents, that when they thought they were 60 Leagues from *Pernambuco* East and West, at the River of *Virtues*, on the Coast of *Brazil*, they found themselves 400 Leagues to the Eastward ; so that the Currents deceiv'd, and drove them 340 Leagues from the Point they had settled by the Degree of Latitude. *Sarmiento* discourses largely upon this Effect, charging the Sea-Charts with Falshood, and being ignorantly laid down. Dreadful Tempests ensu'd, till on the 28th of *April*, on the Coast of *Guinea* he discover'd *Sierra Liona*, abounding in Gold, and Blacks. Then the Islands they call of *Idols*, and beyond them those of *Vixagaos*, inhabited by stout Black Archers, who shoot poison'd Arrows, wherewith, such as are wounded, presently dye raving. On the 8th of *May* they all fell sick on the Coast of *Guinea*, of Fevers, Lameness, Swellings, and Imposthumations in their Gums, which in that Country prove Mortal, by Reason of the Excessive Heat, and then for Want of Water ; but Heaven reliev'd them with seasonable Rain. When they labour'd to make the Islands of *Cabo Verde* for some Refreshment, the Winds drove them off. They bore up without finding Land, or any Ship, till on the 22d of *May*, being in 15 Degrees 40 Minutes of North Latitude, they descry'd two Sail. *Sarmiento* believ'd they had been *Portugueses*, and was desirous to make up to have them ; but upon better Observation perceiv'd, the one was a Tall Ship the other a Sloop, both of them *French*, who pursu'd and endeavour'd to get to Windward of him. The Sloop came foremost to view our Ship, which made good its Advantage. When they
were come in Sight of the Island of *Santiago*, the *French* held up a Naked Sword, and then fir'd some Shot. The *Spaniards* answer'd with their Muskets, which was then done by both Sides, and several *French* Men fell, tho' on our Side never a Man was kill'd, but some wounded, and then they fled more swiftly than they had pursu'd. Those on the Island beheld

the

the Ingagement, and thinking it had been Counterfeit, and both the Ships *French*, they ftirr'd not out to Succour either. When the Pirate was quite fled, a *Caravel* of *Algarve* arriv'd coming from *Portugal*, which difcover'd the Pirate's Name, and Strength; declaring he had 85 Men in the Ship, and 25 in the Sloop, and among them a *Portuguefe* Pilot. That he had plunder'd four other Ships, and the faid *Caravel*, at Cape *Blanco*, on the Coaft of *Africk*; and at the Ifland of *May*, not far from *Santiago*, had funk another *Caravel*, belonging to the Royal Navy, which was failing for *Brazil*, in order to People *Paraguay*; where the *Englifh* had of late Years built Towns, intermarrying with, and being attracted by the Love, and Children they had by the *Tapuyer Indian* Women.

Sarmiento at Cabo Verde.

Sarmiento Landed at *Cabo Verde*, the Cuftom-Houfe of which City yearly is worth to the King 100000 Ducats. There are always in it 20000 Blacks, becaufe of the fettled Trade for them. Before he Anchor'd, there came Boats from the Shore, to view his Ship, and he telling them, he came from *Peru*, through the Streights of *Magellan*, they were amaz'd. They return'd to give an Account to their Governor *Gafpar de Andiade*, and told him, That thofe that came in the Ship, were Men of feveral Shapes, Deform'd, and Ill-look'd, and others with long tangled Hair and Locks. Thefe were fome *Indians* of *Peru* and *Chile*. As for the Reft *Sarmiento* has thefe Words, *As to our being Ill-look'd, they did not wrong us; for befides that we had no effeminate Countenances, the Powder and Sweat of our Volleys of fmall Shot, a little before, had not fet us off to any Advantage; and, in fhort, we had more mind to fome Water than to look like Beaus.* However, neither he nor his Men went Afhore, till they had fatisfy'd a Pratick Mafter that none of them were infected with the Plague. The next Day they Landed bare-Foot, in Proceffion, with Croffes, and Images, repairing to the Church of our Lady of the Rofary, where they gave Thanks, Alms, and other effects of their Vows, with extraordinary Joy; for every Storm is fo much Honour, when recounted in fafe Harbour. They Confefs'd, and receiv'd the Bleffed Sacrament at a Mafs they had Vow'd to caufe to be faid. The Governor, Don *Bartholomew Leytao*, Entertain'd, and made much of them, tho' at firft he would not believe they had pafs'd the Streight. The Sick were Cured, and the Ship and Boat which were much fhatter'd, re-fitted. The main Defign of this Voyage, which was to Fight *Drake*, and provide the proper Defence againft the Defigns of the Enemy, had not been compafs'd; and therefore *Sarmiento*, having fought the *French* Ship, and Sloop, which appear'd again, alarming that Coaft, and both of them flying back with all fpeed, after being Shatter'd and Beaten, to the Ifland *Mayo*, or of *May*, the common Shelter of Robbers; He redoubled his Watchfulnefs, and went on to get Intelligence of the *Englifh*, as well thofe that pafs'd the Streight with *Drake*, as of thofe new Planters in *Brazil*, or *Paraguay*; as alfo of the Inclination of the Subjects of the Crown of *Portugal*, to fubmit to King *Philip*, or Don *Antony*.

Intelligence he receives.

A Pilot of *Algarve* inform'd him, That the Year before, betwixt *Ayamonte* and *Tavira*, two *Englifh* Merchants, fpeaking of the *Indies*, affured him, that *Drake* was gone thro' into the *South Sea*; and by the Time, the News agreed with what the *Indians* of the Streight had fignify'd to him by Signs; and that he arriv'd fafe in *England*, with two Ships traught with Gold and Silver of that notable Robbery,

which

which he prefented to the Queen. She fitted out five o her Ships, with three Years Provifion, to return to the Streights of *Magellan*, to feek out thofe that had been loft there, and *Drake* eight more. That the firft five were already gone in *Decemb.* laft. That the Merchants had entrufted him with that Secret, taking him for a *Portuguefe*, and who, as fuch, would not difcover it to the *Spaniards*. By the *French* he was informed, That as foon as they had brought off fome Ships with Blacks from *Cifbo Vedre*, they would go over to the Ifland *Margarita*, and thence to the North-ward, from the Ifland of *Santo Domingo* to *Yaguana*, whence they came not above four Months fince, Loaded with Hides, and Sugar. That they had kill'd Captain *Barbudo*, in the Ifland *Margarita*, in Revenge for the *Englifh* he had flain. That having taken the Governor of *Brazil*, they again fet him at Liberty. That all their Pilots are *Portuguefes* He was alfo told by o-

Englifh in Paraguay. thers who came from thence, and by Captains of Reputation, who were returning thither, that in the Bay of *Paraguay*, near *Rio de Janeyro*, which is in 21 Degrees, 12 Minutes South Latitude, there had been for eight Years laft paft, Colonies of *Englifh* among the *Tapuers*; with whom for the three laft Years, the *Portuguefe* were at War, and had kill'd moft of them.

That it is fuppos'd the Natives, who are Man-Eaters, had devour'd moft of thofe that fled up the Country. He pick'd up other Intelligence from *England*, concerning their Navies. their Colonies in thofe Parts, and Defign of Ufurping the *Molucco* Iflands with all their Strength, and to render themfelves Invincible Mafters of the Spice. They difpatch'd a Boat, with thefe Advices to the Viceroy of *Peru*; for *Sarmiento* could not return himfelf by the way of *Brazil* and *Paraguay*, becaufe the force of the Currents had drove him away into the Main Sea, Eaft-ward. Before his Departure,

Sarmiento Strangles his Enfign, and Punifhes others. he caus'd his Enfign to be Strangled, as a Traytor to his King, to the Difhonour of his Poft, and an Obftructor of the Difcovery. Two other Soldiers he Bannifh'd, one of them from the *Indies*, and fhew'd Severity to fome of the Company, on Account of the fame Crime, which, it was believ'd, had not been fo fully prov'd upon them, as is requifite for inflicting the ufual Punifhment.

Advice-Boat fent the Viceroy of Peru From this Port he fail'd to the Weftward, till he came to the Channel between the Ifland *Fuego* and that of *Santiago*, where one of the Ships that came out with him ftay'd. Steering Norweft, one Point over or under, for that is the Courfe to the Ifland *S. Anton*, he thence difpatch'd the Advice Boat for the Viceroy of *Peru*, with eight Men, commanded by *Ferdinand Alonfo*. In thirteen Days more he pafs'd betwixt the Ifland *Graciofa*, one of the *Azores*, fmall, but fruitful, and populous, and that of *S. George*, in which he faw prodigious high Fires. Thofe he afterwards found verified

Conflagration in the Ifland of S. George. by the Bifhop, at *Angra*, where he refides. That on the firft of *June* that fame Year, there were dreadful Earthquakes in the Ifland of *S. George*, Voices of Devils were heard, and among other wonderful Effects, the Earth open'd in three Places, whence Streams of Fire ran as far as the Sea. Thofe continu'd, and feven more broke out, cafting forth as many Rivulets of Liquid Fire; one of which ran round an Hermitage, and nine Men running to fave fome Bee-Hives from being burnt, another Mouth open'd, which fwallow'd feven of them, and fing'd the other two. So much Afhes fell like Rain upon the Earth, that it was cover'd a Span deep, and in fhort, all
the

the Island was on Fire Sarmiento held on his Courfe, and on the 18th of *June*, arriv'd at the City *Angra*, on the Island *Tercera*, the Chief of the *Azores*, where alfo came in a Ship from the Town of *Bernambuco*, and another from *Baya de todos of Santos*, in *Brazil*. Thefe being afk'd, What 'they knew of the *Englifh*, affur'd him, That in *November* laft paft there came five White Men, with fifteen *Indians*, who were going to *Ifleos*, and the *Portugufe* Towns by Land; and going along the Shore, they on a fud-den, at *Rio de las Cuentas*, lighted upon an *Englifh* Sloop. Seven of the Men were afhore drying their Sails, and as foon as they faw the Travellers they fled. The *Portuguefe* perfifted purfuing them; but the *Englifh* letting fly fome Arrows, held on their Flight, two of them up the Mountain, and the other five along the Coaft, till they got into the Sloop. They cut their Cables, and left behind them two large Carriages for Guns.

Some Eng-lifh in Bra-zil.

The Travellers defir'd them to come afhore, and offer'd them Meat, and all other Neceffaries, affuring them they meant no Harm. They anfwer'd, they would not come, and fhow'd Mufkets, Crofs-bows and Pikes, pointing a fmall Gun, to fire at them. It was then Ebb, and they departed fix Lea-gues from thence, to fail near the River *de las Cuentas*. That at the Island *Cape*, over-againft *Camamu*, another *Portuguefe* Ship, that knew nothing of this Sloop, lighted on it, when there were only three *Englifh* Men left in her, the reft being kill'd afhore, with Arrows by the Natives. In fhort, the Sloop was caft away, five Men of it being taken, who declar'd, that it came with a Squadron of ten Ships, in which a certain great *Englifhman* pafs'd the Streights of *Magellan*. That they return'd thence Coafting a-long, to plant a Colony in the moft convenient Place for their Purpofe, the Admiral having 500 Men aboard for that End. Four Hundred of them were Soldiers, the reft Seamen, and other Mechanicks. That all this Squa-dron Anchor'd in an Island of *Cainbals*, or Man-Eaters, and a Storm rifing, nine of them fail'd away, but the Admiral not being able to get from her Anchors time enough, was Caft away, none being fav'd but thofe that came in the Sloop, and they efcap'd by being then gone to Water. One of thefe five was 35 Years of Age, and an able Mathematitian. He affirm'd, That thofe who efcap'd the Storm, would foon return to the Coaft of *Brazil*, with a numerous Fleet. Among other Particulars, he told them, that they found an Infcription with the King of *Spain*'s Arms, in that part of the Island *Cananca*, where they were, which their Commander in chief took away, and fet up in the Place of it another, with thofe of *England*. Be-fides all this, three of thofe Ships that efcap'd the Storm, coming before the *Portuguefe* Town of *Rio de Janeiro*, to make the Cape, and find out the other fix, the Governor of that Place, fent out four *Canoes* to take Cogni-fance of them, which on a fudden fell in with another Long-Boat belong-ging to the *Englifh*, who, as foon as they fpy'd the *Canoes*, made away, but could not do it fo faft as to fave all. They took Three, and the Governor fent them to *Bahia*; but the Ships made away with all their Sails. The Prifoners own'd, That in cafe they met with their Ships at the Cape, they were refolv'd to go to *Parayba*, or *Pernambuco*. In other Refpects they a-greed with the Account given by thofe in the Sloop. The *Englifh* arriv'd at *Brazil* about *November*, 1579, at the fame Time that *Sarmiento* was fee-king

An Englifh Squadron.

The Admi-ral caft-a-way.

Englifh at Brazil.

king for the Streight; and this agrees with the confuse Signs the Brutish *Indians* of those Parts made to him, as he Touch'd on their Coasts. His chief Care being to enquire into these Matters, he was inform'd by the *Corregidor*, that is the Governor in Civil Affairs of *Angra*, that on the second of *November*, that same Year, another *English* Ship was Cast-away at *Gualva*, a Town two Leagues distant from that City, with six Men in it, two whereof, and a Black were sav'd. It appear'd there had been 300 Men in the Ship, and much Wealth, which was thrown into the Sea, during the Storm   That they were going to plant Colonies in *India*, and most of the Men dy'd on the Coast of *Guinea*; and perhaps this might be one of the nine Ships aforesaid. The People of *Gualva* drew out of the Sea fifteen heavy pieces of cast Iron Cannon, but could not get out several others. The fifteen are of an extraordiary Magnitude, as it were for some settled Fort. To conclude, he was inform'd, and Time has since verified it, that they were preparing in those Northern Parts to rob us of the Treasure of Metals, and Spice there is in those Countries, and in exchange to Introduce their Sects. The final Success of both the *Spanish* and the *English* Admirals, was that they arriv'd safe in their respective Countries, forsaken by the Vice-Admirals. *Drake* return'd to *London*, with an immense Treasure, which the Queen seiz'd, alledging, That *Don Barnardino de Menoza*, then the *Spanish* Embassador at that Court, demanded Restitution, as belonging to his K. and the rest of it taken from his Subjects; but she adjudg'd it to her own Cofers, in Recompence for the Dammage sustain'd, when the *Spaniards* supported her Rebels in *Ireland*. *Drake* was not enrich'd by his Robberies, nor did he gain any Reputation by his Actions; but on the contrary he was slighted in *England*, either because they knew what he did was not Honourable, or that generally a Man's own Country is ungrateful to him. *Sarmiento* departing from *Angra* with a fair Wind, discover'd the Coast of *Spain* on the 7th of *August*, and arriv'd at Cape *S. Vincent*, full of Intelligence and News from so great a Part of the World, and of the Designs of several Nations, and the Crown of *Portugal*. His Arrival, and Account produc'd the fitting out of other Fleets, and fresh Preparations in *Spain*, and in the *Indies*, which extended to the Relief of the remotest Parts. One of them was the Reducing of *Ternate*, and the sending over one hundred *Spanish* Families, arm'd, provided and examin'd, as to Quality and Virtue, to be the first Inhabitant of those Desarts upon the Streight. They carry'd Tools, Arms, Instructions, and all Necessaries to fortifie the narrow Parts of it. *Sarmiento* went as Chief, and Governour of those Dominions. This Project prov'd unsuccessful, and in the general Opinion of all Men, it was through the Fault of the General *Sancho Flores*. Afterwards *Sarmiento* was taken, and set at Liberty in *England* where he had Conferences with the Queen and *Drake* upon this Subject, whence he drew Information for the Execution of greater Designs.

This Year King *Henry* Dy'd in *Portugal*, when he had Reign'd but thirteen Months. Five Governours had the Administration during the *Interregnum*, and were disturb'd by the Arming of *Don Antonio*, within the Kingdom, and by King *Philip*'s Forces already advancing into the Frontiers. So that neither Government could do any more than consult about the present Exigencies; which at that Time were neither perfect Peace nor open War, there being Hopes that they would lay down their Arms, and joyn

with

Ship of theirs cast-away.

Drake's Treasure seiz'd.

Sarmiento in Spain.

King Henry of Portugal dyes.

with their true Prince, whom the *Portuguese* is wont to Love, as a Father, rather than as a King. However there were some Troubles, and Commotions. Private Discord is an inseparable incident to all Governments, and that draws the Thoughts of Men after it, and is often the Original of general Calamities, tho' it be moderated, or justify'd by a sincere Zeal.

King *Philip* enter'd *Lisbon* supporting his Right by his Power, and whilst the other Provinces, which compose that Monarchy in *Spain*, *Africk*, *Asia*, and the *East-Indies* submit ed to him, he bestow'd Favours, gave Laws, confirm'd the Old, ratified Priviledges, and gain'd Affections by his Presence, and a General Pardon, which he extended to those who had offended him. On the 15th of *November* 1582, he swore to observe those Laws establish'd by his Predecessors, and particularly by King *Emanuel*, as then next Heir to the Crowns of *Spain*, for himself and his Son, Prince *Michael*, whom God took to a better Kingdom in his Infancy. Those Laws were afterwards sworn to by King *Sebastian*, and all of them imported, that all Honours, Employments, Benefices, and the Management of the Revenue of the Crown, with all other Commands by Sea and Land, in *Portugal*, *Africk*, *India*, the Islands and all other Parts already conquered, or to be conquer'd by that Crown, shall be in the Hands of Natural born *Portugueses*. And by the 24th Chapter of these Laws, it was establish'd, that in fitting out Fleets for *India*, or otherwise for Defence of the Kingdom, or suppressing of Pyrates, the King should take the necessary Measures with the Kingdom of *Portugal*, though he should use the Assistance of his Majesties other Dominions. They were sensible that this favourable Law, without infringing the Antient Laws, made way for employing the Forces of the Crown of *Castile*, in the Recovery, or Preservation of the Kingdoms of the Eastern *Archipelago*, where at that Time the Christians suffer'd Martyrdom, without any Opposition. And the King for the Recovery of *Ternate*, especially consider'd the Conveniency of the *Philippine* Islands, which lie more opportune than *India*; the Justness of which Reflection has been confirm'd by the Event. *King Philip the II. at Lisbon.* *He Swears to maintain the Laws.*

India at this Time was govern'd by the Viceroy *Fernan Tellez*, to whom King *Philip* the second Writ, representing how favourable an Opportunity he had to do God good Service, to secure the Tranquility of Christendom, and settle Peace, which inestimable Advantages would be owing to his Fidelity and Care, if through them those Provinces should be united to the Monarchy, without any Trouble, by continuing Loyal, and providing that the Tributary Kings should do the same. He put him in Mind that Services become the more valuable by the surmounting of the greatest Difficulties, and gave him good Hopes of a Reward, which would have been fulfill'd, had he come home to see the Effects of them and his Services. But *Fernan Tellez* had no need of any such Promises, or of the Perswasions which are as good as Commands, contain'd in Letters from Ministers of State, and sent with the King's Letter. These being sent over Land, came to his Hands in six Months, and he either preserving, or gaining their Affections had so much Forecast as to confirm the King, Princes, and *Sangiacks*, who, in those remote Parts, pay subjection to the Crown of *Portugal*; before he knew any thing of the Orders sent him, or of the additional Estate the King was pleas'd to confer on him. By his Authority he disappointed *India submits to him.* *Tellez the Viceroy Loyal.*

dilappointed fome Projects of Confederacies, fet a foot for the recovering of their Former Liberty, hoping by the Example of the King of *Ternate*, that the Revolutions in *Europe* might turn to their Advantage. But in defpight of thefe Contradictions and Changes, *Fernan Tellez* fo far prevailed, as that the Religious Mendicants, and the *Jefuits*, continu'd the preaching of the Gofpel, with fuch Fervour, that they defy'd even Tyranny it felf. The Converfions of Idolater Princes are truly and elegantly related in the Writings and Books of the Miffions of the Society, and other Ecclefiaftical Hiftories ; fo that they excite, and inflame Devotion in the Breafts of fuch as read them. There may be feen, how the Truth was embrac'd, with all poffible Affection ; how haftily, and eagerly they learn'd the Catechifm ; what Rejoycings the Catechumens made on the Day they were baptiz'd ; Queens, and Princeffes worfhipping the Images of Saints ; and fweeping the new Churches, and Chappels with their own Hands ; with what Attention, and Exactnefs they honour'd the Ceremonies of the Church, and laftly, how they frequented the Sacraments, and improv'd in Chriftianity.

All this was Perfecuted, and Extirpated by the King of *Ternate* ; who was now fo far from enduring any neighbouring Empire, that he ftruck a Dread into the remoteft ; infomuch, that tho' they were all fenfible they ought in all good Policy to fupport the Kingdoms of *Tydore* and *Bachian*, yet they became lookers on, as it were on a Stage, to behold the Affaults given, and the Cruelties acted at the Sieges. And in the latter of them, whilft throughout *India* the Standards were difplay'd in fubmiffion to *Spain*, the King of *Ternate* enter'd *Bachian*, and prefs'd on fo vigoroufly, that he took the Forts by main Force, and made the principal *Sangiacks* Prifoners. At the Taking of the City of *Bachian*, the King of the Ifland was flain in Fight, with all the *Portuguefes* that affifted him ; and the Prince, his Son, taken, who was then a Chriftian, but foon after, having taken an Oath of Fealty to the Conquerer, and Apoftatiz'd from the True Religion, he was miferably Reftor'd to his Kingdom, exchanging the Hopes of his Souls Salvation, for the Pernicious Fables of the *Alcoran*, to which he has adhear'd till this time ; tho' in Temporals he now owns the fovereign Dominion of our King. The War with the *Tydores* lafted longer, the two Navies fighting with indiff rent Succefs, and Victory changing fides, according to various Accidents. Thefe Princes method of making War depends on Ambufhes, and Stratagems, where Subtilty fupplies the place of Strength. It is rare that either fide is much weakned ; becaufe as foon as fenfible of the others Advantage, the Weaker flyes, and referves himfelf for better Fortune ; nor do they look upon it as Difhonourable to fly, for in thofe Parts they have but rude Notions of the Laws of Honour. The laft Action, after they had fuftain'd the Siege with extraordinary Magnanimity, was a Sally made by the *Portuguefe* and *Tydores* from the Fort, with much Order and Conduct, Attacking the Enemies Camp with fuch Bravery, that tho' they were much fuperior in number, they could not ftand the Fury of the King of *Tydore*. The *Ternates* being put to Flight, imbark'd after a great Slaughter of their Men, and never ftopp'd till they came to *Talangame*, fo they call the Harbour of *Ternate* on that fide. The *Tydores* purfu'd, and being flufh'd with Victory defpis'd the Succours the *Ternates* had

King of Bachian kill'd.

Molucco way of Fighting.

Battle of Tydores and Ternates

ready

ready in that Place, which Addition made them renew the Fight with fresh Vigour, and wreft the Victory which then inclin'd to the *Tydores*. These without breaking their Order, retir'd and imbark'd; and hasting back in their *Carcoas* came to *Tydore*, where they fortify'd themselves against what might happen. The King of *Ternate* return'd to this City in Triumphant Manner, making a Show of some Prisoners.

The News of the Union of *Portugal* to *Castile*, was now known throughout all those Eastern Parts, and so well receiv'd, that instead of offering at any Oppofition, they all joyfully submitted, hoping they should be protected by a more powerful Arm, than they had been before. Nor were they deceiv'd in their Expectation, for, pursuant to what the King had sworn at *Lisbon*, concerning the Fleets, for suppreffing of Pyrates, and Garrisoning the Coasts of *Africk*, he granted his Royal Order, for all the Governours of the *Philippine* Islands to take Care to relieve the *Moluccos*, and all other the Dominions in *India*, belonging to the Crown of *Portugal*, making use of *New Spain*, and all other Kingdoms subject to the Crown of *Castile*, there being more conveniency for supplying them from thence, than even from *India*.

The King of *Ternate*, being sensible of the Change of Times, and how much greater Forces threatned him than before; and that he should not be suffer'd to reign, without submitting to a Superior, he grew better advis'd, and sent an Ambassador to *Lisbon*. The Ambassador was *Cachil Nayque*, well known for the Antiquity of his Family, and brave Actions. *Nayque* signifies a *Tribune*, or Commander. He embark'd with much Wealth of those Parts, as Porcelane, *Chinese* Silks, Calico's and Muslins, Spice, Fruit, Aromatick Woods and Barks, and Preferves of the same; and paffing between the Islands of *Pangicaz* and *Manado*, near to that of *Celebes*, keeping off from the Equinoctial, coasted it and crofs'd the Line again, till he came to *Borneo*. There he visited the King, who was at *Tayaopura*, and deliver'd him Letters from his Master, attempting by Word of Mouth, to unite him to the *Molucco* Nation against the Crown of *Spain*. Contenting himself with the first Hopes, he pafs'd on betwixt *Cremato* and *Surato*, and crofs'd the Islands *Pulo* and *Linga*, in sight of the greater *Java*, thence thro' the Streight of *Malaca*, by the great Ones of *Banca* and *Bintam*, in the Port whereof were then the 20 Ships, which are sent from *Sumatra* every Year, loaded with Pepper. He barter'd away much of what he had in his own Ship, and propos'd a general Revolt to all Nations. There are two Streights there; the one of *Sincapura*, so call'd from that City built on the Coast of *Malaca*; and the other of *Sabao*, from an Island of that Name, and this leads to *Sumatra*. *Nayque* steer'd this Course, and soon put into the Harbour which lies going out of the Channel.

This great Island, oppofite to *Malaca*, and divided from it by a Bay full of Ridges, of Rocks and Shoals, and above a thousand smaller *Islands*, was formerly a *Peninfula*, and contiguous to *Malaca*, as *Sicily* is said to have been to *Italy*. Ancient Geographers call'd it *Trapobana*, the Modern *Sumatra*. The Ancients also call'd it, the *Golden Cherfonefus*, and the most curious Searchers into Antiquity, *Ophir*, whence *Solomon* gather'd that vast Mass of Treasure. According to the *Portuguefes* it is 80

Nayque Embassador for Spain.

His Voyage.

Streights of Sincapura and Sabao.

Sumatra deferib'd.

O

Leagues

Leagues in Length, and 30 in Breadth. (Here seems to be some Mistake in the Author, for the Island is well known to be above 80 Leagues in Length.) *Italian* Writers say it is 2100 in Circumference. The *Dutch*, who have traded and made War there, do not contradict it, and all agree it is the largest in all the East, and the most fruitful we know of. It lies thwarting from North to South, in the *Torrid Zone*, and the Equinoctial Line cuts it in the Middle; so that one Part falls to the Northern Hemisphere, and takes up five Degrees, and the other to the Southern, extending seven Degrees. This Island is, according to some, divided into four Kingdoms; others say ten, and some 29; but we know of eight, which are, *Pedir*, *Pacem*, *Achem*, *Camper*, *Menancabo*, wealthy in Gold Mines, and *Zaude*; and up the Inland the other two of *Andragide*, and *Auru*, the Natives whereof are Idolaters and Man-Eaters. They devour, not only Strangers, but their own Brothers, and Fathers. In short, among these barbarous People, Hunger produces the same Effects as Passion. The King of *Achem* is the most Powerful of them, and they all pay Homage to the Crown of *Portugal*.

Nayque stirs up Princes to revolt.

Nayque enter'd the Court of *Achem*, attended by his own Men, and follow'd by the Multitude of *Chinese*, *Japonese*, *Malay*, *Persian*, and *Turkish* Merchants; all of them flattering themselves with the Expectation of new Commotions. He first worshipp'd the King in a Temple, where there were monstrous Idols, notwithstanding that the People are *Mahometans*. He had afterwards private Conferences with him at Court, and in a few Days brought him over to his Party, with his Wealth, as if he had been a poor Man. After delivering his Master's Letters, he told him, that before he went over into *Europe*, whether he was sent to discover the Power of *Spain* in its Origin, or Source, at a Time when it was distracted by such Revolutions, it was convenient that most wealthy Part of *Asia* should be restor'd to its former Condition, a Matter of no Difficulty, if they were firmly united among themselves. That none were so able to overthrow the Neighbouring Monarchy, which from *Malaca* had, as it were, fetter'd so many Provinces, as the Kings of *Sumatra*, if they, considering of what Moment it was to them, would stand by one another. That since he had successfully besieg'd that hateful City, assaulted its Walls, and Forts, and valu'd himself on being an Enemy to the *Portugueses*, he ought not to let slip so favourable an Opportunity, which offer'd him compleat Victory. That he should remember the several Expeditions of the Viceroys against *Sumatra*, and that they always breed up *Adelantados*, or Lords-Lieutenants, with their Soldiers in Pay against those Kingdoms. And that since, till then they had not been able to make him uneasy, it was too much Forbearance to suffer a perpetual Threat of Thraldom to subsist so near him.

The King of Achem complies.

The King of *Achem*, listen'd to him with Satisfaction, as one, who, with all his Nation, hates the Haughtiness of the *Portuguese* Behaviour; yet he neither promis'd, nor perform'd any more than obstructing the Trade of *Malaca*, till he had reduc'd it to Want. Nor did he keep the Secret, for they had soon an Account at *Malaca* and *Goa* of these Contrivances. He farther promis'd, That whensoever the King of *Ternate* should make a greater Invasion, or go about to extend, or enlarge himself, as far as he pretended he had a Right, he would continue to give the Diversion, as far as stood with his

Conve-

Conveniency, and that he fhould have the Liberty of his Ports, and all Supplies for his Ships in his Kingdom. *Nayque* return'd Thanks, and extended his Negociation, endeavouring to bring in the other Tyrants of *Sumatra*, as for the Publick Good. Then failing away through the Streight of *Sunda*, fo call'd from the Name of a City in the furtheft Part of the Province, beyond the Line ; he proceeded to the greater *Java*, no lefs Fertile than the other in the fame Medicinal, and Odoriferous Growth, at the Time when *Thomas Candifb*, an *Englifb* Commander was arriv'd there, coming from the North-Sea, by the Way of *New Spain*.

Nayque went up the Country to vifit, and found him in a populous City, where he was loading Pepper, which is excellent in *Java*, with that King's Leave, he being a Friend to the *Englifb*, who had already fetrled a Factory. He found him on the Banks of a River of fuch a Nature, that it prefently converts any Wood whatfoever caft into it into Stone, as folid and hard as our Pebbles. He bore the *Englifbman* Company to the Port of *Sunda Calapa*, view'd his Ship, and made as much of him as he could. Among other Things he prefented him a Pavillion, artificially wove all with fweet fcented Cloves, and not black, which was not only fit to keep out the exceffive Cold of *England*, but even to dry up over moift Bodies that flept under it. There is daily Experience of its atractive Virtue at *Ternate*, by placing great Veffels full of Water in the middle of the Rooms where the Cloves are kept, and in the Morning they find the Heaps of Cloves damp, and the Veffels empty and dry. The fame Effential Heat is in the Skeins of *China* Silk, which therefore thofe who deal in it keep at a fmall Diftance from the Water, yet they fuck it, without touching, and by this Fraud they weigh the heavier. Captain *John Lopez de Ribera* carry'd fuch a Pavillion of Cloves, as is above mention'd, and prefented it to the Earl of *Coruna*, who was then Viceroy. *Nayque*, like a Flafh of Lightning which burns all that ftands in its way, endeavour'd to ftir up thofe who before were kept peaceable by the Valour of *Fernan Tellez*, and to encourage the Turbulent, but without ftaying to fee the effect of his Negociation, he made directly towards the Cape of *Good-Hope*, yet it is more likely, and even pofitive, that he went firft to *Malaca*, and thence in the *India* Ships to *Spain*.

Candifb in Java prefented by Nayque.

Clove a-tracts Water, as does China Silk

Whilft *Nayque* was at Sea, the Marques *de Santa Cruz* had in the Ocean fought the Fleet Commanded by *Philip Strozzi*, in which was *Antony* the Baftard, Pretender to the Crown of *Portugal*, and deftroy'd it, Chaftizing the *French*, who with real, or counterfeit Commiffions from their King, had oppos'd King *Philip*'s juft Poffeffion. He arrived victorious at the Ifland of *S. Michael*, cut off the Heads of the *French* Gentlemen, and condemn'd the Reft to the Galleys. *Strozzi* dy'd of his Wounds, and *Don Antonio* efcap'd in a Boat, and return'd to *Zealand*, to folicite frefh Succours in *England* and *France*. In the mean while, the King of *Achem* perform'd his Promife. His Kingdom lies next the firft Promontory of the Ifland, in four Degrees and a half of North Latitude, and confequently his Ships eafily made themfelves Mafters of all the Streight between *Sumatra* and *Achem*, which they fo entirely poffefs'd, that they fuffer'd none of the Ships to pafs to *Malaca*, which brought Merchandize and Provifions from *China*, *Jipan*, *Camboxa*, not even from the *Moluccos*, obliging them to

Antony the Baftard Defeated.

Kingdom of Achem

Coaft

Coaft about feveral Iflands, to the great Lofs of the Merchants. But the *Portuguefe* Dealers in the City of *Pedir*, eight Leagues from *Achem*, fuftain'd much greater Dammage. Moft of them fled to *Malaca*, and tho' *Fernan Tellez* was then upon his Departure, he gave the neceffary Orders at *Goa* for their Relief. He funk fome of the Enemies Ships, and took one loaded with Daggers, they call *Crizes*, made at *Menancabo*, and a numerous Artillery, a Thing well known, and caft in *Sumatra*, many Years before the *Europeans* brought them into thofe Parts. This appears by the Victory the *Portuguefes* obtain'd over that Nation, during the Blockade of *Malaca*.

Monftrous Piece of Cannon.

The King of *Achem* fending a Daughter to be Married to the King of *Zor*, not far from *Malaca*, in the Country of *Siam*, among other rich Gifts, by way of Portion, prefented him a Brafs Cannon of fuch a bignefs, that the like had never been feen in *Europe*. This prodigious Gun, and the Princefs that was to be Queen of *Zor*, fell into the Hands of the *Portuguefes*. The taking of this Prize, and fome others, clear'd the Sea of that Fleet; and that extraordinary piece of Cannon, which ferv'd to Ballaft a Ship, was brought as a Prefent to the King of *Spain*, for its Monftrous Size, but a Storm oblig'd them to leave it in the Ifland *Tercera*, where it is now feen and admir'd. The City *Zor* was alfo Taken by the *Portuguefes*, and in it they found 1500 pieces of Cannon, Artificially Caft, with curious Figures and Flowers of Rais'd-Work on them.

Molucco Embaffador at Lisbon.

The *Molucco* Embaffador being come to *Lisbon*, obtain'd Audience of the King; who, tho' he was fully inform'd of the Embaffadors Falfhood, and the Practices of his Nation, yet gave him a favourable Hearing, after he had fhew'd his Credentials to the Minifters of State.

His Speech.

He in a long Speech recounted, from its Original, the conftant Fidelity of the *Molucco* Kings, and how particularly Remarkable it had been in *Sultan Aerio*, and that the wicked Commander in Chief in putting him to Death, had equally wrong'd the Crown of *Portugal*. That fince the Murderer was not punifh'd, to fatisfy the dead Man's Children and Kingdoms, it might well be concluded, that fo Cruel and Undeferv'd an Execution had been by the Direction of fome higher Power than the Governor *Mefquita*, and that even in cafe the Crime had been Notorious it had been more Prudence to charge it upon fome private Perfon. That King *Cachil Babu* intreated his Majefty to punifh the Offender in fuch manner as might give Satisfaction, and be an Example and Security to all the *Afiatick* Kings, that own the Dominion of *Spain*. In Return for that Favour, and Juftice, he promifed to Reftore the Fort of *Ternate*, and his other Kingdoms, which were Alienated, and that they would return to their former Subjection, as they had promis'd to the Governor *Pereyra de la Cerda*; fo remarkably correct their Behaviour, that there fhould be vifible Effects of a Royal, and Humble Gratitude, both in refpect to his Majefties fervice, and the fecurity of the Garrifons, and to the Advantage of the neighbouring Provinces, belonging to other Kings, who were his Subjects, about *Malaca*, the *Philippine* Iflands, and Parts Adjacent. He alfo ingaged to Reftore the Churches, and Chriftian Religion, and much more than had been agreed upon with *Pereyra*. The King having heard his Requeft, as if he were ignorant that the *Ternates* did not deferve the fatisfaction they requir'd, fince they had taken it themfelves fo fully, that it exceeded

exceeded even the bounds and examples of Revenge, he Answer'd, That all the Accessaries to that Fact should be found out, it being prov'd that the Principal was already Dead, and none of them should escape Unpunish'd, as would have Leen done by King *Sebastian*, had he Liv'd. That *Cachil Babu* must prepare to Restore all Things into the same Posture they were in before, if he intended to partake of the general Amnesty, which blotted out all past Offences throughout the Dominions of that Crown. *Nayque* had some private Audiences, and some Ministers of State had Conferences with him, with a Design to find out how the People of *India* were dispos'd. *The King's Answer.*

At this same Time *Don Gonzalo Ronquillo*, pursuant to the Orders he had receiv'd from *Spain*, sent the Ensign, *Francis de Duenas*, from the *Philippine* Islands, where he was Governor, to the *Moluccos*, to pry into the Inclinations of the Kings, and People, Governors, and other *Portuguese* at *Ternate*, *Tydore*, and *Bachian*, as to submitting to the King of *Spain*. He set out in the Habit of a *Chinese*, and was much assisted by his Knowledge of those Countries, and their Languages, and much more by his bold Spirit, sufficiently try'd in those Wars. He artfully Learnt what Hopes there might be of the Recovery of *Ternate*, and how firm the People of *Tydore* stood. He first inquired what Leagues were carrying on in the *Archipelago*, what Intelligence they had with, and expected from the Northern Fleets, with whom they had now familiar Correspondence. He Travell'd about the Islands, like a *Sangley*, or *Chinese*, in the *Jangwas*, or Trading Vessels of the *Malay*, and *Philippine* Merchants, and had the Opportunity of viewing them all, so far as to take the Dimensions of strong Places, compute what Stores and Ammunition the Barbarians had, and discover the Humours and Inclinations of the *Portugueses* who Traded, or Govern'd there; and returning to the *Philippine* Islands his Account, and Relation, first Encourag'd and gave Hopes that more Advantagious Enterprizes might be undertaken in those Parts, than about *Malaca*, tho' it were but only Supporting the *Portugueses* and *Tydores*, then hard press'd by the King of *Ternate*. King *Philip* receiv'd this Intelligence at *Lisbon*, whence the *Molucco* Embassador was then gone, ill-satisfy'd with the Answer he had; but *Sultan Babu*, on whom the Word of so great a Monarch, and the Authority of his Promise might perhaps have had great Effect, dy'd long before the said Embassador could come to his Presence. The small Remains of Christianity still left in his Kingdom, took a little Heart, and had our Arms but appear'd upon the Revolution caus'd by his Death, the only Noise of them might have gain'd the Victory. It is Reported that furious King *Babu* dy'd by the excess of his Love, or rather of his inordinate Lust, in the Arms of one of his Mistresses. Some say she kill'd him with Charms, or Poison, which is the Tyrant-Slayer among those Nations, impatient of one Mans long Rule. He was Succeeded by his Brother, who was Illegitimate, as we are told by *Cachil Tulo*, in the Letter, which, as we shall see hereafter, he writ to the Governor of the *Philippine* Islands. The new King took the Name of *Cachil Sultan Nait Dini Baraca Xa*, before whom *Cachil Madiaca* ought to have been preferr'd, as being Son to the principal Queen. As soon as Enthron'd he offer'd Peace to his Neighbours; on this Security, and that of a clear Conscience, *Cachil Gava*, King of *Tydore*, paid him a visit. He was received with publick Rejoycings *Ensign Duenas from Philippines to the Moluccos.* *The Intelligence he got.* *Sultan Babu Dies.* *Sultan Nait succeeds.*

cings

cings in one of the greateſt Squares of *Ternate*, and attended to a mighty lofty Arbour, provided to offer Sacrifize in, a (Chappel ſuitable to the Prieſthood) and there to decide Controverſies, and give Audience to his Subjects. When the firſt Complements were over, and the King of *Tydore* leaſt ſuſpected any thing, the *Ternate* Guards, hearing the Signal given by their K. drew their *Campilanes*,or Cymiters,and without allowing the Gueſt time to cry out, fell upon, and cut him in Pieces; tho' he was the Man thro' whoſe Means the K. of *Ternate* had the Crown given him, contrary to the Opinion, and Deſigns of his Unkles. But whenſoever great Returns are due to a Favour receiv'd, Ungrateful Souls convert the Obligation into Hatred, and nothing can occur to them more odious than the Sight of the Benefactor. Next he turn'd his Fury againſt that murder'd Princes Family, and ſuch of his Servants as could not make their Eſcape to *Tydore*, were either Kill'd, or remain'd Priſoners at *Ternate*, or abſconded whereſoever Fortune, and their own Confuſion lead them. This cruel Fact, which ſome aſſign'd to his Father, *Cachil Babu*, Reconcil'd the Murderer and his Unkles. But he immdeiatly acquainted them, how he expected to be Invaded on two Sides; that it was of the utmoſt Conſequence, that Subjects ſhould own their Sovereign, and fortify his Iſlands, eſpecially all the upper Parts; and that ſince he had ſuch Powerful Unkles, it was Reaſonable, and Convenient, the People ſhould be acquainted how firmly they were United to their Nephew. Then extolling their Valour, he with the ſweetneſs of their Commendations ſo blinded and amuſed them, that they could not perceive the profound Jealouſie he ſhrouded under them. Thus he divided them, that they might attend the Fortifications in diſtant Places; whilſt he in Perſon carry'd on the War againſt the *Tydores*. They preſently ſet up a Brother of their late King in his Stead; who, tho' he govern'd with Bravery, and ſtuck cloſe to the *Portugueſes*, yet had ſome ſtrong Places taken from him by the King of *Ternate*, which were afterwards reſtor'd, in our Kings Name, by *Don Pedro de Acuna* to the King now reigning. This Prince lived but a ſhort Time, yet ſo long that *Cachil Mole*, who was a Child when the King his Father was murder'd, grew up, and in him the Revenge of the Injury receiv'd. He never thought, or talk'd of any other Thing, till he brought it to Execution.

In the mean while the new King of *Tydore*, aſſiſted by the *Spaniards* he had in his Forts, provided to oppoſe, and attack his Enemy. They all expected Succours from *India*, where it was certain they muſt think it neceſſary to ſupport *Tydore*, in order to recover *Ternate*. Their Behaviour was ſo brave, as to defend themſelves, tho' ill furniſh'd with Arms and Proviſions againſt thoſe who attack'd them with Plenty of all Things. *Hector Brito* was come with a Galleen from *India* to their Aſſiſtance, and it being known at *Tydore* that a Storm had oblig'd him to ſtay on the farther Coaſt of *Borneo*, the King fitted out four *Carcoas*, and went to meet him, but was forced back to his Iſland by contrary Winds. He of *Ternate* watch'd to improve all Opportunities againſt his Enemy, and therefore would not let this Slip, nor truſt to any other; but Man'd out nine *Carcoas*, and going in Perſon fell upon him. The *Tydores* wanted not Courage to defend themſelves, and the Fight began with that Fury, which always arms thoſe two Nations againſt one another; but tho' the *Tydore* fought

Murders the King of Tydore.

New King of Tydore.

He is taken by him of Ternate.

deſperately

desperately, he was taken, and his Men either kill'd, or dangerously wounded. This Misfortune griev'd the *Portuguefes* no lefs than the *Indians*, becaufe they all lov'd him, For this reafon they gather'd the Remains of that Difafter, and all the other Forces they could make, offering their Service to *Cachil Aleazen*, Brother to the Captive King, a very hopeful Youth. *Fidelity of* He thank'd them, and was fo dexterous in gaining the Affections, and con- *the Tydo-* firming the Fidelity of the Subjects, that through his Care, no Man was *res.* wanting to his Duty. This Induftry was of good Ufe, for the-Conqueror did not return immediately to *Ternate*; but went about to his Enemies Iflands, perfwading the People in each of them to take an Oath of Allegiance to him, fhowing them their Captive King, whofe Life was at his difpofal; but the *Tydore* Towns, being furnifh'd with all Neceffaries, and believing they might with Safety practice that Hatred and Rage Nature has fill'd them with, would not give Ear to his Propofals, though they were mix'd with Intreaties, and Threats, and on the contrary difmifs'd him with their ufual Fiercenefs. He perceiving that the Oftentation of his Victory, and the Sight of the Captive King availed him but little, Sail'd away for *Ternate*. At his Arrival, he was received with Trumpets, Kettle-Drums, and Bafons they beat on, and with Songs they make for fuch like Occafions. The Heads and Limbs of the *Tydores* flain in Battel, were fix'd *Cruelties* upon the Spears they have advanc'd in the *Carcoas* on the Poops and Prows, *of* Terna-and other high Places of them, and particularly the Kings. This is their *tes.* way of erecting Trophies. Of the Skulls they make Cups to drink out of; like the *Scithians*, who, according to *Herodotus*, practife the fame; or like the *Germans*, as *Tacitus* tells us, of the Heads of the *Uri* they flew, and that was a Token of Nobility. He would not truft the keeping of the King in any of his Forts; but turn'd a ftrong Houfe into a Goal, and appointed him a Guard of *Gilolo* Iflanders, well arm'd. Sometimes he fhow'd Severity, and otherwhiles Tendernefs; but all Men knowing his Difpofition, expected the End of the Captive King; tho' at the fame time they believ'd, he would mitigate his Revenge out of Refpect *Hector* to his Sifter, the Princefs of *Tydore*. *Hector Brito*, Commander of a *Galeon*, *Brito at* came now to *Tydore*; but his Arrival did not much mend the Pofture of *Tydore,* Affairs, tho' thofe in the Fort were Encourag'd to hold out, and at leaft he added fome Reputation to the Caufe, and inclin'd the *Ternates* to liften to fome Overtures. However what could not be compafs'd by force of Arms nor Treaty, was effected by the Refolution of an Amorous Soul.

The Princefs *Quifayra*, Sifter to King *Gapabaguna*, that was the Pri- *Remarka-* foner's Name, had fo great an Opinion of herfelf, as to hope that her *ble Story* Beauty would prevail to bring about that good End, which was then of *of the* Confequence to all Parties, on feveral Accounts. She knew fhe was be- *Captive* lov'd by the King of *Bachian*, by him of *Sian*, a brave Youth, by him of *King's Li-* *Ternate* her Enemy, and by other prime *Sangiacks* of his Kingdom, and his *berty.* Kinfmen, who all publickly vy'd in doing her Honour. She was difcreet enough dexteroufly to feed them all with fuch Hopes, as lay no Ob- *Contri-* ligation on the Party that gives them, and yet encourage thofe who *vance of* value them. She gave out that fhe would marry none but the Man that *Quifayra,* fhould fet her Brother at Liberty, and deliver him to her alive, or dead. *Princefs of* This Part of the Declaration, tended to the Promoting of her Defign. *Tydore.*

The

The Promise work'd upon all her Admirers; tho' it was most certain, that her naming herself as a Reward of the Enterprize, proceeded from the Affection she bore *Ruy Diaz d' Acunha*, a *Portuguese* Gentleman, and Commander in Chief of the Fort of *Tydore*. She thought he would attempt the Rescuing of the King, and that such Success would entitle her to marry him, tho' many suspected there was already a mutual Obligation, as well as Desire, and that they were reciprocally in Love. It was known, that they had discours'd together several Times in the House of *Quinchana*, a great Lady, Aunt to *Quisayra*, whether *Ruy Diaz* was wont to go frequently; and that with her Interposition the Matter had been so far concerted, that the Princess promis'd she would embrace Christianity to marry him. This made not his Rivals dismay, and the King of *Ternate*, upon these profer'd Hopes, offer'd to give her Brother his Liberty. However he was not regarded, because *Quisayra* was as averse to be beholding to him, as she was desirous to be oblig'd by *Ruy Diaz*. This powerful Passion informs barbarous Minds. Her Disdain caus'd the King of *Tydore* to be more close confin'd, and his Body to be loaded with heavy Chains, being more narrowly observ'd than before.

Cachil Salama, a Subject and near Kinsman of his, well known for his Valour in the Wars, was more deep in Love with *Quisayra* than all the Rest, and listen'd to all the Reports of their endeavouring to comply with her Expectation. He entirely keeping his own Council, a Thing rare in Lovers, to be secret without Affectation, that no Notice might be taken of him, one Night fitted out a *Baroto*, so they call a Sort of small Boat, putting into it five *Tydore* Soldiers, he could confide in. Thus he crofs'd over the Channel to the Leeward, and landed on *Ternate*; where he left the Boat ready, but hid on the Shore. Then *Cachil Salama*, conceal'd among the Croud of trading People in the City, went to the chief Part they call *Limathas*, and set Fire to a House in that Ward he thought stood most convenient for his Purpose. The Flame, which had taken hold of the Roof gathering Strength, threatned a greater Conflagration. Having done this Mischief, whilst the People flock'd together, and endeavour'd to put a Stop to it with Water, and other means, *Cachil* return'd to his Boat, on the Inside the Ridge of Rocks there is about the Island, and went away to the other Side of the Fort, where he began to beat an Alarm, to cause the greater Confusion. This done he went ashore again, with only his *Campilan*, or Cimiter, ordering three of his Men to follow him at some small Distance. He found the King's Prison almost abandon'd, the Guards being gone to help at the House that was a Fire. He went in boldly, breaking open Doors, and Bolts, till he came to the Prisoners Chamber, who scarce believing what he saw, ask'd him, with much Amazement, how he came thither, and whether the Fort of *Tydore* was loft? *Cachil* answer'd, he must be quick, and go along with him, and should afterwards be satisfy'd as to his Questions; for if he refus'd he would strike off his Head. Then laying hold of the end of the Chain, and the other three *Tydores* being now come up to them, they forc'd their Passage out of the House, making way with their Swords and killing such as offer'd to oppose them. The same Valour and good Fortune carry'd them through the Streets, to the Port, and leaping into their little Boat, put all their Hands to the

Oars.

She is in Love with the Portugue Commander.

Cachil Salama a Lover of Quilagra, his Bravery.

He rescues the King of Tydore.

Oars. In thofe Iflands it is ufual for Kings to row, without being compell'd to it by Neceffity; for as in *Spain* the Nobility learn to ride, fo the Ifland Princes in all thofe Eaftern Parts value themfelves upon handling the Oars, and Sails. They crofs'd over the Streight, and being purfu'd too late, by the light Veffels of *Ternate*, arriv'd unexpected at *Tydore*. The Fame of his arrival was foon fpread abroad, and when certainly known, the Cannon was fir'd, the flat Drums in the Temples were beaten, and the Bells rung, the Sound whereof ufes to draw the People of the *Moluccos* together, and in fhort there was a general Rejoycing, without quitting their Arms. All Men cry'd up *Cachil Salama* to the Skies, calling him the Deliverer of *Tydore*, and *Neza Maluco*, *Neza* fignifies a Spear, and *Maluco* a Kingdom, and both together the Spear, that is, the Defence of the Kingdom.

Only *Quifayra* was troubled at this Event, becaufe the general Promife *Quifayra* fhe had made of marrying, whofoever perform'd it, was only defign'd for *contrives* *Ruy Diaz de Acunha*. She was not able to conceal this Truth; efpecially *to murder* when *Cachil Salama* boldly prefs'd the Performance of the Promife, the *Cachil Sa-* King himfelf feconding him. She delay'd him, alledging fome fpecious *lama.* Pretences to gain Time. She would willingly have made her Complaint to *Ruy Diaz* himfelf, either to fhame, or provoke him to Paffion. She eafily compafs'd to meet him at her Aunts, where, as foon as fhe began to Difcourfe, there was nothing but Tears, Complaints, Excufes, and Contrivances to murder *Salama*, to conclude a Reconciliation. *Rocque Pinheyro* the Commander's Nephew, and a Soldier of reputed Valour, was prefent at this Difcourfe. *Quifayra* trufting him with her fecret Thoughts, he *Pinheyro* boldly, and with Art, gave her to underftand that his Unkle was as flack as *undertakes* before; and fince he had been fo in the other Affair, what could be ex- *to murder* pected from him in what he now promis'd. He faid, if fhe could prevail *him and his* upon her felf to be fenfible of the Ingratitude of *Ruy Diaz*, and to fubfti- *own Unkle.* tute him in his Place, he would not only murder *Cachil*, but his own Unkle too. That out of the Refpect due to her high Qualities, he had not till then prefum'd to let her know how deeply he was in Love with her Beauty; but that he now thought himfelf abfolv'd from all human Tyes, and wholly confin'd by that. *Pinheyro* had a full hearing, an Advantage not far remote from being admitted; and tho' he was not commanded to murder his Unkle, yet he perceiv'd he had not left him fo well in the Princeffes Efteem as he was before.

In the mean while, *Cachil Salama* was not idle, preffing the Bufinefs hafti- *Salama* ly, and having got fome Inkling, or fufpecting the Caufe of the Delay, like *convey'd* a true Lover who is feldom deceiv'd in this Sort of Jealoufy, he found out *into Qui-* the Truth. By the Contrivance of one of *Quifayra's* Women, he durft *fayra's* prefume to hide himfelf in her Bedchamber; and in the dead of the Night, *Bed Cham-* he fuddenly appear'd before her, his Fiercnefs being overcome by a Superi- *ber.* or Power. The Princefs was furpriz'd, but diffembled it, and prepar'd to defend herfelf in Cafe Violence were offer'd. She threatned to cry out; utter'd Complaints with Tears, and bewail'd the lofs of her Reputation, faying, how could they think her Innocent, who faw him either come in, or go out Salama all the while in humble Pofture, and on his Knees, af- fur'd her he had no other Defign, than to put her in Mind of the Obliga- tion fhe lay under, and that fince it was known he was to be her Hufband,

P

his

his being seen was of no Consequence. That her Reputation suffer'd more, by the delaying of the marriage; and that to convince her of his Affection, he would be gone as obediently as he had always done. He went

He gains her Affection. out immediately, comforted with Thanks, and Hopes; and deliver'd her from the Fear she had conceiv'd of him. She was so taken with this Courteous Action, that revolving it in her Mind, it wrought so much, as to settle her Affection on *Salama*; so that she would have marry'd him, tho' he had not oblig'd her before.

Pinheyro murders his Unkle, and is kill'd by Salama. At this time *Pinheyro*, who was already engaged in her Love, either to obtain its Reward, or because his Unkle did not Favour him as he expected, or for both Reasons, contriv'd his Death. As he was going one Day to the Palace, to acquaint *Quisayra* that the Murder was already committed, *Cachil* happened than to come from a Fort to see his Mistress. He seeing *Pinheyra* coming out of her Apartment, drew his *Campilan*, or Cymiter, and tho' the Youth fought Manfully, and like a Lover, yet *Cachil*, who had the same Qualifications, and was Jealous over and above, at the first onset clove his Head, so furiously, that he dropt down dead of the Wound.

He marries Quisayra. Then proceeding as he had begun, he went in where *Quisayra* was, whom he easily perswaded to be gone with him, and leaving the Palace full of Confusion, they Imbark'd in the *Baroto*, or small Boat that brought him. They Marry'd with the good liking of the King and Kingdome, and the Loss of those two Gentlemen's Lives. And since among the *Portuguese* Nation, as much Account is made of Honour gain'd, or lost in Love Affairs, as was formerly of Victories obtain'd in *Greece*, at the *Olympick* Games, the Vindication of these Lovers shall be left to the Management of those who are well skil'd in that Matter, to whom we refer our selves.

A Portuguese hang'd. The *Portugueses* were much griev'd at this Disaster, as being Publick, and the King was so incens'd, that one of them having accidentally kill'd a Horse he had a great Value for, he caus'd him to be Hang'd, without hearkning to any thing that could be said for him. This gain'd *Cachil Mole* so generally the Affections of all Men, that tho' *Cachil Cota* was Elder, and Son to the principal Queen, by them call'd *Putriz*, under colour that the latter was a Friend to the King of *Ternate*, and about to contract Affinity with him, the other gain'd the greater Party, which advanc'd him to Succeed in the Throne of *Tydore*, as we shall soon see.

Nayque returns to Ternate. The *Portuguese* Galeons arrived at *Malaca*, and in them *Cachil Naique* returning from *Spain*, and having stay'd there some Months for the *Monsons*, he had a good Voyage, and arrived safe at *Ternate*, when he had by the way sollicited the *Javaneses*, and the People of *Achem* and *Borneo*, not to admit of the *Spanish* Domination. He brought no acceptable Answer from King *Philip*, and found the King who had employ'd him Dead, and in his Place another, so different from the Former, that he entertain'd no Thoughts of restoring the Forts to the *Portugueses*, but on the contrary, aim'd at casting off all Obedience, and obliterating their Name.

English at Ternate. To this effect he Confederated with the *English*, who, with other Northern Nations, Lorded it in the Island. Five Leagues from it lay at Anchor an *English* Ship, waiting for two others that came out with her. They Anchor'd in the Port, and went ashore, as if they had been in *London*, being well receiv'd by the *Sultan*, with whose Leave they settled a Factory in

the

the City, where they left Officers, who under the name of Trade, were more absolute Masters of it than the Natives. They dispers'd to gather in the Clove for the Goods they brought to Barter; and on the 21st. of *August* dispatch'd their Ships, loaded with that Spice, and with those Nuts they call of *Molucco*, and excellent Preserves of them both. In these Ships went Embassadors to Queen *Elizabeth*, and to the Prince of *Orange*, carrying Presents suitable to those Persons, of the most valuable Things in *India*. They were order'd to offer the Queen his Kingdome in Vassalage, and his Friendship to the Prince of *Orange*. The Advantage of these Embassies afterwards appear'd; yet he did not on that Account give any hopes of Restoring Christianity; for besides that the Persecution grew more violent, he had at that time brought over into his Kingdome, a great number of Mahome-*Arabian* and *Persian* false Prophets, all of them *Mahomet's* Priests and Mi-tan *Prea-*nisters, to strengthen that Sect. Besides, being inform'd by his Spies, That *chers at* it was given out in the *Philippine* Islands, That they would make War on *Ternate.* him that way, and that in *Spain* the King promis'd the Union of the two Crowns should produce the Conjunction of their Power and Arms, for the punishing of disobedient Tyrants, he slighted no Alliance, nor contemn'd the Weakest Enemy. For this Reason, he gave Entertainment, and allow'd the planting of Colonies to *Europeans*, and Leagued with *Idolaters* and *Mahometans*, who hate *Spain*, as their common Enemy. The *English* Ships now frequented *India*, facilitating the Passage, and shewing an Example to the *French* and *Dutch*, which encourag'd them all to venture out far from their Countries, and seek for Treasure in strange ones.

Sultan Capabaguna did not long enjoy his Liberty at *Tydore*. He was *King of* taken ill at an Entertainment. Some believe he had a slow Poison given *Ternate* him; because he was very moderate in Eating, and those motions of his *dies.* Arms, the gnashing of his Teeth, and losing of his Senses, which attend the Falling-Sickness, and are Simptoms of Apoplexies, could not naturally proceed from his Temperate way of Living; but are always caused by much Excess, which Occasions this violent Distemper. He came to himself after that first Fit, but his Vigour wasted, and he linger'd on to the end of his Life. *Cachil Cotta* should have Succeeded him, but they were suspicious of his Correspondence with the *Ternates*; and they all so openly favour'd his Brother *Cachil Mole*, that there was not the least Difficulty made about the Succession. He often remember'd his Fathers unfortunate Death, and in Regard that this raging Desire of Revenge, might prove in-strumental for the Recovery of *Ternate*; as soon as his Unkle Dy'd, which was on the 24th of *April* 1599, the *Portuguese* Commander in Chief, *Ruy Gonzalez de Sequeyrao* repair'd to his Palace, and by Means of the *Portu-* Cachil *guese* Power and Arms, caused *Cachil Mole* to be sworn King, as being a Mole *King* most faithful Friend to his Nation, and no less an Enemy to the *Ternates*. of Tydore. He immediatly dispatch'd Captain *Palma* with this News to *Manila*, and with it an Account of the *Molucco* Islands, of their Neighbours, and of their Preparations; because they were then providing in the *Philippine* Islands for this War, to extirpate this Receptacle of Sects, where all sorts of Apostasies are admitted, and particularly the vile Doctrines of *Mahomet*. Ever since the Year 1555. when the *Dutch* enter'd those Seas, they have

not,

not, till this Time, ceas'd bringing in Sectaries, and Captains of Pyrates: These Men carry away the Wealth of *Asia*, and in Lieu of it leave behind them that false Doctrine, which renders the Conversion of so many Souls Fruitless.

Moluccos flighted at Coa. The Forgetfulness, or Contempt the Governours of *India* show'd for the *Molucco* Islands, seem'd fatal; since they refus'd, or with-held the usual Succours, abandoning the Commanders, and Forts, for so many Years, as if they had not been in the World. This was not remedy'd by the Union of the Crowns of *Spain* and *Portugal*; on the contrary, the great Success of the *Adelantado*, or Lord Lieutenant *Legaspe*, in the Islands *Luzones*, which he call'd *Philippines*, being known in *Spain*, King *Philip* the IId. thought fit as we shall soon see, that the *Molucco* Islands, and Parts adjacent, whither he was Zealous to send Evangelical Preachers, should be sensible of the Advantage of his Neighbouring Empire. This was

Relief order'd from the Philippines, and why. speedily order'd, and tho' the Effects were not sutable, by Reason of the many Accidents great Undertakings are liable to, yet Time has shown how convenient it was to fix that Resolution. For the better understanding of the Reasons on which it was grounded; since one of them proceeded from the various Disposition, Qualities, and Interests of the Nations throughout those Seas and Lands; it will be absolutely necessary in this Place to make them known, before we come to Particulars.

Description of China. The Country of the *Sina*, whom we call *Chinese*, is the uttermost of the Continent of *Asia*. On the East and South it is encompass'd by the Ocean, which the Ancients call'd *Sericus*. On the West, it reaches to the Borders of the farther *India*; and on the North to those of the *Massagetes* and *Scythians*. Their Ancient Annals, Writings and Traditions informs us, that the *Chinese* extended their Empire much further. This is verify'd by the Remains of sumptuous Structures; and not only in Ruins, wherein their former Magnificence is still apparent, but even in Cities, which Time has preserv'd, tho' not inhabited, and yet to be seen in the Provinces they have excluded their Limits. There are many which take there Denomination, and own their Original from *China*. For that immense Empire finding it self labouring under its own Power, and overburden'd with its Magnitude, like a judicious Patient, to prevent more Harm, it breath'd the Veins, and brought down the Redundancy of the Body. The same we read the *Carthagenians* did, when in the like Condition, and for the same Reasons. It confin'd it self to a narrower Compass, proportionable to the Extent of humane Providence, that so their Prince's Light might reach to shine over, and be communicated to them; which cannot be, when the Circumference is too great for the Darting of the Beams. They publish'd indispensable Decrees against such as go out

Chinese contract their Empire. of *China*, without leave from the Magistrates. They abandon'd vast Provinces, which being left expos'd to Tyranny, and Infidelity, after tedious Wars, submitted to the most Potent. Hence the Kings of *India* took their Original, being oblig'd never to lay down their Arms, nor keep any Faith, so to support themselves one against another, till a greater Power subdues them.

15 Kingdoms in China. In *China* they reckon 15 maritime Kingdoms, or Provinces of an extraordinary Extent, with each its Metropolis, or Capital; the rest are up the Inland.

Inland. The moſt Part of it lies within temperate Climates, and receives into its pure and open Boſome the Sun's vital Rays, having a healthful, and ſerene pleaſant Air. This favourable Diſpoſition renders it ſo fruiful, *Fertility,* that it yearly yields two or three Crops. The great Induſtry of the Tillers, *Air, Popu-* is a conſiderable Addition to its Fertility. The Number of them is infi- *louſneſs.* nite, being a People that daily multiply exceedingly, becauſe they are forbid going into Foreign Countries. Neither is any among ſuch a nu- merous Multitude of Men allow'd to live idle Idleneſs is not only expo- *Idleneſs* ſed to private Contempt, and the Scoffs of Neighbours, but puniſh'd by *puniſh'd.* publick Cuſtome and Law. Thus the Peaſants leave not the leaſt Spot of Ground untill'd. The Hills and deep Bottoms produce Vines and Pine- Trees ; the Plains, Rice, Barley, Wheat, and other common Grain. Thoʳ they do not preſs the Grapes for the Wine, as we do, yet they keep them *Product,* to eat ; and of the Herb call'd *Chia,* they make a wholeſome hot Liquor. *Tea.* This they drink, as do the *Japoneſes,* and it preſerves them from Colds, Head-Aches, Rheums in the Eyes, and makes them live long and healthy. Some Parts of the Country want Olive-Trees, but they are not deſtitute of other Plants, which yield a Liquor to anoint them. There is a perpe- tual Abundance of Paſture, Fruits, Flowers, and all the Products of Gar- dens. There are many Navigable Rivers, carrying Ships of great Bur- *Rivers,* den, and full of excellent Fiſh ; the Banks cover'd with perpetual Greens, *Ports, &c.* ſpacious Harbours, and a Trade in them of all Things neceſſary for humane Life. The Fowl are of various colour'd Feathers, and pleaſant and nou- riſhing to eat; great Numbers of large Deer ; vaſt Lakes, Woods and Mountains, and Mines of Gold, Silver, Iron, and other Metals; beſides Pearls and precious Stones. Its Purcelane, or Earthen Ware, is not to be imitated in the World ; and it affords rich Furs againſt the Cold, Silks, Wooll, Cotton, and Flax ; nor is there any End of its Sugar, Honey, Am- ber, Vermilion, and Lake. Musk, whereof no mention is found among *Greek* and *Latin* Authors, is more plentiful in *China* than in other Parts.

The People are moſt paſſionately addicted to Delight, and Laſciviouſ- neſs. They alone always ſell all Things; they buy nothing that Nature *The People.* or Art affords, either for Suſtenance, or Cloathing, except ſome Perfumes for their Cloaths, and Pepper out of *India* ; nor would there be any Place for Foreign Trade, did not an inſatiable Avarice of Gold and Silver predo- minate among the *Chineſes.* What they draw out of the Bowels of the Mines, they conceal as carefully as if it were ſtill in them ; and even that they bring from remote Provinces, they heap up, and bury. Their publick and private Structures would make up a Narration of ex- traordinary Length. We are told of 200 Cities of an extraordinary Mag- *Cities.* nitude, and many more of inferior Degree, beſides Towns, Caſtles, and Villages, containing above 3000 Families each, built of Bricks made of the ſame Clay as our Purcelane, or *China* Ware, and theſe encompaſs'd with continu'd Woods, Springs and Rivers. In all theſe there are Towers with ſtately Pinnacles, Pleaſure-Houſes, and Temples, thoʳ hideouſly painted, yet coſtly, with Variety of deform'd Images, through which the Devils give their Anſwers. But theſe are not in all Parts, for many of them know no God, nor Religion. Life, they ſay, was from Eternity

common

Barbarous Opinions. common to, and alike in all living Creatures. That at first Men drank humane Blood, and eat raw Meat. That afterwards the Use of Reason provided for Necessity, and Pleasure; inventing the Ways of dressing, and seasoning Meat at the Fire, in Vessels and other Utensils. The same, they say, happen'd in Regard to Man's Nakedness. So that Man is indebted to himself alone for what he enjoys, and therefore whosoever lay'd on him the Burden of Religion, and the owning of a Cause Superior to Nature, only aim'd at the dejecting him, and exercising a Tyranny over his Liberty. With these impious Notions, and destructive Atheism, they oppose their Eternal Salvation, which our Arms, and our Preachers invite them to. They only regard Generation; but not without Distinction. Lawful Matrimony entitles Women to be Mistresses of their Families. The Matrons

Chastity. value themselves upon being highly Chast. Concubines are kept in Houses apart. They do not want for Plays, and such Representations; and they delight in seeing their Traditions, whether true or fabulous, acted on the Stage. They use Entertainments, and have Tables and Chairs of *Ebony*, and other precious Materials, as also Shipping, Shows, Carts, Horse-Litters, and the Exercise of Arms, and Riding.

Customs, and Manners. It were no difficult Matter to give an Account here of their private Customs and Manners, were they to our Purpose. Something shall be said of the Publick and Political, for the better Understanding of some Things that happen'd in the *Philippine* Islands, from whence the Recovery of the *Moluccos*, in our Times, had its Beginning. They call their great

Government. Men *Loyties*, from among whom the King chuses his Judges and Counsellors. There is almost an infinite Number of inferiour Magistrates, who exercise the Regal Power and Authority, even in the most inconsiderable Cases. In every Town there are five, that have the greatest Power, and these are Strangers in the Place, that they may be free from Partiality.

Tutan a Viceroy. The Head of them all, is call'd *Tutan*, being the same as a Viceroy in *Europe*. The next in Dignity is the *Poncasio*, who has Charge of the King's

Poncasio. Taxes, and Royal Treasure, with a great Number of Clerks, and other Officers; and he pays all Salaries and Pensions. Next follows the *Ancasio*,

Ancasio. who is chief Justice, in Criminal Cases of Consequence. The *Aitan* has

Aitan. the Inspection of all Martial Affairs, he musters the Armies, builds the Ships, and his principal Duty is to observe the Guards, that no Stranger

Luitisio. may pass into the Inland Country. The *Luitisio* is next to the *Aitan* in Dignity, and is to be expert in War, in which he is employ'd by the *Aitan*. I know there are other Magistrates, and their Names and Dignities, which I must pass over in Silence. All of them except the *Luitisio*, keep great State. There are ten chosen Persons of the Council, tho' not equal in Authority. Five of them sit on the Right, the others on the Left. The King often thrusts in among the Judges and Parties in Disguize, to pry into the Causes, and their Decisions, and be certainly inform'd of both. When he thinks fit, he sometimes makes himself known; and the Moment he discovers himself, they all stand Mute, full of Respect and Astonishment, listening to what he shall command. Then he commends or reproves either Party, and rewards, or punishes before he

Mandarines. departs the Court. His *Mandarines*, and Prime Ministers are so highly respected, that no Man dares look them in the Face, and they always look fo Stern, that it would be thought a great Diforder to lofe the leaft of their Gravity, tho' it were but with a modeft Smile. This they obferve, when they pafs thro' the Streets, in Sight of the People. The greateft Honour among them is to wear a Cymiter with a gold Pommel, and a yellow Hat.

When the Prefident of the Council Dies, the eldeft Judge fucceeds him. *Judge.* Thefe go Circuits thro' the Provinces, and reform Abufes, and all of them wear the King's Badge on their Shoulders, and Breafts, being a Golden Dragon wove in the Cloth. When they go thefe Progreffes, they fave, or leffen the Charge by circumfcribing the State. When firft elected, at their taking Poffeffion of their Pofts, they generally go out attended by Troops of Horfe and Foot, with all Sorts of Mufick, and Splendour. Their Pomp appears in the Hanging, and other Ornaments of the Streets and Houfes. All the expence of Law Suits, Courts, and other Perquifites is allow'd out of the King's Exchequer. The *Mandarines* are Governors, and Viceroys. In *China* there are no Dukes, Marqueffes, or Earls, nor do they own any Dignity, but what is deriv'd from the King's Authority. Though in the Parts next to *Scythia*, or *Tartary*, fome People are *Mahometans*; yet in all *Religion.* others they are either Idolaters, or look upon the Notion of a God as a meer Jeft. They believe the Life and Death of Men and Beafts are alike. There is nothing they are more attentive to, than the obftructing of any foreign Religion, and this under the politick Pretence, that they are jealous of Innovation. But above all they oppofe the true Religion, hating that they know nothing of; and are as much afraid of it, as if its Minifters went arm'd to preach it, and with the Noife of Drums, and Trumpets, and regular Armies. They are frighted at a few bare-foot, and almoft naked Men who profefs Poverty, and preach up Morality, and fupernatural Virtues, grounded on Humility and Peace. They have fuch an Averfion for them, that were it proper to our Subject, or were there not printed Relations thereof already, we would recount feveral Inftances, to fhow their unreafonable Hatred. Hence may be inferr'd, how much more Need of the fpecial Grace of Heaven thefe Nations ftand in, with thofe in the Neighbourhood, which are expos'd to the Infection and Danger of their Obftinacy. The Reader ought alfo to confider, that tho fometimes, the Avarice, and other Crimes of our Commanders, and Soldiers interfere with the Preaching of the Gofpel, yet their Offences do not leffen the Iuftice of the Caufe. He is alfo to reflect, that, allowing his Majefty, for weighty Reafons of State fhould, as we have faid was propos'd, refolve to abandon thofe Parts of *Afia*, as the *Chinefes* did, and circumfcribe the Compafs of his Monarchy; yet the Caufe of Religion would not permit it. Our Kings are its Minifters, and Sons of the Catholick Church, and any War made for the Propagation of the Gofpel, is of the greateft Confequence, and highly gainful, tho' it be to acquire, or recover defert Provinces. Befides that the *Philippine* Iflands have fhown us how tractable their Natives are, and how much they improve with the Example, and Society of the *Spaniards*, and how affectionately they have imbrac'd the Faith, and affift the Religious Men, who dilate, and carry it over into *China*, *Japan*, *Camboxa*, *Mindanao*, the *Moluccos*, and other Iflands, where ftill Idolatry continues, or the Friendfhip with the Devils left them by their antient Mafters, when they excluded
them

them their Dominions, or elfe the *Mahometan* Fictions, which they have since imbrac'd.

This is the Principal End of keeping those Provinces; and the Revenues and Wealth which is confum'd upon them, and feveral others, are laid out upon the Forces, and Preparations *Spain* makes for the Preaching and Security of the Minifters of the Church. Befides, that as Times have alter'd,

Rumours of Chinefe *Invafions.*

fo they have often in *China* chang'd their Opinion, and fhow'd they repented their having diminifh'd their Empire. No Year paffes over without Threats of *Chinefe* Armies; of their Lifting Men; of building Ships; of their folemn confecrating, or dedicating them to their carv'd Gods, or to the Sun, Moon, and Stars, which are ador'd in fome Parts, begging Succefs in their vain Prayers againft the *Spaniards*, who are poffefs'd of thofe Countries they abandon'd, thro' their own Indifcretion. This fhort Account of the *Chinefes*, or *Sangleys*, is here inferted, for the better underftanding of thofe Actions we fhall foon treat of. They not only oppofe the Truth; but tho' they are wholly addicted to their Intereft, and Slaves to Gain, and tho' it be fo abfolutely requifite for the attaining of thofe Ends through their Induftry and Trade, to maintain Amity with their Neighbours, yet there is nothing lefs to be reliy'd on than their Faith, or to give it a more proper Name, their Diffimulation Happy thofe People, if when *China* withdrew its Dominion, it had alfo withdrawn the Errors of its Worfhip.

The End of the Fourth Book.

THE
HISTORY
OF THE
DISCOVERY and CONQUEST
OF THE
Molucco and *Philippine* Iſlands, *&c.*

BOOK. V.

THE Iſlands *Luzones*, or *Manilas*, which are both of them anti‑ent Names, having been diſcover'd by *Magellan*; after his Death, and various Accidents befallen his Companions, *Sebaſtian Cano* return'd to *Spain* in that renowned Ship, call'd the *Victory*, as it were to expreſs her Voyage, which is not ſo likely as true. *Sebaſtian Cano*, was born in the Town of *Guetaria*, on the *Pyrenean* Moun‑tains, as we are told by *Maffæus*, in his *Latin* Hiſtory, where he extols *Cano*'s mighty Reſolution, and skill in the Art of Navigation. He tells us with what Reſpect and Admiration all Men look'd on him, as the firſt that went round this Globe, which is the Habitation of Mortals. And in Truth what value ſhall we henceforward put upon the Fabulous *Argonauts*, *Tiphys*, *Jaſon*, and all other Sailers, ſo much celebrated by the *Greek* Eloquence, or Vanity, if compar'd with our *Cano*? He was the firſt Witneſs of the Communication of the two Seas, to whom 'Nature diſclos'd what ſhe had till then reſerv'd for his Diſcovery, ſuffering herſelf to be entirely lay'd open, as a Beginning of ſuch Bold Enterprizes of that Law which ſerves, and renders us Immortal.

Margin: Sebaſtian Cano the firſt that ſail'd round the World.

Magellan being dead, the Iſlands *Luſones*, which ought to have inherited his Name for being his Place of Burial, as the Streight did for his diſco‑vering and paſſing it, in the year 1565, chang'd theirs for that of *Philip‑pines*, tho' thoſe of that Eaſtern *Archipelago* bear the ſame. The *Adelan‑tado*, or Lord Lieutenant *Michael de Legaſpe*, ſent from *New-Spain*, by the Viceroy *Don Lewis de Velaſco*, with a *Spaniſh* Fleet arriv'd at theſe Iſlands. He firſt conquer'd that of *Zebu*, and its Neighbours, where he ſpent ſix Years. Theſe Iſlands, as there are ſeveral Names given to divers of thoſe Parts, are call'd *Pintados*, becauſe then the *Indians* went naked, and their Bodies wrought and painted of ſeveral Colours. He left a Garriſon there,

Margin: Iſlands Luſones call'd Philip‑pines.

Margin: Legaſpe the firſt Conqueror

and

Luzon Island subdu'd.

and went over to poffefs himfelf of *Luzon*, 150 Leagues from *Zebu*. He fought the Barbarians, who after the firft Surprize, caus'd by our Arms, Ships, and Countenances, differing from theirs, was over, were encourag'd by that very Novelty. *Legafpe* ran into a Bay, four Leagues over at the Mouth, where is an Ifland now call'd *Marivelez*. The Bay runs thirty Leagues up to the City *Manila*, and is eight Leagues over, lying North-Weft, and South-Eaft. The Inhabitants of this City oppos'd him with more Bravery than the *Pintados*; becaufe they had Cannon, and a Fort, but as foon as they faw that taken by the *Spaniards*, they fubmitted. This was done fo expeditioufly that the Country had not time to come in; and thus he enter'd *Manila*, a Place ftrong by Nature. At a Point of it, which is fhut in by the Waters of the Bay, a confiderable River empties it felf, which rifes in the Great Lake call'd *Vay*, five Leagues Diftant. This Point which at firft is narrow and fharp, prefently widens, becaufe the Sea-coaft

Manila City.

runs away to the South-South-Eaft, and the River Weft, leaving a moft fpacious Spot for the City, which is all encompafs'd with Water, except that part which lyes to the South-Weft. *Legafpe* then built it of Wood, whereof there is great plenty in thofe parts. The Roofs he cover'd, or Thatch'd with the Leaves of *Nipa*, which is like our Sedge, or Sword-Grafs, and a fufficient Fence againft the Rains, but a Combuftible Matter, and the occafion of Great Conflagrations, which have often hapned.

Luzon Island defcrib'd.

Luzon is more Populous than any of the other Iflands, which in Honour of King *Philip* the Second, were call'd *Philippines*, and which fome affirm are in Number 11000. The Compafs of *Luzon* is 350 Leagues. It runs without the Bay 100 Leagues to the Northward, as far as *New Segovia*; and from where this Province commences, which is at Cape *Bojador*, and 70 Leagues from it, turns to the Eaftward, to the Promontory *del Engañno*; from thence along the Coaft to the South, 80 Leagues; then turning again to that they call *Emborcadero*, or the Mouth, being the Streight againft the Ifland *Tandaya*, 40 Leagues, and this is 80 from the Bay. So that it bears the fhape of a Square, and in it feveral Bays, and few good Harbours. It lyes in 160 Degrees Longitude, reckoned from the *Canaries*, the Southermoft Part in 14 Degrees of North Latitude, and the Northermoft in 19. On that Side of it lyes *China*, feparated from it by the Sea 60 Leagues over; and the Iflands of *Japan*, 250 Leagues diftant. On the Eaft is the Vaft Ocean; on the South is the greateft of all the *Archipelagos*, divided into five, and thofe again rent into fo many Iflands, Kingdoms, and Provinces, as if Nature had refolv'd that Man fhould never determine their Number. The moft known are the two *Javas*, our *Moluccos*, *Borneo*, and *New Guinea*. On the Weft of *Luzon*, at 300 Leagues, and greater Diftances, lye *Malaca*, *Siam*, *Patan*, *Camboxa*, *Cochin-china*, and feveral other Provinces on the Continent of *Afia*. The *Chinefes* forfook their Habitations in our *Philippine* Iflands, but not the Trade. Neither did the Worfhip they had introduc'd ceafe, nor their Fertility.

Product, and Trade.

They produce plenty of Corn, and other neceffary Grain; Deer, Cows, Buffaloes, Goats, and Wild Boars, Fruit, and Sweets; and if any be wanting the *Chincheo Chinefes* bring it, as they do Porcelane, and Silks. The Wine they ufe, and always drank, is drawn from the Palm, or rather *Coco* Trees, cutting off the Clufters of the Fruit they produce, when Green,

a i d

and taking off the Nipples of them, they gather the Water that runs from them, and Boil it in Jars, till it becomes so strong, that it makes Men drunk, in the same manner as the strongest *Spanish* Wine. Of its Natural Growth, the Island has Oranges, Lemmons, and most delicious Cittons, of *Spanish* Fruit, Figs, and Pears. There are Numerous Breeds of Sparrow-Hawks, Birds like small Herons, and Eagles, besides sundry Sorts of Parrots, and other large and small Fowl. In the Rivers and Lakes there are many Monstrous Crocodils, or Alligators. These easily kill the *Indians*, and especially Boys, who happen unadvisedly to come where they are, and the Cattle that goes into the Water to drink. It often happens, they lay hold of their Snouts, or Noses, and draw them under Water, where they are drown'd, without being able to defend themselves; then they drag the Carcass to the Shore, and devour it. An Alligator being kill'd a whole Buffaloes Head has been found some times in the Belly, and yet in that Country they are as big as the largest Ox in *Spain*. The Alligators lay Eggs as the Tortoises do, about the bigness of Goose-Eggs, and so hard that they will scarce break, tho' struck against a Stone with main Force. They are Hatch'd by burying in the Sand, near the edge of the Water; the moisture whereof, with the Heat of the Sun, forms the young Ones. There are some *Indians* so brave, that as fierce as these Creatures are, they kill them with their Hands. They arm the left up to the Arm with a Glove of Buffalo's Hide. They hold in it a Stick, or small Stake, somewhat above a Foot long, and as thick as a Man's Wrist, and sharpned at both Ends, with which they go into the Water up to the Waste: The Crocodile makes up to the *Indian*, gaping to swallow him, and he holding out his Arm that is arm'd, and the Hand with the Stake in it, for the Monster to bite at, claps it across his Mouth, so that he cannot shut it, or make use of his Teeth to hurt him. The Alligator feeling the hurt of the sharp pointed Stick, is so dismayed that he neither makes resistance, nor offends, nor dares so much as move, because the least strugling gauls him: Then the *Indian* holding fast the Stake, with a Ponyard he has in his other Hand, Wounds the Creature so often about the Gills, till it bleeds to Death. Then he drags it ashore with Ropes and Nooses, many *Indians* joyning to draw, and there is need of many, considering the Bulk of those Crocodiles. They are shap'd like Lizards, but arm'd with such strong Shells, that a Musket-shot makes little Impression on them, and they are scarce to be hurt, but only about the Gills, and under their short Legs, where Nature has plac'd a sort of sweet Odour, which the *Indians* make their Advantage of. These Islands, besides the Cattel, produce all that is found in *Africk*, as Tygers, Lions, Bears, Foxes, Monkeys, Apes, Squirrels, and some of them Abundance of Civet-Cats, which are much Hunted, in order to be sent into several Countries, with other Commodities of *China*, Callicoes, Silks, Porcelane, Iron, Copper, Steel, Quicksilver, and many more Yearly Transported from those Countries. The Religion and Government is now the same as in *Spain*; but in those which are not yet subdu'd, they follow an Extravagant Idolatry; believing the Soul Immortal, but wandering from one Body to another, according to that ridiculous Transmigration invented or publi'd by *Pythagoras*. They are much addicted to Trade, and forwarded in it by the Commerce

Birds.

Alligators.

How the Indians fight the Alligators.

Beasts.

Commodities.

with

with *China*. The *Philippine* People are braver than their Neighbours; the *Spaniards* and their Breed do not degenerate from their Original.

An Army was now forming of all thefe Sorts of People, by Order of the King, to attempt recovering the Forts of the *Moluccos*. *Don Ronquillo de Pennalofa* was then Governour there; and tho' he had receiv'd fome Intelligence brought him thence by Spies and Traders, yet not fatisfy'd with it, he fent thither another Soldier. He difguifed himfelf, and being like the Natives in Countenance, and fpeaking their Language to Perfection, got to *Tydore*. He found our People very earneft to forward that Enterprize, and that King ready to fupport it with all his Power. Thence he pafs'd over to *Ternate*, among Merchants, where he view'd the Forts, the Shoals of the Harbours; obferv'd their Correfpondence with the *Englifh*, and took notice how they Landed, and Traded in all Safety, or rather with Authority. Nor was he unacquainted with the Numbers of conceal'd Chriftians, who would take up Arms when a feafonable Opportunity was offer'd, or any other Particular, which belong'd to a Judicious Spy to enquire into. Hereupon *Ronquillo* gather'd about 300 *Spaniards*, and above 1500 Natives of the *Philippines*, with Ammunition, Provifions, and Seamen, and at the proper Seafon fent them for the *Moluccos* in three Great Ships, and a confiderable Number of Small Ones. *Peter Sarmiento*, a brave and experienc'd Officer, ftill living in thofe Iflands, when this was writ, went as General. He had Courage, and Force to deftroy any of the Enemies that then frequented thofe Seas. His Majefty had fome time before beftow'd the Government of *Ternate*, if it were Conquer'd, on *Paul de Lima*; and allow'd his Brother *Francis de Lima* to make two Voyages to the *Moluccos*, in Confideration of their Services, and thofe of *Henry* their Father. *Paul* was Marry'd to a Chriftian, and devout Lady, tho' a Kinfwoman to the King of *Ternate*, who was not fo. For this Reafon, and beoaufe he had been poffefs'd in *Ternate*, of the ancient Inheritance of the Villages of *Guita, Mofaquia, Mofaguita, Pavate, Pelveri, Sanfuma, Takane, Mayloa*, and *Soma*; and in the Ifland of *Machian* of *Sabele, Talapao, Talatoa, Mofabonana, Tabaloga, Tagono, Bobaba*, and *Molapa*; and in Regard the King of *Ternate*, had expell'd him moft of them, as alfo of *Bitua* in *Tydore*, and feveral other Places, he went over to *Manila*, as a Banifh'd Man, where he confer'd with the Governour, about the means of facilitating the Conqueft, juft before it was put in Execution. His Advice was of u'e, and he gave it, as one fo nearly concern'd; for befides the Inheritance the King of *Ternate* wrongfully with-held from him, he hop'd to recover the Ifland of *Moutil*, which belong'd to his Forefathers. The Enterprize was farther Authoriz'd by the Prefence of *Don John Ronquillo*, the Governour's Nephew, who had equal Power with *Sarmiento*, both by Sea and Land. If any thing was wanting, they thought the Defect would eafily be fupply'd by the Valour of the Soldiers, the Celerity of the Paffage, and the Enemies Surprize; but the divided Command was an Obftacle to their Hopes.

The Weather prov'd not very crofs, yet neither was it fo favourable, as that they could come directly to anchor at *Ternate*, as would have been moft convenient to deceive the Watchfulnefs of the Enemy. They arriv'd at *Moutil*, and fought a Parcel of *Janguas* in Sight of Land; which

were

Ronquillo's Preparations for the Moluccos.

The Forces fent under Sarmiento.

Paul de Lima rich in the Moluccos.

Don John Ronquillo joyn'd with Sarmiento.

Spaniards arrive at and take Moutil.

were taken, and the Chriſtians in them ſet at Liberty. *Paul de Lima* being well acquainted with the Bays, and there being no ſufficient Force in the Iſland to withſtand a Fleet, it eaſily ſubmitted, when attack'd in ſeveral Parts. The Natives came out with Palm, Citron, and Clove-Tree Branches, in Token of Peace, and to beg Pardon. Both were granted, and *Paul de Lima* appointed their Lord, tho' his New Dominion turn'd to little Account, for within a few Days, all the People ſlipp'd away, either becauſe they thought themſelves ſafer at *Ternate*, or to meet the Enemy, who of Neceſſity muſt carry the War over into that Iſland, as it happen'd. Here *Sarmiento* refitted the Ships, and being over-joy'd with this Succeſs, obtain'd without the Loſs of one Man, arriv'd at *Talangame*, paſſing amidſt the Enemies *Carcoas*, which they had fitted out in a Hurry. The King expected him long before in the Fort, well furniſh'd with our Cannon, particularly the Baſtion they had enlarg'd, and call'd *Cachil Tulo*, from the King's Uncle, who made it, and theſe Preparations ſeem'd to threaten any Diſaſter. Our Men landed on that Side, and were oppos'd by the *Ternates*; but Night put an End to the Fight, and both Parties retiring to their Faſtneſſes, our Cannon was landed, and planted in the Place, and after ſuch Manner as *Paul de Lima* directed, and ever ſince he commanded it in the Fort of *Tydore*. The King of this Iſland was willing to joyn our Camp, as had appear'd by ſome of his Actions, and his Promiſes to the Enſign *Duennas*; but he miſtruſted the Fortune of the *Spaniards*, as if he had not had ſufficient Experience of it. The Opportunity and Fidelity now invited him, and yet he forbore; his Doubtfulneſs is thought to have been prejudicial to the Succeſs. *Sarmiento* having planted his Cannon, intrench'd himſelf, and taking ſome Priſoners, of whom he learn'd what Proviſions and Amunition the Beſieged had, began to preſs on, and batter them furiouſly; yet they were not diſcourag'd, but anſwer'd boldly. It was found convenient to poſſeſs the upper Grounds, which over-looking the Place, tho' they have been ſince levell'd, our Men much incommoded the Enemy, and had they continu'd it, that would have put an End to the War. However there was ſo much Sickneſs in the Camp, that no Remedy was found againſt it, but going off ſo to ſave themſelves for a more favourable Seaſon. The Succours which came as Duties from *Tydore*, were very inconſiderable; the Allies were cold, and all Things weak; what other Cauſes there were Heaven knows. It is likely there were ſome of more Moment, for in ſhort the Army broke up, and reimbark'd for *Manila*, without doing any thing but adding to the Enemies Reſolution.

At that Time, only the *Engliſh* Nation diſturb'd the *Spaniſh* Sovereignty in thoſe Eaſtern Parts; for this Reaſon, King *Philip* was deſirous, not only for the preſent to curb them by Force of Arms, but to make them an Example to all other Nations, that they might not ſpread themſelves abroad to attempt ſuch Invaſions, as we are Eye-Witneſſes to. This Work was undertaken in the Year 1588, but firſt happen'd what we are now to relate. Queen *Elizabeth* of *England*, after a tedious Impriſonment, beheaded *Mary Stuart*, Queen of *Scotland*, for ſome Politick Reaſons, or Fictions. The then King of *Scotland*, and ſince of *England* alſo, Son to the Martyr, arm'd his People, ſtrengthen'd his Garriſons, and invaded the Dominion of the Enemy, who had caus'd him to be Motherleſs, and
more

Sarmiento in Ternate.

King of Tydore dubious.

Fort of Ternate batter'd.

The Siege raiſed.

State of Affairs in Europe.

more particularly the Marches about the River *Tweed*, and thofe of *Anandale*, water'd by the River *Solway*. The Queen call'd Home the Earl of *Leicefter*, who was in *Holland*, appointed him General, and War broke out in all thofe Northern Provinces, with apprehenfions of greater to enfue.

Queen Elizabeth's Practices. After many Events, which do not belong to this Place, Queen *Elizabeth* ftrengthned her Alliance with the *Dutch*, encouraging thofe Provinces to perfift in their Difobedience to the Church, and to King *Philip*, and advifing them, fince the King had forbid them trading in all the Reft of his Dominions, to go over into *India*, there to raife Commotions, and rob him of the Spice. The more fafely to compafs her Defigns, fhe fupported the *Flemmings* Obftinacy, flattering herfelf with the Hopes of a new Monarchy, for the acquiring whereof, fhe propos'd to make ufe of the Wealth yearly brought from the North and South Seas, for *Spain*, the Robbing of which had already made an Addition to her Power; as alfo of the Factories erected for Trade in the *Moluccos*, *Banda*, *Sumatra*, *Ceylon*, and the two *Javas*; where fhe kept Garrifons, in order to convert the Friendfhip into Sovereignty.

King Philip's mighty Fleet. King *Philip*, whofe great Soul ever entertain'd both Forbearance, and Counfel, refolv'd to cut off the Heads of this *Hydra* at the Neck they all fprung from. He gather'd, for the Conqueft of *England*, the mightieft Fleet that has been feen on the Ocean in our Days. Twenty Thoufand fighting Men were put aboard tall Ships, befides 9000 Sailors, with 1730 Pieces of Cannon, Abundance of Ammunition, and Pikes and Fire-Arms for the Catholicks, who it was hop'd, as foon as they faw the *Spanifh* Colours, would joyn our Army. Don *Alonfo Perez de Guzman*, Duke of *Medina Sidonia* commanded in Chief, and was to joyn the Prince of *Parma*, **And Army againft England.** then Governour of *Flanders*, who had Commiffion to raife another Army of 30000 Horfe and Foot, with the Neceffary Provifions and Ammunition, which he was to tranfport at a fit Seafon to that Point of *England*, where the *Thames* falls into the Sea, to march thence to *London*, and there Arm the Catholicks. But it was firft requifite to beat the *Englifh* at Sea, where they were then powerful, and well acquainted with the proper Times to fail and keep at Home. At the leaft they were to be terrify'd, that they might not dare to obftruct the Paffage of the Troops, the Prince of *Parma* had in readinefs at *Dunkirk* and *Newport*, or hinder their embarking, when the *Spanifh* Fleet fhould come thither to waft them over. this Fleet fail'd from *Lisbon* on the 29th of *May*, 1588, and as foon as out fuffer'd much by the Weather, fo that three Gallies were caft away, on **They fuffer by Storms.** the Coaft of *Bayonne*. Abundance of the Powder blew up; and the General was oblig'd to return to *Corunna*, to refit; whence he could not get out till the 2d of *July*.

Arrive at the Lizard Being come into 48 Degrees of Latitude, he fent away Don *Lewis de Guzman* to give Advice to the Prince of *Parma*, and on the laft of the fame Month arriv'd himfelf at the *Lizard*, in *Cornwall*, where he lay by. and was certainly inform'd, that all the Enemy's Ships, being fifty in number, lay in *Plymouth*. The *Englifh* Admiral at Break of Day difcover'd ours, **Spanifh Ship taken.** and tho' he wanted neither Strength, nor Experience in Sea Affairs, he refolved to draw off and avoid ingaging, but his Ships being lighter incommoded us in the Rear. In the Catholick Fleet, a great Ship of *Guipufcoa* blew

blew up, and another of *Andaluzia* spent her Main-Maft, in which Diftrefs, two *Englifh* Ships attacking her, and thofe afterwards feconded by others, in one of which Sir *Francis Drake* was, they took her. There *Don Pedro de Valdes*, a *Spanifh* Commander of known Valour, and then Lieutenant General, was made Prifoner, with whom they fent to *Plymouth*, a great Quantity of Crown Pieces, and fifty Great Guns. About 4co *Spaniards* were kill'd, and taken. On the 2*d* and 4*th* of *Auguft*, the Lord *Howard*, and *Drake* joyn'd their Squadrons, fome write they had an hundred Sail, all well Mann'd, and light, with which they infefted ours, which were heavy, and encumber'd, particularly the *Portuguefe* Galleon, call'd the *S. John*, being the greateft in the Fleet, and in it were *John Martinez de Recalde*, the Count *de Paredes*, the Marques *de la Favara*, and other Commanders of Note. However they got to the Ifle of *Wight*, whence the Duke fent away two Meffengers to the Prince of *Parma*, who was then at *Bruffels*, defiring he would furnifh him with Powder and Ball, for the Defence of the Fleet, and imbark what Troops he had ready. But he, either prevented by invincible Obftacles, or for other Reafons, which have left that Prince's Reputation *Difap-* expos'd to Cenfures, mov'd fo flowly, that what had been fo maturely con- *pointment* certed took no Effect. The Enemy boafting, that the Sea and Winds had *of the Fleet* fought againft us, in Vindication, as they faid of their Caufe, made pub- lick Rejoycings, firing their Cannon; and foon after the Queen put forth a Proclamation to the fame Effect, againft which a certain *Englifh* Religious Man writ learnedly, by the Name of *Andrew Philopator*.

The *Dutch* who were in Confederacy with Queen *Elizabeth*, feeing this Succefs, were encourag'd to afpire to greater Matters, renouncing their Re- *The Dutch* ligion, and their Sovereign, attempting to ufurp the Treafures of the Eaft, *afpire.* Mines, Spice, Drugs, and Silks, as appears by their bold Voyages, wherein they have endeavour'd to follow the frefh Examples of the *Englifh*, and the ancient fet them by *Columbus, Albuquerque, Magellan, Gama*, and *Cortes*, as we fhall fee hereafter. But, both they and the *Englifh*, if they try the Juftice of their Caufe by the Succefs of that Fleet, muft be oblig'd to pre- fer the Caufe of the Gentiles, when God for his Secret Judgments permit- ted his own chofen People to be over-thrown. Deftruction is more glori- ous than Profperity; and a religious Soul will rather chufe to be caft down than Victorious, if an angry God is to give it the Victory.

After this *Santiago de Vera* govern'd the *Philippine* Iflands, and by fpe- cial Order, arm'd againft *Ternate*, where the *Englifh* from that Time tra- *Another* ded with all poffible Security. All Nations had fettled Factories except *Expedi-* the *Javanefes* and *Lafcarines*. Above 2500 *Mahometans* from *Mecca* preach'd *tion from* their Abominations. They fear'd nothing from *Portugal*, all their Ap- *the Phi-* prehenfion was from the *Spaniards*, who were newly ingag'd to feek Re- *lippines.* venge. The King of *Ternate* well knew that *Sarmiento* and *Ronquillo* would have taken it, had not Difeafes prevented them. When the News of frefh Preparations came to *Tydore*, it was carry'd over by Spies to *Ter- nate*. That King prefently call'd together his Subjects, efpecially the Iflanders of *Machian* and *Homer*, who came in 40 *Carcoas*, becaufe their Iflands were very populous. The Number had been greater, but that the *King of* King would not fuffer more to be fitted out than he demanded, for he could *Ternate* nct conceal his Fear that they would rebel, thofe Parts being full of Chri- *prepares.* ftians,

ftians, and the Taxes he laid on the People intolerable. *Santiago de Vera* appointed *John Morones* General, who wanted not for Conduct, nor his Men for Valour, nor the Fleet for Cannon and Ammunition. But whether Natural Ambition, or any other Accident was the Occasion of it, there were such Divisions among them, that they had sufficient Grounds to miftruft the Event, before they left *Manila.* They fet fail with fair Weather, and pafs'd the greateft Dangers of the Sea, and when they thought themfelves fafeft, all the Elements feem'd to confpire againft the Fleet. They loft the Light, and their Reckning, the Veffels were fhatter'd, and the greateft of *Spanifh* them funk, and all the Men loft. This was the Galleon *S. Hellen*, which *Fleet lofes* carry'd the Guns to batter the Fort, and many other Neceffaries and Stores. *a great* For all this, they infifted upon proceeding, and the King of *Bachian* affifted *Galleon.* them with what Forces he had rais'd, under Colour of clearing the Sea of fome Enemies ; and being a Chriftian baptiz'd, lamented his departing from our holy Faith, on Account of Perfecution, and promis'd the Reftitution of his Soul.

Spanifh   The Weather growing calm, when they were in Sight of *Ternate*, the *General* *Carcoas* durft not ftand them, but fled at the firft Difcharges, which they *refufes the* can do without receiving any Damage. Therefore the two Kings, and *Paul* *beft Advice* *de Lima*, advis'd to fall on in feveral Places. *Ferdinand Boto Machado*, Captain of a Galleon, was of the fame Opinion; but the General fufpecting the former, on Account of his Affinity, and the latter for the Friendfhip he had lately contracted with the King of *Tydore*, whom he was not well fatisfy'd with, would not follow their Advice; alledging, That it was not convenient, by dividing the Forces, to weaken them more than the Storm had done. He laid Siege to the Fort, but the Befieged being acquainted *Befieges* with the Condition of our Troops, oppos'd all their Affaults courageoufly, *the Fort of* and fcoff'd and laugh'd at the infignificant Batteries. However our Men, *Ternate.* whom the Storms had depriv'd of Neceffaries for that Work, vented their Spleen upon the *Javanefe.* Thefe valu'd themfelves upon fallying out to Skirmifh, being diftinguifhable by their Arms, and manner of drawing up. The *Spaniards* handled them fo roughly, that they did little more during the War. Some Months were fpent in Fruitlefs Attempts, and if they had attack'd the Country, but a Culverine-Shot fhort of the Fort, at the Bay of *Limathao*, and march'd thence to attack the Fort behind, as the moft underftanding defir'd, it had been of good Confequence. But the General *Morones*, putting all upon Experience without Forecaft, was fatisfy'd with fronting next the Sea, doing much Harm, which was caus'd by that firft, and obftinate manner of attacking; and that gave Way for Succours to go into the Natives, at other landing Places, tho' thirty Men at a fmall Diftance might have prevented it. This both the Kings maintain'd, whofe Valour, which ought to be commended even in Enemies, if our General had pleas'd, might have given Succefs to this Undertaking. Befides that experience has fhown that fifty *Spaniards* have done as much upon Occafion, as whole *Roman* Legions well arm'd and difciplin'd.

Sends fome   *Morones* now perceiving that neither his Arms, nor his Propofals had *Men to the* any effect upon the Rebels, he refolv'd to pafs over fome of his Men againft *other Fort.* the other Fort, which, tho' feated on a Ground of difficult Accefs, feem'd to be pregnable, becaufe built in Hafte, a League from the former on a fteep Hill.

Hill. On the Land Side of it is the Mountain, and on the Back a Lake, and is of no ufe, becaufe it does not defend the City, which is open, and is only regarded for being near the old Fort. Our Men went on chearfully, and the Defendants receiv'd them as well firing their Cannon, which gave a Check to the *Spanifh* Fury. Thofe in the other Fort, tho' they made little ufe of Fire-Arms, being compell'd by Neceffity, ventur'd to fally out to the Shore. To draw them to this Refolution, fome of our Men on a fudden fet Fire to the *Junks*, in which a great Namber of *Javanefe Indians* had come thither. The Veffels, which were old blaz'd up, without any Obftruction from thofe who guarded them, but they referr'd the Remedy to their Weapons. They were in all about 3000 fighting Men, 1000 of them had Muskets, whereof 200 were expert at them ; the reft neither Pikes, nor Lances, nor any other long fort of Arms, but only thofe they call *Toranas*, about a Fathom in Length, like Darts, and fome like Arrows, which they caft by main Strength, with Canes and Strings, wherewith they unexpectedly wound unarm'd Men in Fight; becaufe they fly not out of a Bow, but are thrown ftrait forward, or over their Heads. Others had only their *Campilanes*, or Cymiters, and Shields. Many of them fought the more obftinately, confiding in their Coats of Mail, and Head-Pieces, bought of the *Portuguefes*; but as foon as they clos'd with our Men, they broke their Order, and loft Courage. This Accident prov'd a very great Obftacle, becaufe it diverted our Men from their double Defign of preffing both Forts at the fame Time, fo that the very Commanders were forc'd to ingage. *Morones* knew how to behave himfelf upon all Occafions, and the Spaniards made fuch a Slaughter, that almoft all the *Javanefos* lay upon the Spot. Thofe in the Forts had not the Courage to fall in upon the Rear, tho' they pour'd a Volley upon the Forces of *Tydore* and *Bachian*, but with little Harm. This Victory was not gain'd without Effufion of Blood, yet they took Heart to hope for one more compleat, at the Arrival of the Galeon from *India*, and believ'd that Addition of Strength would make amends for what they loft in the Storm.

Javanefe Ships burnt

Bloody Victory gain'd by the Spaniards.

The Galeon arriv'd at *Tydore*, better provided to carry on the Trade, than the War. For this Reafon, and becaufe many of our Men were Sick, or Wounded, *Morones* was oblig'd to raife the Siege, and difmift thofe Kings, to whom he afterwards fent Prefents of *Spanifh* Commodities, fome Horfes and Silks. It was fince known that tho' the *Ternates* will endure much Hardfhip, they were then fo near prefs'd, that Hunger muft have fubdu'd them, could our Men have ftay'd a little longer. They embark'd in Sight of the Enemy, who prefently appear'd in the Field rejoycing, with Mufick, and other Tokens of Victory. The *Afiatick* Traders reforted to their Ports, and others from *Europe*, but particularly their new Friends the *Englifh*, with whom they communicated the Joy of their Succefs.

The Siege rais'd.

They never made a good ufe of Peace and Quietnefs at *Ternate*, as foon as that was now reftor'd, the King was again at Variance with his Unkles; which Fortune fo improv'd as to furnifh an Opportunity that might have been advantageous to our Defigns, had not fhe thwarted it. *Cachil Mandraxa* was the nobleft of Sultan *Aerio's* Sons, as born of the Queen hey call *Putriz*, which is the Chief. His Father would have had him fucceed in the Throne, but was difgufted at a Boldnefs which does not ufe to be mif-

Notable Practices.

R   lik'd

lik'd among Politicians. *Cachil Mandraxa* was defperately in love with *Filola*, his Niece, Daughter to the King his Brother ; and that Princes did not refufe her Unkles Courtfhip. The Father one Day found them talking together, in the Apartment referv'd only for himfelf; and tho' he was fatisfied their Converfation was within the Bounds of Decency, took fuch an Averfion, that he depriv'd him of the Succeffion.   The illegitimate Ne-

phew Reign'd, againft the Will of all the Unkles, who were near confpiring to kill him ; but the fubtle King knew how to difappoint their Defigns, and fecure himfelf without difcovering the Contrivance. He call'd *Cachil Mandraxa* to him, and repeating all paft Diftates, told him, how defirous he was to remove all manner of Jealoufies by a perfect Reconciliation, which he thought might be done by means of the Princefs *Filola,* and fince there was fuch a good Correfpondence between them, all the Reft would be eafie. However before he gave her to him to Wife, he muft reflect that fhe was promis'd to the King of *Tydore*, to whom he was not willing to adminifter frefh Caufes of War, or to be the Occafion of interrupting that fhort Tranquility they enjoy'd.   That fince all they difcours'd there would remain in their Breafts, he would have him to take his Advice.   *Mandraxa* was befide himfelf, with that unexpected Satisfaction, and yet had he been truly Mafter of himfelf, he might eafily have feen thro' the Fraud of that plea-

fing Change in his Condition, wherein he found the King fo much his Friend, who but juft before had been his Enemy.   He thank'd him for the Favour, and putting his whole Dependance on the Words of his Mouth, defir'd he would give him the Advice he fpoke of.   The King anfwer'd, *I have contriv'd a Way, which will fatisfie you, and the King of* Tydore *will have no Caufe to complain.   For the attaining of both thefe Ends, I will keep Council, as is requifite, and do you any Night fteal away the Princefs, the Way you fhall beft like, fo it be with Regard to my Reputation, and in all Refpects giving fuch outward Tokens, that all Men may believe it was open Violence, and no Contrivance, or at leaft known to me.   I, on my Side, will pretend to be very Angry, and will complain of the Injury as loudly as is requifite to fatisfie the World of my Innocence.   For why fhould I, Unkle, wifh for the Felicities of this World, but to make them common to our Family? I will retain the Cares of the Crown, and do you enjoy the Satisfaction the Kingdom affords.   Mandraxa* could not forbear Weeping for Joy, he fell down at his Nephew's Feet and kifs'd them, without difguizing any thing of his Paffion, yet fuppreffing the Joy of his new Hopes, the beft he could, he found Means to acquaint the Princefs, and to appoint the Hour, Place, and Confidents for expofing herfelf to be ftolen away.

To this Purpofe they pitch'd upon a Garden, which looks out upon the Sea, adorn'd with its Natural Trees, whence the Ships are feen, and among them, on the Day prefix'd they fpy'd a *Carcoa,* with all the Men that Row'd curioufly drefs'd and they and the Soldiers wearing Garlands, plainly fhow'd the Defign of their Voyage, tho' they row'd without the Mufick they ufe to have at other Times.   *Mandraxa* and a fmall but brave Number of his Friends landed as filently, and they after the manner of *Talafio*, and the ancient *Romans*, when they forc'd away the *Sabine* Women, laid Hold of *Filola* and the Reft, and run them aboard with all poffible Speed, conveying them to a ftrong Place in the Ifland, where having fortify'd himfelf,

like

like a Soldier, *Mandraxa* devote himself to Love. Fame the utter Enemy to Secrecy divulg'd the Fact, and convey'd it over to the King of *Tydore*'s Ears, with the King of *Ternate*'s Complaints. He magnify'd the Affront, and every Man spoke of it, according to his own Notion. The King who had contriv'd it, and by whose Breath all the Machines of that Tragedy were mov'd assembled the prime Men of his Kingdom, most of them Enemies to the deluded *Mandraxa*, and ask'd their Assistance and Advice in so notorious a Violence, and pretending extraordinary Concern. They all Voted to a Man, that it was absolutely necessary to make such an Example as might deter others from the like. When the Consultation was over, the King dispatch'd Messengers to his Unkle, intreating him to repair to Court to stop all Mouths by fair Means, and appease the Neighbouring Princes. *Cachil Mandraxa* made no difficulty to obey, as well knowing that none of his Actions had been contrary to the King's Orders. Only the Princess advis'd the Contrary; for tho' young, as little above 20 years of Age, she was better acquainted with her Brother, and well knew he never kept his Faith, particularly with his own Family, and that he could not have any Kindness for them as being jealous of the Crown. *Mandraxa* made no Account of all that, but went to Court, and enter'd the Palace attended by his Family, and relying on the King's Promise, but more especially on the secret Mystery of that Affair, known only to them two, Unkle and Nephew. When he came to kiss the King's Hand, he looking as stern as if he had not advis'd the stealing of the Princess, said he knew not what Course to take upon so notorious an Affront offer'd to his Crown and Palace, but to cut off his Head. *Mandraxa* thinking at first that had been all Counterfeit, and according to what had been agreed between them, when he perceiv'd it was barefac'd falsehood, would have spoke loud in Defence of his Innocence; but was not permitted, and the King making a Sign to a Sturdy Black he had prepar'd for that Action, he drew his Cymiter, and hew'd him down barbarously. The poor Prince fell, without being reliev'd by any Man; for at that Time his Brothers *Cachil Tulo*, and *Cachil Sufur* were not at *Ternate*, the former being Governor, the latter Admiral. Nor did they come to *Ternate* in a long Time after, tho' they took Care to protect the Widdow Princess, who was left with Child, and afterwards brought forth *Cachil Amida*, who dy'd Young.

The whole Truth of this Matter was soon known, with all its Particulars, and Circumstances; and the *Cachiles* conferring together, *Tulo* resolv'd to go over to the Service of King *Philip*, to which Purpose, when *Duarte Pereyra* was Commander in Chief at *Tydore*, he went thither to treat with him, and with *Antony de Matos*, who went first for the same End to *Bachian*, but forasmuch as what was concerted among them, will better appear by the Letter *Cachil Tulo* sent from *Tydore* to the Governour *Santiago de Vera*, we will here insert it, translated from the *Malaye* Language, by the King's *Naguatatos*, so they there call the Interpreters.

Cachil Babu, *my Brother, late King of* Ternate, *writ to the King of Portugal, to desire he would do him Justice, upon a Man, who murder'd his Father and mine; upon receiving which Satisfaction, he would again deliver the Fort of* Ternate *to his Majesty, it being then out of his Possession.*

Base false-hood of t'e King.

He murders Mandraxa.

The King's Unkles conspire against him.

Cachil Tulo's Letter to the Governor of the Philippines.

His present Majesty succeeding in the Throne of Portugal, *answer'd my Brother's Letter, by* Cachil Naique, *his Embassador; but when he return'd my Brother was dead, which was the Reason we did not then deliver up the Fort, because a Bastard Son had succeeded him, being proclaim'd King by the People of* Ternate, *with the Assistance of the King of* Tydore, *tho' he had no Right to it. He would not perform what his Father had promis'd, and he was oblig'd to; nor follow the Advice given him by me, and by my Brother* Cachil Mandraxa, *the rightful Heir of the Crown; which was that he should deliver up the Fort, as his Father had promis'd, to the Portuguese; and this, not because he could not defend himself against them, and his Majesty; but expresly because his Father, and my Brother had so order'd, for we did not suppose it could be taken from us by Force of Arms; but we knew it was his Will to serve his Majesty, by delivering up the Fort to him. He finding we persisted in this Opinion, resolv'd to murder my Brother, and his own Unkle, the true Heir of the Crown, cutting him in Pieces, by the Hands of a Slave, when he came upon his Word, and had his Security and mine. Wherefore considering the Injustice of my Nephew upon this Occasion, and that he will not perform what his Father, my Brother and I promised to his Majesty, I am resolv'd from this Time forward, to become his Majesty's sincere Subject and Servant. And I do by these Presents, oblige my self, and swear by my Law, as I did swear, and do not depart from it, to the Father Vicar* Antony Ferreyra, *to give all my Help and Assistance, towards the taking of the Fort, with all my Kindred and Friends, till it shall be in the Possession of his Majesty's Commander, or whosoever shall come with the Portugueses, or Spaniards that attend him; upon Condition, that the Commander, or Commanders, shall, in his Majesty's Name, perform what* Duarte Pereyra, *the Commander in chief promis'd me and sign'd for him, I having given him a Counterpart; which is, that I shall be proclaim'd King of* Ternate, *as soon as Possession is taken of the Fort for his Majesty; both in regard it belongs to me in Right of my Father, and of the Service I now do, and hereafter hope to do his Majesty. I therefore beg it as a Favour of your Lordship, and require you in his Majesty's Name, that you take Care to send the greatest Number of Men you possibly can, and with the greatest Expedition; to the End that this my Intention, and Will to serve his Majesty herein may be effectual, which I hope will be without the Expence of Lives; notwithstanding the Fort is well fortify'd, as your Lordship may have been inform'd. The Commander in chief, will write to your Lordship, what Season and Order those Forces are to observe. Given at* Tydore, *to which Place I am come to this Intent, as will be testify'd by the Father Vicar* Antony Ferreyra, *and the Judge* Antony de Matos, *whom, as Persons of such Note, I desir'd to sign for me. May the 23d.*

Nunno Pereyra's Perswasions to the same Governor. At the Bottom of the Letter, the Vicar and *Matos* certify'd his Hand and Subscription. With this came another very long one, wherein *Duarte Pereyra* gives the Governour a more ample Account of what is here deliver'd briefly, representing to him the Opportunity offer'd in forcible Terms. He tells him that *Mandraxa* a little before his Death, had propos'd the same thing to him, that his Brother *Tulo* now did; and that they were desirous to fulfill what they promis'd *Nunno Pereyra.* That the Island

Ifland of *Machian*, the moft fruitful in Clove, Efpous'd the Party that was againft the King. That they could no longer endure their Oppreffion. He perfwaded him to Arm 400 *Spaniards*, if they were come from *Mexico*, anto Ship them off for the Expedition upon *Ternate*, giving out, that they were going to clear thofe Seas from *Javanefes*, whofe Friendfhip the People of *Ternate* value more than they do ours. That befides the good Succefs he expected by the Help of thofe Forces, they would at leaft fecure thofe Ports againft the *Englifh*, the People of *Ternate* having always a Fleet in Readinefs. That the Enterprize might fucceed with Fifteen Frigates, and one Galeon, provided they went to ftay a Year at the *Moluccos*, and brought a Number of *Philippine*-Pioneers. He fays, the *Javanefe* Ships are lefs than the Frigats, and there are Forty Soldiers in each of them, who lye Aboard Eight Months, and live a Year upon 300 Bufhels of Rice. That in Cafe the Frigates could not hold the Men, they fhould bring fome Junks, which are neceffary Veffels to Tranfport Provifions from the Iflands of *Burro* and *Bachian*. He complains of the King of *Tydore's* ill Behaviour, and his Avarice; of *Sancho de Vafconcelos*, and *James de Azambuja*, who built the Fort of *Tydore* in an ill place. He commends the King of *Bachian*, and fays he in private lives like a Chriftian. Among thefe Things he intermixes many more, all of them tending to perfwade the Expedition of *Ternate*, to blot out the laft Difgrace, without any Expence to the King, through *Cachil Tulo's* Contrivance.

The Governour receiv'd this Difpatch, and he would willingly have put it in Execution immediately; but as it went on flowly, and the Death of *Cachil Tulo* happened in the mean while, it was requifite to delay the Defign, and attend to the Prefervation of the *Philippine* Iflands, againft the Machinations of the *Chinefes* and *Japonefes*, againft whofe Robberies and Burnings they are never fecure. Each of thefe Attempts harafs'd the Province with the Expence of Treafure, and Power, fo that there was a neceffity of breathing to recover both. It was thought the moft proper Advice to join from the *Philippines* and *Malaca*, with equal Force, coming from both Parts to Arm in the *Moluccos*, which was the Boundary of both Provinces. This took Effect fome Years after, Captain *Andrew Furtado* coming from *Malaca*, of whofe Actions it will be proper to begin to fpeak to give a Reputation to his Perfon.

Andrew Furtado de Mendoza might have Ennobled his Family, had it not been of antient Quality. He was the Terror of thofe Eaftern Parts, where he ferv'd the King ever fince the Year 1576, fubduing Barbarous Nations. In the Year 1587 he was Governour of the Fort of *Rachol*, till he came to have that of *Malaca*. Whilft he was in the firft, fome Villages of Gentiles rofe up againft the Minifters of the Church, difturbing Chriftianity with Warlike Diforders. *Furtado* pacify'd them with Severity, and his Authority. In 1591 *Furtado* was Commander of the *Portuguefe* Soldiery in that *Archipelago*, and was very earneft to employ them in the Recovery of *Ternate*; but was hinder'd by other Wars, which he concluded Victorioufly. In *Auguft* that fame Year, he was inform'd that Eighteen Galeons had put out of *Cunnal*, Commanded by *Cutumaza*, affifted by *Raju*, with a Defign to Befiege the Fort of *Ceylon*. This *Cutumaza* had the Year before Burnt a Ship of ours, Sailing for *China*, and made

The Projects for executing the Defign.

Andrew Furtado his Actions.

difmal

dismal Havock on the Coast of *Coromandel*. *Furtado* went out in Search of the Enemies Fleet, and by the way reliev'd the Fort of *Ceylon* ; and on the Coast of *Malabar* he met three Ships Bound from *Mecca* for *Cunnal*. He fought them, and Sunk two, the Sea running so high, that the Vessels which Row'd could not attack them. The other after a long Dispute yielded to him. This Victory was a sufficient Revenge for the Burning of our Ships. Continual War is maintain'd in these Parts, which Neighbour upon *Malaca* ; and that in *Ceylon* never ceases, contrary to the Advice of Persons that are well acquainted with *India* ; because the best Product of that Island being the Cinnamon, a Commodity of less Durance than the Mace, Clove and Pepper, they look upon almost all the expence laid upon *Ceylon*, as good as thrown away. Besides that the greatest Commanders are employ'd in suppressing the continual Rebellions of those most inconstant People, without stretching out, at least as far as the *Moluccos*, by their Absence encouraging their Tyranny, and giving Opportunity to Nations that are our Enemies to fix themselves in our Forts

Ceylon *describ'd.*   *Ceylon* is one of the most Remarkable Islands in the World, and the most fruitful. It lies opposite to Cape *Comorin*, Nobly Inhabited, and cultivated. In it grow all Plants, known in all other Parts of the World, Nutmegs, Pepper, Cinnamon, and the most Excellent call'd *Mosyllion* grows in this Island. Here is Wild and Garden Fruit, *Spanish* Figs, and Grapes, and the best Oranges in all *Asia*. There are whole Woods of mighty Palm-Trees. The Variety of Flowers, would take up much Time to describe it ; as also of Grain known to us, Wheat, Rice, and Flax, of which and their Cotton, they make wonderful Webs. It has all sorts of Precious Stones, Gold, Silver, Steel, Tin, Iron, and Seed Pearl.

Product.   Several Christaline Rivers, and Fountains moisten it, with delightful and Medicinal Waters, of Excellent Qualities. And among the rest there are Springs of Liquid Bitumen, thicker than our Oyl, and some of pure Balsam. There are Burning Mountains continually blazing, and casting out Clods of Brimstone among the Crags of the Hills ; where there are Groves

Birds.   of Tall Trees, on whose Branches are to be seen all sorts of Birds that fly in other Parts of the World, and among them our Turkys, Wild Hens, and Pidgeons. It abounds in Deer, Wild-Boars, Tygers, Lions, and

Beasts.   Elephants of so Noble a Kind, that all others submit to them. Those that are bred in this Island have such an Extraordinary Natural Instinct, that it

Elephants.   verifies what *Aristotle*, *Plutarch*, *Athenæus*, *Ælian*, *Pliny*, and others, who have Writ Natural History testifie, and is, that whether it proceeds from Knowledge, or Habit, they partake of the Wit, Sense, and even of the Prudence of Men. We are told they have so much Sense of Honour, that they will not go Aboard a Ship, if they imagine they are carry'd to serve Princes in strange Countries, and that they obey, if their Owners swear they will bring them back to their own. That they are concern'd at abusive Words given them. That they pay a sort of Religious Respect to the Sun and Moon. That they remember such Things as they conceive ; and *Gellius* perswades us we may believe, that at Night they bewail their Servitude with doleful Complaints ; and if any Man happens to come near in the Height of their Lamentation, they with shame suppress their Sighs ;

and

and in short, they seem sensible of the Iniquity of their Fate. In this Country it is their Part to load and unload Ships, the Weight of Commerce, whether Arms, Metals, Provisions, or other Commodities whatsoever hanging on their Teeth, or lying on their Necks. They are more willing to carry Arm'd Men on their Backs, in great Castles built to that purpose They serve the *Chingalas*, not as they did in *Rome* at publick Shows, but in Battel, as they did the *Carthaginians*, and afterwards the *Romans*. The People of *Ceylon* believe their Country is the Terrestrial Paradise. They call the Top of a certain Mountain *Adam's Point*, and on it, they say, is to be seen the Print of his Foot, and that there he did Pennance. Upon this Belief, the *Jognes*, who are penitent Pilgrims, visit that Point, where they affirm there grows a thick Tree, of an indifferent Height, with small rough Leaves, of a dusty Colour, the Bark Ash-colour'd, which in the Night shines, and dispells Darkness Under Colour of this Superstition, all the Gangs of strowling Players or Actors, come out of this Island, and travel throughout all *India*, representing their Fables, with odd Gestures, and Dancing to little Flat Tabors, Bag-pipes, and Rattles of small Bells. Abundance of Pearls are found about it. The Gold and other Metals are kept untouch'd in the Mines, by publick Law, and yet notwithstanding this Precaution, they are not free from War and Oppression. The Natives are call'd *Chingalas*, and resemble the *Malabars* in Customs and Countenances. They have broad Noses, but are not so black, and go naked, but not to immodesty. Formerly they had but one King, who was dispossess'd by Force, and Treachery, and the Kingdom divided among many. Division having thus weaken'd them, a Barbarian, call'd *Raju*, tyrannically expell'd the King the Island ; one of whom was by the Magnificence of the Kings of *Portugal* bred at *Goa*.

Raju was a subtle Soldier, and jealous even of those that supported him. He had some Years before, besieg'd the Fort of *Columbo*, with a great Body of Foot, Elephants and Horse. *Andrew Furtado* being in search of the Enemies Fleet, in Prosecution of his Revenge for the Ships lost, to relieve the Fort of *Columbo*, doubled Cape *Comorin*, thro' the Streight of *Ceylon*, at the Time when it is usually most difficult and dangerous for Tall Ships, much more for such Vessels as use Oars. He came to the Fort so opportunely, that had he stay'd never so little longer it had been lost, for most of the Garrison had mutiny'd against their Commander in Chief *Simon de Brito* who was wounded by them with two Musket Balls. *Raju* was marching with all Expedition by Land to *Columbo* for fear of slipping the Opportunity offer'd him of taking Possession of it. *Cutumuza* lay with all his Fleet in the River *Cordiva*, distant from the Fort ready to attack it by Sea, when *Raju* fell on by Land. *Furtado* was before-hand with him, and getting in, dispos'd all Things for its Defence. He quell'd the Mutiny, punish'd the Ring-leaders, satisfy'd such as had just Cause of Complaint or had been wrong'd, and with all possible Speed went out to find *Cunnale's* Fleet. Nor was he disappointed, for the Enemy did not offer to fly, but met him, with his Ships drawn up in good Order, and after Cannonading, they laid one another aboard, where there was an obstinate Fight on both Sides, till *Cunnale's* Navy was defeated. *Furtado* took 14 Galeons, with all their Artillery, and Men, besides Abundance kill'd. The Admiral

Opinion that Paradise is in Ceylon.

Strange Tree.

Players.

King's expell'd.

Furtado relieves Columbo.

Beats the Indian Fleet.

ral

ral fled with only four Ships of 18 he had, and made to *Raju's* Country. This Victory was sufficient Satisfaction for the Damage receiv'd by that rebellious Fleet, the ill Success whereof discourag'd *Raju* from coming to besiege *Columbo*, so that he retir'd and dismiss'd his Army.

Not long after, *Furtado* was inform'd by his Spyes, that the King of *Jasanapatan* had concluded a League with *Raju*, pressing him to return to the Siege of *Columbo*, whilst he did the same to *Mana*. That his Presumption might not want such Punishment, as became the Honour of the Crown of *Portugal*, and the Reputation of its Grandeur, which is more prevalent in those Parts than Force, *Furtado* gathering what Power he could, with all possible Celerity attack'd that King. He was not unprovided, but drawing

Routs him, and sub-dues his Kingdom.

up without the Walls of that City, offer'd him Battel, his Men, Elephants and Horses covering spacious Fields. *Furtado* playing both Parts of a Commander, and a Soldier, drew up his Forces, encourag'd them in few Words ; and both Sides coming to the Charge exercis'd their Force and Fury ; but at Length the King's Troops were routed, and he slain entering the City, in which abundance of Brass Cannon was found, besides the Plunder, which was considerable. He took Possession of it, and seizing the Forts and Garrisons, carry'd on the War there in such Manner, that the whole Kingdom seeing such severe Execution, and feeling it so heavily within its Bowels, submitted to the King of *Spain*. By his Authority, when the Sword was put up, he appointed a Kinsman of the late King, to whom of Right it belonged, to reign in *Jasanapatan*, he having been taken in the last Battel. He caus'd him to swear and plight his Faith, that he would be a perpetual Vassal to his Majesty ; imposing on him the Payment of a yearly Tribute, which still subsists. The Writings containing this Settlement were sent by him into *Spain*, where and at *Goa*, all that had been done was approv'd of by the Viceroy, and the Conqueror, who had concluded it so happily, highly applauded.

Ternate the Cause of Rebellions.

He next Strengthned the Fort of *Columbo*, with Four Ships of his Fleet, and 100 Soldiers ; and Supply'd *Cosme de la Feta* with Eighty Men, under Two Captains, to prosecute the Affair of *Candia*, which was committed to him, and sorted good effect. No Rebellion broke out in those Parts, but what was either supported by *Ternate*, or proceeded from its Example, and great Celerity was requisite in the Commanders for suppressing of it.

Coast of Pearl Fi-shery Re-bells, and is reduc'd.

At this same Time all the Coast of the Pearl Fishery rebell'd, and among other sudden Destruction usually made by Seditious Men in Arms, the Subjects of *Viapanaique* burnt Twenty five Christian Churches. *Furtado* made all possible speed to chastize them before the Rebellion grew to a Head. The Mutineers not being well Strengthned, sent Embassadors to him, begging Peace, and colouring their Guilt with Excuses, which *Furtado* admitted of because it was convenient for his Majesties Service ; upon Condition they should make good all the Damages occasion'd by their Revolt. He commanded them to rebuild the Churches they had destroy'd, and to grant the Society of the *Jesuits*, who had then the Charge of the Christians in that Country, all the Liberties and Immunities demanded by those then residing there ; taking sufficient Hostages for the Performance

These

These and other no less notable Actions, he perform'd in the space of four Months; but as Envy seldom fails to oppose Valour, when he came to Cochin, and was there ready to set out for the Conquest of the Moluccos, and particularly of Ternate, he received Letters from the Viceroy, Matthias de Albuquerque commanding him to deliver up the Fleet to Nunno Vello Pereyra. He obey'd, and when he came to Goa, was Imprisoned, and put to Trouble. As soon as it was in his Power, he resolv'd to depart India, and remove himself from the ill-will of those he thought were not his Friends; but the City of Goa conjur'd him not to forsake it, and in vain endeavour'd to procure a Reconciliation betwixt those Commanders. This happened in the Year 1592, when, and some Years after, Ternate might have been reliev'd, as Furtado desir'd, had not the Animosities reigning obstructed it. However they were so far from employing him, that, tho' Furtado several times Offer'd himself, with his own Ships, and at his proper Cost, where there was such Necessity of suppressing Cunnale, yet he was as often Rejected, and that Victory envy'd him, which afterwards he had granted by Heaven, as we shall see in its Place. *(margin: Furtado ill us'd would depart India.)*

At this Time Santiago de Vera was discharged of his Command of the Philippine Islands. He had signified his Intentions to Andrew Furtado, and received his Answer, That he would comply with his Desires; but Fortune disappointed these good Beginnings, embroiling Furtado with those who did not love him, and removing Santiago from his Government. His Successor was Gomez Perez de las Marinnas, Knight of the Order of Santiago, or St. James the Apostle, a Person of high Reputation, born at Betanzos, in the Kingdom of Galicia. He arriv'd at the Philippines in the Year 1590, and brought with him his Son Don Lewis, Knight of the Order of Alcantara. The new Governor found Manila open, without any Form of a City, and without Wealth to Improve it. Above 200000 Pieces of Eight were wanting for this Purpose; yet he compass'd the Work by Projects, and Contrivance without any Dammage to the Publick, or to private Persons. He Monopoliz'd the Cards; he laid Penalties on excessive Gaming, and punish'd such as Forestal'd the Markets, and on Victuallers, and other Retailers of that Sort that were guilty of Frauds; with these Fines he built the Walls of Manila, which are 12849 Geometrical Foot in Compass, each Foot being the third part of a Yard. He apply'd himself diligently to this Work, and the Inhabitants attended it, being willing to forward it on Account of the Intreaties and Example of their Chief. The City had but one Fort, and that ill built, wherefore he Erected another at the Mouth of the River, calling it Santiago, and enclosed the old one. He finish'd the Cathedral, and built from the Ground the Church of St. Potenciana, Patroness of the Island, for Women that have retir'd from the World. Then he apply'd himself to casting, and brought able Artists, who furnish'd the Place with heavy and small Cannon; built Galleys to Cruize and Trade, whereon depends the Welfare of those Countries; and pursuant to what he had promis'd in Spain, bent his Thoughts towards Ternate, and all the Moluccos; reflected on the Disreputation of the unfortunate Expeditions of his Predecessors, who attempted the Conquest of that flourishing Kingdom, and how he might punish those who Tyranniz'd in it. *(margin: Gomez Perez Governor of the Philippines. He Walls Manila; Builds Forts, &c.)*

He imparted his Thoughts by Word of Mouth, and by Letters to Zealous Persons,

S

Persons, and more particularly to *F. Marta*, a Priest of the Society of *Jesus*, and a grave and active Man, whose Experience and Doctrine had been very Advantageous in those Parts. This Religious Man furnish'd him with Intelligence, Advice, and proper Ministers to prepare and carry on the Work; one of whom was Brother *Gaspar Gomez*, a *Spaniard*, and Lay-Brother of the said Society. Among the many Conferences there were to this Effect, I find an Exhortation of *F. Antony Marta*, in a Letter he writ to the Governor from *Tydore*, which, because it is an Original, and conducing for the better Understanding of this Affair, I will here insert, translated out of the *Portuguese*. Grant me this Liberty, since the Speeches which are generally Fabulous, pretended to be made by Generals and Consuls, in the Greek and Latin Histories, are allow'd of. *F. Antony Marta* says thus;

In fine, your Lordship is resolv'd to undertake this Expedition. You will have a spacious Field for dilating the Glory of God very much, and rendering your Name famous to Perpetuity. By it your Lordship will acquire to his Majesty a most Large and Wealthy Kingdom, since all this Archipelago of the Moluccos and Amboina, as far as Banda, which is above 130 Leagues in Length, and 70 in Breadth, is an inexhaustible Source of Clove, Nutmeg, and Mace, which will afford his Majesty a Yearly Income of 200000 Crusados, which is about 27000 Pounds Sterling, then a considerable Sum, in India alone; besides that of other Islands, which produce no Clove. Nor will it require any Expence, because the Country it self will freely afford it on its very Mountains; and what is yet much more, your Lordship will gain above 200000 Souls to God, all which, in a short time, after subduing the Kingdom, will become Christians, without any, or with very little Opposition; whereby your Lordship will have a burning Flambeau in this World, to light and conduct you to Heaven. Besides, you will magnify and perpetuate your Name, with a Title nothing inferior to those of the ancient Roman Generals, such as those of Germanicus, Africanus, *and the like. It is not now requisite to touch upon the Method your Lordship is to observe for compassing this Enterprize, to your eternal Praise; for, as we understand, there is no want of Experience with you for Warlike Affairs; yet if your Lordship should be any way Dubious,* Jerome de Azevedo *is able to inform you of such things as you shall desire to know. He is well acquainted with the Strength of the* *Moluccos, and of their Enemies. However I would have your Lordship look upon this War as considerable and difficult, because it is very convenient to come well Provided, and Resolv'd. You are not to Fight with the* Ternates *alone, but with all the Moors of this Archipelago. Hitherto the Fort of* Amboina *had to do with the* Ternates, *that are at* Veranula, *and this of* Tydore *with those in the Island* Ternate; *but now, of late we are to fight with those of the Islands of* Banda *and of* Seram. *All the Moors in those Parts Assembled last year, and Resolv'd, That for the future the War should be carry'd on under the Name of their Religion. And for the more Security, and better Establishing of this Point, they chose those of* Banda *for Chiefs of their Law; and took an Oath to lay down their Lives, or expell the* Portugueses. *Accordingly the last Year, those of* Banda *came with the* Ternates *of* Veranula, *with a great number of* Carcoas, *to Besiege the Fort of* Amboina; *and in the Engagement they had with us, took one of the two Galiots we brought from* Goa, *tho' it was not their Valour, but our Negligence that*

that

that occasion'd the making of that Prize. It plainly appear'd, that our Lord did it to punish our Pride. This so far Encouraged them, that they durst afterwards daily Cruize in sight of the Fort, took the Fishermen that went out in the Morning to follow their Trade, and laid a Ground some Carcoas on the Shore. They erected a Mosque opposite to the Fort, as in a safe Place, and thus they kept the Fort Besieged with Contempt, for the space of a Month. At the end thereof, the Galley going out, with one Galiot we had left, made them fly, every one to his own Country, giving out, and threatning, That they would Return the next Year with a greater Fleet, which will be about September. We are certainly assured that the People of Banda, left 50 of their prime Men at Amboyna, as Hostages for the performance of their Engagement. This is also known by a Man of our own, who fled from Banda, having been carry'd thither Prisoner from Amboyna. We are informed, that 25 Carcoas would set out, so many being Launch'd, and they were to Sail after their Lent, which is at the End of this Month of July, and to joyn the Seyrves, and the rest of the Confederates, in order to return again before the Fort of Amboyna. If they come with such a Force, I am very suspitious that the Fort will be lost; because the Enemies method is to take in all the Towns that are Subject to it; and when this is left alone, wanting the Support of its Neighbours, it must of necessity Surrender. Antony Perez, the Governor of that Fort, is a Man of Courage, and well Fortified; and yet there are Circumstances to be consider'd, some of them very Difficult; as that the Enemies are Numerous, and there will come some Confederates with them, who are fit for any piece of Treachery; besides, that they cannot be Reliev'd from any Part whatsoever, for the full space of five Months, that is till the beginning of January next. We cannot but apprehend some great Mischief will happen; for supposing they do not take the Fort, still this War is Dangerous, as being Universal, with all the Moors; stirr'd up by means of the Caciques; Concerted under solemn Oaths; and Declar'd to be Religious, with full Remission of Sins to all that Die in it. There is no want of Fomenters, and those Caciques of Note, and great Authority among the Moors, in Banda, Amboyna, Ternate, and Tydore. These Men urge their Religion, and the Honour of Mahomet, and by that means manage the People as they please; as I have found by Experience this Year, and in this War we had at Amboyna, in which I was. For formerly the Moors were soon weary of being at Sea, and when any Man of Note happened to be kill'd in Fight, they presently retir'd, looking upon it as an ill Omen. Now they continue all the seasonable Months at Sea, without flinching; tho' the Portugueses slew 150 of their Men, and among them their Admiral, and others of the prime Commanders they had in their Fleet. To this must be added, That this is a general Conspiracy of all the Moors against us; insomuch, that two who were our Friends, and had Assisted us several times, with their Fleets, against the Ternates, being those of the Island Burro, these being summoned by the Commander to Sail with him in the Navy, as they had done at other times, did not only refuse it now, but would not so much as receive the Message, or suffer him that carry'd it to Land. The Tydores did the same, for the Commander of Amboyna demanding Assistance of them, they would not go, alledging that their Fort was in as much Danger. And the King of Tydore being inform'd of your Lordships coming,

General Conspiracy against Christians.

S 2   his

his Subjects declare before hand, and perhaps at the Instigation of their King, That they will have no Spaniards in these Parts; which makes us look about, where they will raise Moors to Destroy us. Therefore all Delays, in this Affair, will be very dangerous; because we are Inferior to the Moors, and must of Necessity Fight them, since it is for Religion, and Honour, on both which Accounts they are become our mortal Enemies. By this your **F. Marta** *Lordship will understand what need we are in of your Succour and Relief;* **presses for** *and may compute how many are to draw their Swords against you, since they* **Relief.** *are all our Enemies in general, and have Conspir'd against us. However, it will be Discretion first to Dissemble with the Tydores, that they may not joyn the Ternates, and by that means render the War more tedious and difficult. I do not speak to all the rest in particular, according to my Notion, because I refer it to Jerome de Azevedo, who will give a very good Account. But let this be Established as a Maxim, That your Lordship has a mighty Enterprize in Hand; and I trust in God he will give you Wisdom, and Strength to go through it with Ease; since you come to Revenge the Injuries formerly, and now offered by these Barbarians, to God and his* **Irreveren-** *Saints. For we know that the Ternates still drink out of the consecrated* **ces to Re-** *Chalices, and make use of the Patens to Offer, or Receive any thing, as on* **ligion.** *profane Salvers; and of the Vestments, and Ornaments of Altars, they make Cloaths, and Hangings for their Houses. The People of Banda, most of them, wear Ornaments of the Blood of above 3000 Christians, they Treacherously Murder'd, at several times, in their Ports, as they went thither to Trade with them; and in that Island, and part of the Sea, there are Streams of Spanish and Portuguese Blood running. Your Lordship came to spread the Catholick Faith, and that you may the better conceive what Jerome de Azevedo will say to you touching this Affair, I send you by him a Draught of all this Archipelago, as well of the Moluccos, as of Amboyna, and Banda. In it your Lordship will see what a large Kingdom we loose, when it might be recover'd with little Cost. It only remains, That your Lordship come, with all possible Expedition, because the greatest Danger is in Delay; and when you are here you will find brave Commanders, who will assist you with their* **Good Offi-** *Swords and their Advice Among them is Sanhco de Vasconcelos, who was* **cers and** *Commander at Amboyna, has often fought with these Infidels, and obtain'd* **Soldiers.** *signal Victories over them. Here is also Thomas de Sousa, Commander of Molucco, and of most Southern Parts, a Man expert in Martial Affairs. In Tydore and Amboyna, you will also find brave Soldiers, and there will not want to Pay them, for the Riches of the Country will be sufficent for that, and to satisfy them with Gold, precious Stones, and other Booty; besides you will find many sorts of Arms. We Religious Men daily offer up our Prayers,* **Gomez Pe-** *and will so continue to do with Fervour; and tho' the Unworthiness of the* **rez pre-** *Ministers might be a Hinderance, yet we hope they will prove Advantageous.* **pares.**

The Governour receiv'd this Letter; which, with the Discourse he had more at large with *Jerome de Azevedo*, made him put the last Hand to a Work of so much Importance to the Service of the Christian Commonwealth, which had been neglected in those Parts. *Gaspar Gomez* had conferr'd with him long before, and by his Means, and the Accounts of other knowing Persons, the Governor was so well acquainted with the Kingdoms, and Seas, the Seasons and Dangers of the Undertaking, that he had no great need of *F.*

Marta's

ta's Map. He difpatch'd *Gafpar Gomez*, a Man of Secrecy and Activity, trufting him with the Defign, becaufe he was recommended by feveral grave Fathers of that Order. He gave him particular Inftructions, with which, and his own Experience, he wander'd about the *Archipelago*, and learnt as much as was convenient. He vifited *Ternate, Tydore, Mindanao*, both the *Javas*, and fcarce omitted any Place, as far as the Point of *Malaca*, but what he took a View of.

Gafpar Gomez fent as a Spy.

In the Year 1593, King *Philip* the 2d beftow'd the Government of *Cartagena*, in *America*, upon *Don Pedro Bravo de Acunna*. To take this Employ, he quitted that he had in the *Spanifh* Galleys; he was Captain of the Admiral Galley, and Vice-Admiral of them all, under the *Adelantado*, or Lord Lieutenant of *Caftile*, his Kinfman. He had ferv'd his Majefty many Years by Sea and Land, in the *Mediterranean*. No Action of Note was perform'd without him, fince the Expedition of *Navarino* againft the *Turks*, and the others that enfu'd in thofe Parts, in *Naples*, in *Portugal*, and all thofe that occur'd before, till his Majefty was put in Poffeffion of that Crown. Laftly, When he commanded the *Spanifh* Galleys he fought thofe of the *Moors* and *Turks*, with the Galiots, and Brigantines of the *Levant*, and *Englifh* Ships, and took and funk feveral of both Sorts. He took a great Number of Slaves in *Barbary*; particularly at *Zangazon, Benegicar*, and *Alcazar*. He defended *Cadiz* from the Invafion, and Rapine of *Drake*, the *Englifh* Admiral, who attempted it with a mighty Fleet. This was done by only four Galleys, but two of which were clean, yet the Bravery of the Commander made amends for all. How great an Action this was, and what Reputation *Don Pedro* gain'd by it, appear'd afterwards, when the *Englifh* again poffefs'd themfelves of *Cadiz*, at the Time that all the Galleys in *Spain* were in the Bay, and the Fleet then preparing to fail to the *Indies*. In each of thefe Actions, moft whereof were victorious, there are many remarkable Particulars, and they all deferve large Encomiums; but fince they do not belong to the Subject of this Hiftory, it would be blameable to infert them here.

D. Pedro de Acuna Governor of Cartagena.

His brave Actions.

The King for thefe Reafons conftituted *Don Pedro de Acunna*, his Captain General, in the Province of *Cartagena* and *Tierra Firme*, and Commander of the Galleys on that Coaft; which Commiffions had never before been united in that Government. He gave him a Galley, and Orders to receive the Royal Fifths of the Pearl-Fifhery, at the Ifland *Margarita*. He fet out from the Port of *Sanlucar*, on the 27th of *September*, in a Pink, with 12 Soldiers, fome Religious Men, and his Servants, the Galley, and another Ship following. The Winds foon rofe, and the Sea fwell'd, and the Veffels were difpers'd. In one of them there were 20 Soldiers, and 40 Slaves at the Oar, this was fo far drove away, that they faw it no more, till five Days after they came to *Cartagena*. The Storm ceas'd, and *Don Pedro* arriv'd at *Gran Canaria*, but would not go into the City. He took in two hundred Cask of Water. The Governour *Don Lewis de la Cueva* was not in the Ifland; but it being known in his Family that *Don Pedro* was come, they fent to welcome him. The Vifit was follow'd by fome Horfes loaded with Abundance of Fowl, Game, Sheep, Wine, Pears, and moft ftately Quinces, befides Abundance of other Provifions. He fail'd thence with a favourable Wind, which foon turn'd againft him, and tho' he was at enough off, drove back the Ships in Sight of *Teneriffe*. After being tofs'd about for

His Voyage.

fome

some Days, there happened such a tedious Calm between two Islands, as made Amends for the Violence of the Storms, and yet he had others afterwards as violent as those before. Many Days after, when they had lost their reckning, they arriv'd at the Island *Metalinon*, inhabited by unconquered *Indians*, where they took in Water without Opposition, for the Rest of the Voyage. Thence he had fair Weather to the Island *Margarita*. As soon as he landed in the Harbour, *Don John Sarmiento de Villandrando*, the Governour of the Island came to meet him, having hourly expected him, since he knew he was to come. The rejoycing, and Entertainment was such as became Friends, and Friends of that Quality.

An English Ship near the Island Margarita

An *English* Ship of above four hundred Tun Burthen, with thirty Pieces of Cannon of five thousand Weight each, and Abundance of Men, had been 30 days in a Harbour but two Leagues from the Island *Margarita*. *Don John Sarmiento* telling *Don Pedro*, what Insolences that Ship committed, and how much to his Disreputation she oppress'd the Islanders under his Government, desir'd he might attack her with his Galley. *Don Pedro* perswaded him to desist from that Enterprize, since it did not belong to him, and it was an unpardonable Fault to attack her, without an equal Force. *Don John* persisted so long, that he carry'd it against *Don Pedro*'s Opinion. They made to the Place where the Ship lay, passing by dangerous Rocks, and being come in Sight of it, perceiv'd it was stronger, and better provided than they had been told. Our Men, in Order to fight, turn'd out all the Women, most of them Wives to those that came in the Galleys. Twenty Soldiers came from the Island *Margarita*, by their Governours Order, who being ship'd they appear'd by Break of Day in Sight of the Enemy. The Wind then

The Islanders oblige Don Pedro to Fight her.

blowing fresh *Don Pedro* advising with the Natives of the Island *Margarita* and their Governour told them, it was requisite to expect a Calm, in Order to take the Ship, since the Galley could wait for it under Shelter, without any Danger. The Islanders being provok'd by the Dammage they had receiv'd, and to flatter *Don John Sarmiento*, answer'd, That they had two of the Prime Men of that Ship Prisoners in the City, by whose Account they were inform'd of the Distress she was in, and that she must surrender, as soon as attack'd. This Opinion being bandy'd about with Obstinacy, came to be Positiveness in Don *John*. *Don Pedro* looking upon it as such, and concerned to see his Friend engag'd in such a Piece of Madness, with those Hot, but unexperienc'd Men, said to them, By my long Experience in several Seas, I know it is the worst of Conduct to attack a Ship, when she has the Wind; but let us fall on; that the People of the Island *Margarita* may not have it to say that I deferr'd engaging out of Fear, and not out of Discretion. This said, he order'd his Galley to weigh Anchor. He arm'd himself, and *Don John*, and just as the Sun appear'd they attack'd the Ship

The Engagement.

with Fury and Violence. The *English* were not backward; they speedily cut the Cables of three Anchors they had out, and leaving them in the Sea, set their Sails. The Wind was fair and soon fill'd them. The Men were brisk and ply'd their Cannon without ceasing. Our Galley did the same, and fir'd five Shot, before it receiv'd any Harm. Then she ran her Beak against the Poop of the Ship, but could not grapple, nor board. Some Men went down to the Boats which were tow'd by the Ship, and cut the Ropes. The Ship, and Galley fell a firing again, without Intermission.

Don

Don Pedro receiv'd a Musquet Shot on his Target, which glancing off broke in Pieces a Board of the Stern Lockers, and wounded those that were next it. A Cannon Ball took off the Head of one of our Slaves, and scatter'd his Brains in *Don Pedro's* Face; but another Ball touch'd him nearer, when it threw *Don John Sarmiento* into the Sea, who being sunk by the Weight of his Armour, was never seen again. Fourteen Soldiers of the Island *Margarita*, and nine Spaniards were kill'd, and many wounded, of all whom *Don Pedro* took Care, without neglecting the other Duties of a Commander. Some Persons of Note were also kill'd, as *Alonso de Anduxar*, a Youth about twenty Years of Age, of the Order of Christ, and *Antonio Santiso*, who had been a Captain in *Flanders*. The Ship holding on her Course, made the best of the fair Wind, and was seen to fly, as if she had been victorious; tho' she threw many dead Bodies over Board, in Sight of our Men. *Don Pedro* return'd to the Island *Margarita*, lamenting the Death of his Friend, and his Wife's Widow-Hood, amidst the Tears of other Widows, and Fathers left Childless. He comforted the afflicted the best he could, received the King's Boxes of Pearls, and went on much griev'd at the Event, and to see how little his Precaution had avail'd.

Don Pedro at Cartagena.

Don Pedro had a prosperous Passage thence, to the Island *Curazao*, to *Rio de la Hacha*, and so in Sight of *Cartagena*. Being descry'd from the City the Galleys went out to meet him, whose Musick and Guns, with those of the Fort made a Mixture of Harmony and Noise. He enter'd upon the Government and immediately took a View of the Galleys, Warlike Preparations being of the greatest Consequence in those Parts. He found them shatter'd, and almost gone to Ruin, refitted one, and furnish'd another with Slaves, and all other Necessaries. All things were before in such Disorder, and Confusion, that it was hard to distinguish betwixt the Galley Slaves and the Soldiers, the former going about as free, and gay as the latter. He blam'd this Liberty, and order'd the Heads and Beards of the Slaves to be shav'd, and that they should be chain'd. Next he took in hand the Divisions, Manners, and civil Government of the City, and there was soon a Reformation of Abuses, and publick Crimes, all this he perform'd by his Valour, and Example. He also review'd the Horse and Foot; repair'd the Fortifications; attended all Martial Affairs; had his Gates always open to decide Controversies; without Distinction of Persons; and tho' he had here considerable Opportunities offer'd him, and much Matter to discover his Capacity, and the Greatness of his Soul, yet he found in himself greater Hopes and Desires, above what was present, and exciting him to advance farther, and to make known to the World that generous Restlessness, which was afterwards serviceable to the Church, by restoring its former Honour, in the remotest Provinces.

The End of the Fifth Book.

THE
HISTORY
OF THE
DISCOVERY and CONQUEST
OF THE
Molucco and *Philippine* Iſlands, *&c.*

BOOK. VI.

Gomez Perez builds four Galleys, and makes Slaves wrongfully

Taes of Gold their Value.

IN the mean while *Gomez Perez*, ſtill carrying on his Preparations, conceal'd the Deſign, without ſparing any charge for Shipping, Proviſions, or Men. Among other Neceſſaries, he built four choice Galleys, and for the manning of them, took a Method which was look'd upon as ſevere. He Order'd, That as many *Indians* who were Slaves to other *Indians* of Quality, as would ſerve to Man the Galleys, ſhould be bought up, and Paid for by the *Spaniards*, who were Proprietors, out of their own Money, ſetting the Price of each Slave at two *Taes* in Gold, each *Tae* being little above an Ounce, which was the Price Slaves had in former Times been valu'd at among them. He promis'd, that the Proprietors ſhould afterwards be Refunded what they laid out, from the Kings Revenue. Yet this did not ſeem to mollify the Rigour of the Order, becauſe he improperly call'd thoſe *Indians* Slaves, for their Lords uſe and love them like Children, ſet them at their own Tables, and Marry them to their Daughters; beſides that, Slaves then were worth more Money. The Concern of thoſe

Diſcontent in the Philippines.

that were to be Sold, was attended by that of the Proprietors, who were to contribute out of their Eſtates, to defray Charges they look'd upon as not very Neceſſary, and to Diſguſt their Vaſſals, by taking them away forcibly, being never likely to recover the Money they laid down, which they

The Governors excuſe.

were well aſſur'd of. The Governour gave out, That thoſe Galleys were to ſecure the Country, and defend it from the Danger that threatned; becauſe he knew the Emperor of *Japan* was coming to Invade it, with a numerous Fleet; and that it could not be Defended without Galleys, and therefore it was abſolutely Neceſſary to Man them with Slaves, ſince they had no others to Row. That theſe were not to be Fetter'd in the Galleys, nor Treated like Slaves, but ſo kindly uſed, that they themſelves ſhould prefer their Entertainment, before that of their Lords, whom they look'd upon as Parents, or Fathers-in-Law. Theſe

These Allegations, and the absolute Necessity of defending themselves, silenc'd both Parties; but could not stop the Mouth of Fame, for it was already known, what Engagements he made before he came from *Spain*, to the King, the Ministers, the Kindred, and Fomenters of the Expedition of *Ternate*, so that whatsoever he conceal'd, was divulg'd by uncertain Authors. However some advis'd him not to rely on the *Chineses*, or *Sangleyes* for the Defence of the *Philippines*; because no natural or civil Tye had ever gain'd, or attracted their Affection towards them. That he ought to remember the fresh Instance of what they did, when his Predecessor employ'd them, and consequently should be watchful over them. That he sending a Supply of Men, Ammunitions and Provisions to the Fort and Town of *Cagayan*, which is on the Coast of that Island of *Luzon*, 80 Leagues from the City *Manila*, and there being then no Ship to send it in, Necessity pressing, he thought he might relieve that Want, by making use of one of the *Chinese* Ships that were then at Anchor in the Harbour, and clear'd in Order to return to *China*. He commanded the Supply to be put aboard her, and the *Chineses* to carry, and in the Way, to land it where he directed, since it was no let to their Voyage; promising to requite and gratify them for that Service. They undertook it with extraordinary Tokens of good Will; but their Artifice appear'd by the Event, and show'd how Men that are upon the Watch, improve Opportunities. The *Chineses* set sail, and the second Day after, when the *Spaniards* were asleep, as believing themselves safe among trusty Friends, they fell upon them so unexpectedly, that they had not Time to stand upon their Guard, but were all murder'd and cast into the Sea. They plunder'd all they carry'd, and dividing the Spoil, sail'd for their own Country. They only sav'd one unhappy *Spanish* Woman, that went with our Men, and took her along with them. They spar'd her Life, but after having insolently abus'd her, they set her ashore, in a Sea-Port Town of the first Part of *China* they made. She presently had Recourse to the Magistrates, whom she acquainted with the Villany those Men had committed, and the Wrongs they had done her; but tho' favourably heard by those Judges, she had no Satisfaction for her Wrongs, nor could she obtain Justice. However they appointed Officers to carry her up the Country, remitting her to other Supream Magistrates. In this Journey, which was many Leagues, she endur'd more than she had done before, till some of the Governours taking Compassion on her and her Tears, carry'd her to the City of *Macao*, where the *Portuguefes* reside, and set her at Liberty. Thus the whole Matter came to be known, and it was at *Manila* in the Mouths of all Men, who now magnify'd it, upon Occasion of the New Enterprize.

In short, all the Slaves demanded by the Governour *Gomez Perez*, were raised with much Trouble and Oppression, and in the same Manner they were put into the Galleys, where they continu'd some Time before they departed, and many of them dy'd, as not being us'd to that sort of Life. All those Slaves were not sufficient to Man the Galleys, and the Admiral Galley remain'd without Rowers. This, and the Necessity of finishing the Work produc'd a more rigorous Practice than the former. The Governour order'd that 250 of the *Chineses*, who resort to the *Philippines* to

The Design against the Moluccos takes Air.

Falshood of the Chineses.

Spanish Woman abandon'd in China.

Chineses put into the Galleys.

T   Trade,

Trade, fhould be taken to Man the Admiral Galley, and each of them to
be allow'd two Pieces of Eight a Month, out of the King's Revenue. He
affur'd them, they fhould not be chain'd, but at Liberty, and with their
Arms, to ferve as Soldiers ; and that they fhould only row in the Galleys
when there was any Calm, and to weather fome Capes. The *Chinefes* being acquainted by their *Chinefe* Governour with this Refolution, pofitively
refus'd it, as an intolerable Burden. But our Governour preffing to bring
about his Defign, the *Chinefe* affembled his People, to treat about the Affair, and contrive how 250 might be chofen out from among them all,
threatning that he would take every Tenth Man out of their Houfes.
Thefe Words provok'd them to fuch a Degree, that the next Day they
fhut up the very Windows of their Houfes, and the Traders their Shops,
and ftopp'd the Provifions which run through their Hands. Our Governour feeing this Proceeding, and alledging that they mutiny'd, caus'd
about 50 of thofe that came next to hand, to be feiz'd, and put to the
Oar in the Galley. The others terrify'd by this Action, met, and drew
from among them all, the 250, and becaufe no Man would be of that
Number, they divided 20000 Pieces of Eight among thofe that would comply, and gave every *Chinefe* that would go in the Galley 80 Pieces of Eight,
befides the King's Pay. By Means of this good Encouragement, there
was no Want of *Chinefes* that lifted themfelves to row, but the 20000
Pieces of Eight were confum'd among them, or rather among the Officers.
Thefe 250 *Chinefes* were form'd into five Companies, under five *Chinefe*
Chriftian Captains, who pafs'd Mufters and Reviews, with Pikes and
Catanes, which differ little from Cymiters, and exprefs'd Joy and Sa-
tisfaction.

P. Gafpar
Gomez
brings In-
telligence.

Whilft thefe Things were in Agitation, Brother *Gafpar Gomez* came
to *Manila*, full of Intelligence, whereof he gave the Governour an Account, at feveral private Conferences. He faid, the King of *Ternate's* Affairs were in no ill Pofture ; tho' fomewhat weak'ned, by not agreeing
with the Prime Men of his Kingdom ; and that many of them threatned,
they would Rebel, on Account of his Tyranny, and becaufe he rais'd intolerable Taxes. That then, neither the *Javanefes*, nor the *Lafcarines*,
nor the *Moors* of *Mecca* frequented *Te. nate*, as they had done at the Time
when Captain *Morones* arriv'd there, under the Government of *Santiago*
de Vera. He gave very particular Information concerning the two Forts

Strength of
Ternate.

of *Talangame*. That the King of *Ternate* had then about 3000 common
Soldiers, 1000 Mufquetiers, and a great Number from his other Kingdoms. That they fought with Darts, *Campilanes*, or Cymiters, and
Shields ; and others had Coats of Mail, and Head-Pieces they got from
the *Portuguefes*, in exchange for Spice. That they had Abundance of
Ammunition, all of their own making, of the Materials the *Javanefes*
brought to barter for Clove. That the Principal Place was the City *Ter-*
nate, where the King and all his Court refide, and therefore it is beft fecur'd, and from thence all others are fupply'd, fupported, and encourag'd.

How to be
attack'd.

He advis'd that our Men fhould affault it before Break of Day ; becaufe all
Attacks made upon thofe People in the Morning Watch had been fuccefsful. That, if our Fleet came unexpected, it would certainly fucceed ; but
that the faid King had his Spies fpread abroad in almoft all thofe Iflands,

as

as far as thofe of *Canela, Sariangan* and *Mindanao*. That a good Number of Brafs Sakers, and other great Guns might be brought in the *Carcoas,* from the Fort of *Amboyna,* and the Kings of *Sian,* and *Tydore.* That the People of *Amboyna* would fend them upon Command, thofe of *Sian* and *Tydore,* upon very fmall Intreaty; becaufe befides their owning the Crown of *Spain,* they are Enemies to *Ternate.* That the neceffary Preparation for finifhing the War, even in cafe the King of *Tydore* fhould fail, and it might be fufpected he would not willingly fee his Enemy utterly deftroy'd, confifted in Artillery and Shipping, which was ready, and above 1200 Soldiers well arm'd, with their Coats of Mail and Head-Pieces, till they went over to the Ifland of *Banda,* to put in the neceffary Garrifon there. That there fhould be a Number of Light Veffels to take the Enemy flying; *Light Veffels of* for by that Means the War would be quite concluded in a fhort Time, and *fels of* without Bloodfhed. That even the Malecontent *Ternates* declar'd, and *good Ufe.* publifh'd as much, and own'd, that if a confiderable Number of Fighting Men fhould come into their Country, they would all come in and fubmit without ftriking Stroke. Hence he inferr'd, that there were conceal'd Chriftians in the *Molucco* Iflands. That the Conqueft of the whole Ifland of *Banda,* was very advantageous and profitable, and not hazardous, and that the Neighbourhood of *Amboyna,* which was ours, would be of great Confequence for maintaining it. He further affirm'd, That the *Portuguefes* very much facilitated the Enterprize, and magnify'd the great Benefit it would be to his Majefty; and that *F. Antony Marta,* of whom the Governour had fo great a Conceit, was of the fame Opinion. Brother *Gafpar Gomez* added fo many Circumftances to thefe particular Accounts, that he wholly inflam'd the Governour's Heart.

At this Time, *Landara,* King of *Camboxa,* fent the Governour an Embaffy by two *Spanifh* Commanders, attended by many of his Subjects, with *King of* fuch Splendor as the Occafion of it requir'd. That barbarous King thought *Camboxa* fit his Embaffadors fhould not be natural born Subjects, becaufe of the Oc- *fends Spa-* cafion his People had given him to fufpect their Fidelity. He chofe them *niards Em-* of Different Conditions, to the End that fuch Variety, the Diverfity of In- *baffadors* clinations, and Oppofition, might produce the better Effect. The one of *to the Go-* them was a *Portuguefe,* his Name *James Velofo,* the other a *Spaniard, vernour.* *Blas Ruyz de Fernan Gonzalez.* They brought *Gomez Perez* a Magnificent Prefent, a great Quantity of *Ivory, Benjamin, China* Ware, Pieces of *Their Pre-* Silk and Cotton, and an *Elephant* of a generous Temper, as afterwards *fent.* appear'd by Experience. They deliver'd their Embaffy, the Purport whereof was, to defire Succour againft the King of *Sian,* who was march- *Subject of* ing againft him of *Camboxa,* with a numerous Army; offering in Return *their Em-* for his Affiftance to become fubject to *Spain,* and embrace Chriftianity. *baffy.* That the King concluded, that fo brave and gallant a Gentleman as *Gomez Perez,* would not on Account of any other Diverfion refufe to perform an Action, which muft redound fo much to the Glory of God, and the Advantage of the Crown of *Spain.* The Governour receiv'd the Prefent, making a Return with another of fome *European* Curiofities; and by way of Anfwer, thank'd that King for the Confidence he had feem'd to place *The An-* in him; but that, for the Prefent, he could not poffibly afford the Succours, *fwer.* nor divert thofe Forces, which he was getting ready, to punifh the King

of

of *Ternate*, and recover that Kingdom, and the rest of the *Moluccos*, which had Rebell'd, so much to the Dishonour of the *Spanish* Nation. That his Highness should place his Confidence in the Goodness of God, and persevere in the Design of serving him in his Holy and True Religion, and as soon as the Expedition of *Ternate* was over, he would convert his Forces to the Relief of *Camboxa* The Embassadors were dismiss'd with these Hopes, which the Governours Son, *Don Lewis de las Marinas*, afterwards made good ; and to give them entire Satisfaction, and justify the Delay, it was found necessary to make Publick the true Design of that Fleet, which till then had been kept secret.

Mighty Preparations against Ternate.

The Governour, in fine, resolv'd to set forward, and endeavour'd to take along with him all the Men he could get. All were listed that could be prevail'd upon either by Force or Intreaties. The Proprietors and Soldiers were extravagantly expensive, upon the Ships, Provisions, and Gallantry , and the *Philipines* being well furnish'd with all Things, they did more than had been imagin'd, or could be in the Governour's Power. He sent his Son *Don Lewis*, with all the Soldiers that were in Pay, to the Island of *Zebu*, where the Fleet was to rendevous, and there he continued six Months, waiting for new Orders. *Gomez Perez* stay'd at *Manila*, ordering Matters of great Moment. Two Days before his Departure, being invited by, and supping in the House of *Peter de Rojas*, his Lieutenant,

Prediction of ill Success.

where diverting himself with Gaming, and much Pleasure, he grew so merry, contrary to his Custom, and the Harshness of his Temper, that many interpreted it as a good Omen of his Success. He said in Discourse, that *F. Vincent*, of the Order of St. *Francis*, had told him, the Enterprize could not succeed, because the Army was made up of Men that were carry'd away by Force, and particularly the marry'd Men were so. He departed *Manila* on the 17th of *October*, with six Royal Galleys, one Galleon, one small Vessel call'd a *Foist*, one little Frigot, and several other Frigots, Carcoas, and Bireyes, which are another Sort of

The Fleet sets out.

Vessels of the Natives; all which, being part the Kings, and part belonging to Subjects, who offer'd to serve him with their Lives and Fortunes, amounted to an hundred. There were a Thousand *Spaniards* well arm'd ; above four hundred Musqueteers of the Territory of *Manila* ; a thousand more of those they call *Visaias*, Men arm'd with Lances, Shields, Bows and Arrows, and above four hundred *Chinefes*, of those that dwelt in the Island, besides a good Number of those that came to Trade taken into Pay ; but many more Compell'd than Voluntiers. The Galleys carry'd Abundance of Provisions for the Army, over which he appointed his Son *Don Lewis Perez*, his Lieutenant, and sent him before, as has been said, with Orders to make for the Island of *Zebu*. He embark'd himself aboard the Admiral-Galley, which had twenty eight Benches for the Men to row, and was mann'd with the 250 *Chinefes* for the Oar. Eighty *Spaniards* were put aboard it ; they touch'd at *Cavite*, sail'd thence on the 19th, and with them some Vessels, in which there were private Persons, who follow'd at their own Expence, coasting the Island of *Manila* as far as *Balayan*. They parted, because the Vessels kept in Sight of Land, and the Governour put out to Sea. On the 25th he came alone to pass the Night, at the Point call'd *de Azufre*, or of Brimstone, in the Island of *Manila*,

opposite

Its Force.

oppofite to that of Caza, where the Current, and the Drift of the Water from the Land run ftrong, and the Breezes then blowing, the Galley could not weather it. He anchor'd under the Shelter of it, and yet dragg'd a little with the Force of the Current. They made the *Chinefes* row exceffive Chinefes *at the Oars ill us'd.* hard, to bring her up again under the Land. In fhort, they row'd very faintly, either becaufe they were not us'd to that Labour, and forc'd to the Oar, or becaufe they were then tir'd, and incens'd with the Command. Other contrary Winds ftarted up, which again obftructed their Voyage, and to weather fome Points of Land, it was neceffary to ply the Oars, and to vex the Crew, with the ufual Severity and Punifhment commonly inflicted aboard the Galleys. They thought this hard, and contrary to what the Governour had affur'd them, which was, that they fhould be kindly treated; but neither the Lafh, nor the Threats, nor the ftemming of the Currents, with the Vigour and Sweat of their Bodies, feem'd fo intollerable, and injurious to them, as to hear the angry and ftern Go- *The Go- vernour threatens them.* vernour himfelf bid them row manfully, for if they did not, he would put them in Chains, and cut off their Hair. This to the *Chinefes* is an Affront that deferves Death, for they place their Honour in their Hair, which they cherifh and preferve very fair, and value themfelves upon it, as the Ladies in *Europe* us'd to do, all their Delight and Reputation being in keeping it curioufly comb'd. Hereupon they refolv'd to mutiny, to *The* Chi- nefes rebel and kill the Spaniards. prevent fuch an Affront and Contempt. The next Night, which was the 25th of *October*, being appointed for the Execution, when the tir'd *Spani- ards* laid themfelves down upon the Benches, and other convenient Places in the Veffel, the *Chinefes* did fo too, but cunningly dividing themfelves, every one lay down by a *Spaniard*, pretending to be afleep. In the dead of the laft Watch, which they thought the propereft and fafeft Time, feeing the *Spaniards* found afleep, the *Chinefes*, upon hearing of a fhrill Whiftle, which was the Signal agreed upon between them, ftarted up all together, and every Man with wonderful Celerity put on a white Veft, or Shirt, that they might know one another in the Height of their Fury, and the Darknefs of the Night, and fo diftinguifh where to make the Slaughter, tho' for the more Security, they alfo lighted abundance of Wax-Candles, which they had conceal'd wrap'd up in thofe white Vefts. Then they drew their *Catanas*, which are keener, and more crooked than our *Cymiters*, and began without any Noife every Man to hew his next *Spaniard*; fo proceeding in their Fury, and killing all thofe that flept. Above 60 Perfons had imbark'd in the Admiral-Galley, fome of them being the Governour's Servants, and other old Soldiers, who fuffer'd Inconveniencies to oblige and divert him. They had play'd all the Night, and being tir'd, and the Heat very violent, they lay naked, fome on the Gang-Way in the middle of the Galley, others on the Benches, and the greateft Favourites, who had more Room allow'd them, in the Poop, and to that Purpofe the Governour retired into the Cabin. The *Chinefes* continu'd the Execution, on thofe who flept, without any Miftruft, which was done fo expeditioufly, that when fome of thofe who flept in the Poop awak'd, the other *Spaniards* were all kill'd. The Watch heard nothing of it, tho' their could be no Excufe for that Neglect, becaufe there had been Inftances and Warnings enough before. Others awak'd, and feeling themfelves

Many of them drowned.

Only 12 eſcape.

ſelves wounded, in the Confuſion leap'd into the Sea, where moſt of them were drown'd; ſome few caſt themſelves into the Sea before they were hurt, and were alſo ſwallow'd up by it, tho' they were near Land, becauſe the Current being ſtrong, they could not ſtem it; twelve eſcap'd, and many Bodies were found along the Shores.

The Gover-
nor kill'd.

The *Chineſes* now grown bold, drew out the Pikes they had hid under the Benches, and finiſh'd their Treacherous Work with Noiſe. The Governor, who was under Deck, Sleeping, with a Candle and Lanthorn by him, Awak'd; and that he might do ſo, they made the greater Noiſe; and the *Chineſes* themſelves cry'd out to him, deſiring he would come up to pacify a Quarrel there was among the *Caſtillas*, ſo they call the *Spaniards.* He, for this Reaſon, or believing the Galley dragg'd, as it had done at other times, getting up in his Shirt, and opening the Scuttle, look'd out, lifting half his Body above it: At the ſame time the *Chineſes* fell upon him with their Cymiters, and wounded him Mortally, clutting his Head, and running him through with their Pikes in more than barbarous manner. Seeing his Death near he drew back, and took up the Prayer Book of his Order, which he always carry'd about him, and an Image of our Bleſſed Lady, and ended his Life between thoſe two Advocates, which were afterwards ſeen bathed in his Blood: Yet he dy'd not preſently, for they afterwards found him in his Bed, imbracing the Image, where he Bled to Death, and about him the Bodies of *Daniel Gomez de Leon,* his Valet de Chamber, *Pantaleon de Brito, Suero Diaz, John de Chavez, Peter Maſeda, John de S. Juan, Carrion Ponce,* and *Francis Caſtillo,* all of them his Servants, and four brave Slaves, who had the ſame End. This was not known till it was Day; becauſe none of the *Chineſes* durſt go down where the Governor was that Night, fearing leaſt ſome of the 80 *Spaniards* that were in the Galley, had retir'd thither; ſuch was the Dread of their own Guilt. None were left

Two ſav'd alive.

alive in the Galley, but *F. Francis Montilla,* of the Barefoot Order of *S. Francis,* and *John de Cuellar,* the Governors Secretary, who lay under Deck, whether the fainthearted *Chineſes* durſt not go down in three Days, when their firſt Fury was over. Then they afterwards ſet Aſhore, on the Coaſt of *Ilocos,* in the ſame Iſland of *Luzon,* that the Natives might ſuffer them to Water; and becauſe the Frier and the Secretary had Capitulated, having their promiſe that they would do them no hurt, before they ſurrendered. The *Chineſes* being ſatisfy'd that there were no more ancient Chriſtians left, began to Shout and Roar for Joy that they had gone through with their Work, and had no Man more to ſtand in Awe of.

The Chine-
ſes ſail for
China.

The *Spaniards,* who were in the other Veſſels, near the Shore, tho' they ſaw the Lights, and heard a confus'd Noiſe aboard the Admiral, thought it might be on account of ſome Work belonging to the Galley, or the like. When, a long time after, they underſtood how matters went, from thoſe who ſav'd themſelves by Swimming, they lay ſtill, not being able to redreſs it. They were but few; had not Strength enough; and the Miſchief was done. They ſtay'd till Morning, and when Day appear'd, perceiv'd that the Galley had ſet her Shoulder-of-Mutton-Sail, and was ſtanding for *China,* but they could not follow her: The Wind favouring, ſhe ſail'd all along the Coaſt of the Iſland, till they got clear of it, the *Chineſes* all the way Celebrating their Victory.

The

The Frier and the Secretary, who were among them, being fully perswaded they would soon kill them, and fearing it would be after some of their cruel Methods, holding up their Hands, begg'd they would allow them some Time to make their Peace with God; and in case they would put them to Death, that it might be by Beheading, and not any other Inhuman Way. One of the *Chinefes* bid them not Fear, for they should not Dye. They all lay'd down their bloody Weapons, and proftrating themselves, return'd Thanks to Heaven in moft humble manner, beating Drums, and ringing Bells they carry'd, according to their Cuftom. The two Chriftians being then bolted to a Bench in the Galley, during 15 Days their Captivity lafted, were fed with a fmall Proportion of Rice, boi'd in Water, without Salt, continually looking upon the Blood of their Companions that had been fpilt, wherewith all the Deck was Stain'd. They fhed Abundance of Tears on it, befides thofe they hourly let fall with the Apprehenfion of Death, thofe *Chinefes*, like faithlefs falfe Men, defigning to take away their Lives, in fome ftrange manner. They weigh'd, and failed between the Iflands of *Mindanao* and *Luban*, towards *China*, and Coafting along *Manila* towards *Cagayan*, fome contrary Winds happening to blow, and Calms fucceeding, they were much concern'd, fearing, that if the News of their Treachery reach'd the *Philippines*, they would fend after and overtake them. This Dread made them have recourfe to their Gods, and call upon them, offering feveral forts of Sacrifices, Perfumes, and Prayers, which the Devil often anfwer'd in formal Words, by the Mouths of fuch as were Poffeffed, whom he Enter'd to that Purpofe, for there never wanted two or three fuch, all the time thofe Chriftians were in the Galley. What they faw was, that when leaft they thought of it, and on a fudden, the Perfon poffeffed began to quake, from Head to Foot. The others feeing him in that Condition, faid, *Some God was coming to Speak to them.* Then coming up to him, with Tokens of Refpect, they unty'd, and fpread abroad his Hair; and ftripping him quite naked fet him on his Feet, and he prefently fell a Dancing to the Noife of fome Drum, or Bell, they beat or rung. They put a Cymiter, or Spear into his Hand, and as he danc'd he brandifh'd it over all their Heads, with no fmall danger of hurting them, which they were not the leaft apprehenfive of, alledging, that their God, tho' he did fo, would never hurt them, without they were guilty of fome Sin againft him.

Before the Devil had poffefs'd any in the Galley, the *Chinefes* were concerting to murder the Chriftians, believing they were the Occafion, why God did not give them a fair Wind for their Voyage; but that watchful fovereign Providence, without whofe Direction the leaft Accident does not happen, making Ufe of the Devil himfelf as an Inftrument, prevented it by Means of thofe very Perfons who offended it. The Perfon poffefs'd ask'd for Ink and Paper, which being prefently brought him, he made certain Characters and confus'd Scrawls, which being expounded by the others in the Galley, they found fignify'd, that thofe two Men were harmlefs, therefore they fhould not kill them, which was no fmall Incouragement to the Prifoners. However this lafted not long, for fome others who were poffefs'd after the firft, tormented them cruelly, efpecially one of them, who was the maddeft. He told the *Chinefes*, that if he fhould happen to hurt thofe Men, as he brandifh'd the Weapon he had in his Hand over

them,

The two Prifoners beg an eafy Death, and are promis'd their Lives.

The Chinefes *invoke their Gods.*

Some of them poffefs'd.

Chriftians preferv'd by Means of the Devil.

them, making Eſſays, as if he cut and ſlaſh'd; then they muſt kill them immediately; becauſe it would be a certain Sign, that their Gods requir'd it, and that their being in the Ship was the Occaſion, why they gave them not a fair Gale. All the Men in the Galley aſſembled, to behold that Spectacle, and the Perſon poſſeſs'd having for a conſiderable Space walk'd about the Gang-Way, with extravagant Geſtures, went then to the Place where the Religious Man and his Companion were; there growing helliſhly inrag'd, he commanded all the reſt to ſtand aſide, and being left with only the two Priſoners, began to make hideous Faces and Grimaces at them, *Horred* when getting upon the Table in the mid Part of the Galley, he thence *practices* threw his Cymiter at them, with ſuch Fury, that it ſtuck in the Deck, be-*upon the* tween their Feet. Seeing he had not hurt nor touch'd them, he ask'd for *Priſoners.* it again to make a ſecond and third Tryal, ſticking it every Time ſo deep, that the others could ſcarce draw it out from the Planks. This done, he bid them give him a Parteſan, with which he hack'd, hew'd, and thruſt, in ſuch frightful and dangerous Manner, that the *Chineſes* themſelves were aſtoniſh'd. He kept them above an hour in that Dread and Affliction, without daring to ſtir, or beg for Mercy; believing it would not avail them, but that on the contrary, whatſoever they could ſay might be prejudicial. Thus having plac'd all their Hopes, and Confidence on that ſovereign Lord, who even when he delays does not fail to give Aſſiſtance, they call'd upon him, and offer'd themſelves up to him in fervent Prayers; particularly the Religious Man, repeating ſome Pſalms and Verſes, which his former Devotion, excited by the preſent Danger, brought into his Mind, and were ſuitable to that Occaſion, and ſuch like Exigencies; by which, as he afterwards ſaid, he receiv'd great Comfort, and Addition of Courage. This ſort of miſerable Life, and theſe Torments laſted all or moſt Days during therein Captivity.

At length, the *Chineſes* perceiving they could not poſſibly perform the *The Chi-* Voyage they deſir'd, by Reaſon the Wind was contrary; they reſolv'd to *neſes land,* land on the Iſland of *Ilocos,* not far from *Luzon,* at the Port they call *Sinay.* *820 of* They being there aſhore to Water, the Natives knowing they had murder'd *them are* the Governour, laid an Ambuſh and kill'd twenty of them, and might have *kill'd.* deſtroyed above eighty that had landed, if they had not wanted Courage; becauſe at the very Shout the Men gave, when falling on, they were ſo daunted, that they all fled ſeveral Ways in Confuſion, throwing down their Arms, endeavouring to ſave their Lives, by leaping into the Sea, ſo to get off in the Boat. The *Chineſes* meeting with this Diſaſter, and thinking one of their own Men had been the Occaſion of it, becauſe he advi-*They* ſed them to put into that Port, they reſolv'd to ſeize and put him *drown one* to Death,. They did as had been reſolv'd, and at Night, by unanimous *of their* Conſent, threw him into the Sea, then weighing their Anchors, they got *own Men.* out of that Harbour, and put into another, three Leagues off, on the ſame Coaſt. There the Devil entering into one of them, as he us'd to do, commanded them immediately to return to the Port, where they had ſuſtain'd thatLoſs of their Friends and Companions, and that they ſhould not depart thence, till they had ſacrific'd a Man to him, without appointing which he would have. They immediately obey'd the Command, one of the Chief *Chineſes* making Choice of one of the Chriſtian *Indians* of the *Philip-*

pines they had Prisoners, to be Sacrifiz'd, and ty'd his Hands and Feet, stretching them on a Cross, which they rais'd up, and the Christian being bound against the fore-Mast, one of those possess'd by the Devil came up to him in Sight of them all, and playing the part of an Executioner, ripp'd up his Breast, with one of those Daggers they use, making a wound so large, that he thrust in his Hand with ease, and pluck'd out part of his Entrals, whereof, with horrid Fury, he bit a Mouthful, and casting the rest up into the Air, eat what he had in his Mouth, and lick'd his Hands, pleasing himself with the Blood that stuck to them. *An Indian cruelly Sacrifiz'd.*

Having committed the Murder, they took the Cross, and him that was on it, and cast it and the Martyr into the Sea, which receiv'd that Body, offer'd in Sacrifize to the Devil, then to be cloath'd in Glory, by him that has provided it for those who suffer for the Confession of the Faith. This dreadful Spectacle struck Horror, and rais'd Emulation in the two Christians, who beheld it with Zeal, and had expected as much before. The Inhuman Sacrifice being over, they put out of the Harbour, and having for some days Coasted the Island with Difficulty; one of them, by command of the Possess'd Person, who had order'd the Sacrifize, with the consent of them all, set at liberty the Religious Man, the Secretary, and all the *Indians* they had Prisoners, putting them ashore in the Boat, and then the *Chineses* stood out to Sea. They endeavour'd to make over to *China*, but not being able, put into *Cochinchina*, where the King of *Tunquin* took all they had, and among the rest two heavy Pieces of Cannon, that had been put aboard for the Expedition of the *Moluccos*, the King's Standard, and all the Jewels, Goods, and Money. He suffer'd the Galley to perish on the Coast, and the *Chineses* dispers'd, flying into several Provinces. Others affirm, that King seiz'd and punish'd them. *They cast him into the Sea.* *The Secretary and Frier set at Liberty.*

The *Spaniards* that escap'd, went to carry the News to *Manila*, where some griev'd, and others, who hated the Governour for his Severity, rejoyced; but that ill Will soon vanish'd, and all generally lamented him; more especially when some of the Bodies were found and brought in. Among them were those of the Ensign, *John Diaz Guerrero*, an old Soldier, and Governour of *Cebu*; of the Ensign *Penalosa*, Proprietor of *Pila*; the great Soldier *Sahagun*, whose Wife ran roaring about the City; of Captain *Castano*, newly come over from *Spain*; of *Francis Rodriguez Peruleio*; of Captain *Peter Noyla*; of *John de Sotomayor*; of *Simon Fernandez*; that of his Sergeant; of *Guzman*; of the Ensign and Sergeant of the Company brought by *Don Philip de Samano*, who being sick transferr'd it to Captain *John Xuarez Gallinato*; and those of *Sebastian Ruis* and *Lewis Velez*, these two Merchants, all the rest old Soldiers; whose Funerals renew'd the Sorrow for that dismall Accident. *Spaniards that escap'd came to Manila.* *Bodies found.*

This News being brought to *Manila*, and no Papers of the Governour's appearing, wherein he nam'd, who was to succeed him, tho' it was known he had the King's Order so to do, believing it might be lost in the Galley, among much of the Kings, his own, and private Persons Goods, the City therefore chose the Licentiate *Rojas* for their Governour, and he was so forty Days. But the Secretary *John de Cuellar* returning to *Manila*, in a miserable Condition, with F. *Francis da Montilla*, gave Notice, that *Gomez Perez*, before his Departure had appointed his Son *Don Lewis* to succeed, and that this would be found at the Monastery of S. *Augustin*, in a Box, *Rojas chose Governour by the City.*

U among

DonLewis among other Papers, in the Custody of *F. James Munnoz*. *Rojas* had al-
das Marin- ready sent Orders to *Cebu*, for all the People employ'd in the Expedition,
nas Gover- to return, as was accordingly done. So that *Don Lewis* coming, notwith-
nor. standing some Protestations, he, by Virtue of his Father's Authority, succeeded him in the Government, till *Don Francis Tello* came.

Character Such was the End of that Gentleman, whose Actions were valuable in
of Gomez themselves, and the more for the Zeal he did them with. He wanted not
Perez. for political and martial Virtues, nor for Prudence in both Sorts; but he
would not regard Examples; and contrary to what those taught him, durst
promise himself to succeed, so that he became confident, if not rash. But
his Christian Piety makes Amends for all.

The Fleet *Don. Lewis*, his Kindred and Friends, wou'd fain have prosecuted the Ex-
dismiss'd. pedition to the *Moluccos*, and to this End *F. Antony Fernandez* came from
Tydore; but he succeeded not. The Fleet was dismiss'd, and it was a singular
Providence for the Security of the *Philippine* Islands; for presently after, at
the Beginning of the Year 1594, there came thither a great Number of Ships
from *China*, loaded only with Men and Arms, and brining no Merchandize,
as they are wont to do. Those Ships brought seven *Mandarines*, being some
of the chief Viceroys and Governours of the Provinces. It was believ'd, and
Arm'd prov'd certainly true, that they knowing *Gomez Perez* went upon that Expe-
Chinefes dition, to which he took with him all the *Spaniards*, concluded the Coun-
in the try was left defencelefs, and therefore came with a Design to Conquer, or
Philip- plunder it, which would have been very easy, had they found it as they ex-
pines. pected. They went out of their Ships but twice to visit *Don Lewis*, with
great State, and much Attendance. He receiv'd them affectionately, and presented every *Mandarine* with a gold Chain. They told him, they came by
their King's Order, to pick up the *Chinefes*, who wander'd about those Islands
without his Leave, but this was look'd upon as a meer Pretence; because
there was no Need, for that Effect, of so many *Mandarines*, nor such a Num-
Mandari- ber of Vessels arm'd and furnish'd for War. The *Chinefes* who murder'd
nes visit *Gomez Perez*, were of *Chincheo*, and therefore *Don Lewis*, as knowing the
DonLewis certain Criminals, sent his Kinsman *Don Ferdinand de Castro*, in a Ship,
to give the King of *China* an Account of that Treachery; but his Voyage
miscarry'd, and all was left in Suspence.

King of At this Time *Langara*, King of *Camboxa* made Instance for the Suc-
Camboxa cours, and requir'd *Don Lewis* to perform his Fathers Promise made to him
demands not long before. He therefore, in Pursuance to it, and to the End that
the pro- those Forces, or some Part of them, might continue in the Church's Ser-
mis'd Suc- vice, since they were provided for that End, in the Design of *Ternate*, re-
cour. solv'd to support that King with them.

Camboxa *Camboxa* is one of the most fertile of the *Indian* Regions. It sends
described. Abundance of Provisions to other Parts, for which Reason it is frequented
by *Spaniards*, *Persians*, *Arabs*, and *Armenians*. The King is a *Mahometan*;
but his Subjects the *Gusarats* and *Banians*, follow the Precepts of *Pythago-*
ras, perhaps without any Knowledge of him. They are all sharp witted,
Opinions and reputed the cunningest Merchants in *India*. However they are of Opini-
of the Na- on, that after Death, Men, Brute Beasts, and all Creatures, receive either
tives. Punishment, or Reward; so confus'd a Notion have they of Immortality.
The City *Camboxa*, which gives its Name to all the Country, is also call'd
Champa,

Champa, abounding in the Odoriferous *Calambuco* Wood, whose Tree call'd *Calamba,* grows in unknown Regions, and therefore has not been seen standing The Floods upon those great Rivers bring down Trunks of it, and this is the precious *Lignum Aloes. Camboxa* produces Corn, Rice, Peafe, Butter, and Oyl. There are made in it various Sorts of Cotton Webs, Muslins, Buckrams, Calicoes, white and painted, Dimities, and other curious Pieces exceeding the finest in *Holland.* They also adorn their Rooms with Carpets; tho' they are not like those brought out of *Persia* to *Ormuz.* They weave others for the common Sort, which they call *Bancales,* not unlike the *Scotch* Plads. Nor do they want the Art of Silk-Weaving, for they both weave, and work with the Needle, rich Hangings, Coverings for the low Chairs us'd by the Women of Quality, and for the *Indian* Litters, or *Palanquines,* which are made of Ivory, and Tortoife-Shell, and of the same they make Chefs-Boards, and Tables to Play, Seal-Rings, and other portable Things. In the Mountains there is found a fort of Christal, extraordinary transparent, whereof they make Beads, little Idols, Bracelets, Necklaces, and other Toys. It abounds in Amethists, Garnets, the Sort of Saphirs call'd Hyacinths, Spinets, Cornelians, Chryfolites, Cats Eyes, properly call'd *Acates,* all of them precious Stones; There are also those they call Milk, and Blood Stones, pleasant, and medicinal Fruits, Opium, Bangue, Sanders, Alom and Sugar. *Indigo* is incomparably prepar'd in *Camboxa,* and thence fent to feveral Provinces. The living Creatures are the fame *Asia* affords in those Parts, Elephants, Lions, Horfes, wild Boars, and other fierce Beasts. It is in Ten Degrees of North Latitude. The River *Mecon* waters all the Kingdom, and in it falls into the Sea ; being look'd upon as the greateft in *India,* carrying fo much water in Summer, that it floods, and covers the Fields, like the *Nile in Egypt.* It joyns another of lefs Stock, at the Place call'd *Chordemuco.* This River, for fix Months runs backward. The Reafon of it is the Extent and Plainnefs of the Country it runs along. The Southern Breezes choak up the Bar with Sand. The Currents thus damm'd up, fwell and rife together, after much Struggling one againft the other. The Bar looks to the South-ward, both Waters at first Form a deep Bay, and finding no free Paffage out, but being drove by the mighty Violence of the Winds, are forc'd to fubmit and bend their Courfe the wrong Way, till a more favourable Seafon reftores them to their natural Courfe. We fee fome fuch like Effects in *Spain,* where the *Tagus* falls into the Sea of *Portugal,* and the *Guadalquivir* into that of *Andaluzia,* oppos'd by the fuperior Force of the Sea Waves, and of the Winds.

About this Time, in the remoteft Part of this Country, beyond impenetrable Woods, not far from the Kingdom of the *Laos,* was difcover'd a City, of above fix thoufand Houfes, now call'd *Angon.* The Structures, and Streets, all of maffy Marble Stones, artificially wrought, and as entire, as if they had been modern Works. The Wall ftrong, with a Scarp, or Slope within, in fuch Manner, that they can go up to the Battlements every where. Thofe Battlements all differ one from another, reprefenting fundry Creatures, one reprefents the Head of an Elephant, another of a Lion, a third of a Tiger, and fo proceed in continual Variety. The Ditch, which is alfo of hew'd Stones, is capable of receiving Ships. Over it is a magnificent Bridge, the Arches of it being fupported by ftone

Lignum Aloes.

Manufactures.

Product.

Beafts.

Mecon River.

Angon City Difcover'd.

Its Magnificence.

U 2   Giants

Giants of a prodigious Height. The Aqueducts, tho' dry, show no less Grandeur. There are Remains of Gardens, and delightful Places, where the Aqueducts terminate. On one Side of the Town is a Lake above thirty Leagues in Compass. There are Epitaphs, Inscriptions, and Characters not understood. Many Buildings are more sumptuous than the rest, most of them of Alabaster, and Jasper Stone. In all this City, when first discovered by the Natives, they found no People, nor Beasts, nor any living Creatures, except such as Nature produces out of the Breaches of Ruins. I own I was unwilling to write this, and that I have look'd up n it as an imaginary City of *Plato's Atlantis*, and of that his Common-Wealth; but there is no wonderful Thing, or Accident, that is not subject to much Doubt. It is now Inhabited, and our Religious Men, of the Order of St. *Augustin* and St. *Dominick*, who have Preach'd in those Parts, do testify the Truth of it. A Person of Reputation for his Learning, conjectures it was the Work of the Emperor *Traian*; but tho' he extended the Empire more than his Predecessors, I have not ever Read that he reach'd as far as *Camboxa*. Were the Histories of the *Chinefes* as well known as ours, they would inform us, why they abandon'd so great a Part of the World; they would explain the Inscriptions on the Buildings, and all the rest that is unknown to the Natives themselves. I know not what to say of so Beautiful a City's being buried in Oblivion, or not known. It is rather a Subject of Admiration than Reflection.

Three Spanish Ships sent to the Relief of Camboxa.

Don *Lewis* being zealous to bring those Nations into the Bosom of the Church, and their Wealth, and Kings under the Subjection of the Crown of *Spain*, fitted out three Ships, under the Command of *John Xuarez Gallinato*, born at *Tenerife*, one of the *Canary* Islands, with 120 *Spaniards*, and some *Philippines*. They Sail'd from *Cebu*, but there rose a Storm immediately, which dispers'd the Ships. *Gallinato* drove on by the Fury of the Winds, arriv'd at *Malaca*, and the other two at *Camboxa*. Going up the River, they were Inform'd, That the King of *Sian* had defeated him of *Camboxa*, his Neighbour; who, with the wretched Remains of his Army, fled into the Kingdom of the *Laos*, a Neighbouring but Inhumane Nation, and that, whilst he was begging Compassion among those obdurate Hearts, the King of *Sian* had set up *Prauncar*, Nick-nam'd, *Wry Mouth the Traytor*, Brother to the vanquish'd Monarch, for King of *Camboxa*. This Accident did not obstruct the Succours which the *Spaniards* carry'd under Colour of an Embassy. They came to the City *Chordumulo*, 80 Leagues distant from the Bar, and leaving 40 *Spaniards* in the Ships, 40 others went to the Country where the new King was. They made Application to visit him presently, but he would not be seen that Day, tho' he order'd they should have good Quarters, and be told, he would give them Audience three Days after. But *James Velofo* and *Blafe Ruyz*, either that they were formerly acquainted with the Country, or some new Subtilty occurring, looking on that delay as suspicious, visiting a beautiful *Indian* Woman, of the King's Family, she told them in private, That being admitted into that Tyrants Secrets, he being fond of her, she knew he intended to Murder them all; and that during those three Days he had assign'd them, as it were to Rest, after their Journey, the Men and Means for Executing that Design were to be provided. The *Spaniards* return'd Thanks for the Intelligence, not without promise of Reward.

King of Camboxa routed by him of Siam.

Design to murder the Spaniards.

They

They were not difmay'd at the Danger; but repeating their Thanks to
the *Indian* Woman, for her Intelligence, came to this magnanimous, it it may
not be term'd a rafh Refolution.   They agreed to attack the King's Palace
that fame Night, and to withftand the whole Army, if Need were.   They
prepar d themfelves for that Enterprize, which was above human Strength,
fet Fire to the Houfe where the Powder lay, and the People running to
help, or to fee the Mifchief, the *Spaniards*, during the Confufion, enter'd the
Palace, and being acquainted with the royal Apartments, made through
them, till they came to the King's Perfon, whom they run thro', and kill'd
after cutting his Guards in Pieces   He defended himfelf, calling out
for Help, but thofe who came to his Affiftance found him bloodlefs.   The
Report of this Action alarm'd the other Guards, and then all the City,
which contains above thirty thoufand Inhabitants, who where all running to
Arms; above 14000 Men took up fuch as Occafion offer'd, and came upon the
Spaniards with many war-like Elephants   Our two Commanders drew up
their little Body, and retir'd in great Order, always fighting and killing
great numbers of their Enemies.   The Fight lafted all the Night, with
wonderful Bravery, the next Day they got to their Ships, and imbark'd,
leaving that Kingdom full of new Divifions.

Defperat of Bravery of the Spaniards.

They kill the King of Camboxa.

Retire before 14000 Indians.

The fecond Day after, *Gallinato* came in, with his Ship. He landed, having
been before inform'd of what had happen'd, and thinking he did not perform
his Duty, unlefs he fuccour'd the *Spaniards*, when he heard the Drums and
Bells, and faw the Streets and Port full of trading People, now in Arms.
He gave ftrict Orders to thofe that attended him, to behave themfelves very modeftly, fo as to conceal their own Concern, and deceive the People of
Camboxa, both by their Looks and the Sedatenefs of their Words.   The
principal Men of *Camboxa* vifited him, in peaceable Manner; whom he
treated very courteoufly.   He might have perform'd fome great Exploit,
but finding his Strength too fmall for fuch an Enterprize, and that now Affairs had taken another Turn, and were in a different Pofture, he thought
fit to be gone.   Moft o thofe great Men oppos'd it, promifing him the
Crown, as being well affected to the *Spaniards*, and a foreign Government.
Hence came the idle Report, that *Gallinato* was King of *Camboxa*, which
was believ'd by many in *Spain*, and acted on the Stage with Applaufe, and
good Liking. And it was the Opinion of Perfons well acquainted with thofe
Countries, that had *Gallinato* laid Fold of the Opportunity offer'd him, he
might then have poffefs d himfelf of *Camboxa*, and united it to the Crown
of *Caftile*.

Gallinato at Camboxa.

The great Men offer him the Crown.

I have feen Letters of *Vellofo*, and *Blafe Ruiz*, to the Council at *Manila*,
after this Action, wherein they fpeak to this Effect, and complain that
Gallinato fhould blame what they did.   But *Gallinato*, whofe Judgment,
and Valour, had been try'd in the greateft Dangers of thofe Eaftern Parts,
and many Years before in *Flanders*, would not fuffer himfelf to be eafily
led away by popular Affection, and honourably rejecting that Opportunity,
fail'd towards *Manila* He took in fome Refrefhment in *Cochinchina*. *Blafe
Ruiz* and *James Vellofo* had landed there before, and went alone by Land
to the Kingdom of the *Laos*, which lies Weft of *Cochinchina*, to feek out
the depos'd King *Langara*, and reftore him to his Throne. They found he
was dead, but had a Son living, who being told how they had kill'd the

The depos'd King's Son reftor'd.

Ufurper,

Uſurper, his Uncle and Enemy, he ſet forward immediately for his Kingdom with *Velloſo* and *Ruiz*, and 10000 Men, the King of the *Laos*, contrary to all Expectation furniſh'd him. He attack'd *Camboxa*, where *Ruiz* and *Velloſo* faithfully ſtuck to him during the War, and afterwards in his Government. Then he ſent another Embaſſy to the *Philippine* Iſland, asking Supplies of Men to quell the Troubles in his Country, and that he and his Subjects might receive the Faith of *JESUS CHRIST*; promiſing a conſiderable Part of his Dominions to the *Spaniards*, to ſubſiſt them. This Embaſſy came to *Manila*, when *Don Lewis* had quitted the Government, and reſign'd it up to *Don Francis Tello*, which gave Occaſion to *Ternate* to grow more ſettled in its Tyranny.

D Pedro de Acunna *fortifies* Carthagena.

Don *Pedro de Acunna*, who govern'd *Carthagena* in the *Weſt-Indies*, in this Year 1595, either becauſe it was his natural Inclination, or the Neceſſity of the Times requiring it, fortify'd the Place with Faſcines, Planks, Piles, and Ditches, working at it himſelf in Perſon. Thus he oblig'd the Biſhop, Clergy and Religious Men, to put their Hands to the Work; the very Ladies of Quality, their Daughters and Maids, did not refuſe to follow ſuch an Example. It was wonderful to ſee with what Expedition and Zeal the Work was brought to Perfection, of ſuch Force is a good Example. Soon after came to *Puerto Rico*, the Ship call'd *Pandorga*, or *Borgonna*, that was Admiral of *Tierra Firme*, and *New Spain*, with three Millions in her. The whole under the Care of the General *Sancho Pardo*.

56 Engliſh *Sail ſent to rob the Weſt-Indies.*

At this Time there came into the *Weſt-Indies* a Fleet of 56 Sail, ſent by the Queen of *England* to plunder them, under the Command of *John Hawkins* and *Francis Drake*. Captain *Peter Tello* defended the three Millions ſo bravely with the *Spaniſh* Frigots, that he ſav'd the Prize. *Hawkins* was wounded in the Fight, and dy'd of it before he could come to the Firm Land. *Drake*, with that Fleet, enter'd *Rio de la Hacha* and *Santa Marta*; and being one Night in Sight of *Carthagena*, took a Frigate belonging to that Coaſt, by which he was inform'd, how well the Governour had fortifi'd it; therefore making a Compliment of Neceſſity, he ſent *Don Pedro* a Meſſage by the Men of the Frigot, whom he therefore ſet at Liberty, ſaying, He did not attack his Works and City out of Reſpect to him, and becauſe he honour'd his Valour. The Truth of the Matter was, That *Drake* call'd together his Captains to conſult what was to be done, and they all adviſ'd him to attack the City, promiſing to do their utmoſt, and be anſwerable for the Succeſs; alledging it ought to be attempted, for being a Place of vaſt Wealth and Conſequence. Only *Drake* oppos'd it,

Drake's *Actions there.*

ſtrength'ning his Opinion by ſaying, His Mind did not give him, that the Enterprize could have the Succeſs they would aſſure him, becauſe they were to have to do with a Knight of *Malta*, a Batchelor, nothing weakned with Womaniſh Affection, or the Care of Children; but watchful, and intent upon defending the Place, and ſo Reſolute, that he would dye on the Spot before he would loſe it. This Opinion prevail'd, and the *Engliſh* ſtanding in Awe of *Don Pedro*'s Reputation, went away to the Town of *Nombre de Dios*, and took it. *Drake* afterwards deſigning to do the ſame at *Panama*, was diſappointed, meeting Oppoſition by the Way, which had been provided upon the Advice ſent by *Don Pedro*, that the *Engliſh* were moving againſt that City.   But

But let us return into *Afia*. Still the People of *Camboxa* perfifted to ask Succours at the *Philipine* Iflands, upon the ufual Promife of Converfion and Vaffalage. *Don Lewis de las Marinhas* undertook the Enterprize in Perfon, and at his own Coft. He fet out from *Manila* with *Don James Jordan,* an *Italian, Don Pedro de Figueroa, Peter Villeftil,* and *Ferdinand de los Rios Coronel, Spanifh* Commanders, the laft of them then a Prieft, who had alfo been in the firft War of *Camboxa.* A Storm took them out at Sea, which lafted three Days, with the ufual Fury. The Shipwrack was miferable, two Ships were ftav'd in Pieces, and the Sea fwallow'd up all the Men, Provifions and Ammunition. Of all the Soldiers and Seamen on Board the Vice-Admiral, only five fwam afhore on the Coaft of *China.* Some Soldiers were alfo fav'd out of the Admiral, and among them Captain *Ferdinand de los Rios,* the Veffel remaining founder'd under the Waves. The other Ship got to *Camboxa* almoft fhatter'd to Pieces after many Dangers. She found in the River of *Camboxa,* eight Juncks of *Malayes,* and the *Spaniards* feeing they defign'd to carry away fome Slaves of the King of *Camboxa,* to whofe Affiftance they came, inconfiderately boarded the *Malayes,* who being well furnifh'd with more than ordinary Fire-works, foon burnt our Ship, and moft of the *Spaniards* perifh'd in the Flames or Smoke. *Blaze Ruiz,* nor *Vellofo* were not there at that Time, but foon after in the Country, where they were attending the King, being befet in the Houfe where they lodg'd, were barbaroufly murder'd. Thofe few *Spaniards* that efcap'd, got into the Kingdom of *Sian,* and thence to *Manila.* Heaven was pleas'd this fhould be the End of all thofe mighty Preparations made for the Recovery of *Ternate,* and the other *Molucco* Iflands, whofe Tyrant triumph'd at the News, concluding it was the Effect of his good Fortune, and looking on it as a Teftimony of the Juftice of his Caufe, and accordingly he confederated a new with our Enemies.

D. Lewis de las Marinhas goes to relieve Camboxa.

Is caft away.

Spanifh Ships burnt.

Don Francifco Tello, a Gentleman of *Andaluzia,* fucceeded *Gomez Perez* in the Government of the *Philippine* Iflands, and came to *Manila* in the Year 1596. His firft Care was to inform himfelf of the Condition his Predeceffor had left them in, and to fupply the Garrifons; becaufe the Emperor of *Japan,* having in the Year 1595, executed thofe glorious Martyrdoms, the Memory whereof is ftill frefh, on the Religious Men of the Order of *S. Francis,* it gave him Jealoufy, that he might have a Defign againft the *Philippine* Iflands.

D. Fran. Tello Governor of the Phil.

The Natives of the Iflands of *Mindanao,* hate our Nation as much as thofe of *Ternate,* and upon any Occafion take Arms againft it, as they did in the laft, at the faid Ifland of *Ternate.* For this Reafon, *Stephen Rodriguez de Figueroa* enter'd into Articles with the new Governour, *Don Francifco Tello,* by Virtue whereof he made War on the People of *Mindanao* and *Ternate,* at his own Expence. *Stephen Rodriguez* was fo rich, that he might fafely undertake this Affair. He liv'd at *Arevalo,* a Town on the Ifland *Panaz,* one of the *Philippines,* and fet out with fome Galleys, Frigots, Champanes, and one Ship, in which there were fome *Spaniards,* and above 1500 of the Painted Natives, call'd *Pintados,* who were to ferve as Pioneers. He arriv'd at the River of *Mindanao,* on the 20th of *April,* 1596. and as foon as the Inhabitants of the Town, peculiarly call'd *Mindanao,* faw fuch a fightly Company, they fled up the Side of the

People of Mindanao hate the Spaniards.

Stephen Rodriguez makes War on Mindanao, at his own Expence.

the River, abandoning the Place, to the Fury of the Soldiers Most of them reforted to the Town of *Buyahen,* then the Refidence of *Raxamura,* King of *Mindanao,* who being under Age, had yet no Charge of the Government, which was wholly in the Hands of *Silonga,* a Soldier, and Commander of Reputation. Our Men following up the River, came to *Tampacan,* five Leagues from the firft. That Place was govern'd by *Din urihot,* Uncle to *Monao,* the true Proprietor, who was then alfo young.

T'e N- tives fly, and be purfaes.

These two were naturally well affected to the *Spaniards,* and therefore, as foon as they difcover'd their Arms, came out in peaceable Manner, to meet, and offer them their Affiftance. They inform'd them, that the Enemies, for they were fo to thofe of *Buyahen,* had retir'd into the Fort they had there. *Stephen Rodriguez* hearing the News, and having made much of thofe Princes, order'd the Fleet to weigh Anchor, and continue the Purfuit, four Leagues farther, ftill along the River, to *Buyahen.* Being come thither, he landed his Men on S. *Mark*'s Day; which was done by the Col. *John de Xara,* but without any Order, becaufe having had no Engagement at *Mindanao,* they thought they fhould have little to do there ; as if this, or any other Pretence ought to be an Excufe for not obferving Martial Difcipline, *Stephen Rodriguez* would land to rectify that Diforder by his Prefence. He went out in fuch Armour of Proof, that a Shot of a fmall Drake would fcarce pierce it. Only his Head unarm'd, but cover'd with a Cap and Feather, a black carrying his Helmet, and five Soldiers well arm'd attending him. He had fcarce march'd fifty Paces, before an *Indian,* whofe Name was *Ubal,* fuddenly rufh'd out of a clofe and topping Thicket, and running at him, with his *Campilan,* or Cymiter, clove his Head. *Ubal* was Brother to *Silonga,* and Owner of one only Cow there was in all that Country. He kill'd her three Days before this Accident, and inviting his Friends to her, promis'd in that War to kill the moft noted Man among the *Spaniards.* He was as good as his Word, for *Stephen Rodriguez* dropt down of the Wound, and dy'd three Days after, without anfwering one Word to the Queftions that were made him, tho' he did it by Signs. The five *Spaniards,* feeing their Commander fo fuddenly wounded, that the Slayer, appeared, and the Stroke was heard the fame Moment, fell upon *Ubal* and cut him in Pieces. They acquainted Colonel *Xara* with their General's Death ; and he fuppreffing his Concern, drew back the Men, and threw up a Fortification in the moft convenient Place, near the River, where he orderly founded his Colony, to be inhabited by our Men. He appointed Aldermen, and Magiftrates, calling it *New Murcia,* in Honour of the old one in *Spain,* where he was born. Afterwards, defigning to marry *Donna Ana de Ofeguera,* Widow to *Stephen Rodriguez,* he left Things unfettled, and arriv'd at the Ifland *Luzon* about the Beginning of *June.*

Is kill'd.

A Fort erected in Mindanao and call'd New Murcia.

Cap. Miranda fent to Mindanao.

The Governor *Don Francis Tello,* who was then at the Place call'd *El Embocadero,* an hundred Leagues from *Manila,* being inform'd of what had happen'd, and told upon what defign the Colonel *Xara* came, feiz'd him immediately, fending Captain *Toribio de Miranda,* to the War in *Mindanao.* He found his Men were retir'd to the Port *de la Caldera,* in the fame Ifland but 36 Leagues from the Mouth of the River. There there he maintain'd himfelf, till about *Auguft Don Francis Tello* appointed *Don John Ronquillo,* who was Commander of the Galleys, to fucceed in that Poft. He alfo

command'd

commiffion'd *Peter Arceo Covarrubias*, and others, as Captains, to go with him; *James Chaves Cannizares*, Collonel ; *Garcia Guerrero*, Major; and *Chriftopher Villagra* and *Cervan Gutierrez*, Captains of Foot. *Don John Ronquillo* came with his Recruit to prefs upon the Enemy, and did it fo effectually, that being diftrefs'd, they crav'd Aid of the King of *Ternate*, to whom the People of *Mindanao* pay an Acknowledgement, which is little lefs, or the fame as Tribute. *Buizan*, Brother to *Silonga*, went on this Embafly and fucceeded fo well, that the King of *Ternate* fent with him feven *Carfoas*, x heavy Pieces of Cannon, two fmaller, fome Falconets, and fix hundred Men. They failing up the River of *Mindanao*, defign'd to pafs on as far as *Buyahen*; but met with great Difficulties at the Reaches; becaufe at one of them they were threatned by the *Spaniards* chief Fort, the Galleys, and other Veffels; and the other was a narrow Channel, with a Point running out into it, on which was erected a Baftion, defended by forty Men. From thence our Men had artificially laid a ftrong wooden Bridge over to the other Side of the River, clofe to which a Galliot ply'd up and down.

Ternates Succous Mindanao.

The *Ternates* feeing both Sides fo well Guarded, refolv'd to fortify themfelves at the Mouth of the River. They accordingly erected a fmall Fort, and put themfelves into it, with an equal Number of *Mindanao* Soldiers. The News hereof mov'd the General *Ronquillo* to diflodge them; and in Order to it, came down with the Galleys and other Veffels, and 140 Men well appointed. He landed with 116, and the Captains *Ruy Gomez Arellano*, *Garcia Guerrero*, *Chriftopher Villagra*, and *Alonfo de Palma*, facing the Enemy, at about eighty Paces Diftance, on the Bank of the River. The *Ternates* and *Mindanaos* had levell'd all the Front of their Fort, and defignedly left a Spot of Bufhes and Brambles on one Side, where 300 *Ternates* lay in Ambufh, the reft being in the Fort. Both their Parties perceiving how few of our Men came to attack them, were afham'd to be fhut up within Fortifications, and lye in Ambufh, and accordingly making Show of haughty Threats, came out and met the *Spaniards*. They found fuch Oppofition, that without the Help of any Stratagem, or other Caufe but their natural Valour, at the very firft onfet, almoft all the *Ternates* were kill'd, and the reft fled. Our Men follow'd the Chace, till they made an End of them. The people of *Tampaca*, who till then had been Neuters, to fee which Side Fortune would favour, perceiving fhe declar'd for us, took up Arms for our Part. Only feventy feven efcap'd dangeroufly wounded, whereof fifty were drown'd in the River leaping into it in Defpair : Of the other twenty feven, only three furviv'd, who carry'd the News to their King. The *Spaniards* poffefs'd themfelves of the Shipping, Cannon, and Plunder of the vanquifh'd, and were encourag'd to profecute the War.

They build a Fort on the River.

Slaughter of Ternates.

Only three efcape.

Don Francis Tello did not neglect other Affais of this Nature. He underftood by his Spyes, and it was bruited abroad, that the Emperor of *Japan* was gathering a mighty Army, and fitted out a Fleet for it, with Arms and Provifions. It was alfo known, that he was in Treaty to fecure himfelf againft the *Chinefes*, of whom the *Japonefes* are naturally Jealous. Hence it was inferr'd, that he arm'd to carry the War out of his own Dominions. He had already enter'd into Allyance with the King of *Ternate*, and other Neighbours, who were Enemies to the Crown of *Spain*. All

Warlike preparations in Japan.

X thefe

these Particulars gave vehement Cause to conjecture, that the Storm threatned the *Philippine* Islands, and more especially *Manila*, the Head of them. The Governour strengthned himself, and sent Captain *Alderete* to discover the whole Truth, under Colour of complimenting that Emperour, and carrying him a Present. The Embassador set out for *Japan* in *July*, and at the same Time *Don Francisco* dispatch'd the Galeon *S. Philip* for *New Spain*, with Advice of those Reports. These two Ships, viz. that *Alderete* went in, and the *S. Philip*, were together in *Japan*, which the Natives were jealous of. *Alderete* got full Information of the Strength and Designs of the *Japonese*, and his Industry was of Use, for the taking of right Measures in *Manila*, and to prevent their fearing without Cause. He brought back another noble Present to the Governour; and both Sides stood upon their Guard, to be ready upon all Occasions.

In the Year 1598, the sovereign Court was again erected at *Manila*, King *Philip* prudently conferring Dignity on that Province. It was compos'd of the Judges *Zambrano, Mezcoa, Tellez de Almazan*, and the Kings Attorney *Jerome Salazar, y Salcedo*. That great King never allow'd of any Intermission in his weighty Cares, which extended to all the known Parts of the World; having a watchful Eye upon the Designs of other Princes, whether well, or ill affected to the Propagation of the Gospel, which was his main Design. Therefore, about this Time, he made Haste to rid himself of his neighbouring Enemies, that he might have Leasure to attend the remotest Rebels against the Church and his Monarchy. And in Respect that as Age came on, its Distempers grew heavier, he concluded a Peace with *France*, which was proclaim'd at *Madrid*, with Martial Solemnity, after he had withdrawn himself to the Monastery of *S. Laurence*, at the *Escurial*, a Work of his Piety and Magnificence, where he dy'd on the thirteenth of *September* 1598, with singular Tokens of Sanctity. He frequented the Sacrament of Confession, receiv'd the divine Viaticum, and extreme Unction, the last Remedy for temporal, and eternal Health. His Death was in all Respects answerable to the wonderful Course of his Life.

King *Philip* the Third, our sovereign Lord, succeeded him, having been before sworn in all his Kingoms, who, amidst the Tears and Funeral Solemnities, Commanded the Will to be open'd, and what his Father had order'd to be fulfill'd. His Instructions, and the Mysteries of State, whereof he was so great a Master, and which he communicated to his Son till the last Gasp, produc'd the Peace which attended his most happy Succession, which was his Due by Natural Right, the Law of Nations, and his own innate Virtues; the general Submission of his Subjects, and the Fidelity of the Armies that serv'd in the Northern Provinces in *Italy, Africk, Asia*, the *Indies*, and in Garrisons, were a Curb to other Nations. Many of them presented the new King with Protestations of Loyalty, before they had receiv'd Letters and Advice of his being upon the Throne. The same Unanimity was found in the Fleet, and Naval Power, wherein the Treasures and Commodities are transported; a rare Tranquility upon the Change of Princes, The *Roman* Legions in *Germany*, and *Illyricum*, did not show such Respect to *Tyberius*, after the Death of *Augustus*. And tho' the *Spanish* Monarchy is of so great an Extent, that it borders on the unknown World, and it is never Night in all Parts of it, because the

Marginal notes:

A Spanish Embassy thither.

Sovereign Court at Manila.

Peace between France & Spain.

K. Philip the 2d dies.

K. Philip the 3d.

Greatness of the Spanish Monarchy.

Sun

Sun encompaſſes and continually diſplays his Light over it, yet it obey'd without any Commotion, or rather with Pride, as if it knew and were ſenſible of the new Hand that took up the Reins of Government: Excellent Princes have ſeldom fail'd to employ extraordinary Miniſters about their Perſons, to manage and ſuſtain the Burden their Fortune lays upon their Shoulders; ſo *Alexander* the Great had *Hepheſtion*; the two *Scipios*, the two *Lelij*; *Auguſlus Cæſar*, *Marcus Agrippa*; the Princes of the Auguſt Houſe of *Auſtria*, other Perſons of ſingular Virtue; for all moral Wiſdom, and Experience it ſelt teaches us, that the Difficulties of weighty Affairs are not to be duly manag'd, and ſurmounted, by any but Perſons of a more than ordinary Capacity; becauſe Nature has not left any of its Works deſtitute of a proportionable Miniſtry. And conſidering, that it is of great Importance to the publick Welfare, to contrive, that what is neceſſary for the Uſe and Commerce of Mankind may appear eminent in Dignity, for the ſtrengthning of the common Advantage with Authority: The King, I ſay, following thoſe ancient Examples, made Choice of *Don Franciſco de Rojas y Sandoval*, then Marques of *Denia*, and ſince firſt Duke of *Lerma*, a moſt able Miniſter, privately to conſult with him about fundamental Matters and Concerns, for which he had been prepar'd with ſingular Affection in thoſe Times: Beſides the great Antiquity of his Family, which has ally'd him to all the nobleſt of the *Grandees* of *Spain*, all Men own him endow'd with the neceſſary Virtues, that belong to a Perſon in ſo great a Poſt; which ſhine through that pleaſing Gravity of his Countenance, with a ſtay'd Gayity that teſtifies his Capacity, and provokes Reſpect at the ſame Time that it gains Affections. He conſtituted him the firſt of his Council of State, and all the Orders for Peace and War began to run through his Hands. All the Opinions of Councels, which he found ſeal'd, for King *Philip* the 2d to give his Deciſion thereupon, he reſtor'd, without opening them, to the Preſidents of the ſaid Councels they came from, being, perhaps, calculated out of Reſpect, that they might again debate upon them with more Liberty, and ſend them back enlarg'd or reform'd. *Duke of Lerma Prime Miniſter.*

Heaven was now haſtening the Reduction of the *Molucco* Iſlands, and the puniſhing the Perſecution of the faithfull, tho the Tyrants appear'd never ſo haughty; however the Talk of it was diſcontinu'd for ſome Time; becauſe the Enterprize was to be concerted, and carry'd on in the *Philippine* Iſlands, and to be reſolv'd on, and encourag'd in the ſupreme Council of the *Indies*, and it was requiſite that the Preſident and Councellors ſhould be well affected to the Cauſe, which had then no Body to ſupport it, as being deſpair'd of by Reaſon of ſo many unfortunate Attempts: and therefore the Papers of Reflections, and Informations relating to it, lay by, forgotten, in Heaps. This was the Poſture of thoſe Affairs till Providence diſpos'd the Means for bringing it about, that a Matter which was difficult on ſo many ſeveral Accounts, might fall into the Hands of a Sovereign, who being well affected, might with ſpecial Zeal bring it to Perfection. *Neglect of the Moluccos in Spain.*

No Body now diſturb'd the King of *Ternate*. The *Engliſh* ſettled on his Lands, and Trade enrich'd the Sovereign and the Subjects. He, tho' he had many Sons, and the Prince his Succeſſor was of Age to bear Arms, did not ceaſe equally to increaſe his Wives and Concubines. Luſt was never circumſcrib'd by any Laws among thoſe People. The Relations of curious Perſons inform us, That among the reſt of this Kings Wives, there was

Queen of Ternate in Love with the Kings Son. one very young, and singular for Beauty, with whom the Prince her Son-in-Law, whose Name was *Gariolano* fell in Love, and she rejected not his Courtship tho' she was Wife to his Father: But that Nearness of Blood secur'd their Familiarity, and under the Shelter, and Cover of it, she admitted both Father and Son.

Sangiack of Sabubu Father to her. This Queen was Daughter to the *Sangiack* of *Sabubu*, a potent Prince in the great Island *Batochina*, who came to *Ternate*, upon some slight Occasion. He being lodged in the Palace, and entertain d as a Father, and Father-in-Law, easily saw into the Incestuous Life of his Daughter. He resolv'd to be thoroughly convinc'd, yet concealing his Jealousy from both the Lovers, he was satisfy'd of the Truth, learnt who were the Parties privy to it, abhorr'd the Baseness, and condemn'd his own Blood. He pretended one day he would Dine in private, and sent only for his Daughter; who being free *He Poisons her.* from all Jealousy or Suspition, swallow'd a Poison, which soon took away her Life, in that Food which she us'd most to delight in. Endeavours were us'd to help the unhappy Queen, and compose the Father; but he angrily obstructing that last act of Compassion, put away the Physitians, and Women, and being left alone with the King, who, upon hearing the News, was come to give his Assistance, said, *This Woman, whom Nature gave to me for a Daughter, and I to you for a Wife, has, with her Life, satisfy'd a Debt she had contracted by her inordinate Passions. Do not Lament her, or believe she dy'd of any Natural Distemper. I kill'd her, taking the Revenge off your Hands. The Prince, your Son, had a Love Intrigue with her? Being in your House I had full Proof of it, and not being able to endure, that my Blood should wrong you, I could lay aside all Fatherly Affection, and take away the Stain that on my Side is laid upon the Law of Nature, and your Honour. I have honourably finish'd the first Part of this Example. Now, if you think your self wrong'd by your Son, he is in your Power, and I have no Right to deliver him up to you, as I do this false Body. It lies upon you to finish this Work upon the Offender, for I have perform'd all that was my Duty, in giving you this Information, and depriving my self of the Daughter I lov'd best.*

The King was astonish'd, without knowing how to return Thanks, or perform any other Act becoming a King; and having lamented the Misfortune for some time, order'd Prince *Gariolano* to be secur'd; but he, who was no *The Prince Flies.* less belov'd by the Guards than his Father, Guessing at the Consequences, which might certainly be deduc'd from the Queens violent Death, sparing no Horse-flesh, made to the Sea-Port, where he withdrew, with some of his Relations, from his Fathers Presence and Anger, till it naturally cool'd. It *Is Restor'd to Favour.* happen'd as he expected, for he was appeased before a Year expir'd, and the Prince was restor'd to his Favour; the King then making a Jest of the Stains of his Honour, and saying, *He well knew his ill Luck in Wives and Concubines.* But what Laws does he observe, who is guided by his Appetite? And how can he weigh the Duties of Honour, who Thinks that only the common Actions of the Sense have any solid being?

The End of the Sixth Book.

THE

THE
HISTORY
OF THE
DISCOVERY and CONQUEST
OF THE
Molucco and *Philippine* Islands, &c.

BOOK. VII.

THE Governour *Don Francis Tello*, to attend other Neighbour- **D. Francis**
ng Provinces, where greater Commotions were threatned, **Tello neg-**
turn'd his Arms that Way; sending some inconsiderable Part, **lects the**
at several Times to the *Moluccos*; for he never went seriously **Moluccos.**
about recovering those Islands, either because he apprehended,
or had Intelligence of Dangers threatned by the haughty *Japonefes, Minda-*
naos and *Chinefes*, or that he would not tread in the Track of those who
ruin'd themselves in the Expeditions against *Ternate.* Yet our Men
fought that Nation in other Parts; for being the most Warlike, and averse
to the very Name of *Spaniards*, it never let pass any Opportunity of doing
them Harm.

We have already mention'd the first coming of the *English* into those
Seas, and the Care that was taken to obliterate the Example set by their
Voyage, by fortifying the Streights of *Magellan.* It could not be effected,
nor did our Feet succeed in punishing, as was intended, those who had
the Boldness to attempt that unthought-of Passage. Since then, the *Hol-* **Dutch at**
landers and *Zealanders*, supported by Rebellion and Disobedience, have **the Mo-**
sail'd into *India*, possess'd themselves of strong Holds, and erected Factories, **luccos.**
transporting the Drugs, Precious Stones and Silks of *Asia*; and what is worse,
possessing themselves of several Places, and rending the *Spanish* Monarchy.
They have made several Voyages. What Island have they not pry'd into?
What Barbarous Nation have they not encourag'd to Rebellion and
Tyranny;

Tyranny, especially since *Maurice* of *Naffau* is possess'd of those Provinces, by the Title of Governour.

Philip-pines fill'd with Chinese.

The *Philippine* Islands were now appointed for the Place of Arms, considering the great Delays Experience had shown there were towards Recovering of the *Molucco* Islands. In the mean while, notwithstanding that *Don Francis Tello* was warn'd, how pernicious Inhabitants he was like to have in the *Sangleyes*, or *Chinese*, by whom the Islands of his Province began to be much peopled and fill'd, yet he allow'd them greater Liberty than was convenient; and the Municipal Laws which provided against this Disorder being forgotten or contemn'd, in a very short Time there were additional Towns of *Chinese*, *Chincheos*, and other such like Monsters, who were no better than Pyrates, or Incendiaries in that Country, which ought to have taken sufficient Warning by, and been well provided on Account of past Accidents, to shut up all Passages against such Enemy Nations. *Don Francisco* excus'd their Resort, alledging, That they imported Abundance of Provisions and Merchandise, which is what usually enriches all Places; That no Men have such a consummate Mechanick Genius as they; That they are more assiduous and constant at the Works and Buildings than the Natives of the *Philippines*. He said, That all the Jealousy generally conceiv'd of them vanishes, if the Governour administers Justice impartially, and permits no private Cabals. All these are, or appear'd to be frivolous Reasons, without any Force; and the admitting of such an Inundation of those People, prov'd very dangerous, as may be seen in the Sequel of this Work, by what happen'd to the Governour *Gomez Perez*. It was a particular Providence of Heaven, that other Nations did not go about to League with this, or the *Dutch*, who have so strongly fix'd themselves in the *Archipelago*; for they might, without much Difficulty, have given us more Trouble than has been occasion'd by the Rebellion of the Kings of the *Moluccos*; to whose Country, and all others in *India*, great Fleets of *Dutch* resort, ever since the Year 1585, whereof *Dutch* Writers give an Account, and lay down in Cuts, even the smallest Plants they produce.

It does not belong to us to give an Account of the *English*, *Dutch*, or other Nations of *India* and *Asia*, or their Expeditions and Voyages; but only such as relate to the Conquest of *Ternate* and the *Molucco* Islands, or may have some Dependance on this Subject; but be it known, once for all, that every Year, some Northern Fleets appear'd, coming either thro' *New Streights*, still unknown to our Discoverers, or those before frequented and laid down. But before we enter upon this Relation, it seems requisite to say something of *Holland*, the Head of the Neighbouring Islands, as that which is become most outrageous in *India*, and most covets the

Account of Holland.

Moluccos. The Province of *Holland* is almost on all Sides encompass'd by the Sea, and the Ports of the *Maese* and *Rhine*, for about 60 Leagues in Compass. Within it are contain'd 29 wall'd Towns, whose Names and Situation does not belong to us to speak of, nor of those of *Zealand*, or the other Provinces subject to them. The Curious may read *Lambert*, *Hortensius*, and *Montefortius*. The Natives are descended from the Ancient *Catti*; and forasmuch as *Erasmus* of *Rotterdam*, which is in *Holland*, describes it in his *Chiliades*, we will abridge what he there delivers at large,

large, out of Affection to his Country. The Learned, fay, he, agree, and it is a probable Conjecture, that the Island *Tacitus* mentions, lying from the *Rhine* to the Ocean, is that we call *Ho'land*; which I am oblig'd to Honour, as owing my first Breath to it, and would to God we could honour it as it deferves. *Martial* charges it with being rude, or unpolished; and *Lucan* with Cruelty. Either these Things do not belong to us, but to our Anceftors, or we may value our felves upon them both. What Nation is now known, whofe firft Fathers were not more uncouth than their Pofterity? Or when was *Rome* more highly commended, than when its People knew no other Arts but Tillage and Warfare? *Erafmus* fpends Time in proving, that it is the Nature of *Holland*, not to relifh *Martial's* Wit; and that this is not the Effect of Rudenefs, but a Gravity worthy Imitation. Then he makes an Exclamation, faying, Would to God all Chriftians had *Dutch* Ears! And that if ftill any one fhall contend, the Nation is in the Wrong, in having ftopp'd theirs to all Poetical Delights and Allurements, and arm'd it felf againft them; the *Dutch* valu'd themfelves upon being comprehended in that Reflection, which did not difpleafe the Ancient *Sabines*, the Perfect *Lacedemonians*, and the Severe *Catos*. *Lucan* call'd the *Batavi*, that is the *Dutch*, Cruel, as *Virgil* did the *Romans*, Vehement *Erafmus* adds, That the Cuftoms of thefe Nations are Familiar, inclining to Meeknefs and Benignity, and not to Fiercenefs; becaufe Nature endow'd them with a fincere Difpofition, free from Fraud and Double-Dealing, and did not make them fubject to extraordinary Vices, except the Love of Pleafure, and Excefs in Entertainments. This is caus'd by the Multitude of Beauties, which are Incentives, by the feveral Sea-Ports on the Ocean, the Mouths of the two Rivers, *Rhine* and *Maefe*; the perpetual Felicity of the Soil, water'd by other Navigable Rivers; and the Fifh and Foul in the Ponds and Woods. No Province of fo fmall a Compafs, contains fo many Cities of a confiderable Magnitude, and fo Populous, excellently govern'd; fo full of Commodities, Arts and Trade. It abounds in Men indifferently learn'd. *Erafmus* himfelf, in Conclufion, owns that none of them arrives to fingular Erudition. This Account, which in all that is natural muft be own'd not to exceed, affords Arguments to condemn and convince the Author of it, and the Nation it felf. All that Part of the World where Religion and Politenefs flourifh, is acquainted with the Diverfity of Opinions all thofe Nations efpoufe, of *Proteftants*, *Puritans*, *Calvinifts*, thefe the moft Numerous; *Huguenots*, *Lutherans*, and all other Sorts, too long to enumerate, and not to our Purpofe. Since *Erafmus* confeffes that his Country does not produce any Perfons of eminent Learning, why do they take upon them to decide Controverfies in Religion? Why do they incroach upon Councils? If they are of fuch an excellent Difpofition, and have fuch a modeft Genius, Why do they caft off that Piety, whereof there are fuch ancient Teftimonies in our firft Fathers, fo much honour'd by the primitive Charity of the true Church? It is true, as *Erafmus* fays, that they are of a kind Temper, but Tenacious of whatfoever they once efpoufe; the fame moves us to pity them the more, for the Difficulty of dealing with Pofitivenefs in Minds that are not given to change. Let no Man believe but that under that feeming Meeknefs in Behaviour, the higheft Degree of Pride lies
couch'd.

Tacitus l. 20.

Erafmus of the Manners of Hollanders.

The Authors Reflections on them.

A Spanish Author cannot forbear these Reflections.

couch'd. What greater Pride than to scoff at the most ancient Church? At its Apostolical Traditions? At her universal Agreement? At the Miracles God has wrought, to approve the Catholick Doctrine? And what Error can be more inexcusable, than to follow the New Opinions of unlearned and vicious Men, such as the Arch-Hereticks were; and to live under a Necessity of not laying down their seditious Arms only to defend Impiety grounded on Ignorance, and the Extravagancies of their Passions? What House is there in those Cities which *Erasmus* extols, wherein all the Inhabitants profess and follow the same Way of spiritual Salvation? When the Father is a *Calvinist*, the Mother is often a *Huguenot*, the Son a *Lutheran*, the Servant a *Hussite*, and the Daughter a *Protestant*. All the Family is divided, or rather every particular Person's Soul is so, and at best doubts of all. Wherein does this differ from Atheism? It is positive Atheism. This Division, unworthy of wild Beasts, is the Occasion, and a Sort of Mathematical Necessity, that these People cannot be united among themselves in true Peace. For those Things are the same to one

See the latter part of the Preface.

another, that they are to a Third; so that almost all these having different Notions, as to God, they cannot of Necessity be united among themselves, as differing in the most essential Part, which is the having an uniform Notion of God in Religion. Let no Man believe, that because they are not at War among themselves, it is Love that is the Occasion of it. The Ground of their false Tranquility is to be call'd a Cessation, and not Peace. These are the People who have unhing'd Loyalty and the Christian Religion, before settled in the Islands, and remotest Parts of *Asia*, making Excursions from their own Country, as far as *China*, their raging Avarice being grounded on the Advice given them by the Queen of *England*, and on Malice, because King *Philip* the IId had shut up the other Ports of his Kingdoms against them; so to endeavour to reduce them to to the Truth and Submission, by taking from them the Advantages of Trade.

Dutch first sail to the Moluccos.

The first *Dutch* Fleet that came to the *Molucco* Islands, after the *English*, in the Year 1598, shall be here spoken of. Some prime Men, for the Sake of their Country, as they said, and to gain Reputation, met in *Holland* and *Zealand*, and fitted out six Ships and two Brigantines, to sail into *India*. The first Ship they call'd the *Maurice*, the Admiral in her being *Jacob Cornelius Neck*, born at *Roterdam*, and the Master *Gonaert Jansk*; the second was the *Amsterdam*, and in her the Vice-Admiral *Vibrant Darkik*; the other Ships were the *Holland*, the *Zealand*, the *Guelder*, and the *Utrecht*; The bigger Brigantine the *Friezland*, and the smaller the *Overissel*. They carry'd 160 Soldiers, besides Mariners, and sail'd from *Roterdam* on the 13th of *March*. Off from *Sluys*, on the 4th of *April*, they had such a dreadful Storm, as might have discourag'd them from Proceeding, and the Ship the *Holland* was almost disabled; but still they were drove

25 Dutch baptized.

on by the Weather to the *Texel*, and thence to *Debenter*, and in Conclusion they got into the Ocean. They met another Ship returning to the *Low Countries*, which presented them with 10000 Oranges, and having distributed them among the Men, they made a general Rejoycing, for the

Barrels must be a Mistake.

baptizing of 25 Men, aboard the Ship the *Guelder*, on the 10th of *May*. On the 11th they anchor'd at *Barrels*, and on the 15th at the Island

Madera,

Madeira, and again on the 17th at the *Canaries*, *Gomera*, and *Palma*, paſſing by thoſe of *Sal* and *Santiago*, which are thoſe of *Cabo Verde*, they furl'd all their Sails, and drove in a Storm, in 29 Degrees Latitude. On the firſt o *June* they took a Sea Tortoiſe which weigh'd 143 Pounds. On the 15th of the ſame Month, *Gerrit Jans*, either provok'd by Wine or a worſe Spirit, caſt himſelf into the Sea, from the higheſt Part of the greater Brigantine. The next Day, aboard the Ship *Guelder*, in which the new baptiſed Men were, they ſaw a large flying-Fiſh, which clapping too its Wings, fell into the ſaid Ship; but they ſaw the ſame Sort of Fiſhes fall upon their Veſſels at other Times. On the Eighth they croſs'd the Line, and began to diſtribute a Pot of Wine to every ſix Men; but on the 25th of the ſame Month, for Joy of having paſs'd the Ridges of Rocks before *Brazil*, which run to the Southward in 18 Degrees of South Latitude, they allow'd three Pots to every ſeven Men. Such a thick Fog fell that they loſt Sight of the ſmaller Brigantine; the *Zealand* ſoon found her again, and diſcover'd many Cranes ſtanding on the Tops of the Reeds, or Canes, that grew out Tall and of an equal Height above the Water. On the 24th of *July*, they came to an Anchor at the Cape of *Good Hope*, whence they ſail'd again on the 15th of *Auguſt* with Stormy Weather, all the eight Veſſels together, the Sea there boiling up as a Pot does upon the Fire. This Motion, like boiling, was ſeen for about a Muſket Shot in *The Sea* Length, and the Breadth of a Ship, and all this Space was cover'd thick *ſeems to* with Weeds, which they paſs'd over by main Force, without any Dan- *boil up.* ger.

On the 24th they reach'd the Iſland of *Madagaſcar*, or of *S. Laurence*, *Madagaſ-* and ſaw abundance of Whales. Here the plentiful Diſtribution of Wine *car.* ceas'd, and it began to be given out more ſparingly, to lament by this Abſtinence, the Death of *John Pomer*, a ſkilful Sailor. On the 27th they paſs'd Cape *S. Sebaſtian*, and on the 30th Cape *S. Julian*. On the 4th of *September*, it was debated whether they ſhould make for the Iſland of *Banda*, or put into the Bay of *Anton Gill*. They came to no Reſolution at that Time, tho' they afterwards arriv'd ſeparately at *Banda*, and at ſeveral Times. On the 17th they diſcover'd, at a great Diſtance, the Iſland of *Ceine*, by others call'd the *Iſle of Swans*, which is high and mountainous, and for Joy of the Water they expected to take in there, they gave every Man three Cups of Wine. Before that, the Vice-Admiral went aſhore with five Men, in another little Iſland, and taking a View of it, found a Noble Spacious Harbour, well land-lock'd, into which a Rivulet of freſh *They land* Water fell. They put in and refitted their ſhatter'd Veſſels, finding 14 *in a ſmall* Fathom Water. They had not Landed in four Months, and therefore in *Iſland.* Thankſgiving, and becauſe it was then Fair Time in *Holland*, they made a Sort of Chappel, on the Bodies of Trees, and covering it with Leaves, preach'd there twice a Day, in Honour of the Fair. They eat Abundance of Fowl, which they could almoſt take with their Hands, and drank Wine more plentifully. A Native of *Madagaſcar*, who came along with them, and had been taken in a former Voyage, was, by the Inſtruction of thoſe Sermons, made a Chriſtian, and baptiz'd, taking the Name of *Laurence*. They found no Inhabitants in the Iſland though it was Delightful.

On

On the 28th and 29th, they obferv'd they were upon a very Chriftalline
Clear Wa- Water, without any other Tokens of their being near Land, and thofe
ter in the fame Days at Noon, they had the Sun in the *Zenith*, directly over their
Sea. Heads, which had happen'd to them at other Times. Here a Storm feparated the Ships ; the *Maurice*, which was Admiral, by them in *Latin*
call'd *Pratoria*, the *Holland* and the *Overiffel*, tho' they endeavour'd to
Cerne make *Java*, were drove by Strefs of Weather to *Banda* ; and the other
Ifland. five to the Ifland *Cerne*, or of *Swans*, leaving fix other fmaller on the Right
Hand. They enter'd the Port with ten Fathom Water, between two Moun-
tains, which contract the Mouth of it. The Situation of it is in 21 De-
grees of South Latitude, and is five Leagues in Compafs. The Port is
Spacious enough to contain 50 Ships, and fhelter'd againft all Winds.
They were fo well pleas'd with the Ifland, that they chang'd its ancient
Name of *Cerne*, or of *Swans*, for that of *Maurice*, in Honour of Count
Maurice of *Naffau*, Baftard Son to the Prince of *Orange*, fo well known in
our Days. Difcoverers were fent about it, and return'd without finding
any humane Track, nor Signs of any Habitation. They had a doubtful
Tame Birds Proof hereof in the Birds and Beafts ; for they ran into their Hands and
and Beafts. alighted on their Heads, as they might have done on the Branches of
Trees, or had they been bred Tame ; which Boldnefs proceeded either from
their having never feen Men, or being grown very familiar with them.
Strange Among the reft, there are Bats, which have Heads as big, and like Apes,
Bats. and thefe fleep confiderable Numbers of them together, and hanging on
the Trees, with their Legs and Wings extended. The Air and Soil are
fo healthy and fit to be inhabited, that as foon as the Sick were landed,
they recovered. The Land is high and mountainous, full of Woods, and
not being inhabited, there are no Tracts or Paths through them. There
Ebony is an infinite Quantity of Ebony Trees, as black as Pitch, and as fmooth
as Ivory ; the Trunks being cover'd with a rough Bark, preferve the Body
folid. There are other Plants, whofe Trunks are Red, and others Pale as
Wax ; delicious Coco-Nuts, vaft Numbers of Palm-Trees, and fome of
them of fuch Sort, that one of their Leaves covers all a Man's Body, and
defends it againft the Rain. They fpread their Nets, and among the other
Multitude of Fifhes, took a Thornback fo large, that it afforded two Meals
Monftrous for all the Men in the Ships. They faw Land Tortoifes, fo big, that one
Thornback. of them walk'd with four Soldiers fitting on its Back ; and ten of them
Tortoifes. din'd upon the Shell of another, as if it had been a round Table. In a ve-
ry fhort Time they kill'd Abundance of Turtle-Doves, and another Sort of
white Birds, bigger than our Swans, but as round as a Ball, and have on-
Penguins. ly two or three curl'd Feathers in the Tail. There were fo many blew
Parrots, that they might have loaded their Ships with them. *Indian* Crows,
twice as big as the *European*, of three feveral colour'd Feathers.
Wax found They erected Forges, drefs'd all their Tools, and built another Veffel,
with to fupply the Place of the *Utrecht*, which with the other two, had directed
Greek he. Courfe for *Madagafcar*. They again took a View of their *Maurice*
Charact- Ifland, and towards the Inland Part of it, tho' there were no Signs of any
ers. humane Habitation, found about three hundred Pounds weight of Wax, on
which there were plain *Greek* Letters and Characters. They alfo faw Oars,
Nets, and Pieces of Timber, being the Wreck of Ships. The Vice-Admiral,

                                                                      providing

providing a smooth square Board, carv'd on it the Arms of *Holland*, *Zealand*, and *Amsterdam*, and nail'd it on the Top of a Tree, as a Memorial of his being there, and giving the Name of *MAURICE* to the Island, with this Inscription, which being in *Spanish*, denotes their Hatred to the Ancient Faith of our Nation, and being couch'd in one Line over their Arms, was, *THE REFORM'D CHRISTIANS.* Then they plow'd up a large Field, and sow'd it with Wheat, and other *European* Grain; turning lose some Hens, to see what Improvement they should find another Time. They again, for some Days, visited the Hills and Plains, and found no Track of Man.

Whilst these refresh'd themselves at the Island *Cerne*, or of *Swans*, being fourteen Days, the other three Ships arriv'd at *S. Mary's*, a barren Island, S. Mary Island. tho' some Orange and Lemon Trees grow in it, as also Sugar Canes, and there are Hens. About it, and in Sight of Land, there are monstrous Whales. They landed, but not without Opposition from the Natives, with Strange Ransom for a King. whom they fought, and took their King; but he was easily ransom'd, a Cow and a Calf being given them in Exchange for him. They saw the Manner of the Whale Fishery, which is very easy there. The *Indians* make up close to them in their Canoes, and stick them with a Harping-Iron they dart, being ty'd to Ropes made of the Barks of Trees. They stor'd their Ship with their Flesh and Oil, and some Oranges, and went over to the Bay of *Anton Gil*, where the *Madagascar Indian*, would not stay, as he had desired before, being now well affected to the Habit and Drunkenness of his Companions. They were toss'd backwards and forwards for five Days, between certain Islands, destitute of Provisions, and unsafe, by Reason they were in War among themselves.

They set forward with a fair Gale towards *Java*, and on the 26th of *December*, 1598, arriv'd at *Banda*, which is eight Leagues from *Am-* Banda Island. *boina*. This Island is shap'd like a Horse-shooe, and lies in four Degrees of South Latitude. It is most fruitful, with little or no Improvement, in Nutmegs, and their precious Mace; as also Provisions and Medicines for Men, beyond all other Parts of the known World. It is divided into three Parts, each of them three Leagues in Compass. The Capital City is called *Nera*. As soon as they arriv'd, they contracted Friendship with the Islanders; tho' a foreign Ship, to secure the Trade to herself, gave them to understand, that the *Dutch* were certain Pirates who fled the Year before, and had lain conceal'd at Sea, to come again and rob the Island, and therefore they did not fully credit them. This Notion was back'd by Trading *Portugueses*, and others settled there; but the *Dutch* sending their *Abdol*, that is the *Indian* Interpreter, with some Soldiers, and Gifts to present the King, according to the Custom of Merchants that come into his Country, they before him clear'd that Imputation, and defended their Innocence. The King was an Infant, and govern'd by his *Cephates*, that *The* Dutch *settle Trade there.* is his Vice-Roy, Tutor, or Protector, who set all right. They gave the King the Present before him, which he receiv'd very graciously. It consisted of certain valuable gilt Vessels, admirably ingrav'd, Christal Glasses, Looking-Glasses in gilt Frames, and Pieces of Velvet and Taffety. They deliver'd him Letters and Commissions of the States of *Holland*, *Zealand*,

and Count *Maurice*, with their Seals hanging to them in Form. All was accepted, and they lay down flat on the Ground to receive and read the Letters, with profound Reverence. The King promis'd to anfwer them, as he did, and immediately gave leave to Trade; whereupon tne *Dutch* built Factories in the Ifland. They then expos'd in publick Shops great Store of Arms, Silks, Linnen and Cloth; as did the Natives their Spice, *China* Ware, and Pearls, and other Commodities the Neighbouring Iflanders and *Chinefes* bring hither to barter, and fell to one another. Five

All their Ships meet again.

Weeks after, the other three Ships arrriv'd, and the People of the City hearing the Difcharges of the Cannon, and feeing the Auncients fpread abroad, for Joy of the Ships meeting again, came down to the Port, and encompafs'd the Ships in Boats, offering them Plenty of Fowl, Eggs, Coco Nuts, Bananas, Sugar-Canes, and Cakes made of Rice-Flower. This dainty Feeding continu'd every Day, and they gave them a Weeks Provifion for a *Dutch* Man for one Pewter Spoon. However they rais'd the Price of Pepper; but they pay'd for all with Pins and Needles, Knives, Spoons, Looking-Glaffes, and little Tabors; and with thofe fame Commodities, they purchas'd more valuable Goods at *Sumatra*, as alfo Provifions; when four of thefe eight Ships return'd Homewards, the others failing for *Ternate* and the *Moluccos*.

The greateft Quantity, and beft Commodity they took in here, was of Mace. Nutmegs grow alfo in *Ternate* and the adjacent Iflands, but they

The Nutmeg Tree.

are few and weak; but in *Banda* there is a plentiful Crop, and they have much more Virtue. Nature has cloath'd its Mountains and Plains, with Woods and Groves of thefe Plants. They are like the *European* Pear-Trees, and their Fruit refembles Pairs, or rather in Roundnefs the *Melocotones*. When the Nutmegs blofom, they fpread a cordial Fragrancy; by degrees they lofe their Native Green, which is original in all Vegetables; and then fucceeds a Blew, intermix'd with Grey, Cherry-Colour, and a pale Gold Colour, as we fee in the Rainbow, tho' not in that regular Divifion, but in Spots like the Jafpar Stone. Infinite Numbers of Parrots, and other Birds of various Plumage, moft delightful to behold, come to fit upon the Branches, attracted by the fweet Odour. The Nuts, when dry, caft off the Shell it grows cover'd with, and is the Mace, within which is a white Kernel, not fo fharp in Tafte as the Nut, and when

Oil of Nutmeg.

dry is converted into its Subftance. Of this Mace, which is hot and dry in the fecond Degree, and within the third, the *Bandefes* make a moft precicus Oil to cure all Diftempers in the Nerves, and Aches caus'd by cold. Of thefe Nuts they choofe the frefheft, weightieft, fatteft, juicieft, and without any Hole. With them they cure, or correct ftinking Breath,

Virtues of Nutmeg.

clear the Eyes, comfort the Stomach, Liver, and Spleen, and digeft Meat. They are a Remedy againft many other Diftempers, and ferve to add outward Luftre to the Face. The *Bandefes* call the Mace of their Aromatick Nuts, *Buna Pala*. It was not known to the *Greeks* nor to *Pliny*, according to *Averrous*; tho' *Serapion*, whether the true, or the fuppofitious, when he defcribes it, alledges *Gallen's* Authority. It is true the *Chrifabolans* he treated of, agree well enough with the Nutmegs in Colour and Shape.

The

The *Javanefes*, *Chinefes*, and Natives of the *Moluccos* refort to the City *Mera*, to barter for this precious Fruit, and load their Ships with it; and this is the Trade of that People, as is that of Clove to *Ternate*, *Tydore*, and the other *Moluccos*. The Merchants arriving in this Ifland, many of them contribute to make up a Sum, wherewith they purchafe a Woman, to drefs their Meat, and attend them. The *Dutch* did fo from this firft Time. When they go away fhe is left free, till they return the next Year, fo that her Slavery commences with the Return of her Mafters, and their Abfence gives it an Intermiffion. Some of the Natives are Idolaters; but the greater Part *Mahometans*, and fo fuperftitious, that the very Soldiers do not mount the Guard, till they have pray'd in the Mofques, fo loud, that all the Neighbourhood can hear them. Nor muft any Man go into them without wafhing his Feet, in great Veffels of Water, provided at the Door, by the publick. Their Prayers confift in thefe Words, *Eftagfer Al'lah Eftagfer Al'lah, Afgiv'd Al'lahe, Afgiv'd Al'lahe, La Il'lahe Inla Al'lah, Mutamed reful At'lahi.* When they utter thefe laft Words, they ftroke their Faces with their Hands, a Ceremony denoting much Devotion. The Words in *Englifh* are, Pardon O God, Pardon O God. I proftrate my felf to God. I proftrate my felf to God. There is no other God but God, and *Mahomet* his Meffenger: By thofe Words, There is no other God but God, they deny the eneflable Myftery of the moft bleffed Trinity. Then they proceed to feveral Blafphemie. They fay other Prayers, at which they fcarce move their Lips; when they do this they ftand three and three upon a Mat, lifting up their Eyes o Heaven three Times, and bowing down their Heads to the round. The *Dutch* Author, who gives this Account, does not men n any other Religion in this Ifland, nor in any of the others their Fleets touch'd at; tho' it is fo well known, that the Catholick Faith of our Lord *Jefus Chrift* has been preach'd many Years before, throughout them all, with the Glory o Martyrdom; but thofe People conceal it, to what Intent is well known.

The *Bandefes* affemble in the Streets, and publick Places, where they feaft themfelves. It is frequent among them to eat in the Temples and Woods, an hundred in a Parcel; efpecially when they confult together about the publick Weal, or any Danger. There are feven Cities in the Ifland, which are Enemies to one another. *Nera* is averfe to the *Lambethans*, *Combers* and *Veterans*, and maintains Friendfhip with the Inhabitants of *Lontoor*, which is on the other Side of the Ifland, and thofe of two other little Cities call'd *Poleruija* and *Poelvay*. When they are to fight, they always repair firft to *Nera*, to concert Affairs. *Banda* provides their Entertainments on the Ground, in the Streets. The Difhes are made of the Trunks and Leaves of *Bananas*, and other Plants. Every one has a Piece of *Sagu* brought him on them, and a Plate of Rice boil'd in the Broth of Flefh. This they devour, carrying it to their Mouths with both Hands, and eat it with fuch a Relifh, as if they had *Jove's* Brains drefs'd fet before them: fo the *Dutch* Relation of *Paludanus* and *Hugo* expreffes it. Whilft the Meat lafts, till the Multitude are fatisfy'd, the Nobles by two and two, take up their Cymiters and Shields, and fight to the found of Bells, and the Clattering of their Bafons. When weary of this Exercife, they deliver the Weapons to others, which continue it. The Caufe of their Wars, is for that the Inhabitants of *Labetaca*, many Years since, set some Plants in the Territory of *Nera*. The People of this City affronted at this Presumption, made the first War upon them; which is as bloodily prosecuted, as if their Religion, or Honour, depended on it. They attack one another by Day and Night in their Territories, and by Sea in their *Carcoas*.

Banda Tar. In these they do not, like us, fill up the Seams of the Boards with Pitch and Tar, but with Shells of *Indian* Nuts, which they call *Clappos*. They pound those Shells and Rhinds, till they become like a Bitumen, or 'Mass, wherein there remain certain Threads, which resemble Hemp. with this they knit their Seams, and fill up the Crannyes and cover them in such Sort that it resists the Force of the Water They carry two, and sometimes four Pieces of Cannon. The Men use small Fire-locks, Bucklers, and *Their Wea-* large Cymiters, which they call *Padang*, and Lances of a more solid Wood *pons.* than our Box. They exercise all these Weapons from their Child-hood, as they do in casting a sort of Hooks with sharp Points and Edges, which they dart at the Enemies Bodies, and then draw back the Lines they are made fast to. Their Heads they arm with Helmets; and on their Crests wear Birds of Paradise, both for Ornament, and a superstitious Defence. They have Breast and Back Pieces, and call'd them as we did Corselets. When they are to fight at Sea, as soon as the War-like Instruments begin to sound, the Soldiers fall a leaping, and skipping on the Benches, which run round the *Oars like Carceas* from Stem to Stern. The Slaves ply the Oars, which are like *Shovels.* wooden Shovels, make the Vessel fly by main Force, and serve to lade out the Water, when there is Occasion. They are so revengeful, that having *Cruelty of* been in those Days vanquish'd on Land by the *Labetans*, many of them be- *Bandeses.* ing kill'd and wounded, those of *Nera* assembled the next Day in five *Carcoas*, and attacking the little Island *Bayjer*, the Natives whereof had assisted the *Labetans* they slew all they found, without sparing any but a few Women, whom they carry'd Captives to *Nera*, with the Heads of their Enemies before them on Spears; and for four Days, to the Amazement of Forreigners, and particularly the *Dutch*, they show'd their Cymiters embrew'd in Gore, about the Streets. Nay, a Soldier among them, in the Sight of *Burial of* Abundance, took a Fancy to try his Cymiter, he carry'd naked, and with it *Enemies.* clove down one of the Captive Women, from the Shoulder to the Breast. *Heads.* They shew'd themselves Merciful in burying those Heads, assembling together in the House of the *Shabander*, that is the Governor, in the Presence of all the People, which uses to meet to see such Spectacles, every Soldier, as a Testimony of his Valour, laid all the Heads he had cut off on *Their Fu-* a very large Stone, under a Tree: They wrapp'd them up in Cotton Cloths, *nerals.* and carrying them in Dishes bury'd them in a Grove, with much Smoke of Frankincense, whereof they have great Plenty. Had those dead Persons been Natives, their Kindred and Friends would have come immediately to lament with loud Cries, as they use to do, over their Graves, which they dig like us, wrap up the Bodies in Shrouds of white Cotton, and carry them to be bury'd on their Shoulders. They are great Observers, that the Funerals of Men should go before those of Women; place Lamps over the Graves of all, and by their Light pray for them. They cry out furiously, calling the Dead, as if they hop'd they should come to Life at their Call, and perceiving they do not rise again, the Kindred and Friends meet about

the

the moſt ſplendid Entertainment they are able to provide. Being ask'd by the *Dutch*, what it was they ask'd of God in the Prayers they mutter'd over the Graves, they anſwer'd. *We pray that the Dead may not riſe again.* So that the Want of the true Light of Faith, does not hinder them from ſeeing, how much Mankind ſuffers from the firſt Moment of his Life, till the laſt ; but it is rather to be concluded, that they look upon it as a Miſ-fortune to have been born. They were much amaz'd to hear, that the *Dutch* did not uſe the ſame Ceremony towards their dead.

They play at Foot-Ball, which is made of *Spaniſh* Reeds. They that Play make a Ring one ſtanding in the Center, who toſſes the Ball to thoſe about him, and they with a Kick throw it ſo high that it is almoſt out of Sight. If any one miſſes it, they hiſs, and hoot, to ſhame him for his Unskilfulneſs. Men live in this Iſland longer than in any other Parts of the World. The *Dutch* ſaw ſeveral, who exceed 130 Years of Age. They live upon the Product of their Country ; and tho' there is continual War, yet the greater Number lives Idle ; and it is very remarkable that thoſe People, who are ſo much addicted to Sloath, ſhould be ſuch Enemies to Quietneſs. A uſeleſs Life does not deſerve much Age ; and that which is dedicated to Idleneſs ſeldom attains to it. The Women Plow and Till the Land, and follow other manly Profeſſions. They ſeldom go abroad with Men ; they have all the Charge of Houſhold Affairs, and their greateſt Employment within Doors, is uſually uncaſing and drying of Nutmegs. *Foot-Ball.*

Life long in Banda.

Women Till the Land.

The *Dutch* having loaded with Spice, Purcelane, and ſome Rubies, and ſettled Factories, and Amity, ſail'd from *Banda*, on the 14th of *July*, with great firing of Cannon. They ſtood towards the Iſland *Noeſelau*, the Na-tives whereof are *Anthropophagi*, ſo the *Greeks* call Man-Eaters. They pro-ceeded towards that of *Amboyna*, whoſe Weſtern Point they diſcover'd, yet did not touch at it then, but went on to the greater *Java*, notwithſtanding their Admiral was at *Amboyna*. They arriv'd at *Java* and the City *Tuban*, ſent two Boats thither to Diſcover, and know whither they might be allow'd to take in Proviſions. Thoſe who return'd with the Anſwer, brought a-long with them a *Fortugueſe*, who, at the Perſwaſion of the Natives, had re-nounc'd the Faith of *Jeſus Chriſt*, as was known, and call'd among them by the name of the *Renegado*, as a proper Appellative, and not diſhonourable. This Man inform'd the Admiral, That if he would ſtay there three or four Months, he might enrich his Ships to his Hearts Content. They ſent by him to aſk the King's Leave, with ſome Preſents of Copper, Glaſs, and Silk. The next day Merchants came down to the Harbour, with Abundance of Commodities ; and from the King, in Return for their inſignificant Pre-ſent, they brought the *Dutch* 19 great Sacks of Rice. The Trade being ſettled, they went up to the City, where they ſaw ſeveral Horſemen, well Arm'd, Horſes well Accouter'd, on which they value themſelves very much, Shops well ſtor'd, and a free Trade for all Nations. The Vice-Admiral went to kiſs the King's Hand, who receiv'd him Graciouſly ; promis'd to go Aboard the Ships in Perſon, and perform'd it, having firſt order'd them to be ſhow'd all his Royal Apartments, even to his Womens private Lod-gings, his Elephants, an infinite number of Birds in Cages, and his Sta-bles full of excellent Horſes, and many of them. Then the Prince came Aboare the Ships, and after him the King. The Cannon ſaluted them both, and they admir'd, and were pleas'd with the Noiſe. *Dutch de-part from Banda.*

Come to Java.

Portugueſe Renegado.

Preſents to and from the King.

Tuban

Tuban Capital of Java — *Tuban* is the King of *Java*'s Court, the ſtrongeſt of all the Cities in that Iſland, encompaſs'd with a high Wall, divided by ſeveral Gates with Towers on them, contains ſtately Structures, and Squares appointed for the publick Reſort of Traders, the King is extraordinary rich, and in a few Hours can gather a great Number of Horſe and Foot. His Palace is truly Royal, his Family conſiſts of the Prime Nobility, and he is very powerful at Sea. They call their Ships Juncks; which being loaded with Pepper, and other Product of the Country, as Silks and Cloths, the Manufactures *Trade of that City.* — of his People, are ſent to *Balm*, where bartering them for Cloaths, they tranſport thoſe to other Kingdoms, as thoſe of *Banda*, the *Moluccos*, and *Philippines*. Whence, and from other Iſlands, having improv'd their Commodities, they bring Maſtick, Nutmegs, Cloves, and other Spice. All the *Habit.* — Country abounds in Cattle, which graze all Day in the Woods, and are hous'd at Night. Their Habit is the ſame as at *Banda*, and covers their Bodies from the Waſte downwards, the reſt upwards remaining naked. They all wear Daggers, call'd *Criſes*, and the Nobles ſtately long Veſts, the Fullneſs whereof waves in the Air magnificently. None of them goes abroad attended by leſs than ten or twelve Servants, one of which always carries for his Maſter a little Baſket full of the Leaves of a certain Plant they call *Betele*, which they chew with green Nuts, and a little Lime. This Compoſition they call *Ledon*; in chewing, it yields a Juice, which they ſwallow, and then ſpit out the green Subſtance, after the Virtue has *The Kings Dreſs.* — been extracted in their Mouths.

They were ſo overjoy'd at the coming of the *Dutch*, that the next Day they invited them to ſee their Diverſions. The King was preſent a Horſe-Back, clad in ſeveral Sorts of rich Silks, but all Girt about him. To his Belt hung a Cymiter, in a Scabard adorn'd with precious Stones; the Hilt of beaten Gold, with a Devils Head form'd on it. On his Turbant he had abundance of Feathers. All the Nobility follow'd him, Dreſs'd much after the ſame manner, mounted on ſtately prancing Horſes, but ſmaller than ours, with rich Furnitures of *Spaniſh* Leather, ſtudded, and plated with Gold, and Figures of Serpents; and in ſome of the Bridles they had Stones, ſo white that they look'd like Alabaſter. Sometimes they ran ſtreight forwards, and ſometimes in a Ring, caſting their Darts. When the Sport was over, *Commerce ſettled between the Dutch and Javaneſes.* — they attended the King, by whoſe Orders they carry'd aboard the Ships, and to the *Dutch* Men's Lodgings, a great quantity of Rice, Sheep, Goats, Hens, Eggs, Fiſh, and Fruit, as Coco-Nuts, Mangos, Lemons, and delicious Bananas. Then they fell to treating of Trade, and Amity, and thought every Thing cheap except the Pepper, for they not liking the Commodities the *Dutch* offer'd in Exchange for it, lifting up their Hands cry'd, *Lima*, which, in their Tongue, ſignifies five Pieces of Eight. So much they demanded for a Meaſure of theirs. They were well receiv'd in all Reſpects, except in Relation to admitting of their Sect.

Madura Iſland. — They had deliver'd Letters to the King from Count *Maurice*, which he anſwer'd in the *Perſian* Tongue, and the *Dutch* having receiv'd them, left *Tuban*, on the 24th of the ſame Month, with fair Weather, and well furniſh'd with valuable Commodities and Proviſions. Paſſing by the Iſland *Sidago*, they anchor'd between *Java* and *Madura*; ſounded the Depth, and notwithſtanding the Current, and that the Ground was a ſtiff Muddy Hill,

they

they vifited *Madura*, landing on the Eaft-fide; but remov'd prefently to the City *Arosbay*, on the Weft, and afterwards thence to *Jorta*, to get Guides, or Pilots to conduct them to the reft of the *Moluccos*. They fent to Compliment the King of *Madura*, who prefently after the Audience, fent the Vice-Admiral a Sheep, with which went the Renegado, who had brought him a Dagger, they call *Criz*, from the King of *Tuban*, richly adorn'd with Gold and precious Stones, and the King's Head engrav'd on the Pommel. They found a *German* fettled in the Country, rich in Spice, and underftood by him, that at *Arosbay* they had feiz'd 40 of their Companions. The Ifland of *Madura*, next to *Java*, inclines to the Northward. They wear the fame Habit as in the other; but are fharper Witted. It is moft fruitful in Rice, but both in Reaping and Plowing, the Peafants and Buffalos are mir'd up to the Knees, the continual Inundations keeping the Ground fo wet. Few Ships come to it, by reafon of its inacceffible Shoales. They have the fame common ufe of Weapons, Elephants, Horfes, Spears, Campilanes, or Cymiters, and Shields. The *Crizes*, or Daggers, worn by the King's Guards are of Silver. The City *Arosbay* is Populous, and well Wall'd. The *Hollanders* main Defign in coming to it, was, as has been faid, to take in Pilots, and other Neceffaries to proceed to the *Molucco* Iflands; to which Purpofe, and to avoid the Shoals lying betwixt *Java* and *Madura*, they divided their Ships. The Vice-Admiral, with the *Guelder* and *Zealand*, pafs'd the Chanels of *Madura*, in order to joyn, at *Jorta*, the Junks that fail for *Ternate*, and thence to the other *Molucco* Iflands.

The Admiral *Sticht Utrecht*, running along the length of *Madura*, came to an Anchor before *Arosbay*. He fent out a Number of his Men in the Boat, to bring Rice, and other Provifions from Shore. No fooner were they landed, then feiz'd, difarm'd, ftripp'd, and carry'd before the King. Thofe ftaying long, another Boat was fent with only three Men, and the fame befell them. The Prifoners intreated the King to give leave, that thofe three, or any others, might go to give the Admiral an Account. He granted it, but upon Condition, That as foon as they had deliver'd the Meffage, they fhould return to Prifon. They gave Notice of their Misfortune, and the Admiral fent away a Boat to carry immediate Advice to his Countrymen at the City *Jorta*, writing feveral Letters to procure the Prifoners Liberty. The Vice-Admiral came with his Ships, and joyn'd thofe at *Arosbay*. The King demanded the two biggeft Brafs Guns aboard the Admiral, many Pieces of Silk, and one thoufand Pieces of Eight for the Ranfom of the Prifoners. The Admiral anfwer'd, That the Cannon was not his own, but belong'd to all his Nation, and therefore he defir'd him to moderate the Ranfom, and turn it into Money, or take it out in fuch Commodities as he brought. Six Days were fpent in Treating, and the Delay made the Conclufion more Difficult; and therefore the Admiral believing, that his Men were kept Prifoners in their own Boats, or near the Sea, without any confiderable Guard, he order'd all his Men to land at once, and to Refcue them by Force. An hundred and fifty *Dutchmen* attempted it, but faw a great Number of People gathering on the Shore, led by the *Portuguefes*, who carry'd white Colours, in token of Peace, giving out that they came to treat of an Accommodation, which, as *Hugo* affirms, was a Stratagem to gain Time for the Citizens to Arm. The *Dutch* either fufpected, or had Notice

Margin notes:
Madura Defcribed.

Arosbay City.

Dutch taken by the King of Madura.

His Demands for them Ranfom.

Attempt to Refcue them by Force.

Z   of

of it, and forming a small Body with about 20 Musquetiers, contriv'd to have their other Boats draw nearer, that so the Seamen and Officers might come to Fight, according to the appointed Order   More Men came out of the City, at another Gate, to enclose them unawares in the Port.   The *Dutch* saw into the Policy, and were sensible of the Danger, and therefore sent two other Boats to guard the Port.   This Precaution was the saving of their Lives; but they could not escape a Shower of Arrows, wherewith the *Arosbayans* thought to subdue them, not so much by their Force, and the Harm receiv'd, as by keeping the Enemy in Play, that so they might spend their Powder, and be oblig'd to retire to their Ships.   Nor would they have been safe there, for now the Wind and Sea threatned them, and **Dutch De-** thirty six Men belonging to the Admiral, and thirteen to the *Zealand* were **feated.** Drown'd, and the Boats cast away.   Some few escap'd, whom they did not kill, at the Request of the Renegado of *Tuban,* but they were made Prisoners.   These kneeling down, to move Compassion, with their dismal Looks, and Tears, the Conquerors laid a Handful of Earth on their Heads, a Cere- **Ceremony** mony they use towards the vanquish'd, whose Lives they grant.   Perhaps **in giving** they themselves know not the Reason, and Original of this Custom.   Five **Quarter.** and Twenty were lost in this Encounter, fifteen of the Admirals, one of *John Marts,* and nine of the *Zealand.*   The Prisoners were carry'd to a Country Cottage; three Men dangerously wounded, one Trumpeter, and a Herald put into Chains, the others only their Hands bound.   The rest were carry'd far from these, and put into a deep Cellar.   The Herald being brought into the King's Presence, he ask'd him, whether he would stay in his Country, promising, among other Favours, that he would marry him to two of his own Wives.   The *Dutchman* answer'd, returning Thanks, but with Freedom in his Looks, That with his good leave he had rather re- turn to his Companions.   He was therefore carry'd, with the Trumpeter, about the City, and at his going out at the Gate saw all the Prisoners, be- ing fifty one, who were conducting, under a Guard, to another Island.

Prisoners In fine, the Agreement was concluded, and the King discharg'd them for **Ransom'd.** 2000 *Florines.* So they return'd to their Ships, except two, who hid them- selves, taking a liking to that barbarous Way of living.   The Governour *Jacob Marts* Dy'd, his Body was cast into the Sea, and the rest sailing to the Northward, directed their Course for the Island of *Celebes.*   They pass'd **Dutch De-** by *Combay,* six Leagues from it, and beyond that of *Bonton,* and escap'd the **part.** Ridges of Rocks of *Cebessa,* which are not mark'd down, nor taken Notice of in Maps.   There fell mighty Rains, and they steer'd North East for the Island of *Amboyna,* and in sight of *Boora.* A Boy dy'd aboard the *Zealand;* another falling off a Yard, into the Sea, held a Rope's End in his Mouth, that his arms might be at Liberty to swim, and quitted it not, till he had Help, and was sav'd.   The next Day they lay by, and their Preacher made a long Spiritual Discourse upon the Sacraments, to celebrate the solem- nity of Baptizing two Boys, whom he had already Catechis'd.   On the first of *March,* not far from *Blau,* to the Eastward of *Boora,* they saw three other smaller Islands, call'd *Atypoti, Mamba,* and *Gita,* which are not far from **Come to** *Amboyna.* They pass'd by them, and arriv'd at *Amboyna* on the third of the **Amboyna.** same Month.

The Port is small, and at the Mouth of it, they were receiv'd by three
                                                                                                    Boats,

Boats, belonging to the Town of *Matel*, feated on the Mountains. Thence they went on to that of *Ito*. *Amboyna* is about eight Leagues from *Banda*, to the Northward, in the Way to *Ternate*. The compafs of it is fifteen Leagues, moft fruitful in Cloves, Oranges, Lemmons, Citrons, Coco-Nuts, Bananas, Sugar-Canes, and other fuch like Product. The Natives are more open Hearted, and fincere, than thofe of the *Moluccos* or *Banda*; wear the fame Habit, live upon the Trade of Spice; are temperate and abftemious, and great Sufferers of Hardfhip. Their Weapons, are Spears with Sharp *Their Wea-* twifted Ends; thefe they dart fo dexteroufly, that they will hit the fmall-*pons.* eft Mark at a great Diftance. They alfo ufe Cymiters and Shields, and now Mufkets. They make great Maffes of Sugar, Rice, and Almonds, like our Sugar-Loaves, and value themfelves upon being able Seamen. Their *Car-* *coas* are like great Dragons, did thefe fwim with their Bodies extended on *Carcoas.* the Water, and lifting up their two Ends of Head and Tail, which are gilt, and well Carv'd, and ferve for Prow and Poop. At both of them hang Stan-dards of feveral Sorts of Silk, and Colours, which are born up by the Wind, when they do not reach to the Water. The Admiral of *Amboyna* came with three of thefe Veffels full of arm'd Men, to fee the *Dutch*, with a Noife of Kittle-Drums, and Brafs Bafons hanging on the Mufitian's Left-*Mufick.* Shoulder, and ftriking them with the Right-Hand, as they do the Tabors in *Spain*. They fang their fet Airs, underftood by none but the Native *Amboynefes*, tho' attentively liften'd to by the *Dutch*, for their Strangenefs. The Slaves alfo fang to the Noife of their Oars. They fir'd the three Guns every *Carcoa* carry'd, being a Salute, in Honour of their Guefts; who relying on that Reception, dropt their Anchors, pofting many Sentinels, becaufe they obferv'd the Natives had done the fame in all Parts, and there were conftant Fires in many Places.

The *Amboynefe* Admiral afk'd them, What they came for, and who they were, and having heard their-Anfwer, gave them leave to go afhore, and *Dutch per-* expofe their Commodities, allowing them free Commerce, contrary to his *mitted to* Majefty's Prohibition, which us'd to be more punctually obferv'd in this *Trade at* Ifland. The *Dutch* Vice-Admiral went afhore, where he was well recei-*Amboyna.* ved, and conducted to a Seat cover'd with Sails of Ships, fupported by Trees, full of Fruit not known in *Europe*. He eafily prevail'd with the Go-vernors, to allow him full Liberty to Trade. Their Succefs was forwar-*King of* ded by *Cachil Azude*, Brother to the King of *Ternate*, who happen'd to be *Ternate's* there then, celebrating his Nuptials, being newly come with his Bride, who *Brother* was the Daughter of a *Sangiack* of *Batochina*. He had long courted, and *affifts the* defir'd to be marry'd to her, but was oppos'd by the Father, who had pro-*Dutch.* mifed her to the King of *Bachian*. We fhall fay no more of their Love, nor of what became of the Prince, becaufe it is no effential Part of this Hiftory. He prefently repair'd to the *Dutch*, and order'd them to be fur-nifh'd with thofe Loaves made of Sugar, Almonds and Rice, with Coco-Nuts, Bananas, and Wine made of Rice, and this fo lavifhly, that the *Dutch* Relations own they had fcarce Room to lay up fuch Plenty of Provifions. *Plenty of* The fame would have been, had they bought them, for they had fo much *Provifions.* for a Pewter Spoon, that they knew not what to do with it. The *Amboy-* *nefe* Admiral went aboard the Ships again, was pleas'd to fee the great Guns, and the Variety and Plenty of Merchandife. The Prince of *Ternate*

did

did the fame, and both of them at their coming and going were faluted by the Cannon. They had private Conferences with him, and other Noblemen of the *Moluccos*, who attended him. They erected Factories in feveral Parts of *Amboyna*, and agreed that the two Ships, *Guelder* and *Zealand*, fhould Sail for *Banda*, whilft the other two lay two Months to load and reft at *Amboyna*. We fhall mention hereafter what befel thefe in *Ternate*, let us now return to the other two.

Two Dutch *Ships fail for* Banda. They fail'd with a fair Wind, but one of them ftuck in the Flats of *Ceru*, fo that fhe could fcarce be got off. Below *Jealau*, they met a *Portuguefe* Ship at *Naefau*, the Inhabitants of which Place eat Mans Flefh. They pafs'd on merrily by *Poelfetton*, two Leagues fhort of *Banda*, on that Side. It is defert, and uninhabited, infamous, for ftronger Reafons, than the *Greeks* alledge againft the *Acroceraunian* Rocks. There are Cryes, Whiftles, and

Ifland of Devils. Roarings heard in it at all Times, and dreadful Apparitions are feen, with Fires afcending through the Air ; and long Experience has fhown, that it is inhabited by Devils. Therefore Sailors, when they pafs in Sight of it, which feldom happens without Storms, make all the Sail they can to get far off, from the very Wind that blows on it. The *Dutch* chief Pilot knowing fo much, furioufly took fuch faft hold of the Helm, that all the reft could not put him from it ; He drew it to him violently, thinking that

Dutch Pilot *fighted by the Devil.* Force drove on the Ship ; his Face grew fiery, and his Breaft not being able to contain his Wind, he breath'd faft, and groan'd, till being paft the Ifland, the grew merry, and whiftling loud, fcoff'd at the Devil, becaufe he could not caft away the Ship ; yet foon after he was in Diforder again, and dropt the Helm ; they recover'd him, and made all fail to go forward.

Trade at Banda. They arriv'd at *Banda*, near the River, on the fifteenth of the Mouth. Several *Bandefe* Boats came out, offering their Spice. The *Dutch* landed, carrying with them fundry Commodities, which they expos'd in Shops. A rich *Turk*, who was in Efteem, entertain'd them. They built Houfes on the Ifland, and a few Days after hear'd News of their Admiral, by fome *Chinefe* Ships, that came from *Amboyna* ; and were inform'd, that the *Portuguefes* were already at War with the Natives, for entertaining and allowing them Factories.

Return thence. On the fourth of *July*, having fettled Trade at *Banda*, they fail'd thence towards *Noefelau*, along the Channels of *Zeru*, without regarding their Admiral, who was promoting, and fomenting the War at *Amboyna*. They fail'd in Sight of *Routon*, which is in five Degrees of South Latitude, and of the Ifland *Cobayna*. On the twelfth they pafs'd the Coaft of *Celebes*, and on the feventeenth, by that of *Madura*, and again difcover'd *Aroshay*, where the Misfortune we have fpoken of befel them. They ran along the Coaft of *Java*, and in the Evening came to *Iacatra*, where they caft Anchor, fent to vifit the King, and their Compliment was return'd by him with a Prefent of Rice, Fowl, and Coco-Nuts, and a Buffalo for the Vice-Admiral. The *Zealanders*, who had been left at *Banda* in their Houfes and Factories, in the Cities of *Montelonga*, and *Soleparvo*, by Letters of the firft of *Auguft*, acquainted them, how the new Friendfhip was eftablifh'd. From this Time the *Dutch* began, without any Oppofition, to poffefs themfelves of the Provinces belonging to the Crown of *Spain* in *Afia*.

They took Leave of that King, and return'd to *Banda*, with the Natives
of

of which Place they had now contracted such Familiarity, that some Ships belonging to *Bandese* Merchants, which they met by the Way, presented them with a considerable Quantity of Porcelane. At their Arrival the Governour came out to meet them, with 400 Men, inviting them to take some Refreshment ashore, which they refus'd, but made presents to each other, and drank out great Vessels of Wine made of Rice, which is a powerful and strong Liquor. Continuing their Voyage on the tenth of *September*, towards the South West, they thought they were under the Tropick of *Capricorn*. On the thirtieth, they were in 28 Degrees, with the Wind at West, somewhat Northerly, and ran thirty Leagues beyond Cape *S. Roman*, after they had been toss'd among many Islands, in thirty two Degrees and a half South. Next they discover'd Cape *Ploemera*, of the Southern *Ethiopia*, or Land of the *Cafres*. A Storm dispers'd the Ships, but they met again when it ceas'd, at Cape *Anquillos*. On the seventh of *September* they arriv'd at the Island *S. Helena*; the Master went ashore, kill'd many wild Beasts; and furnish'd the Ships with Fruit, there being Plenty of both. The Sick recover'd there: They went into the solitary Church, and on the first of *January*, 1600, they sail'd thence, and being come into five Degrees of North Latitude, on the Thirtieth of the same Month, observ'd an Eclypse. Then they began to discover the North Pole, which had been out of their Sight so long. On the thirteenth of *February* they had Sight of the Island *Mayo*, or *May*, one of those of *Cabo Verde*, and about the End of *March* discover'd the *English* Hills. In fine, they arriv'd at the *Texel*, and thence to *Amsterdam*, where they unladed that spicy Wealth, the like, for Quality and Newness, had never yet been brought to *Lisbon*; at least *Hugo's* Relations tell us, there might have been as precious Oyl drawn from these, as when they were just gather'd. *S.* Helena *Island.*

Whilst these two Ships, *Zealand* and *Guelder*, were sailing Home, the other two, *Amsterdam* and *Utretcht*, being almost naturaliz'd at *Amboyna*, departed thence for *Ternate*, on the eigth of *March*, 1599, in the Company of three *Junks*, full of *Javanese* Soldiers, well arm'd, and hir'd to attack a Fort that was defended by *Portugueses*. Before their Departure, some of them went ashore, and among other Game, took Abundance of green Pigeons, as big as our Ducks. They loaded with Clove, because it is sold in that Island for thirty five Royals a Bar, which is there 150 Pounds. They were inform'd, that the *Dutch*, who had been left at *Banda*, would soon come to joyn them. The *Portugueses* attacking a Fort with ill Success, the *Dutch*, who were before agreed with the Prince of *Ternate*, arm'd, and mix'd with his Men. This was the first Time they ever fought with the Subjects of *Spain*, in those Parts; and the *Dutch* Author, who gives an Account of this Action, says, the Islanders look'd upon it as a Prodigy. *The other* Dutch *Ships depart the* Moluccos.

Green Pigeons.

Having settled Commerce at *Amboyna*, they sail'd away for the Islands of *Ternate*, taking for their Guide, a Captain, who pretended to them, that he was Brother to the King of an Island; and to magnify his Grand-Father, boasted he had kept seventy lawful Wives, besides Concubines; and that his Son, to vye with him, had forty Wives, besides Mistresses. So says the Journal of that Voyage, writ by them who perform'd it. They discover'd the Islands of *Tydore* and *Ternate* on the twenty sixth, and coming to an Anchor at the latter, in fifteen Fathom Water, put out their Colours, Dutch *at* Ternate.

Co'ours, fired their Cannon, and fpar'd for no real or vain Oftentation. The King of *Ternate*, whofe deep known Sagacity is fuch, that he trufts

The King goes to view the Sh ps.
no other but himfelf to obferve what Dangers may threaten, went into his own *Carcoa*, attended by many others, on the 28th of *May*, and fail'd to the Place, where the *Dutch* lay at Anchor. He drew near and in-clos'd the Ships, call'd to the Admiral, and afk'd him, who he was, whence his Ships, and other Particulars. Thefe Queftions and Anfwers held fome Hours, by Means of the *Naguatato's* who interpreted the Difcourfe. The Admiral intreated the King that he would pleafe to come aboard his Ship. He excus'd himfelf, firft alledging, that he did not like thofe Ladders they fhow'd him to go up to them, tho' they had purpofely cover'd them with fine Cloth; and afterwards, that the Sun was fitting, and it was Time for him to repair to his Devotions. Having made this godly Excufe, he fail'd towards the City, the Air refounding with the Noife of his Brafs Bafons, Flat Tabors, Guns, Shouts, and *Perfian* Songs.

He re-turns.
The 29th he drew near to the new Comers again, with 23 *Carcoas*; in which he had 100 Brafs Guns for his Defence, and firing them all at once, to the clattering of Bells, made fhow of his Warlike Preparation. The Confufion of it being over, tho' they fang Verfes, as they do to denote Peace, in the *Malay* Tongue, fo they call the Language of *Malaca*, whence it was convey'd to the *Moluccos*; yet the *Dutch* made ready their great Guns, Mufkets, and half Pikes. They plac'd fome arm'd Men out of Sight in every Ship, as alfo where they might be taken Notice of, fhowing, or at leaft not concealing their Jealoufy, that fo no fudden Sur-prize might find them unprovided. The King's *Carcoa* drew near alone, and thofe who were in it fpoke to the *Dutch* Admiral, by Means of the *Naguatato*, without fhowing themfelves.

Talks with the Dutch.
The King was fatisfy'd with only talking to them, and withdrew; after Noon he return'd with only two *Carcoas*, one of which tow'd a Boat after her. Being come up to the *Dutch*, he began to talk to the Vice-Admiral; enquir'd after their Guns, and order'd the other *Carcoa* to ftand further off, and the Captain going too far, the Boat, either accidentally, or by De-fign, broke loofe from the Stern, and was over-fet by the Waves; the King then defired the Admiral to fire at it with a Ball, that he might fee whether they could hit or fink it. They fir'd immediately, the King being well pleas'd to fee that the Shot had ftav'd the Boat in Pieces. The Admiral laying hold of this Opportunity, took Care, whilft they were commending the Shot, which ferv'd to difguife the Threat, to let him know that he could with as much Eafe fink the *Carcoas*. This Tryal fatisfy'd the King, who foon after gave leave for that Nation to Trade in his Domi-

Gives them leave to Trade.
nions, and barter Cloves, Spice, precious Stones, and Pearls, all which is there to be found, by reafon of the Refort of the *Japonefe*, *Cambowa* and *Chinefe* Ships. Of thefe laft they then faw fome all made of Wood a'one, even to their Anchors, and the Sails of Cane. They came to an Anchor at *Ternate*, where the firft Thing they did, was burying of *Reynart Rey-narts*, a *Dutch* Soldier, fcarce worthy of that Burial, Idolaters and *Ma-hometans* reforting to the Funeral. The King the next Day fent a *Carcoa* to acquaint the *Dutch*, that he would go aboard their Ships, and a Boat

came

came to the Admiral's Side, with only four *Ternates* in a private Habit, who, by their Questions, Curiosity, and Solicitude, seem'd to be Spyes, as they did by all their Discourse, which was on sundry Subjects, and very full of solid Reflection; which was held on, and listen'd to, with Attention and Dissimulation.

When the *Dutch* expected the King would come, they understood he was one of the four then talking to them from the Boat. They signify'd to him that they knew him, and he did not deny it. They pay'd him the Respect due to a King; but then he refus'd to return to the Ship. Notwithstanding these Jealousies, he approved of the Behaviour of that People. On the second of *June* Embassadors went ashore, who carry'd the King a Present, which he accepted of, and treated them courteously. They return'd, full of Admiration of the infinite Quantity of Cloves, and the wonderful Woods of them; and bringing the News, that the *Ternates* would soon come to view and buy the *Dutch* Commodities. *The King visits the Dutch, in Disguise.*

The next Day they came in great Numbers, *Sangiacks*, *Cachiles*, and Commons, Barbarian Ladies, and all Sorts of Women, with Variety of Attendance. The Shores were cover'd with sundry Sorts of People; differing in Habit, Colour, and great Diversity of Feathers; among them many naked, and of various Countenances, for all flock'd out, as if it had been some publick Festival. Tho' they admir'd the Wealth of the Ships, yet they rais'd the Price of the Bars of Clove so high, that they could not come to any Agreement, because that was to be their main Loading. They went ashore on the 10th and 11th, to see whether they abated any Thing of the Price, and to some other Purposes, which do not concern us, tho' they might be some Ornament, but shall be left in the Originals where they were writ. They could not conclude any Thing with the King, or his Subjects, because they were celebrating a Festival, and the *Dutch* were present at the Shows. *Concourse of People to the Dutch.*

A Sort of Combatants, like the *Roman Pugiles*, and *Gladiators*, tho' differing in some Respects, fought in a large spacious Square. These *Ternates* did not move from one Place to another, nor hurt one another, but stood continually upon one Foot, without changing or easing it, on any Account; but the Foot that was lifted up, mov'd about and stretch'd in the Air, without being put to the Ground. Their Mistresses, Wives, or Sisters attended in the Field, with Branches of Flowers, and *China* Dishes full of *Aromatick* Liquors, to refresh those that were tyr'd; but most of them attended the Conqueror. The Sport being ended, the next Day the King repair'd to the Ships, but went not aboard. Discoursing with the Admiral, he ask'd him for a gilt Musket, which he presented him, and the King did not think fit to receive Gratis, because he had ask'd for it; he therefore order'd, that when the *Dutch* paid the Tithe of the Spice, which is the Duty he has from Merchants, they should have two Bars and a half discounted for the Price of the Musket, and that they should be furnish'd with every Thing they had Occasion for besides. He was well pleas'd one Day, that the *Dutch* should see how a Boy of eleven Years of Age, was led about the Streets, with his Hands bound, because he had stolen a *Tubac*, that is, a Leaf of a Frail, with as many Cloves as it would carry; because this was an Instance of their Severity in punishing that Offence. *Indian Gladiators.* *The King asks a Musket, and pays for it.* *Severe Punishment of petty Larceny.*

The

The other Boys, ſhouted and ſham'd him, proc'aiming the Theft with loud Voices.

Triumph of Ternates

About this Time ſome *Ternate* Troops return'd Home victorious, having plunder'd and deſtroy'd a Town in the Iſland of *Tydore*. They march'd into the City on the 20th of *July*, the King being preſent, with their *Campilanes*, or Cymiters drawn, and bloody, with half Heads, Ears, and Hair of thoſe they had conquer'd, or ſlain, ſticking to them. They ſhow'd the Shields and Weapons they had taken from them, their Cloaths and Feathers, and 43 Priſoners, who follow'd dragging Chains, ſome about their Necks, and ſome at their Heels. Among them was a brave Youth, 21 Years of Age,

Priſoners ſacrific'd.

who was a *Sangiack* of Note, and Kinſman to the King of *Tydore*; as alſo a very beautiful *Portugueſe* Lady, Wife to a Captain in that Fort. They walk'd about the City, with all this State and Plunder, till they came to the King's Palace ; there the Captives were ſacrific'd, and the *Portugueſe* Lady ſold for a Slave, a rare Piece of Mercy, and purchas'd by her Tears. The King of *Ternate* honour'd the Chief of the *Tydores*, ſmiling and lovingly encouraging him, as Kinſman to a King. The Youth excuſing himſelf, and pleading Innocence, to gain the Victor's Favour, he return'd a favourable Anſwer, and bid him waſh himſelf. Sweet Water was brought to waſh their Hands, and it was poured over the King's Hands and his, at the ſame Time, out of one Ewer. Then the Captive thus aſſur'd, letting fall his Hands with the Water, which, perhaps, is a Ceremony to denote Peace, and bowing his Head by way of Civility, a Soldier ſtruck him on

Barbarous Perfidiouſneſs.

the Neck with a ſharp *Campilane*, or Cymiter, ſo furiouſly, that the Head dropt at ſome Diſtance from the Body half alive ; then they cut both the Head and Body into ſmall Pieces, all which, to exerciſe their utmoſt Rage, they put into a *Prau*, which is a little Boat, and then ſunk all together in the Sea.

More of their Cruelty.

Four Days after another Parcel of *Ternates* came with ſeveral *Tydore* Priſoners, whoſe Heads they cut off in the Port, as they did that of a Stranger, who came peaceably to the Iſland with Merchandize. All theſe Spectacles the *Dutch* beheld. Such good Uſe do thoſe Barbarians make of Victory. Friendſhip being now eſtabliſh'd with the *Dutch*, and the King

The King aboard the Dutch Ships.

well aſſur'd of it, he reſolv'd to go aboard their Ships. He went aboard the Admiral on the 25th of *July*, with all his Guard, where nothing eſcap'd being narrowly view'd and obſerv'd by him, with a ſeeming willingneſs to buy it. He deſired the Admiral to leave ſome of his Men at *Ternate*, which was refus'd at that Time. He view'd the Ship over again, and going into the Cook-Room, very much admir'd a Pair of Bellows, wherewith they kindled the Fire in his Preſence, and ſeeing the Uſe they were put to, took them into his own Hands, and was a conſiderable Time opening and ſhutting of them ; then biting and preſſing the Nozle with his Lips,

Fooliſh Behaviour of his.

he began to ſwallow the Wind it blow'd out, ſwelling himſelf up, not without much Laughter and Aſtoniſhment of the *Dutch*, who write, they Thought the King was either running Mad, or had no Senſe before. He begg'd thoſe Bellows, and being preſented with them, was highly pleas'd. He return'd ſeveral Times after to the Ships, with a greater Deſign in his Head, which was to try whether he could by any Means contrive to ſeize them. He was pleas'd to ſee how affectionately his Subjects

traded

traded and trufted them with their Spice. At length they prevail'd upon the Admiral to leave fome of his Men, with a good Sum of Mony, to buy up Cloves the next gathering. The firft *Dutch* Factors left at *Ternate*, were *Francis Verdoes*, Father to *William* ; *Diricht F'oris*, *Jacob Lamberts*, *John Jans*, of *Grol* ; *Cornelius Adrians*, and a Boy of *Amfterdam*, who e Name was *Henry Jans*. Thefe laid the Ground for the fecond Enmity, with the firft Rebells of that Nation, who corfpir'd with the *Ternates*, and were afterwards the Occafion of other Fleets and Succours coming into thofe Parts, againft their Natural Sovereign.

Thefe Men being left at *Ternate*, and having receiv'd Intelligence that the Brigan ines were returning from the Ifland of *Banda*, the Ships tail'd from *Ternate*, on the 19th of *Auguft*, paffing by the Ifland *Maca*, among the other *Moluccos*, and that of *Oba*, to the Northward. Then in two Degrees and a half Latitude, they difcover'd fo many Iflands, that they could not count them ; others they faw, not fet down in the Maps, and learnt their Names from fome Sailors. Among them was that of *Banquore*, and its Neighbour *Sabobe*, whofe King refides in that of *Mitara*, and has 30 more within a very fmall Compafs. He furnifh'd them with Provifions, and gave Notice of Dangerous Ridges of Rocks ; to avoid which, they return'd the fame Way they came, in Sight of *Amboyna* and *Celebes*. On the 13th of *November*, they were inform'd at *Jaquetra*, that the Vice-Admiral was already gone from *Banda* ; and had there a great Quantity of Rice, brought but juft before by *Chinefe* Veffels.

On the 17th they came to *Banda*, where at *Montelongo*, and *Soleparvo*, they found the two *Zealand* Ships, which having traded about eight Months with little Profit, defign'd to return. On the 15th of *January* 1600, the Admiral made the Governour of *Banda* fome *European* Prefents, and among them a fmall Boat, all cover'd with fine Scarlet. All the Merchants met and fet fail for *Holland*, on the 21th of the fame Month, and fail'd all *February*, with ftormy Winds, and lofs of fome of their Men, till the Weather mended on the third of *March*. On the 13th of *April*, in the Latitude of 34 Degrees and a half, they found themfelves fomewhat above 20 Leagues from the Cape of *Good Hope*. On the 16th of *May*, they reach'd the Ifland of St. *Helena*, where, at fome Diftance, they difcover'd other Ships. Some Men landed, and admir'd its ftrange Fertility among thofe Mountains. They faw another Ifland, whofe bare Rocks, without Trees or Grafs, look as if they were made of Coals ; and among them are Abundance of monftrous wild Boars, yet nothing could be feen to grow, or any living Creatures they could feed upon. There were alfo large Tortoifes, fome of them weighing 400 Weight. On the laft of *May* they made for the *Texel*, and thence to *Amfterdam*, where they were receiv'd with publick Rejoycing , and they again prepar'd to return to *India*, and continuing their Trade with thofe barbarous Kings, who are Mafters of the Spice, Metals, precious Stones, Pearls, and other foreign Wealth, have at length converted the Friendfhip they kindly offer'd at firft, into Slavery, and Subjection to the Tyranny of *Holland* and *Zealand*. And in the Year 1600, with more Expedition, they fail'd into *Guinea*, and to *S. George de la Mina*, with only two Ships, the firft Time, and ran through the fame Ports and Iflands, throughout our Seas in Safety. They

took

A a

Marginal notes:

Dutch Factory at Ternate.

Dutch depart Ternate.

Come to Banda.

At the Cape of Good Hope.

S. Helena.

Defart Ifland.

took particular Accounts of all Things, whether Natural, or Political,
relating to that vaft extended Country of *Afia*, which is almoft oppofite to
Europe, and under other Stars, and another Pole. The fame Year, being
in fearch of the *North-Paffage*, in 80 Degrees of Latitude, they difcover'd
Nova Zembla, where they found nothing but monftrous white and grey
Bears, which did not run, but rather took little Notice of the Noife of
Cannon, and devour'd Men , there were alfo white Crows, no lefs undaunted ; and in fhort, moft of that Part of the World was defart, and
they found not the Paffage they expected into the South-Sea. Yet they
now fail'd all thofe Southern Parts, at all Seafons, making a Jeft of the
Monfons, the *Portuguefes* fo mightily obferve, as if they had them fhut
up in Skins, like the Fable in *Ulyffes*. Perhaps they buy fair and ftormy
Winds, as is faid to be done in *Lapland*, at fettled Rates, of Witches that
deal in them.

The King of *Ternate* was fo puff'd up with the Friendfhip, and Support
of the Northern Nations, that he durft boldly flatter himfelf with the
Hope of becoming abfolute Mafter of *Tydore*. Accordingly he ftreightned
that King, and the *Portuguefe* Garrifon, without allowing them the leaft
Refpite. Other *Dutch* Ships had come fince the former to that Ifland,
on Account of Trade, by the Way of *India*, with Arms and feveral Commodities. The *Ternate* Embaffadors were treating in *England* and *Holland*, for fettling of perpetual Peace and Commerce. The King had already received Anfwers to thefe Embaffies, and very fpeedily expected an
Englifh Fleet, and many *Dutch* Ships, with whofe Affiftance he promis'd
himfelf to deftroy *Tydore*, and thence to ftretch out to the *Philippines*.
In the mean while, fome *Dutch* and *Englifh* remain'd at his Court, like
Hoftages, with a Factor, whofe Bufinefs was to attend the Bartering, or
buying up of Spice ; to purchafe which they brought him Abundance of
curious Arms. This being known to the King of *Tydore*, and *Ruy Gonzalez de Sequeyra*, Commander of the Fort, who every Year writ to the

Governour of the *Philippines* about it ; they now fent a particular Embaffy
to *Don Francifco Tello*, giving him an Account of the Condition of thofe
Places ; of the Fort ; of the Succours, and how vain it was to expect
them from *India*. That an Affair of fuch Confequence might fort the defired Event, they appointed *Cachil Cota*, the King of *Tydore*'s Brother, a

notable Soldier, and moft renowned Commander of the *Moluccos*, to go
Embaffador. He came to *Manila*, well attended, with Letters from the
King, and the Commander in Chief. Thofe, and he, in a fet Speech, (for
the People of the *Moluccos* do not want Rhetorick to perfwade) return'd
the Governour Thanks for the Supplies he had at feveral Times fent them of
Provifions, and Ammunition. *But what we come to defire*, faid *Cachil Cota,
is that this Work be now effectually taken in Hand, before the* Englifh *and*
Dutch *with their Fleets ftrengthen* Ternate, *and ren er it impregnable.
We cannot but admire, that whereas the* Portuguefe *Arms obtain fuch fignal
Victories, as are thofe of* Calicut , *over the* Turks, *at* Diu ; *over the* Egyp-
tians ; *over the People of* Cananor, *of* Ceylon, *the* Javas, Sumatra, *and
other Nations on that Side , and the* Spaniards *on this, againft thofe of*
Camboxa, Mindanao, Japan, Cochinchina, *and* China, *yet only we of the*
Moluccos, *who lie amidft the Dominions of one only Monarch, fhould be left
expos'd*

expos'd *to the utmoſt Fury of a Parcel of Rebellious Iſlands.   If the King of* S pain *allows, or rather commands, we ſhould be reliev'd by the Way of the* Philippine *Iſlands, Why is he not obey'd ?   What does it avail to carry on a* cool War, *againſt a hot and watchful Enemy?*   The Governour anſwer'd to every Point, and having entertain'd him, and given Hopes of greater Supplies, when he could be ſecure againſt the mighty Preparations then making at *Japan,* he diſmiſs'd him, with a conſiderable Recruit of Artillery and Ammunition, and ſome experienced Soldiers.   However theſe *Another* Succours being ſo much inferior to the Power of the Enemy, and their *Embaſſy.* own Fear, which made them expect much greater, they could not put them out of Care.   This made them ſend Captain *Marcos Dias de Febra,* their laſt Embaſſador to the *Philippines,* during the Government of *Don Francis Tello.*   He carry'd Letters from the King and *Ruy Gonzalez,* to the Governour and Council, which being almoſt all of them much of the ſame Purport, we will here inſert one of them, directed to Doctor *Antony Morga,* one of that Council, writ with the King's own Hand, and in the *Portugueſe* Language.

I was wonderfully pleas'd with your Letter of the 8th of November *laſt,* The King *becauſe by it I underſtood how very ſincere you were in remembring of me,* of Tydores *God reward you for it with much Proſperity in this Life, that you may do* Letter. *Service to the King, my Sovereign, for I underſtand you are by his Order in thoſe Iſlands, and deſirous to improve them ; which I am not ignorant will be no leſs Advantageous to this Fort and Iſland of* Tydore. *I write to the Governour, and to that Council, concerning the Succours I deſire, and have ask'd ſo often, the Neceſſity of it being great, to prevent thoſe Miſchiefs which may afterwards put my Sovereign, the King, to much Trouble and Charge.   God grant you long Life.   From this Iſland of* Tydore, March *the* 8th 1601.   The King of *Tydore, in* Arabick *Characters ; and then what follows in* Portugueſe.   *The Bearer is* Marcos Diaz, *he will deliver you a Powder Flask, with a Charge of fine* Mooriſh Braſs.   *I ſend it you, that you may remember this Friend.*

The Embaſſador return'd to *Tydore* with the firſt *Monſon,* at the Begin- *Embaſſa-* ning of the Year 1602, well pleas'd with the Anſwer he brought, the *dor returns* Supplies of Proviſions and Ammunition he had demanded, and ſome Sol- *well ſatis-* diers ; but much better ſatisfy'd with the Hopes given him, that as ſoon *fy'd.* as an Opportunity offer'd, that Expedition ſhould be undertaken from *Ma-* nila for *Ternate,* with the neceſſary Preparations, and Force to ſecure the Succeſs.

At this Time King *James* of *England,* writ to *Sultan Zayde,* of *Ter-* K. James nate, deſiring him to continue his former Friendſhip, and that the *Engliſh* of England might build Colonies and Factories in the *Molucco* Iſlands.   The *Sultan* Writes *to* would not grant it, and complain'd in harſh Terms, that *England* had ne- *the King* ver aſſiſted him againſt *Portugal ;* and that ſo little Account ſhould be of Ternate there made of the firſt Alliance concluded by Means of Sir *Francis Drake,* when King *Babu* ſent the Queen of *England* a Ring in Token of Confede- racy, by the ſaid *Drake.*   He ſaid, he could not admit the *Engliſh,* con- *His Anſwer* trary to the ſolemn Engagement he had made to Prince *Maurice* and the

Dutch

Dutch Nation, to whom he had made a Promiſe, that none but they ſhould buy up and lade the Product of his Country. All this appears by the Copy of a Letter in the *Portugueſe* Tongue, found among the King of *Ternate*'s Papers, when our Men poſſeſs'd themſelves of his Palace. Where we may obſerve the perfect Hatred he ſhows for the *Portugueſe* Government, ſince he never Names thoſe People without adding the Epithet of *Mortal Enemies*; and in ſpeaking of the *Dutch, My Friends and Deliverers*; adding, That he expects their Fleets with great Satisfaction. This Anſwer he ſent King *James* by *Henry Middleton*, then Admiral of the *Engliſh* Fleet, on the eighteenth of *July*, 1605. The Truth of the Fact is, that this King admitted, and invited to his Dominions, and the Product of them, all other Nations, to arm againſt the *Spaniards*, and oppoſe Chriſtianity; and tho' he then boaſted of the Succours he receiv'd, and expected from the *Dutch*, had he ſeen the Power of their Fleets and Arms decline, he would have excluded them the Trade. All his Religion and Hopes were ſubſervient to the preſent Circumſtances of Times, and his Faith depended on the Advantages he could make.

The End of the Seventh Book.

THE
HISTORY
OF THE
DISCOVERY and CONQUEST
OF THE
Molucco and *Philippine* Iſlands, *&c.*

BOOK. VIII.

ALL the Contents of the Letters, and other Papers, that came from the *Molucco* Iſlands to *India* and the *Philippines*, for the following Years, amount to nothing but Complaints, aſking Relief, and giving Intelligence, not altogether below the Dignity of Hiſtory, were we not come ſo near the laſt Period of it. Particularly there are Letters of the Commander of *Tydore*, *Ruy Gonzalez de Sequeyra*, to the Governor of the *Philippine* Iſlands, wherein he complains, That whereas he had ſent 400 Men, Ships, and Warlike Stores to *Camboxa*, where his Majeſty had nothing to Recover, he had furniſh'd him with only twenty Soldiers. He repreſents to him many preſſing Wants, without any Hopes of Relief from the Viceroy, by the way of *Malaca*; urging the ſcarcity of Proviſions, Arms, and all other Neceſſaries. He informs him, That through his Means *Cachil Mole* had been ſworn King of *Tydore*; and how faithful a Friend he approves himſelf to the Crown of *Siam*, and an Enemy to the *Ternates*; and that he is always ſollicitous for recovering of that Fort. He deſires him to ſend the King a Preſent of great Guns, and other Gifts, and to do the ſame by the King of *Siam*, who is a Chriſtian, and our Friend. He acquaints him how frequently the *Engliſh* and *Dutch* Ships reſort to thoſe Seas, and that he had taken ſome of them.

The Succeſs of a very great and rich Ship of *Zealand*, is moſt particularly Remarkable: This Veſſel putting into *Ternate*, and Trading with

Complaints from Tydore, and other Advice.

that

that Wicked Faithless King, he consented that *Ruy Gonzalez* should contrive to cut her Cables, provided the Booty might be his. He agreed to it, exacting an Exorbitant price for the Villany. The Bargain made, and the Bribe receiv'd, they who had cut the Cables leap'd over-board, and immediately the King's Officers appear'd, who seiz'd all the Loading, the Ship being beaten to pieces, to no purpose. He assures him, That the Enterprize on *Ternate* might be effected with 400 *Spaniards*; and promises to send him a great piece of Amber, as an extraordinary Rarity, from the Isles of *Mava*, which are 60 Leagues from the *Moluccos.* He again gives Advice of Northern Galeons, and that one of them, in four Hours, had batter'd that Fort, shot into it 261 Bullets; one of which he sent him; and that they had beaten down a large Curtin of the Wall, which was then Repairing.

In the mean while *England* infested the *West-Indies*; where the Towns and Ships suffer'd by their Invasions, Robberies, and Burnings. Only that Part, which was the District belonging to *Don Pedro de Acunna*, defended it self, through the Bravery of its Governor, and for the same Reason the Enemy had Regard to it. *William Park*, the *English* Admiral, appear'd upon the strong and garrison'd Coasts of *America*, in the Year 1601. They defended themselves well, yet he prevail'd in some Places. On the Coast of *Cartagena* he took one *Julio*, a Fisherman, whom he afterwards set at Liberty, that he might carry the following Letter, writ in broken *Spanish* to Don *Pedro*.

Being inform'd by Fame, with how much Generosity and Kindness your Lordship entertains Strangers, especially those of my Nation, I would not forbear expressing the Gratitude due to your Lordship for that Magnificence, on my own Part, and returning Thanks, wishing you as long a Life, and as much Health, as to my self. I would not omit writing these few Lines to your Lordship, not only on the aforesaid Account, but to acquaint you with what has happen'd to me during this Expedition. It pleas'd God to make me Master of one of the Kings Ports, call'd Porto Belo, *which I was possess'd of a whole Day and Part of the Night, where I found some Gentlemen, particularly Captain* Melendez, *and some other Soldiers of the Garrison; and plundering the Place had very little Booty. The said Captain* Melendez, *fought like a resolute Soldier, and faithful Servant of his King, and therefore I order'd him to be dress'd by my Surgeon, and to be carry'd out of the House where he was wounded, having laid Wood in all the Houses to fire them, and consume the Town. I do assure your Lordship, and declare on the Word of a Soldier, that being inform'd of your Valour and Renown, by certain Prisoners I took, as Captain* Rolon, *and several others, and at* Porto Belo *by the King's Factor,* Funes, *and other Soldiers, that were my Prisoners, and aboard my Ship, I gave them all their Liberty, and forbore firing the City, only on Account of your Reputation, and the Fame of your good Usage to such Prisoners as fall into your Hands. So that those I set at Liberty, as also the Town, may be thankful to your Lordship for so great an Obligation, as is the Value of the said Town, and their Lives. The Castle, and the Fort at the Mouth of the Harbour, and the Port it self, so well fortify'd and furnish'd with Artillery, and all other Necessaries, did not deter, fright, or daunt me, for I went out with six Ships, and the Castles did me no Harm. Really the Commanders*

and

and Guners were very honeſt Men. I give your Lordſhip Notice of two Engliſh Men, who landed at Santa Marta, *near ten Months ſince, their Names are* Abraham Collins, *and* Thomas Hall. *Theſe are both Spies upon* Cartagena. *I like the Treaſon, but drown the Traitor ; I ſend you ſome poor Men aſhore, whom I took upon this Coaſt, your Lordſhip will favour them as is due, and according to your Cuſtom. And having Nothing elſe, at preſent, to acquaint your Lordſhip with, pray to God to lengthen your Life, with much Health, and Proſperity, and to give me good Luck, as is in his divine Power, is convenient for us, and I wiſh. From aboard my Ship,* February *the twenty eigth,* 1601, *our Stile. Your Lordſhips,* William Park.

Don Pedro anſwer'd in few Words, yet ſo as his Brevity might not exclude Civility, and the Pyrate being ſatisfy'd, proceeded on His Voyage. The King had at this Time appointed *Don Pedro* to ſucceed *Don Francis Tello* in the Government of the *Philippine* Iſlands, deſigning him for thoſe Enteprizes he afterwards perform'd. This his Majeſty judg'd a proper Reſolution, and ſafe in the Execution ; for what Perſon is fit to be pitch'd upon to Govern the utmoſt Limits of ſo far extended a Dominion, but ſuch a one as is endu'd with both Valour and Loyalty, two neceſſary Qualifications to ſecure the Reſpect and Submiſſion due to an abſent Prince, a Matter of much Difficulty in remote Governments? *Don Pedro appointed Governor of the Philippines.*

Since this Gentleman's own Actions, and the great Opinion his very Enemies had conceiv'd of them, are ſufficient Teſtimonies of his Valour, let us proceed to ſay ſomething of his Quality. *Don Pedro* had the Surname of *Bravo,* as being Son to *Don Lewis Bravo,* who ſerving under the Emperor *Charles* the fifth, on the Day the Prince of *Orange* dy'd, aſk'd Leave to aſſault *S. Deſir,* a ſtrong Town in the *Low Countries,* on the Banks of the River *Matrone.* The Hiſtory of that War informs us, that ſome Friends of his Father's, hearing of it, endeavour'd to obſtruct it, either by diſſwading the Son, or prevailing with the Emperor not to grant him Leave. His Father was *Sancho Bravo de Lagunas,* a Gentleman of Quality by Birth, and no leſs by his own Actions, at that Time Inſpector General of the Emperor's Forces by Sea and Land, and one of his Council of War. All Men honour'd, and lov'd him entirely. They conſider'd he had no other Son but *Don Lewis,* and the manifeſt Danger he expos'd himſelf to ; but he perceiving what his Fathers Friends were contriving, took upon him to lead the Van, before they could have Time to prevent his gaining the Honour he expected ; and aſſaulted the Place with Succeſs, tho' not without ſome Imputation of Raſhneſs. His Son *Don Pedro* did not degenerate, for the Brave are the Off-ſpring of the Brave, and the Eagle does not breed Doves. *Don Pedro's Father.*

The Name of *Acunna* he took from his Mother, according to the Cuſtom of the Kingdoms of *Caſtile,* where noble Families, to keep up the Honour of the Quality they acquire by Matrimony, uſe to revive the Names of their Progenitors even in the Grand-Children. *Don Lewis Bravo,* marry'd *Donna Iſabel de Acunna,* Daughter to *Don Pedro de Acunna,* call'd in thoſe Days *el Cabezudo,* ſignifying, either the Head-ſtrong, or Great-Headed, great Grand-Son to the firſt Earl of *Buendia,* a Family of known Antiquity. Among his Sons, *Don Sancho Bravo,* the eldeſt, is *His Mother.*

now

now, when this History was writ, *Adelantado*, or Lord Lieutenant of *Ternate*, and Knight of the Order of *Alcantara* ; *Don Garcia*, is Knight of *Santiago* ; *Don Lewis*, of *Calatrava* ; *Don John*, bred in the principal Colledge of *Alcala*, went thence to be Gentleman of the Bed chamber to the most serene Arch-Duke *Albertus*, and is since Cannon of the Holy Church of *Toledo*, besides other Church Affairs he is always employ'd in. Our *Don Pedro* was Knight of *Malta*, and Commendary of *Salamanca*.

Don Pedro Knight of Malta.

He departed *Cartagena*, leaving that Government disconsolate, and full of the Desire of his Continuance among them. He had a good Passage, and being come to *Mexico*, and entertain'd by the Viceroy, *Don Gaspar De Zunniga y Azevedo*, Earl of *Monterey*, consulted with him about the Expedition and Recovery of the *Molucco* Islands, beginning with *Ternate*, the Head of them. They admitted to their Consultations some experienc'd Commanders in those Countries. The Result was, the Viceroy's being well affected to the Expedition, and to the Governour, who was going to undertake it, which was of no small Consequence, towards rend'ring the Preparations made in *New Spain* effective. *Don Pedro* writ to the King, to his Confessor, to the Duke of *Lerma*, and to other Ministers of State, especially the supreme Councellors of the *Indies*, very largely, in Relation to this War, showing how difficult it was, and how great a Dishonour, to permit a Tyrant to reign so long, he being so near a Neighbour. He said, he could not secure any Ships, nor even the Provinces, against the *Moluccos* ; and that, had he not been promis'd to be enabled to recover them, he would never have accepted of the Government of the *Philippine* Islands. He sent Brother *Gaspar Gomez*, a Jesuit, with these Letters into *Spain*, And set out himself from *Mexico*, for *Acapulco*, the Sea-Port-Town of that Kingdom. Thence he proceeded, with four Ships of *New Spain*, to the Islands *de los Ladrones*, that is of Thieves, otherwise call'd *de las Velas*, or of Sails, from the great Multitude of Little Sails seen about them, belonging to Abundance of Boats that come out to meet the Ships.

Comes to Mexico.

Arrives at the Islands Ladrones.

He directed his Course to the Isles of *Carpana*, and that of *Guan*, that no Time might be lost without doing good to others. His Design was to bring off from among those barbarous People, such Men as had escap'd of the Ship *Margarita*, cast away there the Year before, with above 1200000 Ducats ; and as true Virtue never wants Matter to work on, he deliver'd twenty five Men of the many that suffer'd Shipwrack in that Place. Having perform'd this good Work, in twenty six Days he came to the Mouth of the Streight of the *Philippines*, and anchor'd at *Cabite*, three Leagues from *Manila* ; where he was receiv'd with incredible, and universal Joy. His first Care was to be inform'd of the Condition his Predecessor left the Government in. He view'd every Part, and cast off the *Sangleys*, or *Chineses*, as thinking they exceeded the large Number allow'd of by the King's Order. Some interpreted the Exclusion of those People, was only to condemn the extravagant Liberties they took ; but Time soon show'd, that there were other great Advantages reap'd by it. In *Don Pedro* all Men believ'd the Security of the *Philippine* Islands was come ; for the Governour's Reputation was equal to the Necessities of his Province ; which requir'd the Government of an experienc'd Commander, of great Name, and so vigilant as he was.

Rich Ships lost.

Twenty five Men sav'd.

Don Pedro at Manila.

Don

Don *Francis Tello* refign'd up the Power into his Hands, and flaying there to give an Account of his Adminiftration, dyed in *April*, the following Year. The new Governour was much concern'd to find the King's Treafury empty, and himfelt under an Obligation of fupporting the King's and his own Credit. To this Confideration belong'd the *Moluccos*, the reducing whereof he had in Charge. However he took Courage, believing he might with Induftry and Labour, make amends for the Want of Cafh. He attended all the Works in Perfon, as he had been wont to do, both at *Manila* and in the Country about, building Galleys, and other Veffels, whereof there was then a great Want, to fecure the Sea, at that Time infefted by the Neighbouring Pirates and Enemies, efpecially thofe of *Mindanao*. Next he vifited the Provinces of the *Pintados*, and fupply'd the Wants he found in thofe Parts. In thefe Paffages betwixt the Iflands, befides the Storms, his little Veffel, which had only three Soldiers in it, efcap'd, he fell into another notable Danger. Two and twenty *Englifh* Veffels enrich'd with the Booty they had taken in the Iflands belonging to that Government, attempted to inclofe and take him, but the Tide failing them, they ftuck on Ground, and could not get off. *Don Pedro* faw them throw over-board above 2000 *Spaniards*, and Natives they had made Prifoners, to lighten their Veffels. They alfo caft into the Sea a beautiful *Spanifh* Maid, about 17 Years of Age. Afterwards the Fleet from *Manila* fail'd in queft of them, and chaftis'd fome, tho' the Punifhment was inferior to their Cruelty.

Don Pedro would fain have remov'd all Obftacles that lay in the Way to the Enterprize he had in Hand; but was oblig'd to put off for fome Months that which he was moft intent upon, and to difpatch the Affairs of *Xolo* and *Japan*. *Chiquiro*, a *Japonefe* Embaffador, was newly arriv'd at *Manila*, with a Prefent of the Product and Manufactures of that Ifland, and orders to treat with the Governour, and fettle Amity and Commerce, between the Subjects of the Emperor of *Japan*, whofe Name was *Dayfufama*, and the *Philippines* and *New-Spain*. The Neighbourhood of thofe Provinces, the Power of the *Japonefe* Kings, their natural Difpofition, and other Confiderations, which Experience had fhown to be of great Moment, made againft refufing of that Commerce; and yet there were Opinions to the contrary, for thofe very Reafons. However that barbarous Prince having once efpous'd that Affair, it was not eafy to find out an Expedient to fettle it, without any Jealoufy or Difguft. *Dayfufama* demanded, that the *Spaniards* fhould trade to *Quanto*, a Port in one of his Provinces, and that fuch Friendfhip might be eftablifh'd, that the *Japonefes* might go over to *New-Spain*. That the Governour fhould fend him Shipwrights, and Workmen to build Ships in *Japan*, for performing of that Voyage, upon which *Dayfufama* was very intent, being perfwaded to it by a Religious Man of ours, of the Order of St. *Francis*, whofe Name was *F. Jerome* of *JESUS*, and for whom that Monarch had a great Efteem.

This was a Matter of great Weight, and on feveral Accounts moft prejudicial to the *Philippine* Iflands, whofe greateft Security for fo many Years, has confifted in the *Japonefe*'s wanting of Ships and Pilots, and being ignorant in the Art of Navigation. Men of Experience obferv'd, that

Don Francis Tello dyes.

Don Pedro vifits his Government.

Cruelty of Englifh.

Japonefe Embaffador at Manila.

His Propofals.

Objections to them.

B b   when-

whenſoever the ſaid haughty barbarous Prince has attempted to arm againſt *Manila*, he has ſtill been obſtructed by this Want. They ſaid, that to ſend him Ship-Wrights, and Men to build him Ships after the *Spaniſh* Manner, would be no other than arming him againſt the *Spaniards* themſelves; and that their Voyages would be deſtructive to the *Philippines* and *New-Spain*; for that the making the *Japoneſes* capable of Trading far off, was not only inconvenient, but unſafe. The Governour *Don Pedro de Acunna* ſeriouſly weighing all theſe Reaſons, order'd the Embaſſador *Chiquiro* to be magnificently entertain'd, made him ſome Preſents for his King and for himſelf, and ſent a Ship with another moderate Preſent, left it ſhould be interpreted to proceed from Fear, if it had been too conſiderable. This Ship ſail'd with *Dayfuſama* and his Embaſſador, both of them loaded with Commodities to barter. *Don Pedro*'s Letters contain'd many Compliments, and Thanks for the good Will he ſhow'd towards eſtabliſhing more ſolid Friendſhip; but that, tho' he had ample Commiſſion for all Things relating to the Government of the *Philippine* Iſlands, yet he could not ſatisfy that Part of his Embaſſy, which concern'd the furniſhing of him with Sailors and Workmen to build *Spaniſh* Ships, without acquainting the Viceroy of *New-Spain*, nor could the Viceroy do it, without ſpecial Orders from the King of *Spain*. That he promiſ'd to write to them about it, for promoting the Accompliſhment of his reaſonable Demands; but that he muſt conſider, it would be above three Years before they had an Anſwer, becauſe of the great Length, and many Accidents of ſuch Voyages. It was order'd that the aforeſaid *F. Jerome* ſhould himſelf deliver theſe Letters, to *Dayfuſama*. The Fryar himſelf had a private Letter

Inſtructions to F. Jerome.

ſent him with a Reproof for what he had done, and Inſtructions how to mend it; and that he ſhould ſignify to the *Japoneſe* Monarch, how highly the Governour valu'd the Inclination he ſhow'd to ſettle Peace and Commerce with the *Spaniards*, and his Kindneſs to them; and at the ſame Time perſwade him to continue that good Correſpondence, which the Governour would inviolably obſerve; but that he ſhould endeavour to divert the King's Thoughts from ſuch Deſigns, and never go about to facilitate the Execution of them; becauſe, tho' perhaps the Emperor then reigning entertain'd no ſiniſter Meaning, nor had any farther Thought than promoting a ſincere Friendſhip, yet that might be very prejudicial in the Days of a more miſchievous Succeſſor; who might make an ill Uſe of his Skill in Navigation, and improve it againſt the Perſons that taught it him. The Governour promiſ'd he would ſoon ſend another Ship with Commodities to barter; and he might put the King in Hopes it would carry over ſome *Spaniſh* Ship-Carpenters to build Ships after their Manner. That he ſhould deſire *Dayfuſama* to wait with Patience, and conſider how heinouſly he would be offended himſelf, if any of his Governours ſhould preſume to make any new Settlements in Trade without his Privity or Order.

Japoneſe Embaſſador caſt away.

Chiquiro return'd for *Japan* with this Anſwer; but when he was off the Head of the Iſland *Formoſa*, ſuch a dreadful Storm overtook him, that he was ſwallow'd up, and neither Men, Goods, nor Arms ſav'd; and this happen'd in ſo remote a Place, that it was not known till many Days after. *Dayfuſama*, at the Requeſt of *F. Jerome*, had granted Leave for Preaching of the Goſpel, throughout his Dominions, building of Churches, and ſuch as

would

would profeffing Chriftianity by publick Authority. *Don Pedro* the Governour took the neceffary Meafures, that fo favourable an Indulgence might
not be loft, and that not only barefoot *Francifcans*, but alfo Religious Men
of other Orders fhould go over thither. They made ufe of the *Japonefe*
Captains and Ships, newly come to *Manila* with Meal. The *Dominicans*
fent over to the Kingdom of *Zazuma* four Fryars, and *F. Francis de Morales*,
Prior of *Manila* for their Superior, faying the King of that Province fent
for them, being the only one, who had not yet fubmitted to *Dayfufama*.
The Order of *S. Auguftin* fent two Religious Men, and *F. James de Guevara*,
Prior alfo of *Manila* for their Superior, and thefe went to the Kingdom of
Firando. Thofe of the Order of *S. Francis*, fent *F. Auguftin Rodriguez*,
who had been Witnefs to the Martyrdom of his Companions in *Japan*,
to *Nangafaqui*, for him to go thence with a Lay-Brother to *Miaco*, and
bear *F. Jerome* of *Jefus* Company. Many perfwaded *Don Pedro*, not to
fend away thefe Religious Men; but tho' thofe Perfwafions were well
grounded, and fome Difficulties occur'd againft their Departure, he refolv'd
to difmifs them. The Zeal of true Glory overcomes all Oppofition.
Thefe Religious Men found no Signs of thofe Defires that had been fignify'd to them in the Provinces they went to. Very few *Japonefes* were
converted, and there was lefs Difpofition to advance, becaufe the Kings,
and *Tonos*, which are Princes had no Affection for our Religion, nor were
any Way difgufted with their Idols. They only afpir'd to fettle Commerce, and to trade with the *Spaniards*, for their private Intereft.

Don Pedro fent the Ship he had promis'd to *Japan*, well ftor'd with
Cannon, and call'd it *S. James* the Lefs. The Captain, Officers, and
Sailors were all Men of Experience; and fhe was laden with Commodities to barter, Red-Wood, Deer's-Skins, raw Silk, and feveral other
Sorts. The Govenour order'd them to difpofe of what they carry'd at
the Port of *Quanto*, and to furnifh the Religious Men they found there,
and then return with the Produce and *Dayfufama's* Leave. Thus Provifion was made for all the Affairs of *Japan*, according to the prefent
Exigences. The Ship-Wrack of the Embaffador *Chiquito* was known,
and by the good Management of *F. Jerome*, *Dayfufama* was acquainted
with the Anfwer he carry'd, and refted fatisfy'd; fo that the preaching
of the Gofpel went on in his Dominions.

Don Pedro's Thoughts were all bent upon Recovering of the *Molucco*
Iflands, and his other Bufinefs did not make him neglect that Enterprize.
Andrew Furtado de Mendoza, Admiral of thofe Seas for the Crown of
Portugal had writ him Word, that he had Orders from his Majefty to repair to *Ternate*; but that he did not expect the Viceroy would fet him
out, as was requifite for that Expedition. *Don Pedro* anfwer'd him, to
his Content, with Affurance, that he fhould be fupported. Thefe Letters
came to the Hands of the *Portuguefe* Admiral at *Malaca*, when he was
ready to fet out. He prefently anfwer'd both thofe of the 22d of *Septem-*
ber, and the 22d of *December*, fignifying how acceptable they were to him.
Becaufe, fays he, *I love your Lordfhip entirely, tho' I have never feen you,*
on Account of your being a brave Commander, and fo zealous for his Ma-
jefty's Service; not to mention other Reafons for which I am yours. I was
much troubled for the Lofs of the Ship, and the ill Fortune of the other, for

the

the want you will find of the Return you expected by them. But it is to be suppos'd, that the Viceroy of New-Spain, *seeing how long those Ships were missing, would impute it to some very considerable Causes, and therefore will Assist you Powerfully, for nothing less can be expected from such a Viceroy, who, I am told, is a very worthy Gentleman. I am experimentally sensible of what your Lordship writes to me ; for after being in those Parts five Years, without receiving any Succours from* India, *when I expected these Disorders should end, and considerable Supplies would be sent me, the Viceroy furnish'd me so poorly, as will appear to your Lordship by the List of what he sends, and thence you may infer, how his Majesty is serv'd in those Parts, that your Lordship may acquaint him with it, and we may joyntly so order it, that all this may not be overthrown in one Hour.*

Then he complains, That they have not sent him his Majesty's Letter, nor the Archbishop of *Goa* had not receiv'd his; and says, *He had rather be at Plow in* Old Castile, *than a Witness to the ill Disposition of what is committed to his Charge :* And proceeding, says thus, *Your Lordship tells me, That as soon as I draw near the* Moluccos, *you will do me the favour to have in readiness for me* 300 *Soldiers, with Captain* Gallinato, *and another Captain, and two Galleys, four Brigantines, and all the* Carcoas *that shall be requisite. I know not what his Majesty appoints for me ; but, for the Sins of these Dominions, Time has put Things into such a Posture, that I must be forc'd to repair to the* Moluccos, *as well to recover what is Lost, as to save what is Gain'd, which cannot be done, unless both Powers, from hence and thence, be United. Twelve* Dutch *Ships anchor'd this Year at the Bar of* Goa : *They took the Viceroy so unprovided, that they lay at Anchor a Month at the said Bar, without any Attempt made to remove them. They made great Havock amongst the Merchants Ships on the Coast of* India, *without any Opposition. They came from the other Sea, by the Back of* Sumatra, *to the Streight of* Sunda. *Seven of them arriv'd at* Amboyna, *the others being then parted from them. When they enter'd over the Bar, the Governour sent two Men, to ask, whether* Don Emanuel *was aboard. The Ships hearing of it, went and Anchor'd under the Fort. Then the Governor sent three or four other Men, who made the Agreement for the surrendering of the Fort. When it was sign'd the* Dutch *drew near ; the Gates were open'd to them, and they admitted without standing one Musket Shot, or firing a Cannon. They took an Oath of Fidelity to Prince* Maurice, *and the Governor after committing the Treason, commanded a Black of his own to put him into Irons, saying,* The People of the Town had done it. *Since that he came hither, and skulks about the Mountains, and I am very earnest to take him, that I may make an Example of him. I have already secur'd some of the Marry'd Men that came hither, being fully convinc'd that the Governor and they are Enemies and Traytors. When the* Dutch *were possess'd of the Fort, they put more Cannon into it, with a Garrison of* 140 *Men, and Provisions for two Years. I have also received Intelligence, That they sent five Ships against* Tydore, *and I am very jealous of that Place, because of the Divisions there ; wherefore I immediately sent away two Galiots, well Man'd, Arm'd, and Provided. God grant they find that Fort in the King's Possession. Thus, if his Majesty well send hither the Galeons he writes of, and commands me to serve him in these Southern Parts, I must of necessity go over that way ; for since*

Amboyna

Margin notes:
More of the Letter.

Baseness of a Portugese Governour.

Amboyna *is in the Poffeffion of the* Dutch, *we may conclude* Tydore *will foon follow. If they extend their Dominion, from that Port, which God avert, they will thence put an End to the Affairs of the* Moluccos, *and of* China, *and with the Affiftance of the* Ternates *muft of neceffity Infeft thofe Parts about* Manila; *and therefore we are all oblig'd, as Chriftians, and his Majefty's Subjects, to Oppofe fuch a mig'ty Misfortune. And fince the Lot has fallen between your Lordfhip, and this Soldier of yours, we feem to be in fome meafure both of us under an Obligation to fpare no Pains for the Recovering of thofe Parts of the* Molucco *Iflands. For my part I will Labour for the Succefs, tho' I were to lofe ten Lives, if I had fo many. But becaufe I fhall not have an Opportunity to fend your Lordfhip Intelligence, till a Year hence, I now intreat you to have what Soldiers you can in Readinefs, and the greateft Number of Natives, that we may not fall fhort when the work is half done, and be forced, for want of them, to put our felves into the Hands, and expect the Affiftance of Traytors. The fame I beg, as to Provifions; for there are none where I am at prefent. But fince Captain* Gallinato *has feen all, and knows what is Neceffary in thofe Parts, whereof he has before now given your Lordfhip ample Information, it will be needlefs to repeat it in this, being your Lordfhip tells me in yours, you do me the Favour to appoint him for my Companion; and he is fo able a Commander, that when your Lordfhip orders him to prepare for this Expedition, he will take with him all he thinks proper for it. Tho' his Majefty fhould fend feveral Galeons, and many Men, I fhall not be able to do any thing with them in thofe Parts, becaufe the main Thing there, is to have Veffels that Row, and Men that have Serv'd, whereof I am very deftitute. From* India *none can come, tho' the Viceroy were never fo willing to furnifh me. However, confiding in your Lordfhips Worth, and in what you have fignify'd to me by Letter, I will undertake this Expedition, believing I fhall find all Things in fuch Readinefs, that they will fet out from thence the Moment your Lordfhip receives Advice from me. I am told your Lordfhip expects a Gentleman in thofe Parts, who comes to Conquer* Camboxa. *If he happens to come, I muft put your Lordfhip in Mind, that the beft Conqueft is that of the* Moluccos, *where his Majefty's Forts will be reftor'd, and there the faid Gentleman may fhew his Valour, and merit a confiderable Reward from the King. Before the* Dutch *came to* Amboyna, *two* Englifh *Ships paffed by that Ifland, which fent a Letter to the Governor of the Fort, to acquaint him, that the* Dutch *were coming after them, with a Defign to poffefs themfelves of the faid Fort, and therefore they advifed him to behave himfelf well, becaufe the* Dutch *they fpoke of, were a poor faint-hearted People. That, if they had Occafion for Powder, Ball, and all other Neceffaries, they were ready to fupply him, becaufe they were then at Peace with* Spain, *and the Conftable of* Caftile *was already fent into* England, *by his Majefty, to Ratify it: And the Poft-Mafter-General was Embaffador in Ordinary. This Intelligence leaves the Rebels no pretence to any Excufe.* Furtado's Letter goes on, to other Particulars, recommending Religious Men, and Commanders and he concludes with Abundance of Compliments, and Courteous Expreffions.

Don Pedro having receiv'd thefe Letters, order'd and haften'd all neceffary Preparations, with the utmoft Diligence, preffing the Bufinefs in *Spain,* and with the Viceroy at *Mexico,* and thought all Delays tedious; but the

Approbation

Approbation of his Advice, and the Supplies to put it in Execution, being to come from a Center so remote, and where there lay an Obligation of being no less attentive to all Parts of the Circumference, the Expedition could not possibly be brought about sooner.   Brother *Gaspar Gomez*, whose Intelligence in this Affair, was always very material, had presently Intimation of what had been resolv'd on, by Letters from *Don Pedro*; and he was so diligent in promoting it, that to advance this Cause, he cross'd the greatest Oceans as readily, as if they had been the Narrow-Seas, which part those Islands; having solicited the Viceroy at *Mexico*, and then the Counsellors, and Ministers of State in *Spain*.   His Arguments and Motives were the same we have several Times mention'd in this Work.   Dividing the Wealth of the South into three fixt Kinds, precious Stones, and Pearls, Metals, and Spice, and Drugs ;   all which were distributed among Enemies, *English* and *Dutch*. That the King had no Spice left, but only that of *Tydore*, which must be lost, unless speedily and powerfully supported, and the same Forces would recover *Ternate, Banda, Amboyna*, and what had been held in *Celebes, Batochina*, and the Places wrested by the Tyrants of *Sumatra*.   All this the Jesuit made out by Demonstration, for he grounded not the least Information upon any thing less than Experience.

He was heard in the Council of the *Indies*, and the Council of State for the Crown of *Portugal*, and dispatch'd for the *Philippines*, by the way of *New-Spain*.   By the other Way, the King order'd, that the Captain General *Furtado*, taking with him the necessary Fleet from *Goa*, should sail for the *Moluccos*, by special Commission, by Virtue whereof he afterward sent to ask Assistance at the *Philippine* Islands, as we have seen, and such Supplies were to be furnish'd on both Sides, as being united, might secure the Conquest of the *Moluccos*.   However the Event must of Necessity be tedious, the *Dutch* being already possess'd of all the King's Forts in the *Archipelago*; and their numerous Fleets of all the Ports, Fairs, and Trade, with Factories conveniently settled for their Intercourse between *India* and their own Country.   We shall not enter upon the Account of those Affairs, because no more of them than have been already mention'd, as yet related to the *Moluccos*.   Much Time, and many Precautions were requisite, for these two Commanders to joyn, amidst so many Obstacles: They sent frequent Advice backward and forward, and neither Part was idle in the mean while.

At length, notwithstanding all Difficulties, *Furtado* fail'd from *Goa* with fix Galeons, eighteen Galiots, and one Galley, with the King's Orders, and in his Name those of the Viceroy *Arias de Saldania*, to fight the *Dutch*, and any other Enemy, and to proceed to *Sunda*, to chastize that King, and the Rebels in *Java*.   He was directed to place Garrisons there, and having settled the Affairs of *India*, to proceed to the *Moluccos*.   They went out with good Hearts to undertake that Work, but were hinder'd by Storms and Tempests.   In the Gulph of *Ceylon*, he lost the Galley, and seventeen Galiots that were under the Conduct of *Francis de Sousa*, and *Andrew Roiz*, and in them the greatest Strength he had to compass his Designs.   He was three whole Years without any Succours to proceed on his Enterprize.   At *Malaca* he recruited the best he could ; and in *December*, 1601, Steering his Course for *Sunda*, relying on the Succours he expected from the King of

Palimbam

Margin notes:

Brother Gaspar Gomez forwards the Expedition.

Succeeds in his Negociation.

Furtado Sails from Goa.

Disabled by Storms.

Palimbam, in *Java*, suppos'd to be our Friend and Confederate; but he was deceived, for that Infidel was so far from espousing our Party, that he had taken up with the King of *Sunda*, whom he intended, and afterwards actually did succour with 30000 Men. This did not dismay *Furtado*, but he *Sails for* sail'd on towards *Sunda*, referring the Punishment of the King of *Palimbam Sunda*. to another Time : There, on the Bar, he discover'd seven *Dutch* Ships, which he pursu'd, tho' to little purpose, they being excellent Sailers. However the Galeon Commanded by *Thomas de Sousa Aronches*, fought five of them, killing many *Dutch*, without losing one Man; but her Rigging was torn, and she could not board the Enemy, who fled, drawing our Ships after them in such manner, that *Furtado* could not possibly recover the Bar, tho' he anchor'd in a Road, from whence he might have return'd to the Port.

This was a special Providence, for the Enemy did not seem dispos'd to *Arrives at* stand, and they had already been upon both Bars; and therefore reflecting *Amboyna*. on the Tears, and Groans of the Commanders, and Christians at *Amboyna*, he directed his Course towards those Islands, where he arriv'd on the 10th of *February* without being detain'd by some Victories he gain'd in his Way. The Natives and those in the Fort were alarm'd, believing they had been Enemies, but the Admiral giving a Signal, they knew the Christian Fleet. The Joy spread abroad, and the Shore was cover'd with People expressing it. *Furtado* first apply'd himself to repair the Fort, and refit the Ships. He also built four Ships, two Galiots, and twelve *Carcoas*. Then he set out, without losing Time, to make War on the *Itos*, and other Towns *Subdues* that had rebell'd against the Fort, sending *Joseph Pinto*, with 200 *Portu- the Itos*. *guefes* by Land. The Fleet sail'd round the Island, and lay a Month in the Bay call'd *Bacacio*. *Texeyra*, Commander in Chief of the Fort, went before, with a good Number of *Carcoas*, to reduce some rebellious Towns, especially those which are on the Mountains call'd *Gunos*, where there are excellent sweet Waters, and large Woods of Orange Trees. These Towns *The Gunos* acknowledge their Fault, and came to make their Submission. Seven or *submit*. Eight of the principal Men came from each Town. Every Town brought a Flag, and three large valuable Basons of bright Metal, and in them a little Earth, with Branches of Clove-Trees in Blossom, in Token that they deliver'd up the Land, with the most precious of its Product. Some brought Goats, and Hens, and such Fruit as their Country afforded to denote the same.

Furtado knew there was a private Alliance between the Rebels of *Am- Ten* Dutch *boyna* and the *Dutch*, and that ten Ships were to come to take that Fort, *Ships at* and the other we had left us at *Amboyna*. They were so deeply engag'd in *Amboyna*. this Contract, that those at *Sunda*, seeing *Furtado* set sail towards those Parts, they did the same, and on the 10th of *March*, the ten Ships appear'd in Sight of the Islands, three of them coming on and treating with the Natives; yet for fear of us, they stood off to the Island *Burro*, and the other seven to *Banda*, to sail over to the *Moluccos*. All this was known to *Furtado* by good Intelligence, besides that he receiv'd from F. *Lewis Fernandez*, Rector of the Society of *JESUS*, who was newly come from *Three of Tydore*, with Letters from that King, and the Christians residing there, *them at* bidding him welcome, and pressing that he would come to their Assistance, *Ternate*.

because

becaule three ot the leven Ships that elcap'd from him at *Sunda*, were together at *Ternate*. He was alfo inform'd, that thofe Ships, had found
out a Way to relieve thofe Forts, paffing between *Borneo* and *Macaffar*,
which is a fhorter Cut by a Year; and that they were fortifying *Ternate*
where they would not fuffer the *Dutch* to leave them, but oblig'd them to
ftay and ingage in the War they expected. *Furtado* follow'd that in *Amboyna*, daily reducing fome Towns that had revolted. The Inhabitants
of *Rofatelo*, built on an Eminence, and well fortify'd difcovering our Ships,
and *Carcoas*, fet fire to all their Goods, and then to their Houfes, and fled to
a high Mountain, where their Wives and Children were before. The Way
up to it was by tying to the Trees certain *Rotas*, which are flender tough
Canes, that may be knotted like Ropes, a flow and almoft ufelefs Hold,
which render'd the Mountain never the lefs inacceffible. Yet our Men
making their Way thro' Clefts, attain'd the Top two days after. The
Rebels perceiving they were loft, came to receive the Conquerors with
white Flags, but the King, not daring to truft to that Security, fled to remoter Parts.

The Infidels of *Ito*, puff'd up with the *Dutch* Supplies they expected,
made no Doubt of routing the Chriftians, as foon as they landed; but
perceiving they were difappointed of the Succour of the ten Ships, which
fail'd by without ftaying, and that *Rofatelo* was reduc'd; yet they were
not quite dejected, but committed their Safety to the Strength and Tops
of the Mountains. They abandon'd their chief City, properly call'd *Ito*.
and the Fort there erected by the *Dutch*, retiring with all their Families
to the higheft and moft impregnable Part of the Country call'd *Nao* and
Bemnao, being two Rocks, one above another, like the Round-Tops in a
Ship one over the other; whence the Shore appears near at Hand tho'
half a League diftant, by Reafon of the Windings of the Ways. *Nao*
is all encompafs'd with upright Rocks, with pleafant Planes below.
There are three Ways to get up to it, but all of them fo difficult, that
the very Lizards can fcarce climb it. On thefe three Paffes they threw up
double Trenches, with ftrong Ramparts, and a good Number of Brafs Sakers,
and Demy-Falconets to fecure them. At each of them was a confiderable
Number of Men, with their Colours flying, and all Sorts of offenfive and
defenfive Arms, wherewith the *Dutch* have furnifh'd thofe Southern
Seas. The greateft Danger threatned was from a great Number of mighty
Stones, or Pieces of Rocks, which being roul'd down from fuch a Height
can bear down and deftroy an Army. All the Enemy's Power was now
reduc'd to this fingle Place, and the Town ftanding on the firft of the
two Rocks, being built on a large round Spot it forms, like an *European* City with good large Houfes, after their Manner. All the Country
about beautify'd with Clove Trees, like our Olive Trees, but with greater
Heads. Among which there ran up Branches of the Male and Female
Trees, and underneath all Sorts of thorny Plants, Orange, Lemmon, Citron
and *Zamboa* Trees, with fix, or eight Springs, each of them gufhing out
curious Streams of Water. All the Mountain look'd like a delicious
pleafure Houfe and Garden. On the Top of it appear'd the Town of
Bemnao, which fignifyes, the Son of *Nao*, exceeding the other in Number of Houfes, and Extent of Woods.

The

*A new Paf-
fage to the
Molucco.*

*People of
Ro'atelo
burn their
Town.*

Submit.

*People of
Ito fly to
the moun-
tain.*

*Nao ftrong
place,
whither
the Rebels
fled.*

*Pleafant
Country of
Nao, and
Bemnao.*

The General came to this Place on *Palm-Sunday*, order'd a Trench to be cast up, and Tents to be pitch'd, for a Defence against the Sun, and the Rain, which sometimes falls unexpected. He commanded an Enemy *Am-boynese*, that had fallen into his Hands, attended by some Christians, to go enquire into the Designs of the People of *Ito*, and to guide the Way. When they were come within hearing, and had deliver'd their Message, the Infidels answer'd, *That they were the King of* Ternate's *Subjects, and own'd none but him. That they would trade with the* Dutch, *and all other Nations they thought fit. That they would also sell Clove to the* Spaniards ; *but that the King of* Spain *had a very long Neck.* Having return'd this Answer, they began to fire the Cannon. Our Men were forc'd to put up the Affront, and pass by their Fury ; but the General regarding neither, order'd a Captain, on *Monday*, to view the Situation of the Place; because his Soldiers had gone up disorderly to their Trenches, and been repuls'd with Shot, and throwing of Stones, which made them retire down the Mountain with many wounded. The next Night he sent 200 Men, to possess themselves of a Mount that overlook'd the Enemies Trenches. They did so, and as soon as the Day appear'd, our Musketiers pour'd in their Volleys of Shot, firing at the same Time with two Drakes, they had carry'd up with a Design to cast up another Trench, and thus they put the Enemy to Rout. The Trench was thrown up, and the next Night they remov'd the Drakes to it, drawing nearer, to make the greater Slaughter. *Gonzalo Vaz de Castello-Branco* commanded at this Pass. The Men here that Night talk'd with the besieg'd, and assur'd them, they would take their Fort the next Night, as they actually did.

On *Wednesday* Morning the General order'd the Drums to beat to Arms, to go up himself to the Hill where his Men were, leaving *Trajano Ruiz de Castello-Branco* below, with 50 Men, to guard the Camp; but without any Design of attacking the Fort that Day; but only to order the Men, and assign them their Posts. Whilst he was concerting this Affair with his Officers, *Gonzalo Vaz* came to them with a dangerous Shot in one of the Calves of his Legs, and five other Wounds running Blood. The Soldiers were incens'd, at the Sight of him, and signify'd they would fall on. It was given out, where the General was, that the Victorious Enemy was falling upon our Drakes, and Posts ; and he improving Necessity, cry'd out, with a loud Voice, *Santiago*, that is, *S. James*, the Cry given by the *Spaniards* when they fall on. The Soldiers were so encourag'd by this Cry, that they immediately gave the Assault, with much Fury and Alacrity, climbing those smooth Rocks, upon their Hands and Feet: The Barbarians Drums and Bag-Pipes rattled in their Ears, and the Noise of their Cannon and small Shot eccho'd among all the Rocks. The Enemy threw Stones, which wounded, and knock'd down our Men, and many tumbled, without being able to help themselves : Some single Stones carry'd two or three Men down the Side of a Hill, till they stopp'd at some Tree. A Captain was stunn'd with a Pebble, tho' he receiv'd it on a Steel Buckler ; but he soon recover'd, and was seen upon the Enemies Works. The Cries and Shouts rent the Air. Many tumbling down forc'd out the sharp Pointed Stakes that were drove into the Ground ; and presently after, as if they had flown, were seen Fighting above. Those who were left to guard

the

C c

Furtado encamps at Beinnao.

Haughty Answer of the Itos.

Portugueses gain Ground.

They attack the Enemies Fort.

The Fort taken.

the Camp, look'd on with Emulation.   Among them a Religious Man of the Order of *S. Dominick*, fell on his Knees to fay the Litany, all the Men anfwering, and God heard him, for before it was ended, they faw our Colours difplay'd above, and the Enemies caft down, the Fort and Works being Demolifh'd.

A brave Chriftian, who carry'd the fore noft of our Colours, was laid hold of by an *Amboynefe*, yet he, tho' fhot thro' the Body with a Mufket-Ball, whereof he foon after Dy'd, defended them bravely.   However, notwithftanding his Refiftance, and that his Captain came to his Succour, the Infidel carry'd off a Part of the Staff, which was recover'd when the Victory was gain'd.   The *Amboynefes*, feeing their Works taken, and their Colours dragg'd about, withdrew to the upper-Part, leaving only three Men behind them, who dy'd Fighting, with honourable Obftinacy. They did not fortifie themfelves in that Place, but abandoning their Town and Goods, and flipping down Precipices, and upright Heights with Ropes, made their Efcapes; and though they burnt fome of their Goods, yet many of value remain'd. The General gave Order for curing of the wounded Men, which were above 200, befides thofe run through by the fharp Stakes pitch'd all about the Field.

Amboy-nefes a-bandon their higheft Fort.

The Towns fubmit.

The gaining of this Victory did fo difcourage all the Iflanders, that they refus'd to take up Arms, or hazard an Engagement.   Nine Towns fubmitted at once, the next day, and the Territory about did the fame.   The General came down Victorious, and erected Arbours in thofe Delightful Woods, with an Altar, on which Mafs was fung on Eafter-Day, and all the Office of the Church, with much Solemnity, in Thankfgiving, affigning the Sovereignty to that Lord, who grants, or takes away Victory, according to his fecret Judgements.   The *Dutch* Fort was raz'd, where, in feveral Places, were to be feen Efcutcheons, with the Arms of Count *Maurice*.   The King of *Ito* came and fubmitted himfelf; his Name, whilft an Idolater, was *Talere*, afterwards *Don Melchior*; for he was a Renegado Chriftian, and fled at the taking of *Rofatelo*.   He deliver'd himfelf up, as alfo a famous *Caziz* he brought with him, who was a Man of much Reputation among them.

Dutch Fort raz'd

Veranula City defcrib'd.

To this Victory *Furtado* refolv'd to add thofe he expected at *Veranula*, a large City, and Neighbouring Ifland.   He fail'd from *Amboyna* with all the Fleet, and arriv'd at *Veranula*, and the City of the fame Name, which is populous, and its Territory the moft fruitful in Clove of any in thofe Parts. It is built along the fhore on a high and upright Rock, which look'd like a Wall, with Towers, and Stories.   The Houfes are high Roof'd, with Galleries.   There is a Mofque that has three Ifles, with a ftately Room to read the *Alcoran* in.   Within the City was the *Dutch* Fort, conveniently feated, built of Stone, round, and cover'd.   Beyond that was alfo another Stone Fort, with feveral falliant Angles, Ravelins, and Guerites.   This belong'd to the King of *Ternate*, who was Tyrant of that Part of *Veranula* As foon as our Fleet anchor'd before the City, the Prime Men of it came to acquaint the General, That they were willing to fubmit, but knew not how to do it, for Fear of the *Ternates*; and therefore defir'd he would let them affemble their Council, and they would return the next Day with their Anfwer.   *Furtado* granted their Requeft, fending two *Amboynefes*

boynefes of Note along with them. They return'd no Anfwer, but fled, not daring to ftand the Fury of thofe who came Victorious. They fir'd a Gun for a Signal of what they were doing, and the Gene al being affur'd of their Flight, order'd the Men to land and plunder the City. The In- *fly.* habitants had before fecur'd the beft of their Effects, and yet in fome Houfes they found above the value of 30000 Crowns, and in others lefs, befides many Goods of value; abundance of Brafs Drakes and Mufkets; *China* Ware, and Silks; *Dutch* Glaffes, and great Store of Royal-Cloves. *Veranula* After plundering the City, they fet fire to it, and it burnt for fome Days. *plunder'd* The *Dutch* and *Ternatefe* Forts were raz'd. The General was inform'd by *and burnt.* fome Prifoners, that the People of *Veranula*, had expected mighty Succours againft him from the *Dutch* Ships that were feen; and that there were aboard 100 Men to Garrifon *Viranula*, and 100 more for the Fort he had demolifh'd at *Ito.* Some of our Men purfu'd the *Ternates* as far as *Lacidecavello*, a Town where they imbark'd on many Veffels, for their own Ifland.

People of *Veranula*

After this, the City *Mamala* fent to make its Submiffion, and many others follow'd its Example. *Furtado* having concluded this Affair, re- folv'd to return to *Amboyna*, and being upon his Departure, *Francis de Soufa Teve* came to him, with ten *Portuguefes*, who had been, not long be- fore, taken by the *Dutch* Ships. He had met at *Banda* the five Ships *Furtado* found at *Sunda*, and here gave him fome important Intelligence, fhow- ing how much he would fird the Seas, in his Way to the *Moluccos*, in- fefted by thofe Northern Sailers. The Commander in Chief of the *Dutch* made very much of *Francis de Soufa*, difmiffing him with Arms and Pro- vifions for his Voyage, but at the Price of 500 Crowns, paid for him and his Companions, by fome Heathen Towns in the Ifland; to whom *Furtado*, without any Delay, made good the whole Sum. The *Dutch* General writ very civilly to *Furtado*, defiring he would ufe his Men well, as he would do by the *Spaniards* he met with. *Furtado* return'd an Anfwer, no lefs Courteous, and fent him a *Dutch* Youth, who had been Prifoner at *Ternate.*

Mamala City fub- mits with others.

Having rednc'd thefe Iflands, *Furtado* appointed a Day for the Governors of them to come and fwear Fealty to our King, that he might fave Time, and follow the Courfe of his Victories. They came with much State, and Submiffion; and to fecure their future Behaviour, and their new promis'd Fidelity, deliver'd to the General a confiderable Number of Youths, being the Sons of the Prime Men, as Hoftages. Peace, and the general Pardon, were celebrated with Rejoycings. The Preaching of the Gofpel was again exercis'd with entire Liberty, and many Idolaters, and *Mahometans* were converted. Other Provinces came to acknowledge the Conqueror; with- out expecting the Chance of War. *Furtado* at *Amboyna* prepar'd for the Expedition againft the *Moluccos.*

The con- quer'd fubmit, and give Hoftages.

Thofe who fled to *Ternate*, gave an Account of the Lofs of the Towns and Forts that King had been poffefs'd of at *Amboyna*; and that the General *Furtado* openly declar'd he was making Prepara- tions againft thofe Iflands, and grew ftronger upon his Succefs. The King flighted not this Intelligence, but immediately ftrengthened his Fleet, and his Forts, and call'd in the *Javanefes* and *Mindanaos*, to be in

King of Ternate's Preparati- ons.

readinefs

readiness upon any Attack.　Amidst the Noise of War, and his Treaties with the *Dutch* for maintaining of it, he found Leisure to seek his Satisfaction; concluding a Match with his Queen *Celicaya*, who follow'd him in all his Troubles, even when he last fled from his Kingdom. She was very Young, and so Beautiful, that all the *Indian* Kings courted her for their Wife, and sent to demand her of the *Sangiack* of *Motiel*, her Father; who gave her to him of *Ternate*, as the greatest, most potent, and respected.

His Marriage. The Time for the Nuptials being come, when the Bride was brought to *Ternate*, attended by her Father, Kindred, Brothers-in-law, and many Troops of arm'd Men, she was receiv'd with the Noise of Cannon, Musick, and other Instruments us'd in their Festivals and Solemnities.　These

Queen Celicaya's great Beauty. lasted many Days, with Profusion; but the most pleasing Object, was the Presence of *Celicaya*, her extradiordinary Grace, which drew the Eyes, and Affections of all Men, temper'd with a Sort of Affability, which encourag'd all that convers'd with her.　This Quality very often gave Occasion to suspect her Husband's Reputation, and were not this History confined to such Things as really relate to the Conquest, it might afford us a large Field to treat of the Gentleness of her Disposition, her Love Intrigues, and uncontroulable Power over the Affections, even of those who were most wrong'd; which are spoken of at large in several Discourses and Relations.

Furtado sends for Succours to the Philippine Islands. The Exigencies of the Time, and necessity oblig'd the General *Furtado* to press for the Succours, which were providing for him in the *Philippine* Islands.　*Amboyna* is 200 Leagues from the nearest of them, and that 200 more from *Manila*, he sent thither F. *Andrew Pereyra*, a Jesuit, and Captain *Antony Brito Fogaza*, in *May* 1602.　They arriv'd at *Cebu* on the 25th of *July*, sail'd thence for *Manila* on the 6th of *August*, and came to that City on the 5th of *September*.　Don *Pedro de Acunna* was well pleas'd to see them, asking particularly concerning all the Proceedings of the General *Furtado*, wherein he was very curious, or rather generously emulous, and he having in his Letters referr'd himself to their Relation, they gave it him at large, and perform'd the Duty of their Embassy, each according to his Profession.　Don *Pedro* did not delay their Business; but call'd a Council of War, wherein it was resolv'd, that the Succours he desir'd should be sent *Furtado*, tho' they were forc'd to comply with the Difficulties the Country then labour'd under.　Upon this Determination he sent away to

Succours sent from the Philippines to Furtado. the Provinces of the *Pintados*, ordering Capt. *John Xuarez Gallinato*, who commanded there, to furnish all Things necessary for the Enterprize; and that he, with the best disciplin'd Infantry, should leave *Cebu*, and repair to the Town of *Arevalo*, the place appointed for the Fleet to rendezvouz. *Gallinato* did so, and sent a Ship to *Oton*, to take in as much as it could of the Succours. It arriv'd at *Oton* on the 28th of *October*, and that same Day Don *Pedro* set out from *Manila* for the *Pintados*, in Order to hasten the fitting out of the Fleet by his Presence, tho' it was then almost ready at *Oton*, where he arriv'd on the 13th of *November*, and he was of such a mettled Temper, that never regarding the Expeditions of *Xolo* and *Mindanao*, or that the Natives of those Islands were spread about in Troops among those of the *Pintados*, robbing and murdering his Majesty's Subjects, he gather'd the Supplies, and deliver'd them to *John Xuarez Gallinato*,

Gallinato, appointing him General, and Commander in Chief for this Expedition.

As soon as the General *Furtado* had sent away for Succours to *Manila,* after chastising and garrisoning of *Veranula* and *Amboyna,* he set sail for the *Molucco* Islands, with five Galeons, four Galliots, and 12 *Carcoas,* carrying his Victorious Men, but in those Seas Disasters are so frequent, that neither the Joy of their late Successes, nor the Refreshment receiv'd after their Victories, appear'd in their Countenances. He arriv'd at *Ternate* with this Fleet, on the 10th of *August;* but he only look'd on that Island, and proceeded to *Tydore :* There he view'd the Fort, encourag'd the Soldiers in it, and made use of that King's Person and Interest, as Prudence directed; for that Prince, tho' he labours by Words to convince us of his Friendship and Fidelity, does not confirm it by his Actions; but rather leaves us dubious, when he most endeavours to persuade. *Furtado sails by Ternate to Tydore.*

Furtado left the Galeons at *Tydore,* and with the other Vessels that row'd, went six Leagues thence, to the Island of *Machian,* then Subject to the King of *Ternate,* but so weary of that Vassalage, that as soon as our Fleet appear'd, the Governours flock'd down to the Port, attended by the Natives, with their Wives and Children, and such Gifts as came next to Hand, as also some Colours, which they laid at *Furtado's* Feet, submitting themselves, and delivering up their Country. The Men landed in peaceable Manner, amidst the usual Noise of Bagpipes and Basons; and the *Portuguefes* having in vain sought after some *Dutch* Men, who chose rather to secure themselves by Flight, than to trust to the General's good Nature, were inform'd that they were gone over to *Ternate.* A view having been taken of the Island, *Furtado* erected a Fort with all possible Expedition, in the most convenient Place. When finish'd according to the Rules of Fortification, he put into it a Captain with 50 Men, whom he left well arm'd and provided, and with them a light Vessel, call'd a *Galizabra.* Then he return'd himself, with the Rest of the Fleet, to *Tydore,* where he joyn'd all his Ships, repair'd them, and set out for *Ternate* to the Port of *Talangame,* where he anchor'd, and lay from the End of *October* to the middle of *February,* when the Succours from *Manila* came. *Machian Island submits to Furtado.*
Dutch fly to Ternate.

Some accuse him of lying still very long without attempting any thing; saying, he let slip the Opportunities, without cutting off the Enemies Provisions, or ravaging their Country, when he might have subdu'd them by that Means alone, without firing a Shot. However, when we have before us the Actions of such great Commanders, it is safer to judge they had some sufficient unknown Reason for what they did, than to attribute it to their Fault. Most certain it is, That being inform'd of a Fleet of the Enemies of 22 *Carcoas,* which was not far from the Island *Machian,* he lost no Time, but putting 172 *Portuguefes,* of the chosen Men of his Fleet, into 18 *Carcoas,* under an able Commander, he sent them to find out the Infidels But tho' the Soldiers were so haughty, that every one undertook to fight six *Carcoas,* yet every Officer was for commanding all the Rest, and thus Want of Discipline snatch'd the Victory out of their Hands. The Enemy pass'd by, and they look'd on, without firing a Gun. The Barbarian Fleet, observing their Disorder, stood about nimbly, and pouring in a *Furtado accus'd.*
Portuguefes baffled through their Pride.

Volley

Volley upon the *Portuguefes*, took a *Carcoa*, with fourteen Men in it, whom they flew, in Sight of their Companions, and it was good Fortune that they did not follow their Stroke. This occafion'd the General's erecting the Fort at *Machian*; whilft the King of *Ternate* ftrengthen'd his, with the Affiftance of 20 *Hollanders*, making good Ufe of the Leifure of eight Months given him by *Furtado*. He then caft up Works, and provided Engines, as he did afterwards in the Sight of our Camp.

The Succours fent by Don Pedro de Acunna. When the Fleet was all affembled at the *Philippine* Iflands, the Ammunition and Provifions were deliver'd to *Gallinato*, by the Judges and King's Attorney of the Sovereign Court, being 1000 Bufhels of clean Rice, 300 Bullocks for Flefh; 200 Jars of Wine; 80 Quintals, or hundred Weight of Nails, Hooks, Hinges, and other Iron Work; 40 of Powder; 300 *Ilocos* Blankets; 700 Yards of *Spanifh* Woollen Cloth; 100 Needles for Sails; 30 Jars of Oil; and for the Complement of Men, 200 Soldiers, 165 of them heavy Harquebufiers, and the other, 35 light Mufquetiers; 22 Seamen; fome Pilots; one Mafter; three Gunners of S. *Potenciana*, and 20 Grummets. The whole Expence hereof amounting to 22260 Pieces of Eight a Month. The Governour and Sovereign Court having done thus much, they requir'd F. *Andrew Pereyra*, and Captain *Brito*, to go with that Supply, which was then in readinefs, under *Gallinato*, with the Colours, and Captains *Chriftopher Villagra*, and *John Fernandes de Torres*. The Company belonging to Captain *Don Thomas Bravo*, the Governour's Nephew, and Son to his Brother *Don Garcia*, ftaid behind, but the Captain went himfelf, and ferv'd honourably in the Expedition. The Foot embark'd on the Ship S. *Potenciana*, and the Frigats S. *Antony*, S. *Sebaftian*, S. *Bonaventure*, and S. *Francis*. They fet fail from the Port of *Yloilo*, on the 20th of *January*, 1603, and arriv'd at that of *Caldera*, in *Mindanao*, on the 25th; where receiving fome Intelligence of the Enemy, they continu'd ill the 28th. Then they faild towards the *Moluccos*, and on the 7th of *February*

S. Antony Frigat caft away. defcry'd the Ifland of *Siao*, and the next Morning, by Break of Day, that of *Toalan*, four Leagues from it. There the Frigat S. *Antony* was caft away, on a Shoal of that Ifland, which difcompos'd all the Squadron. *Gallinato* took Care to fave the Men. He fent Captain *Villagra*, who brought them off, with the Arms and Guns; the reft was fwallowed by the Sea.

Gallinato from Manila joyns Furtado. They held on their Voyage, and on the 13th of *February* difcover'd the Ifland of *Ternate*. On the 14th they arriv'd at *Tydore*, where they were inform'd of the coming of *Andrew Furtado*; and therefore ftay'd but a fhort Time to refrefh themfelves, being earneft to joyn him. Setting forward with a fair Wind, they came to *Ternate*, and enter'd the Port of *Talangame*, a League from the Fort, on the 16th of the aforefaid Month. The Fleets faluted one another in friendly Manner, and the Generals did the like, giving one another an Account of their Strength, Tranfactions, and all other Particulars till that Time. The Difcourfe falling out of one Thing into another, came to contefting; for *Gallinato* affirm'd, That the Enemies Provifions ought to have been cut off, by ordering our *Carcoas* to fail round the Ifland, which was in great Want of them, and could be reliev'd by the Opportunity he had given. *Furtado* alledg'd other Reafons to defend himfelf. It was thought convenient before they landed, to take

a

a View of the Enemies Fort, to which Purpose, the Captains, *Christopher Villagra*, and *Gonzalo Sequeyra* were appointed to make up to it in a *Carcoa*, with a white Flag, as it were to speak with the King, and propose Peace and Conditions.

Those two Officers drew near, the Enemy met them, and understanding what they came about, sent to acquaint the King. He answer'd he could not give them Audience that Day, but they might return the next. They returning accordingly, the Inhabitants of the City came out to meet them, and among them *Cachil Sugur*, *Cachil Gogo*, and *Cachil Quipate*, the King's Uncles, who went back to tell him, that those Captains were come by his Highness's Command. This Message was brought him at Nine a Clock in the Morning, and tho' he was close by the City, the Answer came not till four in the Afternoon, and was, That unless *Furtado*, or *Gallinato* came, he would not speak with any other, but that the Captains that were come might treat with his Officers, and he would stand by, and ratify what they should conclude. The *Spaniards* having receiv'd this Answer, and their Design being to view the Fort, Captain *Villagra* set his Resolution, and pretending some Occasion, went into the Thicket, whence he observ'd all that could be seen on that Side, more nicely than could have been expected in so short a Time. They return'd to the Fleet, and gave the General an Account of all they knew. *Two Captains sent to the City of Ternate.* *Villagra views the Fort.*

In fine, they landed, and then again *Gallinato* intreated *Furtado*, to send out the light Vessels a cruising, to cut off the Enemies Supplies, and those which went out upon his Request, sped so well, that they met a plentiful and strong Reinforcement of Men and Provisions, in two *Junks* and a large *Chiampan*, which they took, killing and taking the Men, who were Numerous and well arm'd. They continu'd to round the Island, encourag'd by this first Success, and by that Means cut off all Succours. The Enemy began to want, sicken and dye. They fed on Herbs, and other slight Dyet; and many, but particularly Women, not being able to endure Hunger, fled confidently, tho' compell'd by Necessity, to our Camp; and the rest would have done the same if they could. *The Forces land.* *Famine at Ternate.*

On the 27th of *February*, *Furtado* took a Review of his Men on the Enemies Shore, where our Ships were at Anchor. *Gallinato* said, he was much troubled to see it, because in his Opinion, they were not fit even to make that Show, most of them being Boys, sick of the Distemper they call *Berber*, unskillful at their Fire-arms, and very few of them had Muskets, but only little Fowling-Pieces; so that all seem'd to forebode ill Success. The whole Number of them was 420 Soldiers, divided into four Companies. The next Day, the *Spanish* Infantry of the *Philippine* Islands pass'd Muster, in the same Place, before *Furtado* and his Officers. *Don Thomas* led them in Armour, and with a Pike in his Hand, with all the Musquetiers in the Van. After him the other Companies in Order, according to Seniority. They all form'd three Bodies, being Men of Experience, well equipp'd, orderly, and of such Valour as soon after appear'd. *Christians review'd.*

A Council was held, about landing, on the first of *March*, where the General declar'd by Word of Mouth, saying he never did it in Writing; That he had lain so long, almost idle, wholly depending on the Succour that was come, and that since *Don Pedro de Acunna* had sent it so compleat, *Consult about landing.*

pleat,

pleat, it was not reasonable to lose Time. *Gallinato* answer'd, representing the Greatness of the Enterprize, and that they had provided no Necessaries to begin the Work, hinting at some Home Particulars, which were signify'd to him by the *Portuguese* Commanders. The Votes being taken, it was finally resolv'd to land, because all Things were in readiness ; perhaps they conceited that the Enemies Power was imaginary, and that they would submit at the Sight of our Army. *Gallinato* was always of the

Gallinato against it. contrary Opinion ; because that Weakness he was an Eye-witness to, could not deceive him ; and therefore that nothing might be wanting on his Part, tho' he was under Command, but much respected, he writ a Role of the Things necessary for the Design in Hand, setting down in it even the Hand-Spikes for moving of the Artillery, which had not been provided in all that Time. By which may be seen, said *Gallinato*, how great a Defect there had been in the Rest. When the Council broke up, *Furtado* told *Gallinato*, he had order'd, that as soon as they landed, 200 *Portugueses* should mount the Guard, with one Company of *Spaniards*. *Gallinato* begg'd he would give him leave to lead the Van, saying, he would not go as Chief, but only as a Soldier, as being proud of serving under him. This he requested very earnestly ; but *Furtado*, who knew how to value such Requests, answer'd, That if he went he must accept of his

He begs to lead the Van and obtains it. Company. *Gallinato* reply'd, That he should take the Post due to his Person, since it was of such Consequence, and do him the Favour to grant him the Van. He would not grant it at that Time, but the next Day, he and his Admiral spoke to him, saying, He assign'd him the Van, by the Advice of his Admiral, and therefore desired he would be content it might consist of the Number of Men he had appointed. *Gallinato* accepted the Command, and valu'd it as was due. They landed on the 3d of *March*, and as they were drawing up, *Furtado* would needs place two of his Colours, and one of the *Spanish* in the Van, with 300 Men ; the other three in the Rear ; and the Royal Standard, and himself to be in the main Body ; *Gallinato* was of Opinion, that all the Colours should march with the main Body, but the General follow'd his own Way.

They move towards the Enemy. In this Order they began to move towards the Enemy, Captain *Don Thomas* marching by *Gallinato*, who afterwards, in a Letter to *Don Pedro*, said, *He this Day, and upon other Occasions, gave good Proof, that he was the Son of such a Father, and these grey Hairs of mine were sufficiently honour'd with the Assistance of such a Hand, and I was well defended and secure.* The Enemy being above 700, kept in a strong and safe Post, the Shore on which our Men march'd, being little or nothing, by Reason it was High-Water, and that on the Land Side there was a very high Bank, and above it a rising and close *Zacatal*, which could not be broke through. *Zacatal* is a Field overgrown with such deep Grass or Weeds, that many Men, and much Cattle may be hid among them. These are much thicker

Zacatal what it is. than the Fields of Sedge, or Sheer-Grass in *Spain*. They call it *Zacatal*, from the Word *Zacate*, signifying that Sort of Grass or Weed, which grows up almost as thick as a Reed. Along this narrow Slip of Shore, which was full of Rocks, and uneven, only three Men could march abreast, he that was next the Sea, being partly in the Water. The Enemy was possess'd of this close Pass, and a great Tree cut down for that Purpose, ḷofe, and lying acrofs the Place, ferv'd them inftead of a Trench. Behind it, and upon the Bank, between it, and the *Zacatal*, appear'd all their Men, with Mufkets, Fire-Locks, *Campilanes*, or Cymiters, *Bacacaes*, or burnt Staves, Darts, Hand Granadoes, and Stones which did not do us the leaft Harm. They had alfo five Drakes in this Poft, wherewith, upon fome fhort Attacks, they kill'd five *Spaniards*; and afterwards, as the Action grew hotter, wounded ten *Portuguefes*, in fuch Sort that they dy'd in a few Days. *Gallinato* owns he was this Day in Danger of lofing his Honour; becaufe the Colours, and all the Reft was in the utmoft Peril.

Pofture of the Ter-nates.

The Enemy fought in Safety, and did our Men fo much Harm, that the firft Charge *Gallinato* gave, the *Ternates* fell on fo furioufly, as to drive us from the Ground we had gain'd. *Gallinato* look'd behind him to fee the Colours he had brought with him in the Van, with the 300 Men, and found them at his Back very thinly Guarded. Thus the fecond Time the Shout was given to fall on, and he again oblig'd to retire, becaufe he had fewer Men every time, and the laft they were fcarce twenty. At length fhaming thofe that lagg'd, and as it were infpiring new Vigour into them, he fell on fo fiercely, that he gain'd the Poft, and the five Drakes. The *Ter-nates* loft all, or moft of their beft Men. *Gallinato* follow'd the Chace till he difcover'd the Fort, then he halted, and order'd our Camp to be Intrenched. The work was begun, and the Enemy obftructed it twice, fending out Parties to prevent planting the Gabions, and divert the Workmen; but they retir'd both times with lofs. When the Trench was finifhed, *Gallinato* fent to the General to come to it. He came and took up his Quarters, with all his Men, bringing the Royal Standard, and all the Colours.

Gallinato repulfed.

Gains the Pafs.

Spaniards Intrench.

The next Day he judg'd it convenient to carry the Lodgment forward. *Gallinato* undertook it, and with his Men finifh'd the Trench, within 200 Paces of the Enemies Fort. There they continu'd fome Days; and it being *Gallinato*'s Part only to obey, he fometimes gave his Opinion, and always did what he was commanded. He did fo, when the General told them it would be convenient to carry on a Trench farther, to plant the Cannon. On the Ninth of the fame Month, before the Fort had been well view'd, he went to open the Trench, with his own Men, and 100 *Portuguefes*, a little above 100 Paces from the Walls, which being fo near they all foon perceiv'd the danger of the Undertaking. It was the worfe for the Confufion and Noife in filling the Gabions. The next Day the Cannon was brought thither, being four Guns, two thirteen, and two fixteen Pounders. Thefe fixteen Pounders, which the *Portuguefe* Soldi-ers call Camels, are fhort Pieces, unfit for Battery; befides that the Bul-lets were made of Stone, and broke as foon as they touch'd the Wall; be-ing only fit to fire at the Houfes. *Gallinato* feeing this, told the General that fince before they landed he faid, he had Cannon, he fhould order it to be brought on, and planted in Battery, now he faw how ineffectual that they had prov'd. He anfwer'd, that there was all he had, having left the beft in fome Places he recover'd the foregoing Year; and could not bring any more fuch, by Reafon of the ftormy Weather.

Trenches carry'd on nearer to the Fort.

Stone Bul-lets unfit for Batte-ry.

This being mounted, the Battery began; but being fo improper for this Purpofe, it was canonading the Air; for the Enemy overlook'd, and was ftrengthen'd by a Stone *Cavalier*, which is that of Our Lady, next the Sea,

The Ene-mies Strength.

D d

Sea. Under it was a Ravelin, with seven heavy Pieces of Cannon which did, and threatned greater Harm to our Camp. The *Cavalier* was all Rampard, four Fathom high, and a Fathom and a half broad, all which had been perform'd, and rais'd with Ffpauls, by the Contrivance of the *Dutch*, who forwarded it, ever since they traded with that Tyrant. On the Land Side ran the Curtin of the Wall, as far as the Stone Bullwark, call'd *Cachil Tulo*, fortify'd outwards with Massy Timbers, on which there were three large Guns, and two on the Wall from this Bullwark to that of our Lady All these Works look'd towards that Part, where our Men had taken up their Quarters. These Forts had also a great Number of Falconets, and Drakes, and the *Cavalier* that was batter'd being the strongest Part, where there was more Noise than Effect, the General order'd the Battery to ceafe.

They Sally. On Sunday the sixteenth, between four and five in the Evening, the Enemy sally'd out of their Fort, with most of their Men to attack, and gain the Trench, where our Cannon was planted. They assau'ted it in three Places, dividing their Men, next the Mountain in Front, and towards the Shore. From the Mountainward came above 800 *Ternates*, with *Campilanes*, or Cymiters, in the Van of them almost as many *Javanese*, with Pikes 25 Spans long, all in close Order. The Leader of them was a

Amuxa, gallant Youth, call'd *Cachil Amuxa*, the King's Cousin German, and Son *the King's* to *Cachil Tulo*. Four hundred attack'd in Front, and many more next the *Nephew* Sea, each Body under its own Commander; who all fell on together *leads them.* with such Vigour, that had not they who defended it been in great Readiness, the Enemy could not miss of being Master of it. The Captains *Pinto* and *Villagra* commanded in it, who defended it bravely, but *Emanuel Andres*, Sergeant to *Villagra*, *Alonfo Roldan*, a Corporal, and another *Portuguese*, who behav'd himself gallantly, dy'd fighting, being all run

He is De- through with Pikes. The Advantage soon appear'd on the *Spanish* Side, *feated.* which the Enemy perceiving, they turn'd their Backs, leaving the Commanders their King had the greatest Value for, dead in the Field, and retired to the Fort. This Success gave Occasion to draw another Trench nearer the Fort, to batter the Ravelin, whence they did us Harm, with seven Pieces, notwithstanding our Work, which was carry'd on by the Captains *Villagra*, and *Sebastian Suarez*. On *Thursday* the Trench was almost finish'd, and being near, made them so uneasy, that the Besieged began to batter it, with all their Cannon, but ineffectually, because the *Gabions*, and Rampart on the Inside, could bear much more. However, by this they perceiv'd the Power and Strength of the Enemy, and the Difficulty of the Undertaking.

Council of On the twenty first of *March* the General came to the Trench, and *War held.* calling together the Captains, *Gallinato, Villagra, Antony Andrea, John Fernandez de Torres, Gonzalo de Sequeyra, Sebastian Suarez de Alberguciia, Stephen Texeira, Gafpar Pacheco*, the Admiral *Thomas de Soufa Ronches, Lewis de Melo Sampayo, Jacome de Morales, Don Lope de Almeyda, Ruy Gonzalez, Trajan Rodriguez Castelbranco, Antony de Brito Fogaza, John Pinto de Moraes*, and *Don Thomas Bravo*, and taking out a Miffal, in the first Place desir'd them to take an Oath upon the holy Evangelifts, that they would not speak of, nor any otherwise reveal, what he should
there

there propofe to them, and what fhould be refolv'd upon it, till effected. They all fwore, and then he propos'd the Matter thus.

I have call'd you together, Gentlemen, to acquaint you with the Condi- Furtado's
tion I am in at Prefent, and this Siege has brought me to. It is two Speech to
Years fince I came from Goa, and during my Voyage, have fpent a great the Coun-
Quantity of Ammunition, upon feveral Occafions; fo that when we lan- cil.
ded the other Day we had only ten Pipes of Powder, and 29 Barrels fent
me from Manila. Since I landed, fo much has been confum'd, as is vifible,
in Skirmifhes, and Battery, that I have now much lefs than half that Quan-
tity. The Dead, Wounded and Sick, of our Foot, now wanting in the Camp,
are 130; and the reft, as daily Experience fhows, fall Sick very faft of the
Diftemper call'd Berber. *Our Provifions, tho' we took the Rice the Frigates*
brought from Manila, *are fo fhort, that they can not laft beyond the be-*
ginning of June. *The Ships and other Veffels of the Fleet, in the Opinion*
of the Pilots, run a great Hazard, where they now lie at Anchor; becaufe,
when this Moon is out, there can be no Safety for it, by reafon of the high
Winds and Storms, unlefs they remove to another Place, and there is no other
but Tydore. *We fee how refolute, and well fortify'd the Enemy is, fince*
all our Battery has produc'd fo little Effect, and if they receive any Dam-
mage, it is foon made up by the Multitude of People. The Friendfhip the
King of Tydore *promis'd for advancing of his Majefty's Service, has prov'd*
fo falfe, that he has perform'd nothing of what was concerted with him,
tho' fo reafonable, and beneficial to himfelf, having only been free in Words,
but his Actions have not yet been feen. I have had fufficient Tryal of him.
He has no other Defign, but to deceive, and amufe us, that our Men may be
deftroy'd by Degrees, and fo Time may confume us if the Enemy cannot. When I
prefs'd him to do fomething, to fhow at this Time that he was a Friend,
and his Majefty's Subject, he anfwer'd, he would; but that we muft furnifh
Provifions for all his Men, becaufe he had none. They demand Powder and
Ball, for every trivial Undertaking, that fo they may confume the little we
have left; and when there is any Work to be done, there are no Men for
it. Of the few Amboynefes *I brought with me, for this Purpofe, their La-*
bour being great, fome are return'd home, others gone to the Enemy. Thofe
that remain are not fufficient, and moft of what has been hitherto done is
owing to the Infantry; which is fo harrafs'd, that it can do no Service. The
Enemy expects Dutch *Ships, and knows they are now at* Banda. *I have*
Intelligence that they have fent for them, and if they come they will be a
great Obftacle to our Defigns. Confidering what I have difcours'd of, I defire
you, Gentlemen, and every one of you, ftill under the Obligation of the Oath,
to give me your Opinions, that according to them I may refolve what to do,
in purfuance of the great Duty incumbent on me.

Upon the Requeft of the Captains, the General *Furtado* gave in thefe
Propofals in writing, tho' he oppos'd it at firft. In fhort they were written,
as were the Opinions of the Councellors, among whom the greater Part,
even of the *Portuguefes* oppos'd the General; and tho' I ought to give fome
Account of their Votes, becaufe they had all different Views, yet, in
Regard that moft of them affented to *Gallinato's* Opinion, it will fuffice to
fet down his Anfwer.

John Xuarez Gallinato, *Commander of the Provinces of the* Pintados, *and*
D d 2 *the*

the Officers attending me, do answer to the Proposal made by your Lordship, as follows. That as to the want of Powder you represent, we look upon it as essential, since we can not fight without it, and if that fails, our Cannon and small Fire-Arms, are rather Encumbrances, than Weapon, and therefore it is requisite to resolve and agree, where and when to employ, and how much of what we have may be spent, so as our Enterprize may succeed, since we see how ineffectual that hitherto spent has been, considering, at the same Time, that a great Quantity is to be reserv'd, to fight five Dutch Galeons we expect, which, if they come, part of our Fleet must of necessity go out and ingage. For, if this be not done they will put Succours into the Place, which tho' never so inconsiderable, as but of 100 Muskets, would be very prejudicial to us; besides that, it will be a great Disreputation, not to meet them out at Sea.

As to the Mens sickning, being kill'd and wounded, we say, those are Misfortunes always attending War; and that we are sensible how fast the Army grows weak, for which Reason, it will be necessary to be the more expeditious in the Work we have in Hand; yet so that neither too much Precipitation may expose it to Hazards, nor Delay give Time for all the Army to fall Sick. As for the Scarcity of Provisions, our Opinion is, that an Account be taken of what we have, how much is consum'd in a Month, and thus the necessary Distribution may be made in Time; for otherwise we shall fall short, when we least expect it; and Hunger will do us more Harm than the Enemy.

To the Danger of the Ships threatned by the Pilots, and their Advice to go over to Tydore, we answer. That if the Fleet quits the Station where it is, it will be a manifest Detriment to the Army, which is supply'd from it with all it Wants, and must want every Thing upon its Absence. Besides, that if the Enemy see it once gone, they will take fresh Courage; and if the Dutch come and find the Harbour empty, it is plain they will possess themselves of it. Again, if the Fleet makes off, must not a considerable Number of the Soldiers go for its Security? Now how can it be proper to divide our Forces; especially considering they are so small, and the Men so sickly? Besides that here is no Place to lay up the Provisions, for the Waters destroy them by Day and Night. Whilst aboard the Fleet, the Soldiers have it daily brought fresh and wholesome. Farther, the Pilots, and Natives of Tydore, say the Ships are safe in the Harbour till after the Middle of April.

We have had Tryal of the Enemies Power, and believe they have Men, Ammunition, and Cannon to spare, considering our Condition; and the Commanders, and Deserters from them confirm it. But neither can it be deny'd, that the very first Day we ingag'd, as we have been told by Prisoners, and wounded Men, 1000 of the best Men they had in Ternate came out to stop our Passage with five Pieces of Cannon, and so posted, that only two of our Men could come up a Breast to charge them; and yet they with all these Odds, were beaten off with the Loss of many Men, as appear'd by the dead Bodies, scatter'd along the Shore, where they also lost their Artillery. The same Day we saw them sally upon the Fort of Santiago, where Captain Villagra commanded, and tho' our Men were surpriz'd, yet they repuls'd them and slew the Flower of their Commanders, so that they were certain-

ly

ly much weakned; and streightned by Hunger and Sickness. And tho' with the Help of the Dutch, and their own Hardiness they repair the Breeches, and fortify themselves with Artillery, Means may be found to surmount these Difficulties, for if there were none, it would be no War we are ingag'd in.

We are sensible of the King of Tydore's Want of Faith; but what discreet Commander has not made the best of such Accidents, and wink'd at disloyal, and unsteady Persons till a more favourable Opportunity; Besides, before we landed, Notice was taken of this Princes Indifferency, and that his Design is to protract the War, rather in Hatred to Ternate, than out of any Love to our Nation. We our selves will make amends for the Want of Labourers; we will be both Soldiers and Pioniers, as we have hitherto been; for the Sword and the Spade are equally honourable in so just a War; and we again offer our selves, and our Soldiers, to perform whatsoever shall be for the Service of God and the King.

It is therefore our Opinion, that the Galeons remove immediately; that two of them Anchor between our Ladies Cavalier, and S. Paul, and batter the inside of the Cavalier, and the other two, the House of S. Paul, the Fort, and the Town. Then of Necessity the Defendants within must fly, since the Defence of the Stone Parapet, is but a meer Show, except only where it looks upon the open Country. As soon as the Galeons begin to batter, we will also batter the Ravelin before the Cavalier, where the seven Pieces of Cannon are, which will certainly be ruin'd in two Hours, because our Fort of S. Christopher commands them, and the Thickness is not above a Fathom. To conclude, My Lord, the Want of Provisions, and of Health, the coming of the Dutch, the Resolution of the Besieged, of all other Difficulties will be surmounted by Celerity. We are ready to perform all Things on our Part; it belongs to your Lordship to make Tryal of our Promise. It will not be reasonable immediately to abandon the small Remains of Christianity in the Moluccos, and the Hopes of regaining what has been lost, in vain endeavour'd for so many Years, at the Expence of so many Millions of Money, so many Lives, and the Honour of European Nations, by turning our Backs upon so holy an Undertaking.

This Answer was sent in a Paper signed by the Captains, to satisfy all his Doubts, for they answer'd others by Word of Mouth, which were started by the Portuguese Commanders to perswade drawing off; but the General Thanking both Parties for their Zeal in Advising, broke up the Council; and on Saturday the 22d, came to a Resolution, which he left to be put in Execution the next Day. That Night he drew off the Cannon; and on Sunday Night, at the second Watch, the Forces began to March towards the Shore, where the Ships lay to take in the Men. The Admiral, Thomas de Sousa, led the Van; the General and his Officers, the Main Body; and John Xuarez Gallinato, with the Captains Don Thomas Bravo, John Fernandez de Torres, and Christopher Villagra, and the Musketeers, brought up the Rear. In this Order the Foot were Shipp'd off, and got all aboard by the Morning. At the same time two Dutch Men, of those that were in the Fort with the Enemy, fled from it, and came to the Ships. Among other Intelligence, they told the Spaniards how strong the Enemy were in Men and Cannon: That they had 36 heavy Pieces

Furtado dissolves the Council, and acts counter to it.

The Forces Shipp'd off.

mounted

mounted on the Ravelin near our Ladies; seven on *Cachil Tulo*'s Bastion; three between them; and two on the *Cavalier*; three at S. *Paul*'s; eight in the Main Fort, three at *Limatao*; three more on that Bastion, and four more near it.

Furtado refuses to supply Ty-dore, and other Places.

This Day *Furtado* propos'd to sail away with the Fleet towards *Amboyna*, but wanting Water, put it off for four Days, and during that time *Gallinato* had leasure to Discourse him, since he was going away, about providing the Fort of *Tydore*, which could not be Maintain'd without Supplies. He Answer'd, He was very willing to do it, but could not, and therefore would send Succours from *Amboyna*. Application was made to him to provide for other Wants, which concern'd his Majesties Service, to which he return'd the same Answer. He press'd him to consider, in what Condition he left the Fort of *Machian*, whereto particular Regard ought to be had, because there were 50 Men and a Captain, with the small Vessel, call'd a

Machian Fort raz'd.

Galizabra, and he must either Relieve, or Dismantle it. He said, He had already sent to Destroy it, and did believe it was then Raz'd.

Having taken this Order, and Leave of the Commanders, he set sail on *Thursday* the 27th of *March*, sending a Letter to *Don Pedro de Acunna*, the Governour of the *Philippine* Islands, with an Account of the Particulars of this Enterprize: A small Part of it will suffice to express the Thoughts and Intention of so Discreet a Commander as he has been prov'd by his former and later Actions; for it is not to be believ'd that he would quit the Attempt upon *Ternate*, without substantial Reasons: *The Succours your Lord-*

Part of Furtado's Letter to the Governor of the Philip-pines.

ship sent me, says he, *by Gods Assistance, came in good Time; for it was Providence that furnished his Majesty with this Fleet, and sav'd the Lives of us, who still enjoy them. By what has happen'd in this Expedition, his Majesty will understand how much he is beholding to your Lordship, and how little to the Commander of Malaca; since it is his Fault, that his Majesty was not serv'd. When the Succours your Lordship sent me arriv'd, this Fleet had no Ammunition, as having been two Years out from Goa, and having spent it as Occasion offer'd. Wherefore, that it might not be thought I Obstructed his Majesties Service, I landed; and did it with the Loss of many of the Enemies. I carry'd up my last Trenches within 100 Paces of the Enemies Works, planted five heavy Battering-Pieces; and in ten Days Battery a great part of a Bastion, wherein the Enemies main Strength consisted, was ruin'd. During that Time all the Powder the Fleet had was spent, without leaving enough for one Charge of the Guns, and if it should happen, as I do not question it will, that I meet any Squadron of* Dutch, *I must of Necessity fight them, this being my principal Motive for raising of the Siege, when the Enemy was reduc'd to great Streights, both by Want, and for that many of their best Commanders had been kill'd during the Siege. By this your Lordship may guess at the Condition I am in.* This Letter dilates upon the Complaints against the Governours of *India*. He promises *Don Pedro*, that if he meets with any Succours at *Amboyna*, and is not oblig'd to go relieve the southern Parts, he will return to the *Moluccos*, tho' he be forc'd to go refit as far as *Malaca*. He praises and recommends the Captains *Gallinato, Don Thomas, Villagra*, and their fellow Soldiers, and so concludes the Letter.

Gallinato went to *Tydore*, where he was inform'd, that tho' the Fort of

Machian

Machian was abandon'd, only one Baſtian of it was diſmantled, ſo that if the Enemy would poſſeſs themſelves of it, they might do it with Fale, and were actually about it. Hereupon he ſpoke to the King of *Tydore*, and the *Portugueſe* Commander in Chief, recommending to them, that they wou'd either take Care to maintain, or elſe quite raze that Fort. They commiſſion'd a Captain to do the latter, who going to perform it, loaded the Veſſel, call'd *Galizabia* with 200 Quintals, or a Hundred Weight of Clove, and return'd to *Tydore*, to the great Satisfaction of the *Portugueſes* of that Iſland. At this Time the King of *Ternate* was repairing the Breaches in his Fortifications, and rais'd new Defences, providing againſt Dangers he knew Nothing of yet. His Subjects are Warlike, with whom, and the Aſſiſtance of the *Dutch*, he thought his Kingdome invincible. Great Matters might have been expected could any Confidence be repos'd in the King of *Tydore*; but our Commanders ſay his People, and thoſe of *Ternate* underſtand one another.

Gallinato at Tydore takes Care of Machian.

Falſhood of the King of Tydore.

On the 17th of *April*, the King of *Tydore* acquainted *Gallinato*, that with his Leave he deſign'd to make Peace with the King of *Ternate*. He anſwer'd, He would do well to conſider what was expedient for his own Dominions, without Detriment to his Majeſty's Service. The ſame Day the *Sangiack* of *Nua*, in the Kingdom of *Bachian*, came to *Tydore*. He was a Chriſtian, and laying hold of the Opportunity of ſerving his Majeſty in the laſt Expedition, viſited the Queen of *Tydore*, a beautiful young Lady, Daughter to the King of *Bachian*, who liv'd diſcontented, becauſe the King her Husband was more fond of another ancient Woman, and not ſo well born. The *Sangiack* had Commiſſion and Strength to ſteal her away; and conduct her to her Father, ſince neither Complaints, Intreaties, nor any other Methods had been of Force to reclaim the King. On the 4th of *May*, came a Siſter of the King's, on the ſame Pretence of viſiting her Neice, and reconciling her to the King. The *Sangiack* and ſhe having concerted thoſe Affairs, the young Queen going abroad with them to an Entertainment, and all Things being provided, they embark'd, and ſail'd away towards *Bachian*. The King of *Tydore* was enrag'd, out of Patience, and apprehenſive of a new War; tho' afterwards this Difference was amicably adjuſted, by the Interpoſition of *Cachil Malua*, a principal Perſon of *Bachian*.

The King and Queen of Tydore at Variance.

She is ſtolen away

On the 22d of *May* News was brought to *Tydore*, that the King of *Ternate*, had fitted out 50 Carcoas in his Harbour, and expected the *Dutch* Ships. He, at the ſame Time, made Rejoycings, in a triumphant Manner for the Departure of the *Spaniards*. It was requiſite to leave ſome Men and Proviſions in the Fort of *Tydore*, which being done, *Gallinato*, who had been writ by an Advice-Boat, to the General and Governour of the *Philippine* Iſlands, left the *Moluccos*, and ſail'd himſelf that Way. This was the Event of that ſo long intended and threatned Undertaking, which I have deliver'd impartially, having ſearch'd after, and even gueſs'd at ſome Excuſes to juſtify the Behaviour of ſo great a Commander as *Andrew Furtado*, enquiring of thoſe very Officers who were preſent at the Attacks, and in the Councils. Neither by them, nor by the General's own Memorials and Papers, can be found or made out any more than what appears by thoſe which have been here inſerted; but to judge of theſe Affairs is not the Part of an Hiſtorian. This

Fort of Tydore ſupply'd.

Impartiality of the Author

This same Year, about the beginning of *April*, the Presidentship of the Council of the *Indies* was conferr'd on *Don Pedro Fernandez de Castro*, Earl of *Lemos* and *Andrade*, Marquefs *de Sarria*, Chief of his Family, whofe Royal Antiquity is well known, Nephew and Son-in-law to the Duke of *Lerma*. In his Youth he gave fuch Hopes, as were afterwards fulfill'd by his Actions. He was then Gentleman of the Bed-Camber to our King. The World made the fame Judgment of him, that the Senate of *Rome* had in his Time of *Scipio*, afterwards call'd *Africanus*, when it made a Scruple of entrufting him with Matters of great Difficulty, becaufe he was fo young. But Experience foon made appear in the Earl, as well as in *Scipio*, that Prudence, which regulates all other Virtues, often anticipates grey Hairs. It is no Merit of the Off-spring to be defcended from Noble, or *Plebeyan* Families; but fuch was the Vivacity of this great Man's Spirit, and Judgment, that had he been born Mean, he might by his own natural

Parts have made his Fortune. No Man can fay he wanted publick or private Accomplifhment. In him appears a fettled Magnanimity; with a courteous Sincerity; yet temper'd with that Juftice we extol in the fevere Aufterenefs of fome of the Ancients. Thefe Virtues are interwoven with Religion, a Zeal for its Propagation, and the univerfal Agreement, which is the Product of publick Tranquility. Thus he ferv'd his King, with Care and Solicitude; without Intermiffion, or feeking himfelf and his Advantage. It will be requifite to be brief in this Particular, becaufe his fingular Modefty is not pleas'd with the Soothings of Commendation; but is as averfe to Flattery, as remote from ftanding in need of it.

The Earl found the Council fill'd with zealous and grave Men; the Lords *Benedict Rodriguez Valtodano, Peter Bravo de Sotomayor, Alonfo Molina de Mediano*, Knight of the Order of *Santiago*, or S. *James* the Apoftle, *James de Armenteros, Gonzalo de Aponte, Don Thomas Ximenes Ortis, Don Francifco Arias Maldonado, Benavente de Benavides, John de Villagutierre, Lewis de Salcedo*, and *Ferdinand de Villagomez*; all of them qualify'd by Extraction, noted for Learning, and having taken the higheft Degrees in it. Thefe were Counfellors, and the laft of them Solicitor General of that Affembly. To which alfo belong'd *John de Ybarra*, Knight of the Order of *Calatrava*, and Commendary of *Moratalaz*, and *Peter de Ledefma*, the King's Secretaries. In the Places of the Licenciates, *Molina de Medrano*, and *Gonzalo de Aponte*, whom his Majefty afterwards employ'd in his Royal Council of *Caftile*, and in thofe of fome who dy'd, his Majefty, at feveral Times put in the Licenciates, *Lewis de Salcedo, Gudiel*, and *Don Francis de Texada y de Mendoza*, Doctor *Bernard de Olmedilla*, and *John de Ybarra*, &c. All thefe amidft that Multitude of Bufinefs they dexteroufly difpatch'd, laid all their main Defigns, for the reftoring his Majefty's Monarchy to its Fulnefs, in thofe utmoft Limits of it; a Project fuitable to the Genius of the new Prefident. He enquiring into the general and particular Pofture of all Things then depending, met with that of the *Molucco* Iflands, and finding it of Confequence, and almoft forgotten, inclin'd to give it a helping Hand.

Much about this Time, Brother *Gafpar Gomez* came into *Spain*, being fent by *Don Pedro de Acunna*, to folicite that Enterprize. The Brother at feveral tedious Audiences, gave the Prefident full Information of all that

concern'd

concern'd the *Molucco* Iflands, their Wealth, the great Treafure *Spain* has expended in Attempts to recover them, to reftore perfecuted Chriftianity, where it had been fo much receiv'd; and what Confequence it was, that this fhould be done by Way of the *Philippine* Iflands. The Earl undertook that Caufe, as fuch ought to be fupported, and confulted about it with the Council, with the Duke of *Lerma*, and moft particularly with the King's Confeffor. He never defifted, till it was brought to bear, and in fuch a Forwardnefs, that it might be effectually difpatch'd. The Members of the fupream Council, with the fame Zeal, and confidering the repeated Dif-appointments of this Enterprize, forwarded the Expedition, and all of them agreed that *Don Pedro de Acunna* fhould undertake it in Perfon. This favourable Difpofition of theirs, was fully confirm'd, by the News brought a Year after, of the ill Succefs of the united Forces of *India* under *Furtado*, and thofe of the *Philippine* Iflands, under *Gallinato*. It was writ by *Don Pedro de Acunna*, defcribing it to the Life, with Duplicates for his Ma-jefty, and the prime Minifters, and though he left much to Brother *Gaf-par Gomez*, he was very particular himfelf.

He complain'd that they had let flip fuch an Opportunity of Recovering *Ternate*, and chaftifing the *Dutch*, who refort thither to the Trade of Clove, Mace, and other Spice, and Drugs. He reprefented the Danger the *Philippine* Iflands were in, after that Neighbouring Tyrant's Victory; and that having more particularly weigh'd the Circumftances of that Affair, befides the Neceffity of regaining the Reputation loft there, he found that whatfoever has been yet faid, was fhort. For not to mention the principal End, which was the Propagation of the Faith, but only with Regard to the King's Revenue, he fhow'd, That *Ternate* being reduc'd it would be eafie to fubdue the Iflands of *Banda*, which are above thirty, lying about a hundred Leagues from the *Moluccos*, full of valuable Mace, and poffefs'd by an unwar-like People, would add that Income to *Spain*, and take it from the *Dutch*, who carry all away, with little or no Oppofition. He promis'd the fame as to the Iflands *Papuas*, which are many, not far diftant from *Ternate*, fome of them Subjects to that King, and yeilding him a confider-able Quantity of Gold, Amber, and other valuable Tribute. Then he ex-tended to the Great *Batochina*, or *Gilolo*, defcribing its Fertility, and how that Tyrannical King opprefs'd it. Thofe of *Celebes* 45 Leagues from *Ter-nate*, where he had ftrong Garrifons. The Greater and Leffer *Javas*, whofe Kings would again fubmit to *Spain*, as foon as the *Moluccos* were brought under. He earneftly recommended Secrefie and Expedition. To evince the Neceffity of both, befides the ufual Reafons, he urg'd that as foon as thofe Rebels and the *Dutch* hear of any War-like Preparations, they fpare neither Coft, nor Labour, to make all neceffary Provifion; and that they never fail by the Coafts of *India* without ruining, and plundering them. He affirm'd, that the General *Furtado* was no way to blame for ha-ving abandon'd that Enterprize; for as it plainly appear'd, and Captain *Gallinato* declar'd he had always behav'd himfelf like a brave Gentleman, and difcreet Commander; but that befides the Want of Provifions and Am-munition, he could not relie upon his own Men; and that if the Succours fent him from *Manila* had been more confiderable, he would have hazard-ed all with only them. He faid, the King of *Tydore* had fent him great

Don Pe-dro de Ac-cunna's letter con-cerning the Enter-prize on Ternate.

Complaints againſt the General *Furtado*, and that it was a common ſaying with him, That before he came to the *Moluccos* the King of *Tydore* Slept, and he of *Ternate* Watch'd; but now the Caſe was alter'd, and the contrary might be ſaid. Yet he believ'd he was not heartily ſorry for the Diſappointment. The ſame he urg'd in Relation to the Kings of *Bachian* and *Sian*. He concluded, offering to undertake that Affair in Perſon, provided he might be furniſh'd with what was neceſſary, that he might not be Diſtreſs'd as his Predeceſſors had been. Then he went on, by Way of Anſwer to the Objections, or Accuſations of the *Spaniſh* Commanders, who being us'd to the Wars in *Europe*, deſpis'd all other Enemies, who made War without all thoſe Engines, and Fire-Arms us'd in *Flanders*, *France*, and *England*. He ſays, none of thoſe Eaſtern Provinces wanted any of the Inventions we have in *Europe*; and that beſides the great Numbers they have, and the Dexterity in uſing them of the *Japoneſes*, *Chineſes*, *Mindanaos*, and *Moluccos*, they are no leſs expert at their Bows, and Arrows; eſpecially the *Javaneſes*, who conquer when they fly, and that they are not deſtitute of ſuch Stratagems, that the *Spaniards* have need of all their Valour againſt them, and their numerous Armies. He owns the *Molucco* Iſlands can not ſtand in Competition, with the ſtrong and populous Cities taken in our Parts, but that neverthelefs, ſo many Chriſtian Churches as have been polluted in them; the baniſhing of our Religion; the Perſecution of its Miniſters; the continual Tyrannical Practices; and Alliance of thoſe People, with the *Dutch*, his Majeſties laſt Rebels, ought not to be caſt into Oblivion. And that, were there no other Motive but this, the King ought to retrieve his Honour, which is concern'd for the loſs of ſo many of his Fleets, and Commanders. It is very remarkable, that tho' in theſe Letters he gave an Account of the Poſture of Affairs, either as to Peace, or War, of ſo many ſeveral Kings, among whoſe Territories the *Spaniſh* Arms appear, not without Glory; yet he inſiſts not ſo much on any Point, as that of *Ternate*, which was grown Old by above thirty Years ſtanding, to the Diſcredit of our Nation. From all this may be inferr'd, how neceſſary it is always, in Affairs of great Difficulty, to bend the entire Underſtanding to them, and to be in Love with the Deſign conceiv'd, that ſo the Event may anſwer the Expectation. He at the ſame Time ſent long Reflections, and Projects of the Count *de Monterey*, then Viceroy of *Peru*, relating to the Execution of that Affair, wherein it plainly appear'd, by the Conſonancy of the Reaſons, and the Opinions of Men well acquainted with thoſe Parts, that the Expedition was of greater Concern and Importance, than all the Arguments made uſe of upon the like Occaſions do ever amount to.

Lewdneſs of the King of Ternate *and* Cachil Amuxa   Thus was *Ternate* bandy'd in the Councils of *Spain*, whilſt at home it abounded in Trade, yet ſtood upon its Guard, and particularly the King, whoſe Proſperity gave him Occaſion to indulge his Inclinations, of Cruelty towards the Chriſtians, and private Satisfaction to himſelf. He gave himſelf up to the Love of *Celicaya*, yet being divided among ſo many Women, it had not the uſual Power over him, but allow'd of other Diverſions. *Cachil Amuxa*, the braveſt of his Commanders, and his Couſin German, was newly Marry'd to a Daughter of the King of *Mindanao*, a ſingular Beauty, not of the *Aſiatick* Sort, but of the *Spaniſh* or *Italian*. The King, who was us'd to obſerve no Rules, courted her as a Gallant, and as a King, perſiſting, and preſenting her; and was ſoon admitted by the *Indian*

dian Lady. Her Husband, tho' their Privacy for a while conceal'd his Wrong; at length, by the King's contriving to keep him abroad, and the Interpofition of Time, which reveals all Secrets, found out who it was defil'd his Bed. What could the unfortunate Man do? He durft not kill his Wife, for the Love he bore her, and for Fear of the King's Difpleafure. He refolv'd to be reveng'd; as if it had been in a Money Concern. In order to it, he diffembled the beft he could, and whenfoever he had an Opportunity to talk to Queen *Celicaya*, either feign'd, or profefs'd Love, till he had inculcated it as he defir'd. He bore with the *Difdain* and Threats, which are the Weapons Nature beftow'd on that Sex; and Perfeverance prevail'd, for *Celicaya* rewarded *Cachil's* Love. This Intrigue continu'd a confiderable Time, till the King found it out, and both Rivals took No- tice of it. Tho' the King more deeply refented the Reprifal his Kinfman had made, to be reveng'd; yet they did not fall out on that Accont, nor forbear converfing together. They preferv'd Peace and Friendfhip in their Houfes; and the King ftood fo much in need of *Cachil Amuxa*, for his Wars, which in thofe Parts are no lefs frequent, than Peace, the fpecial Bleffing of Heaven, is among us, that he durft not declare againft him, and what is more, not fo much as difpleafe *Celicaya*. She, as if the Abufe tolerated in Men had been allow'd to Women, juftify'd herfelf by alledg- ing the Wrong the King had done her in courting the other. However, the King being once in the Field, under one of their Arbours, and *Cachil Amuxa* coming in, without his *Campilan*, or Cymiter, the Guards upon a Signal given them, handled their Arms, fell upon, and gave him many Wounds on his Head, Face, Arms and Body, none daring to defend him. He was fenfible of the Occafion, and Revenge, and fuddenly drawing a fmall *Criz*, or Dagger, he happen'd to have about him, did not only de- fend himfelf againft many Cuts and Thrufts, but affaulted the Murderers, and with great Activity, wounded fome, bore down others, and put the reft to Flight, killing four. Nor had his Fury ftopp'd there, but that the King flipp'd away; tho' now his Wounds had weaken'd *Amuxa* by Reafon of the great Quantity of Blood that ran from them. He was left for dead; but an Uncle of his, hearing the Noife, came into his Affiftance, with his Followers; who all bound up his Wounds, and carry'd him to his Houfe, where he was cur'd, by the King's Permiffion. This was the Effect of his Fear, rather than good Nature, for all his Kindred took the Injury up- on themfelves, and began to meditate Revenge; which they would cer- tainly have compafs'd; and made fair Way for the Pretenfions of *Spain*, had not thofe who were apprehenfive of another War foon reconcil'd thofe Animofities. The *Cachil* was cur'd, but with fuch Scars in his Face, and fo many deep Gafhes and Seams in his Head, that he was nothing like the Man he had been before. So fay they who knew him, and have feen him in our Days at *Manila* and *Ternate*. He was reftor'd to the King's Favour, and both of them to that of their Wives, without Notice taken of the Accident, or as if it had been a Secret. So great is the Difference in the Humours of Nations.

Amuxa Cuckolds the King in Re- venge.

The King's Revenge.

The End of the Eighth Book.

THE
HISTORY
OF THE
DISCOVERY and CONQUEST
OF THE
Molucco and *Philippine* Iſlands, &c.

BOOK. IX.

Preparati-
ons in
Spain
againſt the
Moluccos.

T H E continual Application of the Preſident and Council to expedite the Enterprize, ſeem'd to be a Preſage of the late ill
Succeſs at the *Molucco* Iſlands. The true Account of it was
brought in *Don Pedro de Acunna*'s Letters. The King and his
Miniſters were concern'd at it ; but at the ſame Time, it was
a Motive to haſten the Preparations, recover the loſt Reputation, and put
an End at once to that Strife. Some attributed the Miſcarriage to Diſa-
greement between *Gallinato* and *Furtado* ; others ſuſpected the Diſcord had
been between the *Spaniſh* and *Portugueſe* Nations. None urg'd that it
might be for Want of Neceſſaries for carrying on the Work. Theſe Debates ended, and the Preſident eſpouſing the Buſineſs with the Reſolution
that was requiſite, repreſented the Matter in a lively Manner to the King,
recounting what the General *Furtado* had done, the Succours ſent by *Don*
Pedro de Acunna under *Gallinato*, and how, tho' the Officers and Soldiers

The Pre-
ſidents Re-
monſtrance
to the
King.

did their Duty, the Succeſs fail'd. That it was look'd upon as moſt certain, That the *Molucco* Kings, who ſtill continu'd under Subjection, had
acted coldly: That this Failure in them was occaſion'd by a Sort of State
Policy, eaſy to be ſeen thro'; which was the Protracting of the War, and
making uſe of our Arms for their private Advantage, without deſiring it
ſhould be fully concluded. That if Means were not us'd for expelling
the *Dutch* out of *Ternate*, they would become abſolute Maſters of the
Archipelago of the *Conception*, and deprive his Majeſty of all the Revenue

oꞇ

of the Spice, as they had almoft done in the moft confiderable Parts of *India*.

The King having confider'd it, approv'd of what was laid before him ; *The King's* and being fenfible of its mighty Import ance, judg'd the Number of Ships, *Anfwer.* Men and Arms demanded,too fmall; and theretore added more with his own Royal Hand, without fixing a certain Proportion ; and order'd, that no Time fhould be loft, feeming very earneft to have his Decree put in Execution. In the fame Manner he directed, thro° the Intervention of the Duke of *Lerma*, that the Defign in Hand fhould be carry'd on. Hereupon the Council pafs'd the Neceffary Orders, and the Prefident fent Letters and Inftructions to the Viceroy of *New Spain*, and the Governour of the *Philippine* Iflands, that they might with the fame Diligence fulfil the Commands they fhould receive as to this Point. The King in his Order fent to this Effect, declar'd his Will, and the Method he was pleas'd fhould be obferv'd as follows.

Don Pedro de Acunna, *my Governour, and Captain General of the* Phi- *The King's* lippine *Iflands and Prefident of my Royal Court in them. On the* 20th *of* Lettei to September *of the laft Year* 1603. *I writ to you by an Advice Boat, which* Don Pedro carry'd Gafpar Gomez, *of the Society of* JESUS, *to* New Spain, *ac-* de Acunna. *quainting you with the Refolution I had taken concerning what you writ to me from* New Spain, *when you went to ferve in thofe Pofts, relating to the Expedition of* Ternate. *Purfuant to it, I have order'd* 500 *Men to be rais'd in thefe Kingdoms, who fhall be fent aboard the Fleet that is to go th s Year to* New Spain. *I writ to the Viceroy, directing him to raife* 500 *more, that fo you may have at leaft* 800 *fent you for this Enterprize. I have appointed four Captains to carry them from this Kingdom ; one of whom is the Vice-Admiral* John de Efquivel, *to be Commander in Chief of the faid Men ; befides fix in half Pay, who are skillful and experienc'd Soldiers, that in Cafe any of the faid Captains dye by the Way, they may fupply their Places ; and that they may take Charge of the Companies to be rais'd in New* Spain, *as I write to the Viceroy. I have appointed the faid Captains* 40 Captains *Ducats a Month Pay, and the Vice-Admiral* John de Efquivel 60. *Thofe in* and their *half Pay are to have* 25 *Ducats, and from that Time forward, the faid* Pay. John de Efquivel, *in Cafe I order him to have the Title of* Collonel, *fhall have* 120 *Ducats a Month ; and whilft he ferves under the Title of Commander in Chief of the faid Men, to have* 90 *Ducats a Month ; the Captains* 60, *and thofe in half Pay* 40. *The Soldiers, as well thofe rais'd in* Spain, *as thofe from* New Spain, *fhall have Eight Ducats a Month ; the Viceroy* Soldiers *being order'd to fend to thofe Iflands as much Money as is requifite for a* Pay. *Years Pay, according to thofe Rates. And, if they fhall be longer detain'd upon other Occafions of my Service, he fhall alfo furnifh what is Neceffary, upon Advice from you. Concerning which I have thought fit to acquaint, charge and command you, that in Cafe this Pay of the Soldiers can be moderated, with Regard to what is ufually paid there to Men of this Sort,* The Vice- *you accordingly reform it, as may be juftifiable, acquainting me, and the* roy to fur- Viceroy *of* New Spain *with it. However you fhall make no Alteration in* nifh Money, *the Pay of the Vice-Admiral* John de Efquivel, *nor of the Captains, Enfigns,* Powder *and thofe in half Pay. I have alfo directed the Viceroy to furnifh you with* and Can- *whatfoever fhall be requifite, as far as* 120000 *Ducats you have demanded* non.
for

for *this Expedition, six Pieces of Battering Cannon, and* 500 *Quintals, or hundred Weight of Musket Powder. The Men from hence go arm'd with Muskets and Firelocks. You must be very careful that there be due Order, Rule and Method in the Distribution of the said Money, and every Thing besides. You shall endeavour to perform what is intended, as I expect you* **Don Pedro** *will, with the Men sent from hence and from* New Spain, *and those you* **to go in** *may have rais'd in those Islands for the Expedition against* Ternate. *If it* **Person.** *be possible you shall go in Person, as you have offer'd to do, leaving those Islands in the best Order that may be. And in case the Affairs there should be in such a Posture, that you cannot go in Person upon this Expedition, you shall appoint another of sufficient Experience, and well quallify'd, to take the whole Command, for I impower you so to do. And it is my Will, That in Case you should miscarry, either going upon the Expedition, or thro' any other Accident, or the Person you shall appoint for it, that then the* **John de** *Vice-Admiral* John de Esquivel *succeed and prosecute it; and that all such* **Esquivel** *as go upon the said Expedition, as well Seamen as Landmen, obey him, as* **to succeed** *they would you, if there. And I declare that in this Case, and if you* **DonPedro.** *should miscarry, and the said* John de Esquivel *succeed in the Command of the Expedition, he shall be subject and subordinate to my Royal Sovereign Court of those Islands. I have made Choice of the Captains, who have the Command of the Foot rais'd in those Kingdoms, as Persons of Merit and Service; and therefore do command you to honour and favour them as far as may be allowable, and in so doing you will please me; and that you do not reform them, nor take away their Companies, to give them to others, unless it be to advance them to higher Posts. Nevertheless, if they shall be guilty of any Crimes, you may punish them, as their Superior Officer. It is to be suppos'd, That when these Men come to those Islands, and they shall set out in the first Ships that sail from* New Spain, *after the Arrival of the* Flota, *you will have all Things in such Forwardness, that the Enterprize may be* **Charge of** *gone upon immediately. I charge you strictly to undertake it with all the* **Martial** *Precaution, Maturity, and Consideration I can expect from so able a Sol-* **Discipline,** *dier; and that the Men be well disciplin'd and exercis'd, and all Things so* **&c.** *well dispos'd, that you may meet with the wish'd Success, which is of such Consequence, and you are sensible how much is hazarded, and of the great Expence that is made. You are to take Care, as I charge you, that the necessary Order be taken in the Distribution and Management of my Trea-sure; and that all superfluous Charges be avoided. You shall from Time to Time give me an Account of whatsoever happens, as Occasion shall offer. When you have recover'd the Fort of* Ternate, *you shall take the necessary Measures for the Security of the same, and of the Island. I have order'd the Viceroy of* New Spain *to send you Advice, as soon as the Men that go from hence arrive there, if there be conveniency so to do; and that he par-ticularly inform you of what Force he has gather'd there, and will be ef-fective any other Way; as also when they shall sail thence, that you may dispose Things there accordingly; and if you shall think fit that the Men be left any where, before they come to* Manila, *you may order it, or do as you shall think most Expedient in all Respects.* Valladolid, *June the* 20*th* 1604.

Altez

After the Difpatching of this Order, or Letter, the Contents of it began to be executed in *Spain*. In the foregoing Year 1603, whilft *Don Pedro de Acunna* was bufy in making Preparations to this Effect, an Accident happen'd in the *Philippine* Iflands, which threatned the Ruin of them, and greater Calamities. A Fire broke out at *Manila* in *April*, which confum'd the beft Part, and above half the City, without being able to fave the Goods, which had been landed from the Ships newly arriv'd from *New Spain*, and laid up in the fafeft Part of the Houfes, whereof 270 of Timber and Stone were burnt, as alfo the Monaftery of S. *Dominick*, Houfe and Church, the Royal Hofpital of the *Spaniards*, and the Magazines, no Building that lay betwixt them efcaping. Fourteen *Spaniards* were burnt, and among them, the licenciate *Sanz*, a Canon of the Cathedral, with fome *Indians* and *Blacks*. The Lofs was valu'd at a Million. It feem'd to be an Omen of what was to follow, which agreed with the Signs feen in the Sky. *Dreadful Fire at Manila.*

In the foregoing *March*, a *Chinefe* Ship came into the Bay of *Manila*, in which, as the Out-Guards gave the Account, there came three great *Mandarines*, with fuitable Pomp and Retinue, about their Monarch's Bufinefs. The Governour gave them leave to land, and come into the City. As foon as landed, they were carry'd directly to the King's Houfe, in *Palankines* of Ivory, and curious Sorts of Wood gilt, on the Shoulders of their Servants, who were clad in Red. There the Governour expected them, with the Members of the Royal Court, and a great Number of Officers and Soldiers, who alfo lin'd the Streets, and publick Places. When they came to the Houfe, they were fet down by their Servants, and leaving their Colours, Umbrelloes, Launces, and other Tokens of Grandeur, went into a fpacious Room magnificently adorn'd. As foon as they faw the Governour, who expected them ftanding, the *Mandarines*, making their Obeyfance, and performing Ceremonies of Civility after the *Chinefe* Fafhion, made up to him. *Don Pedro* return'd their Courtefy after the Manner of *Spain*. They, purfuant to their Commiffion, with the Interpofition of Interpreters, told him; " That their King had fent them with a *Chinefe*, they brought along with them in Chains, that they might with " their own Eyes fee a Golden Ifland, call'd *Cabit*, near *Manila*, of " which that Subject of his had given him an Account, telling him, it " was not poffefs'd by any Body, and therefore afk'd of him a Number " of Ships, to feize it, promifing to bring them back loaden with Gold, " and if he did not he fhould take his Head. That they were come to " fulfill that Promife to their King, and to fatisfy him of the Truth of " the Exiftence of fo ftrange an Ifland ; which being an Affair of fuch " Confequence, their King would not commit it to any Perfons of lefs " Note than themfelves. *Don Pedro de Acunna* anfwer'd them in a few Words. " That they were Welcome ; that they might reft them in the " Houfe prepar'd for their Entertainment in the City, and they would af- " terwards difcourfe about that Affair more at Leifure. Thus they took their Leave, and at the Door got up again into their *Palankines*, on the Shoulders of their Slaves, who carry'd them to their Lodgings. There the Governour order'd them to be plentifully furnifh'd with Provifions, and all Dainties as long as they ftaid. *Three Chinefe Mandarines at Manila.* *Their Extraordinary Meffage.* *Don Pedro's Anfwer.*

It

Jealousy of the Chinefes.

It is a plain Cafe, that the coming of thefe *Mandarines* muft raife a Jealoufy, and make it be concluded, that they came upon another Defign, than what they declar'd. The *Chinefes* are fharp and miftruftful, and it was not to be believ'd, that their King fhould fend them on that Errand, nor the Fiction likely to be credited by the *Spaniards*. At the fame Time, eight *Chinefe* Ships arriv'd at *Manila* with Merchandize, and declar'd, That the *Mandarines* come as Spies, becaufe the King of *China* intended to break off all Trade with the *Spaniards*, and fend over a mighty Fleet of Ships that could carry an hundred Thoufand fighting Men, to poffefs himfelf of that Place, and that this Expedition would be fome time that Year. The Governour redoubled his Care for the Security of the City, and order'd the *Mandarines* to be well treated, but not to be fuffer'd to go out of the City, nor to adminifter Juftice among the *Sangleys*, or *Chinefes*, as they had began to do, which they feem'd to refent. Then he fent them Word, that they muft difpatch their Bufinefs, and return fpeedily to *China*. All this was done, without any Signs of Jealoufy fhown by the *Spaniards*, or that they faw into their private Defigns.

Second Vifit of the Mandarines, *and the Governour's Anfwers.*

The *Mandarines* vifited the Governour again, and then he was more plain; and making fomething of a Jeft of their Coming, faid to them, That he wonder'd their King fhould give Credit to the *Chinefe* they brought Prifoner; or if it had been true that any fuch Gold were in the *Philippine* Iflands, that he fhould think the *Spaniards* would fuffer it to be carry'd away, the Country belonging, as it did, to the King of *Spain*. The *Mandarines* anfwer'd they believ'd as much; but that their King had fent them, and they were oblig'd to come, and to carry him an Anfwer. That having done their Part, according to their Duty, they would return. The Governour being willing to make fhort Work of it, fent the *Mandarines*, with their Prifoner and Servants to the Port of *Cabite*, which is two Leagues from the City. There they were receiv'd with the Noife of our Cannon, purpofely fir'd at their Landing, which they admir'd, and did not conceal their Surprife and Fear. When landed they ask'd the Prifoner, whether that was the Ifland he had told the King of: He, nothing daunted, anfwer'd, It was. They reply'd, Then where is the Gold? All that is in it, rejoyn'd he, is Gold, and I will make it good. The fame Anfwer he made to feveral other Queftions put to him; and all was writ down in the Prefence of fome *Spanifh* Commanders, and trufty *Naguatatoes*, or Interpreters. To conclude, the *Mandarines* order'd a Basket made of Palm-Tree Leaves to be fill'd with that Earth, to carry it to the King of *China*; and after dining and refting, return'd to *Manila*. The *Naguatatoes* or Interpreters, declar'd, That the *Mandarines* preffing the Prifoner to anfwer directly to the Purpofe, he told them, That the meaning of what he faid to the King was, that there was abundance of Gold, and other Wealth in the Poffeffion of the *Spaniards* and Natives of the *Philippine* Iflands; and if he would furnifh him with a Fleet well mann'd, he having been at *Luzon*, and knowing the Country, would undertake to make himfelf Mafter of it, and return to *China* with the Ships laden with Gold. This, with what the *Chinefes* had faid before, feem'd more likely than the Invention of the *Mandarines*.

The Chinefe *Prifoner prov'd a Cheat.*

He explains himfelf

Don

Don F Michael de Benavides, then Archbishop Elect of *Manila,* who understood the *Chinese* Language, was of this Opinion. He had been in their Country, was acquainted with the Subtilties of the *Sangleyes,* and suffer'd their Torments and Cruelties. It was presently Judg'd, that the *Mandarines* came under that Colour to view the Country, and to lay the Foundation of their Insurrection and Mutiny there. These certain Judgments are grounded on the Irrational Disposition of the *Sangleyes,* or *Chineses,* which, not to mention other Proofs, will sufficiently appear, by some few Periods of the long Letter *Ferdinand de los Rios,* of whom we have spoken before, writ to *Manila,* from the Port of *Pinai* in *Canton,* where he was upon the Service of the Church, and of his King. *For these Infidels,* says *Part of a* he, *have the Light of Nature more clouded than any other People in the Letter World, and therefore there is need of Angels, and not Men, to deal with concerning them. For the better conceiving what a sort of a Country 'tis we are in, I shall the Chine- only say, that this is the true Kingdom of the Devil, and where he may be said ses. to govern with absolute Power. Every Sangley, or Chinese, seems to be possess'd by him; for there is no piece of Malice, or Fraud, but what they attempt. The Government, tho' outwardly it appears good, as to Order and Method, for its Security; yet when you once have Experience of its Practice, you will find it is all a Contrivance of the Devil. Tho' they do not here publickly rob, or plunder Strangers, they do it another worse Way,* &c.

This Jealousy conceiv'd against the *Sangleyes,* who, once for all, are the *Chineses* Chineses so call'd by the *Spaniards* at *Manila,* was verify'd; for it *design the* was afterwards known, that the Captain of the King of *China's Conquest* Guards had begg'd of him the Conquest of the *Philippine* Islands, at the *of the Phi-* Perswasion of that *Chinese* they brought Prisoner. The Governour trea- lippines. ted the *Mandarines* civilly, and mistrusted their Designs, keeping a watchfull Eye over them. However there wanted not some-body that ask'd them, what they thought of that Fellow's Invention, since they had seen that the Place he mention'd was so far from having any Gold, that there were not the least Tokens of any such Thing to be found in it; and since it was so, they ought to make him give it under his Hand, that he had told his King a Lye. One of the *Mandarines* bid him do so, and he taking the Pen form'd three Characters, which, explain'd in our Tongue, signify'd, *If the King The Priso-* pleases, it is Gold; and if not, it is Sand. Being press'd farther, he decla- *ners De-* red, That he had inform'd his King that Gold was produc'd there, to incline *claration.* his Majesty to entrust him with a good Fleet, wherewith he might take Revenge of the Christian *Sangleyes,* who had done him many Wrongs. Little Notice was taken of all this, and tho' the Authority of the *Mandarines* seem'd to corroborate it, all was look'd upon as Folly, for none believ'd that they design'd to carry on a War out of their Country. The *Mandarines* return'd Home, having, as is believ'd, communicated their Project to the *Sangleyes* that were settled there, who at *Manila,* and in the other Islands, were above 30000.

The same was practis'd by the *Chinese* King in the Island of *Aynao,* or *Chineses* *Aynan,* a most fruitful Country, and near to his Kingdom, where the *Chi- take Ay-* neses crept in under Colour of Trade, as they did at *Manila,* and possess'd *nan by* themselves of it to this Day. This Island has such a plentiful Pearl Fish- *Treachery.* ery, that in the Year 1600 the King caus'd 1500 *Arrobas,* that is, 375 Hundred Weight of them to be taken up. This will not seem incredible to such as know, that not long before, in four Months Time, he gather'd 1700 Vessels that row'd, for this Fishery, every one being oblig'd to take a *Pico*, that is, five *Arrobas*, or Quarters of an Hundred, to gather a sufficient Quantity of Pearls to rebuild a Royal Apartment that had been pull'd down in that King's Palace He built it again, covering the Walls and Roofs with Clusters of Pearls, and Birds, Beasts, Fruits, and Flowers, all made of that precious Substance, set on Plates of Gold. The Truth of this Fact appears by an Authentick Writing, which gives an Account of it, for being likely to be judg'd Fabulous, it was requisite to authorize the Relation.

Monstrous Quantity of Pearls.

The Governour did not altogether look upon the Design of the *Mandarines* as a Piece of Vanity and Folly, tho' he conceal'd his Thoughts; for he made some Preparations, and among the rest hasten'd the repairing of the Walls of the City; which having suffer'd much by the Fire, when the Arms were also lost, he made up that Defect the best he could, and the *Sangleyes* were assisting in it. It is to be observ'd, that those People have a separate Government among themselves, in the *Philippine* Islands.

Precautions taken at Manila.

At the Time that *Don Pedro*, the Governour, was most intent upon the War against the *Molucco* Islands, there happen'd such an Accident at *Manila*, as might not only have diverted it, but utterly destroy'd the whole Province. A Man was then living, who stay'd at *Manila*, when the great Pyrate *Limaon*, of whose Life and Actions there are Printed Relations, came to *Manila*. He was then an Idolater, and, as was reported, serv'd the Pyrate in a leud Capacity. His Name was *Encan*, born at *Semygua*, in the Province of *Chincheo*; and was baptiz'd under the Government of *Santiago de Vera*, who gave him his Surname, and he was call'd *Baptist de Vera*. He prov'd a subtile Dealer, and successfully Active, by which Means, following Trade, he gather'd immense Wealth, and was Great with the Governours of the *Philippines*. Through his Interposition, the *Sangleyes* propos'd to *Don Pedro*, that he should allow them to repair a Parapet of the Wall, which was finishing, at their own Expence; for that they, as a Part of the Publick, would do his Majesty that Piece of Service; and every one of them offer'd four Royals, that is, two Shillings, towards the Work. This Piece of Service, and the Favour of the Citizens, *Encan* had purchas'd by good Turns, made the Suspicion conceiv'd of their Conspiracy vanish, or at least be little regarded.

Encan a Chinese of great Subtalty.

He was respected by the *Spaniards*, and belov'd by the *Sangleyes*, had been their Governour several Times, and had many Godsons, and other Dependants. At this Time he cunningly kept within the City, to secure Things by his Presence, but from thence he stirr'd up the People, and laid his Design, by Means of his Confidents. He thought fit to know what Number of People he should find to put it in Execution, and that he might muster them in private, order'd that every one of his Country-Men should bring him a Needle; pretending he had Occasion for them for some Work. The *Sangleyes*, either guessing at the End for which these Needles were gather'd, or else ignorantly obey'd *Encan*. The Needles being put into a little Box, the Number of them was so great, that it encourag'd him to undertake a far different Work than he had propos'd.

His crafty Practices.

The Governour still forwarded the Work of the Walls; rais'd Men; and directed the Justices to furnish themselves with Provisions, and Arms,

to

to relieve the City. Near the *Parian*, which is the Quarters of the *Chinefes*, there was another Ward, inhabited by *Japonefes*, who are Enemies to the *Sangleyes*, with whom they are continually at War in their own Country. The Governour fummon'd the Heads of them, and artfully div'd into their Inclinations, to difcover, what Ufe he might make of them upon Occafion, and whether they would affift him againft the *Chinefes*, in Cafe they came to a War. The *Japonefes*, proud of the Confidence he repos'd in them, and of an Opportunity of ferving againft their Enemy, anfwer'd, they were ready to dye with the *Spaniards*. This difcreet Precaution occafion'd fome Harm, for the *Japonefes* revealing the Secret, or adding fome Circumftances in the Relation, it was given out, that *Don Pedro*, with their Affiftance, intended to cut off the *Singleyes*; and fome of the *Japonefes* told them as much, that they might fly, and reward them for the Intelligence. Many of them had Thoughts of abfconding in the Mountains, the Reft were frighted, and thofe who intended to revolt, found an Opportunity to perfwade the others to joyn with them, and encourag'd the unfettled with fair Promifes. In fhort, moft of them confented to the Rebellion, and appointed *S. Francis*'s Day, when the Chriftians were all at Church, celebrating that Feftival, for the Time of rifing. Others were for having it done at Night, when 25000 of them were to break in and murder our Men. *Don Pedro ftrengthens himfelf*

Japonefes promife to affift the Spaniards, and alarm the Chinefes.

Confpiracy of the Chinefes.

Notwithftanding their Secrecy fome Difcovery was made. *John de Talavera*, Curate of the Village of *Quiapo*, inform'd the Arch-Bifhop, that an *Indian* Woman, with whom a *Sangley*, or *Chinefe*, was in Love, had difcover'd to him the Plot laid for *S. Francis*'s Day. It was alfo reported, that a Woman-Black had faid, there would be a great Slaughter, and another Conflagration, like the former, on *S. Francis*'s Night. Thefe and other Advices were prefently made known to the Governour and Council. A fufficient Proof was to fee the *Chinefes* fell all, to their very Shoes, and compound their Debts, tho' this was rather lookt upon as a Defign to be gone, than to commit any Treafon. To difpell their Fear of the *Spaniards* and *Japonefes*, the Governour made them fome Speeches himfelf, and caus'd the fame to be proclaim'd in all Parts, ingaging the King's Faith and Security; but nothing was of Force to quiet them. Three Days before the Feaft of *S. Francis*, above 400 *Anhayes* Merchants ftay'd in the City, becaufe they could not difpofe of their Goods. Thefe feeing the others in Diforder, on Account of the Report, that the *Spaniards* and *Japonefes* defign'd to maffacre them, fent a Meffage to the Governour, by *Chican*, one of the Province of *Anhay*, or *Chincheo*, whereof that City is Head. He came to him by Night, for Fear of the other *Chinefes*; and acquainted him with the Dread, and Confufion they were in, without knowing what Courfe to take, and therefore they came to him for Advice and Protection. He having hear'd him, gave all poffible Security in his Anfwer, and the next Day went himfelf to talk to his Companions, whom he fatisfy'd in a very obliging Manner, affuring them, that the *Spanifh* Nation never was guilty of executing, or confenting to fuch Villanies. This Difcourfe fatisfy'd them; but ftill thofe who had Mifchief in their Hearts did not defift. *Difcovery of it.*

The Governour's Precautions.

Anhayes in Fear, affur'd.

The *Sangleyes*, or *Chinefes* live there in a feparate Quarter, which the *Arabs* call *Alcayceria*, and the People of the *Philippines*, Parian. On *S.*

Francis's Eve, a great Number of them met in a Houfe half a League from the City, where there is a Sugar Work : The Houfe ftands in a Thicket, which belongs to the *Sangley* Governour. Thofe who began firft to gather there, were the Gardiners of the Quarter of *Parian*. *Don Lewis Ierez de las Marinbas* had Advice of it, from the *Dominicans of Minondo*. *Don Lewis* had Charge of the Chriftian *Sangleyes*, and fent Word to *Don Pedro de Acunna*. *Minondo* is a Town inhabited by *Chinefes* oppofite to *Manila*, the River only parting them. From *Minondo* the *Chinefe* Dwellings run on, as far as another Town of the Natives, call'd *Tondo*; and in the Quarter of the *Chinefes*, there is a ftrong Monaftery of *Auguftinians*, all of Stone. Not far from it the *Dominicans* have two, but wooden Buildings. The Governour, to be fully inform'd of the whole Truth, fent thither *Baptift* before mention'd, Governour of the *Sangleyes*, of whom he had a great Opinion, and all Men lookt upon him as a fincere Chriftian, and loyal Subject to the King. He charg'd him to fpeak to them in his Name, and to convince them how little Caufe they had to fear, as knowing how peaceable the *Spaniards* were. *Baptift* undertook this Commiffion, went to the Sugar Work, which was his own, fpoke to his People as he thought fit, and return'd very late with the Anfwer, telling *Don Pedro*, that he had been in Danger of being chofen their Chief, and that his People would have forc'd him to accept of it . That it was true, they were affembled together, and ftrong, but that it was all occafion'd by the Fear they had conceiv'd of the *Spaniards*; and that they had difplay'd feveral Colours with *Chinefe* Characters on them, which, being tranflated, contain'd thefe Words.

'The *Chief and General of the Kingdom of* China, *call'd* Ezequi, *and another of the Tribe of* Su, *call'd* Tym, *following the Dictates of Heaven in this Affair, that all the* Chinefes *may unanimoufly joyn in this Work, and obey them, in Order to root out thefe Enemy Robbers, are willing that* Yochume *and* Quinte, Japonefes, *in Conjunction with us* Sangleyes, *do conquer this City, and when we have fubdu'd it, we will divide this Country, even to the Grafs of it, equally between us, as becomes loving Brothers.*

He pretended to be mightily concern'd, becaufe they would have proclaim'd him King, and he was forc'd to make his Efcape to fave his Loyalty; and had deceiv'd them, promifing to return. Hereupon the Governour us'd feveral Means to appeafe them, the Danger of fo furious a Beginning increafing with the Number of the Rebells. The firft Mifchief he endeavour'd to prevent was the deftroying of the Rice, which was then almoft ripe. He appointed Colonel *Auguftin de Arceo*, Major *Chriftopher de Azcueta*, and Captain *Gallinato* to go fpeak to them; but *Don Lewis Perez de la Marinbas*, who liv'd at *Minondo* thinking the Rebellion now requir'd fome harfher Remedy, came at Night to advife the Governour to be more watchful, and that all the City fhould do the like. He defir'd he would allow him fome Men to fecure that Town, for he fear'd the *Sangleyes* would burn it that Night, and it was now requifite to make open War; and he muft not believe they could be reduc'd by Meffages, or fair Means. The Governour being impos'd upon by *Baptift*, ftill hop'd all would be compos'd without Effufion of Blood, and at the Perfwafion of *Don Lewis* gave him 20 Soldiers, his own Servants, and fome marry'd *Spaniards*, who were Inhabitants of the fame Town . He diftributed thefe Men into the moft dangerous Pofts of it, that the Enemy might not fet Fire to it, and the Chriftian

Sangleyes

Sangleyes when they loſt their Goods, joyn'd the Rebels. On the other Hand, the Governour privately poſted his Troops, and Sentinels; and all Men expected, or dreaded the Fate of that Night, particularly the General *John de Alcega*, who, by the Governour's Command, was to follow the Orders he receiv'd from *Don Lewis*. Proclamation was again made, that all Men ſhould be peaceable, under Penalty of being ſent to the Galleys for four Years.

This avail'd ſo little, that, excepting 4000 Handicrafts Men, and the *Anhayes* Merchants, all the Reſt aſſembled at the Sugar Work. At one in the Morning, a Party of about 1000 *Sangleyes* march'd out of a Fort, with *Catanas*, or *Cymiters*, Halbards, and other Weapons advanc'd, as alſo with long Staves, harden'd at the Fire at the Points; which they uſe inſtead of Pikes, and are no leſs ſerviceable. Theſe are very frequent among them in their Country, and are made of a ſolid Sort of Wood, call'd *Mangle*. They fell upon the Farm, or Pleaſure Houſe of Captain *Stephen de Marquina*, not far from their *Parian*, and murder'd him, his Wife, Children, Servants, and Slaves. They ſet Fire to the Houſe, and to thoſe of other *Spaniards*, among which were thoſe of Colonel *Peter de Chaves*, and of two Clergymen, who liv'd a retir'd Life, their Names *Francis Gomez*, and *Ferdinand de los Rios*. They alſo kill'd *F. Bernard de Santa Catalina*, Commiſſary of the Inquiſition, of the Order of *S. Dominick*. All theſe defended themſelves, as did many more who eſcap'd, deſparately wounded. Thence they drew towards the Town of *Tondo*, which is divided into Quarters. They fell upon that of *Quiapo*, and ſet Fire to it, after murdering 20 Perſons. Among the Reſt they burnt a Lady of Quality, and a Boy, giving great Shouts, and boaſting that from thence forward, the *Indians* ſhould pay Tribute to them, and the *Caſtillas* periſh.

News being brought on *Saturday* Morning, that the *Sangleyes* were going to enter the Town, and that the Natives had withdrawn themſelves in their Veſſels toward *Manila*, in Order to get in, or lye under the Shelter of its Walls in the River, the Governour diſpos'd the Regular Troops, and thoſe of the City *Militia* about the Walls, viewing the Gates, and all weak Places. He ſent Captain *Gaſpar Perez* with his regular Company to *Tondo*, and order'd him to obey *Don Lewis de las Marinhas*, and to carry no Colours. As ſoon as he came, the 20 Men ſent the Night before, joyn'd him, and *Don Lewis* thinking that too ſmall a Force, ſent to deſire Succours. The Governour knowing he was in the right, ſent the Captain *Don Thomas Bravo*, his own Nephew, 24 Years of Age, who ſerv'd at *Ternate* in the Expedition of *Andrew Furtado*. He went over to the Town of *Tondo*, with another Company of the regular Forces, ſome Voluntiers, and ſeven of the Governour's Servants, leaving the Colours in the City. After him he ſent Captain *Peter de Arcea*, an old Low-Country Soldier. *Don Lewis* ſent Word again, that the *Chineſes* were marching towards *Tondo*, that they were Numerous, and he fear'd they would burn the Town, and a ſtately Church of the *Auguſtinians*. The Governour ſent him 60 Men more, moſt of them arm'd with Pikes, and Halbards, the firſt having been Muſketiers. Theſe were commanded by *Don John de Penna*, till he deliver'd them to *Don Lewis*. When this Company came, there had been an Ingagement at *Tondo*, wherein *Don Lewis* ſlew abundance of *Sangleyes*, and oblig'd the reſt to retire; preventing their burning the Town, which began to take Fire, and the Houſes at the Entrance of it were conſum'd. *Don Lewis* would have purſu'd the Enemy,

1000 Sangleyes ſalley.

They murder ſeveral and burn Houſes.

More Cruelties.

Captain Perez ſent to Tondo.

Captain Thomas Bravo Succours him.

my, who retir'd to their Fort, and *Don Thomas Bravo* endeavour'd to dif-
fwade him, faying, The Men were all fatigu'd, and that as foon as out of
the Town they would meet with nothing but Bogs and Brambles; and fince
the Governor's Orders extended no farther than to keep the Enemy off from
thence, and fave the burning of the Church and Houfes, and that had been
done, they ought to fend him Advice of it, before they proceeded, being only the River parted them, and in the mean while the Soldiers would refresh
themfelves, and they might hear more of the Enemies Defign.   Captain
Alcega faid the fame, but *Don Lewis* being bent upon it, and offended to be

contradicted, afk'd him, *What Hen had cackled in his Ear?* And bid them
follow him, for five and twenty Soldiers were enough to deal with all
China. Alcega anfwer'd, *He was us'd to hear as good Game-Cocks as himfelf Crow*, yet he would do well to confider what he did.   However, tho'
F. Farfan, an *Auguftinian*, earneftly perfwaded *Don Lewis*, falling on his
Knees, to do as they defir'd him, and not to go any farther, yet he could
not be prevail'd on; but having order'd the Captains, *Gafpar Perez*, and *Peter
de Arceo*, to fecure fome Pofts with a few Men, he broke out furioufly, and

began to march, being follow'd by the Men, in Purfuit of the Enemy ; who
had already gain'd the Road, and they overtook them near the Fort, between the Bogs and the Fordable Shoals.   When they came to the Fort,
the Country open'd a litttle more. Here they began to fall upon the Enemies
Rear, and they perceiving how few the *Spaniards* were, as not being above 130,
drew up in a Body with two Points, like a Halt Moon, and lay in Ambufh
among the Grafs.   The main Body of our Men march'd towards the Fort,
and then thofe who lay in Ambufh rifing, enclos'd our Men, and fell upon
them fo furioufly with fharp Stakes, Cymiters, and other Weapons, that
they cut them in Pieces.   Head-Pieces of Proof were found batter'd with a
Stake.   A Mufketier, who ferv'd *Don Lewis*, reported, that a Company of

Sangleyes fell upon him, who havirg enclos'd him, laid about fo implaca-
bly, that they bruiz'd and broke his Legs; after which he fought a confiderable Time on his Knees, till they ftun'd him with their Staves, againft
which a ftrong Helmet could not defend him.   They left the Enfign *Francis de Rebolledo* ftun'd, for Dead, and when the Enemy drew off, he made
a Shift to get up and efcape, with his Head cruelly cut, and was cur'd in
the City, where he told many Particulars of that miferable Slaughter, about
30 more efcap'd, and among them *F. Farfan*, who all got off by being in
the Rear, and light of Foot.   *Don Lewis* was kill'd there by the fame People that had flain his Father, and with him the General *Alcega*, *Don Thomas Bravo*, Captain *Cebrian de Madrid*, and only one of all the Governor's
Servants furviv'd.

The *Sangleyes* cut off the Heads of the Slain, and hoifting them on the
Points of their Spears, run in at their Noftrils, carry'd them to prefent to
their *Chinefe* General, who was in the Fort, and his Name *Hontay*. He,
and the Reft, view'd the Heads, and fet them up with much rejoycing, returning Thanks to Heaven, and the Earth, according to their Cuftom, for
that Victory, thinking they fhould meet with little Oppofition from the
Spaniards after that.

All this Day, being the Feaft of *S. Francis*, and the next, the Enemy
fpent in rejoycing.   At *Manila* they were burning the Suburbs, and Houfes without the Walls, and confider'd what Order they fhould take againft
                                                                    the

the *Parian*; for tho' many Thousands of *Sangleyes* us'd to inhabit it, there were no then 1500 remaining, and among them 500 *Anhayes* Merchants, a peaceable and rich People, of whom there was no mistrust; the rest were Handicrafts, no Way suspected. About 50 of the others were secur'd, who had their Hair shorn, and were mix'd among the Christian *Sangleys*. These gave Information, that they had burnt Monasteries of Religious People in several Places. Some Clergy-Men, with abundance of Women and Children, secur'd themselves in the Church of *S. Francis del* *Christians* *Monte*, and some Companies of *Sangleyes* coming to besiege them, they *defend* went up into a Belfry, where having fixt a Sheet on a Staff, they display'd *themselves* it like Colours, the People appearing at the Windows, the Women and *in a Belfry.* Children ringing the Bells, rating the Enemy, and bidding them come on. Our Men often firing two Muskets, which was all they had, the *Sangleyes* durst not approach, being more afraid than they had Occasion, and accordingly drew off to a strong Post, whence they were to continue the War.

The Governour endeavour'd to prevent the News of the Slaughter *Francis de* spreading abroad, lest it should discourage the Country; and gave out, that *las Missas* the Slain were at *S. Francis del monte*. He warn'd the Justices to get to- *does the* gether all the *Indian* Servants, because there were scarce any *Spaniards* left; *Rebels* and sent the Factor *Francis de las Missas* to cruise upon the Coast, with *much* three Rowing Vessels, towards the Enemies Fort, to cut off all their Pro- *Harm.* visions. The Factor perform'd his Part so well, that he sunk some Vessels, and burnt those that carry'd them Provisions. He kill'd many of their Men at the Mouth of a River that falls into the Sea, about the Fort call'd *Navotas*; look'd for the Clergy-men they were said to have kill'd in their Houses; and sent away to *S. Francis del monte*, a Party of 500 *Japonese*, with three *Spaniards*, and two *Franciscan* Fryers, to gather the Remains of that Slaughter. In his Way, he pass'd by the Enemy's Fort, with a Design to do them some Harm, if he could, and found they had abandon'd it, retiring to the *Parian*, to joyn the rest and besiege the City, being puff'd up with their late Victory. This happen'd on *Monday* the 6th. The *Japoneses* *Japoneses* search'd the Fort, where they found about 200 sick and wounded *kill 200* *Chinese*, whom they slew, and saving abundance of Provisions, burnt *Chinese*, the Fort with all their Warlike Preparations, which could not be service- *and burn* able against the first Owners. They went up to the Monastery, and re- *their Fort.* turn'd thence the same Day to the City.

The few *Sangleyes* in the *Parian* were no less apprehensive, than the greater Number in the Fort, both because they were so near, and for that *Rebels* it was suppos'd they would joyn their Companions, when they saw the *send to stir* *Spaniards* decline. Besides, it was known, that those in Rebellion had *up the* sent to desire them to come over to their Party, giving them Notice of the *others.* *Spaniards* they had kill'd. This was discover'd by a *Sangley*, who swimming over, was taken by the Sentinel on the Vessels that were in the River, who, having confess'd on the Rack, that he was a Spy, and went *Spy execu-* forward and backward with Intelligence, was put to Death. On the other *ted.* Hand, it was consider'd, that though the safest Way was to kill all those People, yet it was not just to execute Men that were not convicted of any Crime: especially since they came to the *Philippine* Islands, to trade upon
the

the publick Faith, and the Governour having engag'd for their Safety, in cafe they were quiet, and intermeddled not in the Rebellion. For this Reafon fome Councils of War were held among the Commanders, at which the Counfellors, and the Archbifhop, were alfo prefent, and confidering, that the Rebels earneftly applying to thofe in the *Parian*, to fide with them, it was poffible they might be perverted, and in cafe they did not revolt, thofe Mutiniers would kill them, it was refolv'd, That the *Anhayes* Merchants fhould be perfwaded to retire with their Effects into the Monaftery of *S. Auguflin*, which is a ftrong Houfe within *Manila*. The Governour having himfelf in Perfon acquainted them herewith, as alfo by fome of the Counfellors and their Friends, yet they were refolute; and tho' fome of them committed the keeping of their Goods to others, they ftay'd themfelves to be Spectators of the Event. The laft Care taken of them, was *Don Pedro*'s going in Perfon to the *Parian* that fame Day; and about an Hour after, many of the Enemies Colours appear'd on the other Side of the River, along the Bank of it. They came from the Fort, which was a quarter of a League from the City.

The Governour would fecure the Anhayes.

Some of the *Sangleyes* began to fwim over to the *Parian*, and others came in Boats and Floats provided for that Purpofe Their Paffage could not be obftructed, becaufe the Galiots and *Carcoas* belonging to the Navy were then among the *Pintados*, to defend thofe Iflands; Intelligence having been brought, that a Fleet of *Mindanaos* and *Ternates* was coming to invade them. The Rebels enter'd the *Parian* with great Cries, bringing the Heads of the *Spaniards* they had kill'd on S. *Francis*'s Day, run through the Noftrils The Governour obferving their Refolution, order'd the Captains, *Gafpar Perez*, and *Peter de Arceo*, who were at *Tondo*, to come over to the City with their Companies. The Enemy being return'd to the *Parian*, with that difmal Spectacle of the Heads, began to perfwade the *Anhayes*, who had not yet declar'd, but not being able to prevail, and finding them pofitive on the contrary, and that they blam'd what they had done, they fell upon and butcher'd above 200 of them. Then they plunder'd Part of their Silks, which made them Cloaths of feveral Colours. They alfo hang'd other Merchants, and fome, being about 80 in Number, hang'd themfelves, to prevent falling into their Hands, which is very frequent in theat Country. One of thefe was the *Sangley* General himfelf, call'd, *Hontay*. F. *John Pobre*, formerly a Captain, fince a *Francifcan* Fryer, and at this Time compell'd by Neceffity to take up Arms again, reported, That the mutinous *Sangleyes*, having perfwaded the *Anhayes* to follow their Example, they appointed *Chican*, a rich *Sangley*, and Mafter of the *Spanifh* Tongue, to anfwer for them. He, before he would fpeak his Mind, told them it would be proper to fet up a Gallows, and the Heads of the *Spaniards* on it, that being in View, they might all take Courage to fight manfully. They approv'd of his Counfel, and the Gallows being fet up, he went up himfelf to range the Heads, and taking out a Rope he had carry'd up unfeen, put it about his own Neck, and hang'd himfelf in the Sight of them all.

Chinefes pafs over to Parian.

The Chinefes murder the Anhayes.

Some hang themfelves to avoid their Fury.

Strange Death of Chican.

The fame Day Captain *Peter de Brito*, being with his Company in the Cathedral, which had been affign'd him the Night before, for his Poft, and obferving that a certain Houfe was not uncover'd, contrary to the Proclamation

mation made the Day before, commanding them all to have the Palm-Tree Leaves and *Nipa*, wherewith they are thatch'd, taken off, for Fear of another Conflagration ; he sent to take it off. The Ensign *Andrew Obiegon* went up to this Purpose to the very Top, and there found *Baptist* hidden with his Sword and Dagger, whom some Women endeavour'd to conceal. Being ask'd by the Ensign, what he did there ? he answer'd, He was taking off the *Nipa*. The next Question he was quite dash'd, and his own Conscience suddenly accusing him, he said, *Do not kill me, Sir*. The Ensign mildly encouraging, bid him go to the Governour, who expected him, and stay'd to take off the Covering of *Nipa*. Then coming down saw some Soldiers, and went up again with them. By this Time certain *Indian* Women had hid *Baptist* in a Chamber, where the Soldiers entering by Force, bound him, and he was cast into Prison among other *Chinefes*. The Tryal was short, as is usual in the Martial Way, and in the mean while the Prisoners were remov'd to Captain *Gallinato's* House. Thither came a *Japonese* Boy, enquiring for *Baptist*. They found his Pocket full of Squibs, and another Boy with a Piece of a Wax-Candle, all which was given them by one of *Baptist's* Slaves. The Squibs were all bloody, perhaps it was some Christian's Gore. He own'd himself he had so great a Hand in the Rebellion, that it was not without good Reason they would have made him their Chief. That the *Sangleys* call'd out upon his Name. That *Hontay* was troubled at his Absence, saying, He must needs be in some Trouble, since he did not come to Head them ; and for this Reason he hang'd himself. Next appear'd the Ring-leaders of the Mutiny, and it was prov'd against them, That they had set up a Pole on the Place call'd *el Cerro*, or the Hill of *Calocan*, and on it a black Flag, with two *Chinese* Characters on it, which imported *CUNTIEN,* the Signification whereof is, *IN OBEDIENCE TO HEAVEN*. Other Colours were found with the Army that fought at *Dilao*, with a Cut on them containing the *Chinese* Figures of *Encan*, or *Baptist*.

Baptift Chief of the Rebels taken.

His Confeffion.

Why Hontay hang'd himfelf.

Several Religious Men, at this Time fought against the Mutiniers ; but among them all, special Praise is due to the Valour of the Lay-Brother *Antony Flores*, of the Order of *S. Augustin*. He was born in *Estremadura*, had serv'd in *Flanders*, was a Slave in *Turkey* above 20 Years, and made his Escape out of the Inland Country by his Valour and Industry. He went over to the *Philippine* Islands, where he chearfully took the Habit, in the Monastery of *S. Augustin* at *Manila*. He always show'd great Humility in Obedience, and lost nothing of his Courage in the Simplicity of a Religious Life. Him the Governour order'd to scour the River, in the Galliot belonging to the Monastery, fighting the Ships and *Champanes* of the *Sangleyes*. One Night after having drove from the Shore above 200 Vessels, burnt some large ones, and sunk others, he stay'd in the Middle of the River *Pasig*, to observe the *Sangleyes*. Between eleven and twelve, he perceiv'd that one of the Rebels was swimming over to the City, and the Darkness causing him to mistake, he lighted upon Brother *Antony's* Galliot. He having seen him before, the *Indian* Servants had the Opportunity of laying hold of him, drew him by the Hair into the Galliot, and carry'd him to the Governour. He was put to the Rack, and there confess'd, That he came to acquaint the *Sangleyes* of the *Parian*, that the next Day those

Brother Antony Flores, a brave Man.

Does good Service.

Takes a Spy.

on the other Side wou'd crofs the River, and then they would all together, with the Engines they had provided, attack the Wall, put all the *Spaniards* to the Sword, and make themfelves Maflers of the Iflands. The Governour having this Intelligence, took the neceffary Precautions for the next Day, and Brother *Antony* return'd to his Monaftery, where he furnifh'd himfelf with Meal and other Provifions for his Galliot. He carry'd two Mufkets for himfelf, and drew his Veffel into a Creek the River makes, that runs by the Walls of *Manila*, among abundance of *Manglans*, which are Trees growing in any watrey Land, and fo thick, that Men may eafily be hid among them, without being perceiv'd. There Brother *Antony* lay in Ambufh

He alone kills 600 Chinefes. fuppofing, or knowing, that the *Sangleyes* muft of Neceffity pafs that Way, as being the narroweft in the River, and neareft to the Wall. Nor was he deceiv'd in his Expectation, for they came very early in the Morning, and were paffing over in great Numbers from the firft Peep of Day, till very late. The Fryer had put above 200 Bullets into two Pouches, and kept firing the two Mufkets from before five in the Morning, at break of Day till fix in the Evening, cooling them with Vinegar; nor did he ever fire at lefs than a Company of 20 or 30 *Sangleyes*, that no Shot might be loft. It was concluded for certain, that he alone that Day kill'd above 600 of thofe Barbarians. The Governour afterwards fent him in purfuit of thofe that remain'd, with a thoufand *Indians*, and he flew above 3000 *Sangleyes*, putting to flight the fmall Remains of them.

Defperate Sangleyes kill'd from the Wall. At this Time many of the *Sangleyes* that had crofs'd the River, appear'd in the Streets of the *Parian*; who ftanding in Sight of the Walls, with their own, or the Weapons they had taken from the *Spaniards* they flew, call'd upon thofe who defended the City, whence they made feveral Mufket Shot at them, wounding and killing many, for they came within good Aim, after a defperate Manner. It was reported, they had taken their *Anfion*, that is, a Compofition of *Opium*, as the *Turks* do, and is alfo us'd by the People of the *Moluccos*, when they are to give Battel; for it does and gives them a brutal Courage. A Piece of Cannon was planted on the Gate of the *Parian*, and did confiderable Execution, and no Man

Opium gives Courage. would have fufpected that any had been there. Some *Japonefes* and Natives of the *Philippines* fally'd out upon the *Sangleyes*, with good Succefs; for they kill'd many of them, and particularly fuch as had been wounded by the fmall Shot, and Brafs Guns on the Wall. They thinking the *Parian* was a Shelter for Cowards, fet Fire to it, and went out to fight the

Japonefes and Indians fight the Chinefes. *Japonefes* and *Indians*. The *Sangleyes* from the Houfes, where they lay conceal'd, kill'd a *Portuguefe* Captain, and wounded three others, with fmall Shot. One of them was *Ruy Gonzalez de Sequeyra*, Commander in Chief of the *Moluccos*. The *Sangleyes* remov'd to the Monaftery of *Candelaria*, that is of *Candlemas*, whence they fally'd more furioufly than from the *Parian*.

Fight of Spaniards and Chinefes. On *Tuefday* in the Morning, Captain *Gallinato* march'd towards the *Candelaria*, with about 500 *Spaniards*, and fome *Japonefes*. The Enemy refus'd not the Engagement, but came out above 4000 ftrong. Our Men made themfelves Maflers of a Bridge, whence they pour'd fome Volleys upon them. Perceiving the Lofs they fuftain'd, they fell back, to draw the *Spaniards* into open Field, and ferve them as they had done *Don Lewis*;

but

but tho' some Soldiers were so bold as to go into the Church, and plunder Part of what the *Sangleyes* had robb'd in the *Parian*, yet some of them retir'd hastily to the Bridge, with the Loss of three *Spaniards*, and five *Japonefes*, besides the wounded, the Enemy charging them in a Body. Of the *Chinefes* 360 of the boldest were kill'd, which made them flinch with Fear. The same Day in the Evening, a Party of them came up to assault the Wall, where it was lowest, bringing scaling Ladders, and other Necessaries, cover'd with Silk; but the Cannon play'd so smartly on them, that they lost their Ladders, and many of them their Lives. This same Afternoon there was an Engagement on the Side of the *Parian*, where the Enemy brought on two great Machines, like Carts, made the Night before, with Wheels, and stuff'd with Quilts, Blankets, and such Materials, to defend them against the Cannon, and small Shot. The Governour was apprehensive that they had some Fire-works, they being great Masters at them; but was soon satisfy'd, for having fir'd at them with the Piece that was over the Gate of the *Parian*, where one of his Servants was Gunner, it carry'd away a considerable Part of the foremost Machine, and with it a good Number of the *Sangleyes* that drew underneath, and were on it. However they advanc'd boldly, till the Gun tore others in Pieces, and they retir'd, abandoning the *Machine*. Still the Fight grew hot about the River, and several Men went out in Boats, and others did Execution thro' the Loop-Holes. The Ensign *John Guerra de Cervantes*, sent out the *Japonefe* and Native Soldiers, and they drew near to the *Parian*, under the Shelter of the Cannon on the Walls, so courageously, that they set fire to the best of it, being the Houses of the *Anhayes*; which quite discourag'd those that were in them, especially when they observ'd they had secur'd the River, and the Boats, and taken their Musquetiers. It was judg'd that above 2500 *Sangleyes* perish'd this Day by Fire and Sword, besides those at the *Candelaria*, and other Straglers. Having lost the Shelter of the *Parian*, they took up in the Church of the *Candelaria*, but the next Morning none of them appear'd. They cross'd the River on *Wednesday*, and some of our Men were drowned pursuing them too eagerly. They took the Way to the Village call'd *Tabuco*, 5 Leagues from *Manila*, which is very populous, and plentiful. Here Captain *Don Lewis de Velafco* found them fortify'd, and defended with Doors and Boards, towards the Lake *Vay*; whence he ply'd them with small Shot, and kill'd many, they no longer able to endure the Damage they receiv'd, kindled many Fires in the Night, to prevent being observ'd, and march'd away towards S. *Paul's*, a Village 16 Leagues from *Manila*, where they came so thin, that they were not above 6000, having lost very many in the Way to *Tabuco*. There *Don Lewis* fell upon them again; and pursuing them after they quitted the Village, was so hot, that they kill'd him four Soldiers, and two barefoot Fryers, the one a Priest, the other a Lay-Brother.

They made a Halt at S. *Paul's*, intending to reap the Rice, which was then almost Ripe, because that is a forwarder Country than *Pampangua*. Before they came to S. *Paul's*, a Detachment of 1500 of them turn'd off from the main Body towards the Mountains of *Pace*. The *Spaniards* and Natives overtook them, and tho' they stood to it, our Men play'd their Parts so well, that they cut them all off, and recover'd Part of their Booty.

Slaughter of the Latter.

Their Machine destroy'd.

The Spaniards fire the Parian.

Kill 2500 Chinefes.

They fly.

And are pursu'd with great Slaughter.

Capt. Velafco kill'd.

Another Slaughter of Chinefes.

G g 2 The

The Fort the *Sangle,es* had rais'd at S. *Paul's* was of Palm-Trees, whence they made Excurfions to fight, reap the Rice, and ravage the Country. They thought it convenient to divide themfelves into two equal Bodies; the one ftay'd in the Fort, the other went away to *Vatangas*, feven Leagues diftant towards the Sea-Coaft, with a Defign, as was thought, to build Ships, for which Purpofe they carry'd Carpenters, Labourers, Tools, Nails, and all other Neceffaries. The Governour reflecting on their Defign, fent fome vigilant Perfons towards the Bay of *Vatangas*, to fecure the Veffels on the Coaft, that the Enemy might not make ufe of them, and get over to other Iflands, which would have been of ill Confequence.

Rebels defign to build Ships.

The Governour believing the Defign of the *Sangleyes* was to gain Time, and perhaps to expect fome Supplies from *China*, which might be promis'd by the *Mandarines*, before they went away; he thought it requifite to bring the War to a fpeedy Conclufion, becaufe the Enemy fortify'd themfelves daily, and made Excurfions from their Forts, to fcour the Country, and gather in the Rice; perfwading the Natives to joyn with them; tho' they were fo far from complying, that they kill'd all they could meet with. There were feveral other Reafons which prov'd that the greateft Safety confifted in Expedition, and therefore abundance of *Spaniards* and Natives, by the Governour's Order, were always in Queft of the ftraggling *Chinefes.* However it was judg'd expedient to prefs them yet nearer, and not allow them Time, as they wifh'd, till the Rice was ripe, fince Hunger muft prove their greateft Enemy. To this Purpofe it was thought Expedient to make ufe of trufty neighbouring People.

The Rebels prefs'd.

Pampangua is a Province ten Leagues from *Manila*, beyond the Town of *Tondo*, over the River *Pafig*, on which the Citizens have convenient fmall Veffels. The Country is fubject to be overflow'd, by reafon of the many Rivers, and becaufe the Natives draw Trenches from them, to water the Rice, and other Grain. The whole Diftrict is of twelve Leagues, all inhabited, and has feven Churches, belonging to the Order of S. *Auguftin.* The Natives are Brave, Docible and Loyal, receive the Chriftian Faith, and are fteadfaft in it; and richer than thofe of other Parts of the Ifland. Captain *Ferdinand de Avalos* was *Alcalde mayor*, or chief Governour of *Pampangua*, and the Governour General having acquainted him by Letter with the Rebellion of the *Sangleyes*, requiring him to fend Provifions and Arms for the War, and not to leave any Enemies behind, he perform'd both Things, with extraordinary Care. He furnifh'd him with great Store of Rice, Palm-Wine, and a confiderable Number of Cows and Calves; and took above 400 *Sangleyes*, who being carry'd to a Creek in the River, bound two and two, and deliver'd to the *Japonefes*, they flew them all. F. *James de Guevara* of the Order of S. *Auguftin*, Prior of *Manila*, who writ this Relation, preach'd to them firft, and only five of them forfook their Idolatry, and were baptiz'd. At the fame Time he fent the Governour 4000 *Pampanguos*, arm'd after their Country Fafhion, with Bows, Arrows, Half-Pikes, Shields, and long broad Poniards. They came to *Manila* with great Shouts, and as if fure of Victory, fell upon the Enemy, who increas'd ftill, the more they were deftroy'd.

Pampangua defcrib'd.

Service done by the Alcayde of Pampangua.

This obliged the Governour, notwithftanding fome Oppofition, to fend a Number of *Spaniards*, and *Japonefes*, with a ftrong Party of the *Pampangua Indians*,

Indians, well arm'd and provided, under the Command of the Captain and Major *Azcueta*, a brave and vigilant Commander, well acquainted with the Country, ordering him to draw near the Enemy; yet not to engage, becaufe they were a desperate barbarous People in their first Onsets, but to alarm them Day, and Night, on every Side, obstructing their Excursions, that so they might want Povisions, and consequently be oblig'd to dislodge, for if he could remove them but twice, he might cut them off, as it happen'd accordingly. The Major departed *Manila*, with these Orders, by the Way of the River. On *Munday* the 20th of *October*, he came in Sight of the Enemy, who was still in the Fort at *S. Paul's*, and there he had some Actions. Having cast up some Works, for his greater Security, in the Quarters he took up, the Enemy's sally'd out of their Fort, and some of those who valu'd themselves on their Bravery advanc'd to fight the *Spaniards* in their Posts, with as much Boldness, as could be expected from Men in Despair, and quite distracted. Thus being cut off from Water, streightned, often alarm'd, never suffer'd to rest, and such as ventur'd out cut off, they dismay'd, and dislodg'd in the Night very silently, marching towards *Batangas*, where their other Body was. However their Departure could not be conceal'd from the Vigilancy of our Men, who march'd after them, *Martin de Herrera*, Captain of the Governours Guard, leading the Van, which confisted of *Spaniards*, and the bravest of the Natives. He overtook the Enemy, and began to fall so hard upon their Rear, that they were forc'd to face about; and after killing above 800 of them as they pass'd a narrow but deep River, our main Body coming up attack'd the rest three several Ways, on an Eminency they had taken, and slew above 1000 more; those that escap'd perishing the next Day, so that only one was taken alive, tho' the Governour would have had many sav'd to serve in the Galleys; but the *Japonefes* and Natives are so bloody, that neither his Orders, nor Major *Azcueta's* Severity, or the other Commanders could curb them.

The Men rested that Day, having travel'd above five Leagues over Grounds full of Sedges, and Bogs; and prepar'd to proceed to *Batangas*, to fight the other Body of Rebels, carrying some Fields Pieces. The Major had dismiss'd the *Japonefes*, becaufe they, alledging they were not Soldiers in Pay, would return to *Manila*. He had only 50 Soldiers left with him, and found the Enemy well fortify'd, and furnish'd with Provisions, as having been Masters of the Country. He spoke to them in peaceable Manner, as he had done before to the other Party, offering good Terms, if they would submit to the Governour; but Obstinacy had stopp'd their Ears, and excluded all Hopes, so that they would not admit of any Accommodation. Our Men drew near, three several Ways with their small Shot, and the *Pampangua Indians*, who were brave, supported by the *Spaniards*, who led and encourag'd them, attack'd the Fort; but the Defendants behav'd themselves so bravely, that they caus'd them to retire, with the Loss of four or five *Pampanguos* kill'd, and some wounded. Our Men came on again, and the Captain of the Guards, who Commanded that Attack, with the Men under his Charge, and others that joyn'd him, fell on with such Fury, that they enter'd the Fort, and put them to the Sword. About 600 escap'd of whom they made an End a few Days after. Some few above a Hundred were saved, who were carry'd alive to ferve in the Galleys. Of our Men eight
Natives

Na ives and fix *Japonefes* weie kill'd in thofe two Actions; but never a *Spaniard*, tho' many were wounded , and among them the Captain of the Guards, who had both his Thighs run through acrofs with a Lance. ,

Encan and others Executed. On the 22d *Encan*, otherwife call'd *Baptift*, was executed, being hang'd and quarter'd, his Head fet up in the *Parian*, and his Goods confifcated. The following Days the like Juftice was,executed on other guilty *Chinefes* ; and had the Laws of their own Country been obferv'd, the fame Punifhment had been inflicted on their whole Families and Kindred.

End of the Chinefe Rebellion. Thus was that Conflagration fupprefs'd, which threatned the utter Ruin of the *Philippine* Iflands, and thus above 23000 *Chinefes*,perifh'd, few above 500 being left for the Galleys, and all thofe Ifles being reftor'd to unexpected Peace. Some affirm, the Number of the *Sangleyes* flain was greater, but that the Magiftrates conceal'd it, for fear Notice fhould be taken of their Fault in admitting fo many to live in the Country, contiary to the King's Prohibition ; yet in vain does Subtilty contend with Truth.

Don Pedro had receiv'd fome Intelligence of his Majefties approving of the Enterprize on the *Moluccos* ; and whilft he expected to fee the Effect of that Refolution, writ all the Ways he could, as alfo through *India*, to folicite thofe who were commiffion'd in that Affair. Being deliver'd of *Ill Effects of the Chinefe Rebellion.* the Trouble of the *Sangleyes*, he bent his Mind to provide all Neceffaries for the Fleet, againft he fhould be commanded to fet out ; but the End of this War, was the Beginning of other Difficulties at *Manila*. All Handicrafts ceas'd, Works were lay'd afide, and Provifions grew fcarce; which Scarcity made all Things dear; whereas before there was Abundance, all Things laborious being done by the *Sangleyes*, by Reafon that the Native *Indians* are neither willing, nor induftrious at fuch Affairs. They had quite laid afide tilling the Land ; breeding of Fowl, and weaving of Blankets, all which they formerly us'd to do, in the Time of their Infidelity. The *Parian* or *Chinefe* Quarter was particularly ruin'd with Fire and Sword. That Place us'd to be fo plentiful and advantageous, that when *Don Pedro* came firft to *Wealth of the Parian.* *Manila*, he writ concerning it to a Kinfman of his in *Spain*, as follows. *This City is remarkeable for ftately Buildings, which have aftonifh'd me. I fhall only mention one Particular, which is the chiefeft, That it has a Suburb, or Quarter, full of all Sorts of Silks, and Gold, and Mechanick Trades, and* 400 *Shops full of this Sort, with above* 8000 *Men generally dealing in them; and at the Time when Fleets come from* China *with Merchandize, which is at this Seafon there are always above* 13 *or* 14000 *Men. They bring extraordinary Things, fuch as are not in* Europe. *Don Pedro* was alfo afraid that the Slaughter lately made would obftruct the Trade, and that the Ships wou'd not come as ufual, with Provifions, from *China*. But the greater and more general Apprehenfion was that inftead of Merchants, Ships of War would come to revenge the *Sangleyes*. He therefore fent away F. *James* *F. Guevara fent through India to Spain.* *de Guevara*, Prior of *Manila*, into *Spain*, by the Way of *India*, with an Account of what had been done, and of his Fears. The many Accidents that befell him in *India*, *Perfia*, *Turkey*, and *Italy*, made him fpend three Years before he came to Court, where he then found other frefher Intelligence.

At the fame Time *Don Pedro* fent Captain *Mark de la Cueva*, with F. *Lewis Gandullo*, a *Dominican*, to *Macao*, a City in *China*, where the *Portuguefes*

guefes refide, with Letters for the Commander in Chief and Council of that City, giving them an Account of the Rebellion of the *Sangleyes*, and the Event of it, that they, upon any Rumour of a Fleet providing in *China*, might fend him Notice of it feveral Ways. They had alfo Letters for the *Tutoner*, or *Tfuntos, Aytaos*, and Vifitors of the Provinces of *Canton*, and *Chincheo*, acquainting them with the Guilt of the *Chinefes*, which oblig'd the *Spaniards* to punifh them fo feverely. The Meffengers at their Arrival, found all the Country peaceably difpos'd, notwithftanding that fome *Sangleyes* flying from *Manila* in *Champanes*, had given an Account of their Commotions. The Coming of thefe *Spaniards* to *Macao* was foon known at *Chincheo*, and prefently fome of the richeft Captains, who us'd *Manila* moft, came to vifit them ; their Names were *Guanfan, Sinu*, and *Guachuan*. They being fully inform'd of the Truth of the Fact, took upon them to deliver the Letters *Don Pedro* fent to the *Mandarines*, who receiv'd them by their Means. The Merchants of *Chincheo* took Courage to trade in the *Philippine* Iflands, and fail'd in their own Ships from *Macao*, with our Meffengers, carrying Abundance of Powder, Saltpeter, and Lead, wherewith the publick *Magazines* were ftor'd. In *May* following 13 *Chinefe* Ships arriv'd at *Manila*, and many more after them, continuing that Trade.

Message to China.

Chinefes trade again at Manila.

Don Pedro fent the Ships that had brought Supplies from the Iflands, to *New Spain* ; The Commodore of them was caft away, and not a Man nor a Plank fav'd. He ceas'd not at the fame Time to ftore the City with Provifions and Ammunition, that he might be at Leafure to undertake the Expedition againft the *Moluccos*. Now arriv'd Colonel *John de Efquivel*, from *Mexico*, with 600 Soldiers, and Intelligence that farther Provifion was making in *New Spain* of Men, Stores, Ammunition, and Money, by the King's Order. All came in due Seafon to *Manila* ; and there at that Time dy'd the Arch-Bifhop *Don Miguel de Benavides*, generally lamented by all the Country. The *Chinefe* Ships that came again to trade, brought the Governour the Anfwers to his Letters, contain'd in three others, all to the fame Effect, from the *Tuton*, or *Tfunto*, that is, the Viceroy, the *Hayton*, and the Vifitor General of the Province of *Chincheo*. Being tranflated by the Interpreters, they were found to this Effect.

spanifh Ship loft.

Efquivel with 600 Men at Manila from New Spain.

To the Chief Commander of *Luzon*. *Having underftood that the Chinefes that went to Trade and Trafick in the Kingdom of Luzon, have been kill'd by the* Spaniards, *I have inquir'd into the Caufe of that Slaughter, and intreated the King to do Juftice, on thofe who had been the Occafion of fo much Mifchief, that the like may be prevented for the future, and the Merchants enjoy Peace and Quietnefs. Some years fince, before I came hither as Vifitor, a* Sangley, *whofe Name was* Tioneg, *went over to* Cabit, *in Luzon, with three Mandarines, and the King's Leave, to feek for Gold and Silver, which was all a Cheat; for he found neither Gold nor Silver, and therefore I befeech'd the King to punifh that Deceiver,* Tioneg, *that the World might fee how impartially Juftice is adminifter'd in* China. *It was in the Time of the late Viceroy, and Funuch, that* Tioneg *and his Companion, whofe Name was* Yanlion, *told the faid Lye. Since then I intreated the King to caufe all the Papers relating to* Tioneg's *Cafe, to be copy'd, and the faid* Tioneg, *and the Proceedings againft him, to be lay'd before his Majefty, and I my felf faw thofe Papers, and was fenfible that all the faid* Tioneg *had faid*
was

Chinefe Letter to the Governour.

Difcovery of the Cheat of the three Mandarines above.

was a Lie. I writ to acquaint the King that the Caſtillas *ſuſpected we intended to make War on them, on Account of the Lyes* Tioneg *had told, and therefore they had ſlain above* 30000 Chineſes *at* Luzon. *The King did what I deſir'd, and accordingly puniſh'd the aforeſaid* Yanlion, *ordering him to be put to Death; and caus'd* Tioneg's *Head to be cut off, and hung up in a Cage. The* Chineſes *that Dy'd at* Luzon *were not to blame, and I, and ſome others have acquainted the King with ſo much; as alſo with the coming of two* Engliſh *Ships upon theſe Coaſts of* Chincheo, *a Thing very dangerous for* China, *that the King may reſolve what is to be done in two Affairs of ſuch Conſequence. We alſo Writ to the King, to order two* Sangleyes *to be puniſh'd, for having ſhown the Harbour to the* Engliſh. *And after having Writ as aforeſaid to the King, he anſwer'd, What did the* Engliſh *Ships come into* China *for? Whether they came to Rob? That they ſhould be order'd to depart thence immediately to* Luzon; *and to tell thoſe of* Luzon *that they ſhould not give Credit to the wicked and lying Perſons among the* Chineſes; *and that they ſhould immediately kill the two* Sangleyes. *As for the reſt we writ to him about, he anſwer'd that we ſhould do our Wills. The* Viceroy, *the* Eunuch *and I, after receiving this Order, do now ſend theſe our Letters to the Governour of* Luzon, *that his Lordſhip may be acquainted with the Grandeur of the King of* China; *for he is ſo Great that he governs all the Sun and Moon ſhine on; as alſo that the Governour of* Luzon *may know how well this ſo large Kingdom is govern'd, whoſe King none has dar'd to offend this long Time. And tho' the* Japoneſes *have attempted to diſturb* Corea, *which belongs to the Government of* China, *that have not ſucceeded; but have been expell'd thence, and* Corea *has remain'd very peaceable and quiet, as is well known by Fame to the People of* Luzon.*

The laſt Year, when we were inform'd, that ſo many Chineſes *were ſlain at* Luzon, *on the Account of* Tioneg's *falſhood, we met many* Mandarines *of us to agree to propoſe to the King, that he would revenge ſo great a Slaughter. We ſaid, that the Land of* Luzon *is poor, of no Value, and that formerly it was the Habitation of none but Devils and Snakes; and that ſo many* Sangleyes *having of late Years gone to Trade with the* Caſtillas, *they are now grown ſo great; the ſaid* Sangleyes *having labour'd ſo much there, building Walls, and Houſes, making Gardens, and other Things very Advantageous to the* Caſtillas. *And ſince this is ſo, why had not the* Caſtillas *conſider'd theſe Things, nor been grateful for theſe good Turns, but on the contrary ſo cruelly deſtroy'd ſo many Men? And tho' we, two or three Times, Writ to the King as above, he being Angry for the aforeſaid Things, anſwer'd us, That it was not convenient to take Revenge, nor make War on the People of* Luzon, *for three Reaſons. Firſt, Becauſe the* Caſtillas *have for many Years paſt, been Friends to the* Chineſes. *Secondly, Becauſe it could not be known, whether the Victory would fall to the* Caſtillas, *or the* Chineſes. *Thirdly, and laſtly, Becauſe the People kill'd by the* Caſtillas *were baſe, and ungrateful to their Native Country of* China, *their Parents and Kindred, ſince they had not return'd to* China *in ſo many Years; which People the King ſaid he did not much value, for the aforeſaid Reaſons; and he only order'd the* Viceroy, *the* Eunuch, *and me to Write this Letter by the* Embaſſador: *that the People of* Luzon *may know the King of* China *has a*

great

Margin notes:

Chineſes puniſh'd for Falſhood.

Japoneſes expell'd Corea.

Spaniards charg'd with the Slaughter of the Chineſes.

great Soul is very Patient and Merciful, since he has not order'd War to be made on the Inhabitants of Luzon. *And his Justice will appear, by his causing the Falshood of* Tioneg *to be punish'd. And since the* Spaniards *are a discreet People, how can they not be troubled for having kill'd so many Men; and repent of it, and be kind to the* Chineses *that are left. For if the Castillas bear the* Chineses *good Will, and restore the* Sangleyes *that have remain'd of the War, and pay the Money that is due, and restore the Goods taken from the* Sangleyes, *there will be Amity betwixt this Kingdom, and that, and Trading Ships shall go every Year; otherwise the King will not give Leave for any Ships to trade; but on the contrary will cause* 1000 *Ships of War to be built, with Soldiers, and Kindred of the slain, and with other Nations, and Kingdoms that pay Homage to* China, *and will make War without sparing any Person, and then the Kingdom of* Luzon *shall be given to those People that pay Acknowledgement to* China. The Visitor General's Letter was writ on the 12th of the second Month, which, according to our Reckning, is *March*; the Eunuchs on the 16th, and the Viceroys on the 22d of the same Month and Year.

Manda-rines Threats.

The Governour return'd an Answer to these Letters by the same Messengers, in Terms full of Civility, and Authority. He gave an Account of the Rebellion of the *Sangleyes* from its first Rise; justifying the *Spaniards* for their natural Defence, and the Punishment they had inflicted on the Criminals. He tells them, no State can subsist without punishing the Wicked, or rewarding the Good; and therefore he does not repent that Execution, because it was to suppress those that would have destroy'd us. That the Visitor ought to consider what he would do, in Case the like had happen'd to him in *China*. That the only Thing which troubled him was, that he could not save some *Sangley* Merchants *Anbayes*, who dy'd among the guilty; but that it was not possible to prevent it, because the severity of War will not allow the killing of some, and exempting of others; especially, they not being known by the Soldiers in the Heat of Action. That using Mercy towards those that were taken alive, he condemn'd them to row in the Galleys, the Punishment substituted among the *Castillas* for such as deserve Death. Yet if it should be thought in *China* that it ought to be moderated, they shall be set at Liberty. But let it be consider'd, said *Don Pedro*, that the not punishing of so heinous an Offence, may be the Occasion of their falling into it again, which would exclude all Mercy. The Goods of the *Chineses* that were kill'd are safe laid up, and to show I had no other Motive, but the Execution of Justice, I will order them to be immediately deliver'd to their Heirs, or to such Persons, as they of Right belong to. Nothing but Justice inclines me to any of these Things. Your saying, that unless I release the Prisoners, there will be Leave granted in *China* to the Kindred of the slain in the Rebellion, to come in Arms to *Manila*, does not move me in the least; because I take the *Chineses* to be so wise, that they will not go upon such Undertakings upon a slight Occasion; especially, when no Provocation has been given them on our Side. And in Case they should be of another Mind there, we *Spaniards* are Men that know how to defend our Right, our Religion, and our Territories. Let not the *Chineses* think they are Lords of the World, as they pretend; for we *Castillas*, who have measur'd every Foot of it, very well know the Lands of the *Chineses*; and therefore

The Governours Answer, to the Mandarines.

H h   they

they ought to underſtand, that the King of *Spain* maintains Wars wih Kings as poweiful as theirs, and checks, and gives them much Trouble. Nor is it any Thing new with us, when our Enemies think they have brought us under, to be waſting and deſtroying their Lands, and never give over till we have caſt them out of their Thrones, and wreſted their Scepters out of their Hands. I ſhould be very ſorry the Commerce ſhould be interrupted ; but at the ſame Time, believe the *Chineſes* are not willing to loſe it, ſince it is ſo advantageous to them, for they carry Home our Silver, which never waſtes, in Exchange for their Commodities, which are ſlight Things, ſoon ſpoil'd. It was diſcreetly done, not to admit the *Engliſh* Ships that appear'd upon the Coaſt, for they are not *Spaniards*, but their Enemies, and Pyrates ; for which Reaſon they ſhould have been puniſh'd, had they come to *Manila*. To conclude, for as much as we *Spaniards* always juſtify our Proceedings, and value our ſelves upon the Worlds not being able to ſay, we Uſurp the Right of others, or make War on our Friends, what is here promis'd ſhall be perform'd. And the *Chineſes* may take Notice, for the future, that we never do any Thing out of Fear, or on Account of our Enemies Threats. *Don Pedro* concludes, offering the Continuation of Friendſhip, upon new Aſſurances of Peace, with the Kingdom of *China*, ſaying, he would, at the proper Time, give Liberty to their Priſoners he had in the Galleys; Tho' he deſign'd firſt to make Uſe of them, and did ſo in his Expedition to the *Moluccos*, which he was then preparing for ; and all this was punctually perform'd.

The Emperour of Japan's Letter. He receiv'd other Letters at the ſame Time, from the Emperor of *Japan*, wherein, after returning him Thanks for a Preſent of Wine of Grapes, which *Don Pedro* had ſent him, with other Things of Value, he Encourag'd him to Trade, and deſir'd he would not ſend him any Chriſtian Preachers, without his Conſent. For, ſays he, this Country is call'd *Xincoco*, which ſignifies, *Dedicated to Idols*; which have been honour'd with much Commendation by our Fore-Fathers, whoſe Actions I alone can not reverſe, and therefore it is not convenient that your Law be ſpread abroad, or preach'd in *Japan* ; and if your Lordſhip is willing to entertain Amity with me, and theſe Kingdoms, do as I would have you. So ſays the *Japoneſe*. *Don Pedro* anſwer'd and appeas'd him, ſo that the preaching was continu'd in his Dominions.

Dutch Squadion. This ſame Year 1604, the Provinces of *Holland* and *Zealand*, according to their Cuſtom, fitted out a Squadron of twelve tall Ships, well equipp'd, with ſome ſmaller Veſſels, and, as if they had been Lords of the Winds and of the Seas, ſet Sail for *India*, the known Way, arriving proſperouſly, in a ſhort Time, at the Cape of *Good Hope*. All the Captains had been there before, and the Pilots valu'd themſelves upon no leſs Experience. The Admiral was *Stephen Drage*. Beginning to viſit their Forts, and Factories, in Order to take ſome Prizes, as well as Trade, they met with two ſmall Ships, loaden with Ivory, at the Bar of *Mozambique* They chas'd them, and tho' *Takes two Portugues Ships.* they fled amain, being purſu'd with no leſs Swiftneſs, the *Dutch* Robbers overtook, and after a ſharp Engagement enter'd them. They burnt the one, and mann'd the other, which was a Reinforcement to proſecute their Robberies. All thoſe Kings, and the Commanders of our Forts, receiv'd them as Friends. In *September*, they came to the Bar of *Goa*, and lay 15 Days at *Bardes*, in as much Security as if they had been at *Amſterdam*, expecting

the

the *India* Ships. Thence they fent away a Ship to *Cambaya*, to exchange the Ivory they had not long before robb'd our People of, acting not like Pyrates, but Merchants who difpofe of the Wealth they pick up by Trade, and fucceeded profperoufly in all their Undertakings. They fent two more Ships to *Bengula*, with other Commodities ; all which return'd in due Time confiderably enrich'd. Perceiving that no Power oppos'd them, they failed down the Coaft of *Malabar*, trading wherefoever they thought fit, and took another *Portuguefe* Veffel, call'd a *Foift*, which had 21 Oars ; and after unlading the Booty, they fitted her up their Way, and took her along with them. *And a Foift.*

After this they bent their Thoughts upon greater Matters, to which End they fent an Embaffy to the *Zamori*, which Name imports as much as *Cæfar* among us, and he is King of *Calicut*, a Friend and Confederate with the *Dutch*. Having agreed upon an Interview, they fell to Trade, and whilft the reft attended Commerce, and private Gain, the Admiral confulted about State Affairs, concerting to carry on the War againft the *Spaniards*, and more particularly the *Portuguefes*. They fettled the Time, and the Forces they were to joyn for that Effect. Then they diverted themfelves with Feafting and Treats. At one of which, by way of Farewel, *Zamori* gave Admiral *Drage* an Emeraud, thought to be the largeft and beautifulleft in the World. They went on, and took fome Prizes on the Coaft of *Java*, and among them a fmall Ship, in which were *Don Manuel de Melo*, Commander in Chief of the *Moluccos*, and his Wife, who was oblig'd to fight as well as her Hufband, and yet they could not efcape Captivity. The nearer they drew to *Ternate*, the more confiderable Encounters they had, for in Sight of *Amboyna* they fell in with a Frigat coming from the *Moluccos* to Anchor in that Ifland, which they took, and in her Captain *Antony Machado*, her Commander. They ftay'd at *Amboyna*, hoping to recover what they had loft, either by Treachery, or Force. The Year 1605 had now commenced, and they began their Work on the 23d of *February*. *Zamori fignifies Cæfar.* *Joins with the Dutch.* *They take a Portuguefe Frigat at Amboyna.*

Eight Ships and fix Tenders enter'd the Port, and the Fort was furrender'd to them without much Difficulty, or Oppofition. They alfo poffefs'd themfelves of the *Portuguefe* Colony. Thofe People feeing the *Dutch* fo ftrong in Men and Cannon, durft not, nor could they well oppofe them. Forty *Portuguefes* took an Oath of Fidelity to the Prince of *Orange*'s Baftard Son. They put the Commander in Chief into Irons, and deliver'd the Fort to the *Dutch*, alledging, for an Excufe, that they had not Ammunition to defend themfelves. There was another greater Mifchief, which was, that the Natives favour'd the *Dutch*, as their Deliverers from the *Portuguefe* Yoke; and they are well belov'd there, and in all Places where they Trade, becaufe of late they have taken this Courfe, not to meddle with their Religion, nor fo much as mention it, unlefs, where any will embrace Chriftianity on their own Accord. They neither wrong'd nor diftur'd any Body; and to fhow they would always maintain them in that Security, within five Days, they fitted out 40 *Carcoas*, to defend the Natives againft any Enemy. *Drage takes Amboyna.* *Fits out 40 Carcoas.*

The Admiral pick'd out three of the Ships, and went himfelf with them to the Iflands of *Banda*, to load Nutmeg, Mace, and Clove, there and at *Amboyna*. The Fame of this Succefs, and the Hatred conceiv'd againft the *Spaniards*, were fo favourable to this Nation, that at this Time the People *Indians well affected to the Dutch.*

H h 2 of

of *Amboyna*, *Ito*, *Veranula*, and other Places, had their Embaſſadors at *Sunda?* to expect this Fleet, which came from Home at their Requeſt.   Before they ſet out from *Holland* they had receiv'd Embaſſadors from the King of *Achem* in *Sumatra*, to the ſame End   For this Reaſon the *Dutch* give out, that they come to revenge the Wrongs, the *Portugueſes* and *Spaniards* have done to the Natives, and to reſtore them to their Liberty.   The Deſigns of theſe perfidious People were no longer a Secret; for the Admiral *Drage* re-fitted five of his Ships, and ſent them to the *Moluccos*, to take the Fort and Kingdom of *Tydore*, the only one that continu'd in Subjection to *Spain*; and it was publickly reported, that the King of *Ternate* would forward the Enterprize with his Ships and Men.   The *Dutch* Vice-Admiral ſail'd with theſe Ships ſtopping by the Way to make his Advantage, take in the Refreſh-ments in their Factories, and lade Pepper, and other Spice.   Every Thing

ſucceeded as they could wiſh, tho' they aſpir'd to ſome Matters which re-quir'd a greater Power than they brought.   They intended to paſs by the Streight of *Acapulco*, and there to lie in wait for the Ships belonging to the *Philippines* going and coming, becauſe they knew them to be Rich, and might take them.   To this End they delay'd Time, till they could be joyn'd by the two Ships they expected from *Sunda*, laden with Pepper, from that plentiful, and ſecure Factory of theirs.

Aboard the eight Ships there was great Store of Bricks, Lime, and ſqua-red Stones, Wheele-Barrows, and other Tooles and Materials for Building;

all which was to be carry'd from the aforeſaid Streight. tho' they had al-ready began to build it at *Amboyna*, and landing a conſiderable Part of thoſe Materials, they left there 130 Soldiers, to carry on the Works, and Garri-ſon the Fort.   At the Heels of this Fleet they expected another to lay Siege to *Malaca*; deſigning from thence to Govern *India*, as the *Portugueſes* have done.   In Order to this, they had before confederated with the Kings of *Jor*, *Achem*, and *Sunda*, with whoſe Aſſiſtance, and that of other Native *Sangiacks*, they were to overthrow the Power of *Portugal*, for they were reſolv'd not to quit *India*, and ſince its Commodities enrich'd them, they would pay for the Expence of the War; beſides, that they were already ſo wealthy, that even in *Flanders* the Soldiers deſerted from the Arch-Duke *Albertus*, to ſerve them.   Notwithſtanding this extraordinary Affection,

wherewith the *Dutch* are entertain'd in all thoſe Countries, before they came to *Amboyna*, two *Engliſh* Ships came to an Anchor near by, and ac-quainted the Natives, that a *Dutch* Squadron was coming to poſſeſs itſelf of the Iſland; but bid them not to fear, for it had none but poor ſcoundrel Men; and therefore they ſhould defend themſelves, offering them their Aſſiſtance, and acquainting them that the Crowns of *Spain* and *England* were then in Amity; and therefore the Subjects of them both ought to be ſo of. Courſe.   They ſlighting this favourable Opportunity, choſe rather to be-

come Subjects to Prince *Maurice*, and undergo the *Dutch* Yoke.   The *Engliſh* demanded Clove, and offer'd them their own Price for it, and were ſo juſt, that they never joyn'd with the *Dutch*.   In ſhort, *Amboyna* remain'd in the Enemies Hands.   The People diſpers'd, many of them went to *Malaca*, and among the reſt, the Commander in chief, *Don Emanuel de Melo*, with ſome *Portugueſes*.   Others repair'd to the Iſland of *Cebu*, part of the *Philippines*

and

and other Places, for they had all their Liberty. They all departed *Amboyna* about the middle of *May*, but without their Goods, or Spice, being positively forbid that Trade, the *Dutch* alledging it was all their own.

One of those *English* Ships sailing along those Coasts, and escaping the Ridges of Rocks, got before-hand to the Port of *Tydore*. They call'd the Commander in Chief of the Fort, *Peter Alvarez Abreu*, and inform'd him, that they left the *Dutch* Squadron fortifying the strong Holds at *Amboyna*; and that when they had reduc'd all in those Seas, they would come to fall upon *Tydore*. The Commander in Chief return'd Thanks for that friendly Intelligence; and among other Civilities that pass'd between them, desir'd to know the Motive that induc'd them to show such Kindness. Then the *English* told him, That their Kings were Friends, and to convince him of it, and the Danger he was in, offer'd him as much Ammunition as he stood in need of. They gave him Six Barrels of Powder, 100 Cannon Balls, and a Number of Head-Pieces. This made the *Tydores* and *Portuguefes* begin to fortify themselves, and was the Product of the late Peace. They give the Intelligence of the Dutch at Tydore.

A Month after, four great *Dutch* Ships, and four Tenders, came to the Island, where two of the King's Galleons lay at Anchor, with the *Portuguefe* Ships laden with Goods and Provisions. The *Dutch* Admiral sent the King of *Tydore* Word, That if he would deliver him that Fort, and expell the *Portuguefes*, he would be his Friend; and desiring he would not start any Difficulties, since he might easily do it, being a peaceable King in his own Dominions; besides that, they had Men and Strength enough aboard that Squadron, to force them to consent to what they now courteously demanded. The King of *Tydore* sent him a Cow, and answer'd, That he neither could, nor ought to put the *Portuguefes* out of their Forts, nor to admit of any other Nation in their Place, till they had either voluntarily, or by Force of Arms, abandon'd their Poffeffion. That whilst they two decided the Quarrel, he would look on as Neuter. The *Portuguefe* Commander in Chief, understanding what Messages pass'd, interrupted them, sending to let the *Dutch* Men know. That it was in vain to talk of surrendring the Fort, whilst he was alive, and present. That he was to treat with him, and the marry'd Men that liv'd in it about that Affair. Four Dutch Ships at Tydore. Their Message to the King. His Answers. Bravery of the Portuguefe Commander.

Being come to this Refolution, the next Morning the *Dutch* Ships remov'd, and went to board the *Portuguefes* that were at *Tydore*, two Cannon Shot from the Fort. They fought above two Hours, and so constant was Fortune to one Side, that in so short a Time, the *Portuguefes* that remain'd alive were fain to throw themselves into the Sea, and their Galleons were taken, one of which they immediately burnt. The next Day another Message was sent to *Tydore*, wherein the *Dutch* directed the King to propose the surrendring of the Fort to the *Portuguefes*, and he would give them the Galleon he had spar'd, to carry them and their Effects, wheresoever they should think fit. The *Portuguefes* taking Courage, where others would be dismay'd, answer'd, That the Loss of the Galleons had not daunted them; for they would rather dye all of them, than deliver up the Fort. The *Dutch* durst not batter it alone, but resolv'd to joyn the King of *Ternate*, who was already set out with abundance of *Carcoas* to that Effect. They met him a League from the Fort, and spending little Time Dutch take two Galleons. Bold Answer of the Portuguefes. Dutch and Ternates joyn and burn a Town.

Time in Ceremonies return'd together, burning a Town of *Tydore* by the Way, came the next Morning before the Fort.

They landed 800 *Dutch* and *Ternate* Soldiers, and having made a Trench with Barrels fill'd with Earth, batter'd the Fort for three Days from that Work, with two Pieces of Cannon. At the same Time they play'd upon it from their Ships, firing above 1500 Shot. The third Day they drew nearer; and the fourth in the Morning began to batter more furiously. They kill'd the Constable of the Castle, and in the midst of the Confusion, the King of *Ternate* and the *Dutch*, that were ashore, advanc'd, drawing the Cannon under the very Fort, having surpriz'd the *Portuguese*, and falling on them unexpectedly. They soon recovering themselves, attack'd the *Dutch* afresh, who turning their Backs, behav'd themselves so basely, that they ran into the Water; abandoning the Guns they had ashore. In the Height of this Success, many *Dutch* being slain, and only four *Portuguese*, on a sudden they spy'd all the Fort in a Flame, which roar'd from the Ground to the Tops of the Houses, till a considerable Part was blown up, and almost all the rest consum'd, and lay'd flat. Six and twenty *Portuguese* were burnt, and it could never be discover'd or guess'd, how, or which Way the Powder was set a fire, to cause that mighty Destruction. The *Portuguese*, who just before were joyful for their Victory, having no Walls to shelter them, were forc'd to retire to the City of *Tydore*, and the *Dutch* and *Ternates* rallying, pursu'd them thither. The King receiv'd them in friendly Manner, and he himself went the same Day aboard the *Dutch* Ship that lay at Anchor before it, and calling the *Dutch* Admiral, propos'd to him the Affair of the Fort, and that if those who defended it had Ships allow'd them, they would go away to other Parts. He agreed to it, and though it cost the *Portuguese* all they had, they accepted of three small Tenders, a Galliot that had been the King's, and a *Dutch* Tender to secure them against the *Ternates*. The *Dutch* settled Amity with the King of *Tydore*; that they should continue in his Dominions; and erect Factories, and Trade for *Clove*, as the *Portuguese* had done. Thus the Conquer'd having bought some Ships dispers'd themselves about those Islands. Many of them went to the *Philippines*, where Don *Pedro*, the Governour, examin'd them, in order to get Information concerning the *Moluccos*.

Antony de Silva, a *Portuguese*, was one of them that escap'd from the Fort of *Ternate*, and came to the Town of *Arevalo* in the *Philippines*. Besides being a Soldier, he was also a *Naguatato*, or Interpreter. This Man gave an Authentick Relation of that Affair, and added, That being brought Prisoner from *Amboyna*, the *Dutch* Admiral having a Sea-Chart before him, look'd for *Mindoro*, *Manila*, and for *Cabite*; and being ask'd by *Silva*, why he look'd for it, was inform'd, That his Design was, in Case he did not succeed at the *Moluccos*, to try to take some of the Ships that trade betwixt *New Spain*, and the *Philippines*. *Silva* reply'd, That he had not Time to meet either; because those that come to the *Philippines* arrive about the 10th of *May*, and the others set out on the 10th of *June*. However that was the Design of the *Dutch* Admiral, who intended to get Intelligence at *Mindoro*, thence to sail to *Macao*, send an Embassador into *China*, and revenge the Wrong Don *Pablos de Portugal* had done them

The marginal notes read:

Batter the Fort and are repuls'd.

The Fort burnt.

Tydore taken by the Dutch.

Dutch defign to take the Ships of the Philippines.

Silva gives Intelligence of it.

them in those Countries. Then to load Pepper at *Patane*; next at the Streight of *Sincapura*, to endeavour to take the *Chinese* Ships that resort to *Milaca*; and whatever happen'd, to hold on his Voyage to *Holland* that Way, loaden with Treasure. All this the *Dutch* Admiral communicated to *Antony de Silva*, as to one that was to go with him into *Holland*, because he was a Soldier, and able Interpreter in both Languages; and therefore *Stephen Drage* made much of him. This Intelligence was confirm'd by some others, who had fought and escap'd the Slaughter at *Tydore*. *Don Pedro* hearing so much, was concern'd, as a Man zealous for the Church, and for his King; and it griev'd him to consider, that the Crown of *Spain* had not a Foot of Land left it in the *Moluccos*; and that a Rebel was in quiet Possession of them all.

All the Moluccos lost to Spain.

Prosperity having embolden'd, and strengthen'd the *Dutch*, *Don Pedro* assembling his Council of War, order'd that the Captains *Antony Freyle*, Commander of the Squadron belonging to the *Pintados*, *Peter Sevil*, *Stephen de Alcazar*, and *Bernardine Alfonso*, should repair to the Forts of the *Pintados*, and other Islands that were in Danger, with their Companies. He refitted the Ships, and prepar'd his Cannon, as being so near a victorious Enemy, who so successfully put in Execution all their Threats. *Antony de Sylva* show'd an Original Letter, written by another *Dutch* Admiral at the Island of *Borneo*, to the King of *Ternate*, and sent by *Philip Bissegop*, Captain of a Ship, with a Present of a Quantity of fine *Holland*; Six Bales of several Vessels with Musk; Twelve Bottles of Rose-Water; Six Pounds of Dutch *Anfion*, that is, Opium, which, as has been said, disturbs the Senses, and is us'd by those People to encourage them to fight, and six Barrels of Powder. He gave him an Account of *Andrew Furtado's* unfortunate Voyage, the Obstacles, Storms, and Enemies he had met with, since his Departure from *Ternate*, till he came to *Malaca*. He gave him the Title of Most Serene Prince, and Potent King of the *Moluccos*, *Bandas*, *Amboyna*, and innumerable other Islands. He congratulated with him for the Event of his Arrival at the *Moluccos*; promising he would return to *Ternate* with a greater Power, he expected from *Holland*, and take Possession of the Forts, to extirpate the common Enemy, the King of *Spain*; and encourag'd him with these Hopes, to hold out till then. He assur'd him, that he should scour all those Seas from the *Moluccos*, and extend his Dominions as far as *China*, without being hinder'd by the *Philippines* or *Japoneses*. To this End, he desired him to renew his Friendship with *Mindanao*, and to acquaint the King of those Islands, that he was a Friend to the *Dutch*, so to give them Admittance to those Ports, Freedom of Trade, and amicable Entertainment, as was requisite for their Undertakings; this being a Thing most Expedient, above all other Politick Considerations. He added, he might observe, and be assur'd, that nothing was so little regarded in *Spain*, as to contrive that their many Provinces should preserve some Sort of Union. That therefore all those which are very remote, and subject to that Crown, ought to take much Notice of the great Delays there, in coming to a Resolution, and sending Succours from *Spain*; because before they believe, or examine the News brought them in order to believe them, Affairs have taken a new Turn, and consequently neither the *Spanish* Councils, nor their Arms come seasonably. That Experience had

Don Pedro's Precautions.

Dutch Letters and Present to the King of Ternate.

had made most of these Things known to his Highness, and his Zeal for his Service oblig'd him to mention them. *Antony de Silva*, added, that he was very sure the King of *Ternate* had not omitted doing any Thing of what the *Dutch* Man recommended to him ; and that he had already propos'd to his People to go abroad to fight, far from their own Islands. Tho' it was never apprehended he would do so, yet at that Time it much troubled *Don Pedro*, because he was so spent with the Affair of the *Sangleyes*, the Want of whom he labour'd so to supply, that no such Mischief might happen again, it being so necessary to support the Trade of the *Philippines* another Way, and procure safety at Home in Order to make War, and keep up a Reputation.

Time, which sometimes gives Hope, and sometimes Despair, comforted *Don Pedro* in his Affliction, bringing in a few Months after some Ships of private Persons from *New Spain*, and then in due Season the usual Fleet.

Men, Money, &c came at Manila from New Spain.

They arriv'd at *Manila*, on the Eve of *S. Matthias*, and in them the *Spaniards* sent from *Spain*, for the Expedition of *Ternate*, with above 200 more from the Marquess *de Montesclaros*, Viceroy of *New Spain*, as also the other Necessaries, and Money, pursuant to the King's Order. Part of this came committed to Brother *Gaspar Gomez*, who was receiv'd with incredible Joy. He deliver'd all his Letters to the Governour, and immediate Care was taken to quarter the Officers and Soldiers, and to distribute them speedily, so that all Men might believe there was no other Design in their coming, but the Security of the *Philippine* Islands, threatned by the Emperor of *Japan*, and the Conspiracies of the *Sangleyes*. This Report was industriously so given out, that it might fly and spread abroad without the Kingdom, left they might receive any Intelligence, who had

Management of the Governeur.

cause to fear. Besides that, as the Fame of those great Preparations was Advantageous to the *Spaniards* in Point of Reputation, so the Reality of the Power they had, added to the Opinion conceiv'd, prov'd the Defence and Security of them all. In *Japan*, only the News that *Manila* was full of Men, and Ships of War, allay'd, or quite banish'd the Disgust of that King, on Account of *Don Pedro*'s refusing him Ship-Wrights. The People of *Chincheo* also forbore meditating Revenge against an Enemy, whose Victories were back'd with such Succours. *Don Pedro* consider'd all these Particulars, and each of them made him conclude, that he might with Safety be absent for some Time from *Manila*. However the King of *Ternate* overjoy'd that he had shaken off the *Spanish* Yoke, made little Account of all that was told him, concerning its Neighbouring Kingdoms, believing they would never recover their Ancient Possessions. The *Dutch* Commanders, who were rebuilding the burnt Fort at *Tydore*, sent him a considerable Number of heavy Brass Cannon, of *Drakes*, and Muskets, and he hired some of the Ingeniers, that came in those Ships, to look to his Fortifications, and reside in them, and in his City. Some accepted of the Habitation, approving of that disorderly, and irreligious Liberty of Life allow'd in that Country ; where considering the frequent Resort of Ships from the North, and the many Factories, they reckon'd themselves as good as at Home, since they could often meet with their Kindred or Friends, or at least with their Country-Men. Banish'd *Spaniards* and *Portuguese* arriv'd daily at the Port of *Oton*, in the *Philippine* Islands, and
among

among them *Paul de Lima*, a Perfon of great Experience, and ftill General of the Artillery at *Tydore*, who, befides the News of the late Deftruction, brought an Account of the Joy wherewith the *Dutch* dug up the Guns he endeavour'd to hide, and how much they were increafed in Strength and Shipping. He was receiv'd with much Honour, in regard to his Quality, and becaufe he was one of thofe who had loft Lands and Goods, taken from him by the King of *Ternate*, and his Information, and Counfel were of Ufe for what afterwards happen'd. All Men attended the Warlike Preparations, in their feveral Stations, but with equal Zeal; building Ships, and gathering Provifions, Arms, and Ammunitions; and *Don Pedro* himfelf was fo diligent and vigilant, that he attended the meaneft Employments, giving an Example, and encouraging; fo that it may be faid, he did every Thing, for he ply'd all Hands.

The End of the Ninth Book.

I i   T H E

THE
HISTORY
OF THE
DISCOVERY and CONQUEST
OF THE
Molucco and *Philippine* Iſlands, &c.

BOOK. X.

Want of Political Reflections whence.

THERE is generally ſome Moral Inſtruction, which lies couch'd under the Actions of Men, and which Judicious Wri-ters uſe to point at in the Relation of Events, as the Advan-tage of Hiſtory ; but what civil Rules, or Precepts for the forming of the Political Life, can we lay down, in writing the Conqueſt and Defence of Barbarous Countries, which all depends on Voy-ages, and reducing of Garriſons; notwithſtanding State Craft has ſome-what inform'd thoſe Nations? Or what can occur in this Subject, which the Reader may not infer, as a neceſſary Conſequence of the foregoing Diſcourſe? Since then the Matter in Hand does not afford us ſuch Re-flection, let us draw to a Concluſion, in Purſuance of our Promiſe made at the Beginning.

Yloilo Poit the Ren-dezvous of the Navy.

Don Pedro de Acunna, now Captain General of the Fleet that was aſſem-bled in the *Philippine* Iſlands, at the ſame time took Care to ſee it fitted out with Expedition, and to provide for the Security of the Province he was to forſake, that he might go upon that ſo difficult Undertaking. Some there were, who look'd upon it as Part of *Don Pedro's* good Fortune, that the *Molucco* Iſlands had been utterly loſt, that ſince he had the more Mat-ter to work upon, his Victory might be the more glorious. He moſt in-duſtriouſly provided all Things requiſite for the Uſe of War ; and even for all the Accidents it might be liable to. The Point, or Promontory of *Iloilo* runs out into the Sea, not far from *Arevalo,* in the Iſland of *Panay,*

forming

forming a Harbour proper and capacious enough to be the Place of Arms, for the Preparations then in Hand. Here the Fleet rendezvous'd, confifting of Six Tall Ships, Six Galleys, Three Galliots, like thofe they call *Galizabras*, belonging to the Crown of *Portugal*; in one of which was *Peter Alvarez de Abreu*, Commander in Chief of the Fort of *Tydore*; the other two, under the Command of *John Rodriguez Camelo*, Commodore, fent from *Malaca*, by the General *Andrew Furtado de Mendoza*, to be aiding with his Courage and Conduct, and to carry him an Account of the Succefs. One flat bottom'd Galliot, to land the Artillery, and in it 300 Bafkets of Rice. Four Foifts built purpofely for carrying of Provifions. Two *Champanes* of Ten Tun Burden each, with 1600 Bafkets of clean Rice. Two *Dutch* Long-Boats, which carry'd over the *Portuguefes* when the Fort of *Tydore* was loft. Seven Frigats belonging to the King, and Seven more to private Perfons, and the like Number of *Champanes*, in all 36 Sail. *Particulars of the Fleet.*

Colonel *John de Efquivel* brought 12 Companies of *Spanifh* Foot, four whereof were rais'd in *Andaluzia*, being his own, and thofe of the Captains, *Paul Garrucho, Peter Sevil*, and *Luke de Vergara Gavira*. Six came from *New Spain*, under the Captains *Don Roderick de Mendoza*, Son to *Don John de Baeza y Caftilla*, and to *Donna Maria de Mendoza*, and by her Grandfon to the Marquefs *de Montefclaros*, and therefore, out of Refpect to his Kinfman, the Viceroy of *New Spain*, he came out of *Italy* to ferve his Majefty in the *Philippine* Iflands; the others were Captain *Pafcual de Alarcon Pacheco, Martin de Efquivel, Bernardine Alfonfo, Peter Delgado*, and *Stephen de Alcazar*. Two other Companies commanded by the Captains *John Guerra de Cervantes*, and *Chriftopher de Villagra*, belong'd to the Forces of *Manila*, and the Province of the *Pintados*. All which, with their Officers, make up 1423 *Spaniards*. Under the Colonel *Don Guillermo*, and the Captains *Don Francis Palaot, Don John Lit, Don Lewis* and *Auguftin Lout*, 344 *Pampangua*, and *Tagalo* Indians; befides 620 others of the fame Nations, for the Sea and Land Service, and 649 Rowers. All the Men in the Fleet, befides the General's Houfehold and Family, amounted to 3095; with 75 Pieces of Cannon of all Sorts, and all other Perquifites for Sea, Landing, Fight, and Battery. *The Land Forces.* *1423 Spaniards.*

Don Pedro fail'd from the Port of *Yloilo*, with all thefe Preparations, on the 15th of *January*, 1606, the Weather being unfettled, but he as refolute as at other Times. He arriv'd at the Ifland *Mindanao*, then in Enmity with the *Spaniards*, and in Confederacy with the *Ternates*, and came to an Anchor in the Port of *Caldera*, to water, where the Admiral's Ship, in which the Colonel *Efquivel* was, began to drag her Anchors, and was forc'd to fet her Sails to get off; but perceiving fhe could not, by fo doing, weather a Point, fhe fired two Guns, in Token of Diftrefs, at the Time when her Rudder ftruck. The Galleys made up to tow her off, and broke fome Ropes to no Purpofe, the Sea and Wind being againft them. Captain *Villagra* was entrufted to fave the Men and Provifions that were aboard; and he, tho' a confiderable Part belonging to the King and private Men was loft, with incredible Induftry fav'd the moft of them, and the Goods, as alfo all the Men, Cannon, Powder, Cables, Rigging, and Sails; and that the People of *Mindanao* might not reap the Benefit of the Wreck, he *The Fleet fails from Yloilo.* *Caldera Port.* *Admiral Ship loft.*

fer

set Fire to the Vessel, after taking out all the Iron Work. This Accident was much lamented, both for its own Consequence, and because the Men, who are often vainly Superstitious, put an ill Construction upon it; but the General's Wisdom made amends for all.

They sail from Caldera. From the Port of *Caldera*, the General order'd the Colonel to sail over to that of *Talangame*, which, as has been said, is in the Island of *Ternate*; and bore him Company himself, with the Galleys, till he was out of the Streight of *Sabuanga*, which is dangerous by Reason of the Currents, and Ridges of Rocks, wherefore they tow'd the Ships, till they were out of Danger, as also because they were becalm'd. The Fleet stood out to Sea; the Galleys coasted along slowly to take in Water enough to last them to *Ternate*, the Men that had been sav'd from abroad the Admiral being distributed among them, and the other Vessels, so that their Burden and Labour was increased. The ablest Pilots in those Seas, had Charge of the Galleys, and yet notwithstanding all their Care, and that of the Captains and expert Mariners, they mistook their Course, and fell in among the Islands of *Celebes*, otherwise call'd of *Matao*, above 60 Leagues to the Leeward of *Ternate*. The Wind was contrary, and the Error was to be retriev'd by rowing. With very much Labour they reach'd *Ternate*, on the 26th of *March*, being *Easter-Day* That Day so joyful to all Mankind, made them forget past Toils, and convert them into Pleasure and Delight.

Through Mistake fall in with Celebes.

Arrive at Ternate.

Superstition of Moluccos as to Eclipses. They were inform'd, that the Day before, an Eclipse of the Moon had been observ'd at *Ternate*, with the usual Concern. No sooner does the Darkness begin to cover the Body of the Moon, than the People with Sighs and Tears begin also to lament that Planet's Mourning; for they believe it forebodes the Death or Captivity of their King, or of some eminent Person, or some Calamity to the Publick. If the Eclipse passes over without any of these Losses, they Repair to their *Mosque* in Procession, Rank and File. Here the foremost carry large *China* Dishes. Those are follow'd by others with Launces, and Hatchets advanc'd, and Muskets rested. Next them follow three Lamps, carry'd on Men's Shoulders, as common Pictures represent the great Bunch of Grapes carry'd by the Discoverers, who went to view the Holy Land promis'd by God to his People. Next comes a Boy, in Royal Robes, and behind him another holding an Umbrello, made of various Feathers, over the Head of the first. Then follow the Women, set off with Flowers and Palm-Branches, without Order; and thus they celebrate their Thanksgiving, in the Streets and Temples, because the Eclipse pass'd over without any Detriment. The *Dutch* told them, That Eclipses were commonly known in their Country, and throughout all *Europe*; which those People either admir'd or did not believe.

Dutch Ship at Talangame. When our Galleys came to the Port of *Talangame*, Don *Pedro* expected to have found the Colonel with the Fleet in it; but only saw a stately *Dutch* Ship, carrying 30 Pieces of Cannon, and 12 Pedreroes. She fought our Ships as they pass'd by, and then drew to the Shore, and defended herself with Part of the Artillery, that was fittest for the Purpose, and being guarded by a great Number of *Ternate* Soldiers, kept close in her Fortification. Don *Pedro* took a View of her, as he pass'd by in the Galleys, tho' she made several Shot at him, and threw 18 Pound Balls into the Admiralmiral Galley, where he was. He thought fit not to ſtay, till he heard of the Fleet which was then at *Tydore*, little above two Leagues from that Port, as was known by ſome Veſſels of the Natives, that came up board and board, in ſailing by that Harbour. The Galleys directed their Courſe to *Tydore*, led by the Joy of this good News, which eas'd *Don Pedro* of much Care he was in, knowing there was a Scarcity of Seamen aboard the Fleet, and he fear'd it might have been drove away elſewhere.

Eſquivel found four *Dutch* Men at *Tydore*. One of them was the Factor who gather'd the Clove for a Company of his Countrymen, that belong'd to the Factories of *Ternate*, *Amboyna*, *Banda*, *Sunda*, and other Places about them ; the other three were Sailers. He examin'd all four, and they gave an Account of the Strength of that Ship, and her Guns, ſaying, She was loden with Clove; and one of the five that fought the *Portugueſes*, when the Fort of *Ternate* blew up. That they expected another Ship, which came with her from *Bantam*, and was parted in foul Weather. That the main Drift of the Agreement made between the King of *Ternate* and the *Dutch*, was their Aſſiſting him againſt the *Spaniards*, and *Portugueſes*. That there were Orders at *Java* and *Sunda* for the *Dutch* Ships which paſs'd by to enquire there, whether there were any News from the *Moluccos*; and if Need were, that they ſhould leave their Loding there, and go ſuccour the King of *Ternate*. Dutch Men at Tydore.

Intelligence they give.

Before *Don Pedro* departed *Talangame*, he conſulted with his Officers, whether it were convenient to attack the *Dutch* Ship before they went upon the Enterprize of *Ternate*. Opinions varied, but it was concluded, that ſince his Majeſties Deſign was to recover the *Maluccos*, and he had order'd the Fleet to be provided for that Intent, it was not expedient to prefer any other Action. Time is ſubject to change, and ſometimes an Accident overthrows the beſt concerted Deſigns. That great Ship, ſo well ſtor'd with Guns, and Mann'd, might have ſunk ſome of ours, by which we ſhould have loſt our Cannon, and Proviſions, or ſome other Miſchief, that could not poſſibly be foreſeen might have happen'd, to the obſtructing of the main Deſign. Beſides that the *Ternates* being their Friends, in Caſe we had maſter'd the Ship, the Men might fly and ſave themſelves among their Confederates, and thus the Enterprize be rendered more difficult by their Aſſiſtance; and it was known by Spyes, that the King already had *Dutch* Gunners, and Soldiers of Courage and Conduct. Ternate to be attack'd before the Dutch Ship.

The King was not at *Tydore* when our Fleet came into his Harbour, being gone to marry a Daughter of the King of *Bachian* ; and tho' the Colonel ſent to acquaint him with his Arrival, and to deſire he would haſten his Coming, as fearing Delays; yet perceiving the Time ſlipt away, he ſet out on the laſt of *March* for *Ternate*, with his Fleet. When they were at Sea, they heard the new marryed King's Bagpipes, Baſons, Trumpets, and Kettle-Drums. He having receiv'd the *Spaniards* Letters, imbark'd, bringing the New Queen along with him, and joyn'd them with his *Caicoas* full of Muſick, and Garlands of Flowers. They met with extraordinary Joy, and the King of *Tydore* expreſs'd it particularly for ſeeing of *Don Pedro de Accunna*, with whom he had before frequent Communication by Letters and Meſſengers He ſhow'd much Concern for the Streights he had been reduc'd to by the King of *Ternate*, with the Aſſiſtance of the *Dutch*. *Don Pedro* King of Tydore and Don Pedro meet at Sea.

Pedro comforted him, declaring his Majesty's Intention, and how he had order'd him to come to his Assistance, from the *Philippine* Islands, whensoever he should require it.   He visited the Bride, paying her all possible Respect; and the King of *Tydore*, telling him, he would attend the Fleet in Person, with his Ships and Men, went away then to his Island, and the next

Orders for the Enterprize.

Morning, at Break of Day, according to his Promise, came into a Bay near *Ternate*, where our Fleet had anchor'd.   The Rejoycings for his coming did not delay the Consultations, and Orders for the Enterprize.   The Governour call'd a Council of War, where it was resolv'd, that all the Strength of the Fleet should be reduc'd to only three great Ships, to secure the Sea and Land.   They were immediately sufficiently mann'd with Sea-Men and Soldiers, under the Command of *Bernardine Alfonso, Antony Carreuno de Valdes*, and *Don Gil Sanchez de Carranza*, all three Commanders of Repute.   Other Orders were issu'd out, and presently put in Execution by the Officers.   Of the three above nam'd, two dy'd in their Return Home, and only *Carreno* out liv'd it.

The Forces land April *the first.*

Don Pedro, and the King of *Tydore* landed their Men, on the first of *April*, at Break of Day, but it being difficult, and even dangerous to march so near the Water, because there was no more ground on the Shore than for five Men in Rank; it was resolv'd to make the Attack with a small Number, gradually along the Sea Coast, without ingaging too far; and at the same Time to make Way over the Top of the Mountain, with some *Pampanguo*, and *Tangalo Indian* Pioneers, and to send another Party of Men that Way, to give the Enemy a Diversion, and oblige them to divide their Forces.   The King of *Ternate*, whom Experience and Fear had instructed in

K. of Ternate retires to his Fort.

the Art of War, perceiving what was aim'd at, to avoid being cut off in the Rear, retir'd to his Fort, as soon as he discover'd our Army.   This was the Reason why our Men met with no Opposition, whereas the General *Furtado* found so much Resistance there, three Years before, at the Seige we have spoken of, when in gaining that Pass, he lost some *Portugueses* and *Spaniards*, being assisted by Captain *Gallinato*.

Gallinato invests the Place.

He now put our Men into good Order, leading the Van, and drew up within Musket Shot of the Wall.   He told *Don Pedro*, in the Presence of the King of *Tydore*, that some Soldiers had, by his Command, taken a View of the Place, and that considering the Nature of the Situation, it was requisite to maintain that Ground till Night, when our Men should intrench, and bring up the Cannon for Battery.   His Advice was approv'd of, and put in Execution; and in Regard that the Enemy did some Harm in the main Body, and Wings, with their Cannon and small Shot; *Don Pedro* to prevent it, order'd the Men to lye down.   It was observ'd that there were

Sentinels on Trees beaten off.

four Eminences cover'd with wild, and full headed Trees, on which the Enemy had their Sentinels, who gave Intelligence how the *Spaniards* mov'd, and of whatsoever they order'd, or perform'd.   A Captain went up to make himself Master of the Trees, and soon brought down the Enemies Sentinels. *Gallinato* perfected that Work, commanding our Sentinels to get up into those same Trees, as was done.   The Enemy endeavour'd to remove them with their Cannon and small Arms, firing incessantly; but could never disturb either those that were on the Top, among the Boughs, who gave the Information, nor the others that stood at the Foot, who receiv'd and carry-

ed

ed it to the Officers. The Enemy was poffefs'd of a Poft near the Baftion of *Cachil Tulo*, on the right Hand of the Wall, a little beyond the Trees, and the General thinking it neceffary to be gain'd, commanded Captain *John de Cubas*, an old Low-Country Soldier, to attack it with 30 Musketiers, and if he thought himfelf too hard fet, to fend Word, and he fhould have a good Supply of Pikes. The Captain went on by the Way of the Mountain, and the Enemy to prevent him, fent a Body of Men out of the Fort next the Sea, whom Captain *Villagra* charg'd. Whilft they were ingag'd, the King of *Ternate*, perceiv'd that *Cubas* was marching to gain his Poft, and being fenfible how prejudicial the Lofs of it would be, fally'd out himfelf to fight him, and the *Spaniards* had enough to do. *Cubas* gain'd the higheft Ridge ; but fo fatigued, that he was forc'd to fend for the Supply of Pikes. The Captains *Vergara*, *Alarcon*, and *Don Roderick de Mendoza* fupported him with 40 detatch'd Men ; and before they came up more *Ternates* and *Javanefes* fally'd out of the Fort, with whom the Fight was renew'd in more furious Manner. Another Party of Infidels was prefently difcover'd next the Sea, for which Reafon, and becaufe, if the Enemy had demanded more Succours, his Pofts would be forfaken, the King order'd thofe who fought with *Villagra* to retire, and went himfelf with them, and fome others to fuftain the Reft. His coming on like a brave, or rather a defperate Commander, oblig'd *Cubas*, to ask for another Supply which the Captains *Villagra*, and *Cervantes* carry'd him, and charg'd the Enemy. *Cachil Amuxa*, of whofe Bravery Mention has been made, went up to Captain *Cubas* after burning the Brims of his Hat, and the Feather in it, with a Musket Shot, and they both fought Hand to Hand for a confiderable Time, the one with his Sword, and the other with his *Campilane*, or Cymiter. The Sentinels on the Trees cry'd out, giving Notice of the Troops on the Shore, and that they came on towards our Van-Guard, and the Front of it. Captain *Villagra* was order'd to charge them with a Divifion of Shot, belonging to Captain *Cervantes*, who commanded all the Halbardiers. Both Parties fought with equal Tokens of Courage, when the Sentinels from the Trees gave Notice, that *John de Cubas*, on the Right, demanded more Succours. The Captains *Don Roderick de Mendoza*, and *Pafcual de Alarcon* went with it immediately, drawing out two Divifions of Musketiers. The Sentinels cry'd out again, that the Enemy, who fought with Captain *Villagra* were retiring towards the Walls, and that *John de Cubas* demanded another Supply of Pikes and Halbards. Captain *Cervantes* fupported him with 50, and *Villagra*, with the Men he commanded.

> *Villagra and* Cubas *fight the* Ternates.

> *The Fight re-doubl'd.*

> *Single Combat.*

Our Sentinels, to whofe Vigilancy a great Part of this Succefs is owing, gave Notice again, that upon the Approach of our Supplies, the Enemy retired in Diforder, and our Men made up to the Wall. The Event of the Battel began now to be out of Doubt, and even in that Pofture requir'd Diverfity of Conduct. *Don Pedro* therefore order'd the Colours with the Reft of the Pikes to march, leaving one Divifion of Mufquetiers, and the Heavy Harquebuffiers in the Rear, to face the Enemy, in Cafe they fhould happen to fally out again toward the Sea. The other Captains and Soldiers went on fighting, and at the fet Time attack'd the Wall, helping one another to climb to the Top. The two firft that got upon it were the Captains *John de Cubas*, and *Cervantes*, who having receiv'd fome Wounds on it, tumbled

> *Ternates retire in Diforder.*

down

down again The Difficulty of this Enterprize increas'd as the Enemy renew'd their Efforts, doing us Harm with their heavy and small Cannon, Muskets, sundry Sort of Fireworks, Stones, and other Contrivances the *Dutch* furnish'd them with; but the Attack was made so furiously, that the *Spaniards* gave not the King, nor his Men Leisure enough to get into the old *Portuguese* Fort, within the Wall; for had they done so, they might have defended themselves some Time, and our Men would have been oblig'd to batter the Walls with Cannon; and tho' the Fort is small, and built in more unskilful Times, it would have cost Trouble.

The Place taken, and Number of the Slain. The Place was taken with little Loss, for we had but Fifteen Men kill'd on our Side, among them was Captain *Cervantes*, who getting up the first upon the Wall, with a Design to display the King's Standard on it, was run into the Eye with a Launce, by a Barbarian, and others coming on, they threw him down to the Ground, whereof he dy'd the seventh Day, much regretted by all Men. He had before said publickly, offering to give the Charge, *Gentlemen, the Bull shall not make his Escape my Way, unless it cost me my Life*; alluding to keeping of him in at the Bull-Feasts. He was as good as his Word both ways, since he dy'd in Performance of it, with his Arms and Legs broken. No Man of any Note, either among the *Spaniards* or *Indians* escap'd unhurt. Many *Ternates* and *Javaneses* were slain, and some *Dutch* shed their Blood, like brave or desperate Men, thinking it a Misfortune, as they said, to owe their Lives to our Courtesy, or Mercy.

Cannon found in it. It was never expected that the Success, would be in all Points answerable to the Justice of the Cause. *Don Pedro* had design'd to batter the Forts, wherein he would have met with mighty Difficulties, because the Cannon was very heavy, and hard to be drawn to the proper Posts for Battery; as also for that there was not Earth to fill the Gabions, and the Rockiness of the Ground obstructed the throwing up of the Trenches, which would have occasion'd the Loss of many Men before the Artillery could be planted. The *Spaniards* pursu'd their Success, and possessing themselves of the Fort, found in it 43 large Brass Guns, abundance of Drakes, and other Arms, besides Ammunition and Provisions.

Prisoners made Slaves. The Men having enter'd the City, every one fell to plunder, and commit Outrages. *Don Pedro* had made Proclamation, that all the Enemies taken within four Days should be made Slaves. The Commanders halted near the ancient Church of S. *Paul*, which was fortify'd by the Enemy with Ramparts for this Service. Opinions vary'd about what was next to be done; Some were for securing what was already gain'd; Others for pushing on, to gain the main Fort. The Captains *Vergara* and *Villagra*, were for the Latter, and the Soldiers were so brisk and eager to run into any Danger, that one of them, of the Province of *Estremadura*, and be-

Eagerness of the Men.

They attack and take the main Fort. longing to the Company of Captain *Sevil*, an *Aragonian*, and notable Commander, who was also for going on, took up Captain *Villagra* in his Arms, and carry'd him above ten Paces, saying, *Good Captain, fall on, fall on*; and then set him down. The Captain struck him, for having taken him up so rudely, at such a Time; and the Soldier bowing, pleasantly and with a smiling Countenance, said to him, *God is my Life, strike again, and fall on.* In short, *Vergara* and *Villagra*, with a few Men attack'd

tack'd the main Fort, and carry'd it, being themfelves the firft that enter'd *They at-*
the Gates, but not the firft that went up ; for as they were running up the *tack and*
Stairs haftily, and juft going into the Hall, *Barela,* and old Soldier, and *take the*
Corporal to Captain *Cervantes,* thruft by their Side, and getting in, took a *main Fort.*
gilt Ewre, made in the Shape of an Urn, curioufly ingrav'd, from off a
rich Cupboard, or Side-board there was in the Hall, faying to the Captains, *Gentlemen, I take this in Token that I came in here with you* ; and *The King's*
carry'd it away, by their Confent. All the Palace was then expos'd to the *Palace*
Avarice of the Soldiers. *Don Pedro* would have given a check to it ; but *plunder'd.*
was not taken Notice of, till almoft all was over.

The King of *Ternate* had forfaken all, and fome of the *Dutch* him, when *The King*
they faw he was going down ; none follow'd him in this Confufion and *&c. fly, to*
Flight, but the *Sangiack* of *Mofaquia,* his Kinfman, who encourag'd and *Gilolo.*
advis'd him, his Queen *Celicaya,* and fome other Women. He embark'd
with them all, Prince *Gariolano* his Son, and a few *Dutch,* in great Hafte,
within the Wall, aboard fome *Carcoas* of *Mofaquia,* and plying the Oars,
or rather Flying, arriv'd in the Ifland of *Gilolo,* at a Fort there, built not
long before in *Sabugu.* The reft of the *Dutch* got off in other Veffels to
their Ship.

The whole Body of the Army now rang'd the Towns and Houfes of the *The Dutch*
Natives, wholly intent upon Plunder, and *Don Pedro* went about, giving *to their*
Orders, and checking the Soldiers, that they might keep in a Body. *Ship.*

The General went on to S. *Paul's* Church, which was unroof'd and
profan'd ; he order'd it to be cleans'd, and immediately adorn'd with *Poffeffion*
Boughs, and other Ornaments, brought thither by the diligent Soldiers, *taken of*
where they devoutly, with loud Voices, fang the Hymn, *Salve Regina,* *the Fort.*
which our Church ufes to call upon the bleffed Virgin. For the com-
pleating of this Victory, they ftill wanted to feize the King, Prince, *Sangi-*
acks, and Commanders that follow'd him. The General took Poffeffion of
the Forts, fetting up and difplaying the Colours, with the Arms of the
Crown of *Spain,* and the Name of PHILIP *THE THIRD, OUR*
SOVEREIGN, the Mufick playing, and Guns firing. He order'd, *King of*
that the next Day Captain *Villagra* fhould fet out in Purfuit of the King of *Ternate*
Ternate, with 100 Men in two Galleys, and the King of *Tydore,* and the *purfu'd.*
Prince his Son, with their Fleet, confifting of two *Janguas,* and 15 Car-
coas, in which were 1000 Men.

The King and Prince of *Tydore,* with Captain *Villagra,* came to the *Tacome*
Fort of *Tacome,* in *Ternate,* on the third of *April,* where they found *Ca-* *Fort fur-*
chil Amuxa, the braveft of the Natives of *Ternate,* Coufin German to their *render'd to*
King, and his Captain General. *Villagra* fent him a Meffage by *Antony* *Villagra.*
de Silva, Interpreter of their Language, and through his Means he furren-
dred, with fome *Dutch* ; all whom he carry'd Prifoners to the City. He
brought them in very honourable Manner, and they had not the dejected
Looks of Men that were overcome. Being come to the City, he deliver'd
them to *Don Pedro de Acunna,* who obferving the fame Generofity, received and treated them courteoufly, and commended their Valour. There
the *Cachil* and Captain *John de Cubas* knew one another again, remember'd
the Wounds they had given and receiv'd, and were good Friends. The
Portuguefe Commanders vifited him, and in his Prefence, after commending

K k

mending the Bravery they had shown in the War, the General, with his own Hands, put weighty Gold Chains about their Necks, as was then us'd among Soldiers, desiring they would accept of that Acknowledgement of their gallant Behaviour, and excuse the Smallness of the Gift ; and they on their Side, made suitable Returns of Courtesy.

Villagra went out again, and by the Way, took the *Sangiack* of *Mofaquia*, and two of his Nephews, without any Opposition. All these having desir'd Audience of *Don Pedro*, told him, they had always been desirous to return to their Subjection under his Majesty, but that their Kinsman, the King, had obstructed it, and ruin'd himself by adhering to his own Opinion, rejecting the safest and best, which was to recover their former Favour. *This Pride*, said they, *has reduc'd him to the miserable Condition he is now in. If you please we will discourse, and persuade him to put himself into your Hands, after you have taken such Security of us as becomes conquer'd Men, and given Commission to such as you can confide in to Article with the King. It is not the Change of our Fortune that moves us to this, for none can daunt those who are prepar'd for the worst ; but it is that Fidelity, which the Circumstances of the Times would not permit us to exert.* Don *Pedro* return'd Thanks for their Zeal, and told them, The Method they had chosen was the best to oblige the King of *Spain* to use that Victory with his innate royal Goodness ; and therefore empower'd them to assure the King, and his Son, that their Lives should be safe. The two *Cachiles* embarking with *Paul de Lima*, who, tho' a Native of *Ternate*, was discreet and a Master of the *Spanish* Tongue, as also well known to the King, and with Captain *Villagra*, they sail'd over together to the Fort of *Sabubu*, in the Island *Batochina*. The King embrac'd, and receiv'd them with Tears ; but when they propos'd his surrend'ring himself, he would not consent without a formal safe Conduct first granted. That Satisfaction was soon given him, for *Don Pedro* sent it, with Assurance of his Life, in respectful Terms, becoming the Person of a King, and all solid and safe, according to the Power committed to him, the Rest being left at his Catholick Majesty's Disposal.

The Instrument, which the General had drawn in Form, being read, the King resolv'd to repair to *Ternate*, with the Prince, and the other *Cachiles* and *Sangiacks*; yet contrary to the Advice of *Celicaya*, of whom he was always desperately in Love. In fine, he put himself into the Hands of *Don Pedro*, and to this Effect embark'd on three *Janguas*, and meeting with *Villagra*, they went over with all the rest into his Galleys, to be carry'd to the General. The King desir'd by the Way to visit his Mother, who was in the Fort of *Tacome*, and having propos'd it to Captain *Villagra*, he comply'd with him, and the Galleys made haste. They came to *Tacome* on the 8th of *April*, where he landed, and his Mother coming out to meet him, encourag'd him, without showing the least Dejectedness. Nothing appear'd in the Discourse between them that could be heard, that had a Womanish Air, or the Resemblance of a Motherly Tenderness, as the Interpreters declar'd. nor did she comfort him with Hopes of Revenge, but only with Reasons persuading to suit himself to his Fortune, which is the Will of Heaven.

From

From this Place *Villagra* sent Advice to *Don Pedro*, that the King was come, and would soon be with him. He having receiv'd the News, sent Major *Ascueta* to bid him welcome. He order'd he should be treated with Respect, and that the Major should in secret bid Captain *Villagra* make haste to *Ternate*, because there was much still to do, and it was not proper to lose Time. The Progress of Victory is not to be interrupted. They set out in the Evening for *Ternate*, where they arriv'd late at Night, and therefore went not into the City. The King stood as it were amaz'd when he saw the Place, and heard the Drums, and other Martial Noises; being sensible of the Yoke he had been so averse to bear. However he diverted himself that Night, as a sick Person uses to admit of the Entertainment he receives from those who are in Health. The next Day the General came aboard, whilst the Army was forming into one great Body, and the Companies were marching, that the King might not stay; that Show being provided for him, and the Design that he should be conducted in through the Midst of the Forces. *Don Pedro* order'd, That before he landed, the King of *Tydore*, who attended in the same Harbour, should go visit him. He refus'd to receive him, as long as he could, and the Colonel and all the Captains intreated him to admit of the Visit, which he at length consented to, either being perswaded, or yielding to Importunity. The Galley made towards the King of *Tydore*'s Fleet, and as they drew near, the Cannon fir'd. The King of *Tydore* stay'd aboard his Admiral, conceal'd between Curtains of Crimson Damask, and when the two Galleys were come together board and board, after a long Silence, the Curtains were drawn. Both the Kings appear'd in their Vessels, looking at one another, for a considerable Time, without speaking a Word. At length he of *Ternate*, as the conquer'd, call'd to one of his Nephews, to whom kneeling, he deliver'd a Message in his Ear for the King of *Tydore*. The Nephew went over to the *Carcoa*, and having made the *Zumbaya*, according to their Ceremonies, with great Tokens of Submission, kneeling, joyning his Hands, and raising them up to his Face, kiss'd the King of *Tydore*'s left Foot. Then he deliver'd him his Message with much Deliberation, all the Standers-by observing the knitting of his Brows, and all the other Tokens of Admiration and Sorrow, wherewith he was heard. The Nephew withdrew as soon as he had done speaking; and after the King of *Tydore* had continu'd a while Thoughtful, he call'd another *Cachil*, who was his Favourite, and Kinsman. He spoke to him in the same Manner, and gave him another Message for the King of *Ternate*, with much Deliberation and State. This Messenger paid him the same respectful Ceremonies, and going over to our Galley, when he came into the Presence of the King of *Ternate*, after performing the same *Zumbaya*, bow'd himself down, and deliver'd the Answer. The King receiv'd it with as much Grandeur as he could have done had he been Conqueror. Then he also stood a while musing, and rising went over to the Admiral of *Tydore*, which, as has been said, was grappled with the Galley. The Prince, his Son, and the Commanders attended him. The King of *Tydore* stood up to receive him. When they met, each of them us'd tedious Civilities, and Ceremonies towards the other, about sitting. He of *Ternate* sat first, and the Prince, by his Father's Order, paid him of *Tydore*, the Respect of the *Zumbaya*,

The King brought to Ternate.

The King of Tydore goes to visit him.

Barbarous Ceremonies of the Kings.

Zumbaya Ceremony.

Meeting of the two Kings.

K k 2   kissing

kifling his Foot. He to prevent obliging his Son to repay the like Compliment to the other, before the King of *Ternate* came, had order'd him aboard another Veffel, and to put out to Sea, that he might not be prefent at the Interview. The two Kings difcours'd about feveral Affairs, and he of *Ternate*, of his Misfortune, tho' in manly Manner.

The two Kings land. It being now Time for the King of *Ternate* to land, both the Kings began to draw near it, but with different Notions. The General waited in the Fort, and faw the Landing from the Top of it. The King of *Ternate* came afhore between and led by the Colonel, and *Gallinato*. After him follow'd the Prince, conducted by Captain *Villagra*, and the Major. The King march'd thro' a Lane of our Foot, and feem'd pleas'd to fee them fo gallant, and orderly. Thus he came to the Fort, the ancient Refidence of his Predeceffors, and not long fince his own, *Don Pedro*, the Governour

Don Pedro receives the King. coming down to the Gate to meet him, unarm'd, richly drefs'd, and with fuch Decency as became his Perfon. He would have kifs'd his Hand, but the King embrac'd him, and they went up Hand in Hand to the Lodgings; in the Statelieft whereof, they found three Chairs, with as mary Cufhions before them, plac'd on a rich Carpet under the Canopy The King fat on that in the Middle, the Prince on the next, and the Governour on the third. After a fhort Silence, the Difcourfe began, *Don Pedro* telling the King, his Highnefs ought to bear his prefent Condition with Refolution, remembering the long Profperity he had enjoy'd. That he offer'd to in-

Comforts him. terceed, and ufe his Intereft with his Majefty, that he might be reftor'd to his Kingdoms; and that the Subject in Hand requiring longer and private Conferences, he for the Prefent would cut it fhort, becaufe the fettling of weighty Affairs, is not to be grounded on the Noife of Promifes.

The King's Anfwer. The King return'd Thanks for the Kindnefs he fhow'd, in promifing his Reftitution, and bewailing his prefent Condition, concluded, faying, That he took Comfort in him, confidering Heaven had referv'd him to be fubdu'd by fo great a Commander; in which particular he reckon'd he was much oblig'd to his Fortune; and that he confided, he would treat him with fuch Generofity and Goodnefs as was due on his own Account, and his being the Minifter of fo great a Monarch, without calling to mind that his own Pride had been his Ruin. The Governour fatisfy'd him as to all Points, and having order'd the beft Houfe in *Ternate* to be furnifh'd, and

A Spanifh Company guards the King. fent to it Plate, Houfehold Goods, Linnen, Beds, Pavillions, and all Things anfwerable to fuch a Gueft, he defir'd the King would be pleas'd to remove thither, and with his leave he would wait on him; and that, with his good liking, a *Spanifh* Captain with his Company fhould guard his Perfon; left the Subjects of the Kingdom of *Tydore*, his natural Enemies, who were then very Numerous in the City, feeing him alone, fhould offer any Rudenefs. The King accepted of it, fmiling in a heavy Manner, to fignify that the Guard was appointed to fecure him, and all the other Prifoners, and that he was fenfible of the falfe Glofs they gave it.

He defires the Company of Captain Villagra. Captain *Peter Delgado* was order'd with his Company to guard the King's Houfe, and attend him, till reliev'd. That Night the King was very melancholy, being among fo many Strangers, and though it was late, would not go to Bed, till he had fent *Sylva*, the *Portuguefe* Interpreter, to defire the General, that for fome Comfort in his Solitude, this being the

Requeſt of a conquer'd Perſon, he would ſend him Captain *Villagra*, whom, as the firſt *Spaniard* he had been acquainted with, he lov'd, call'd him Father and delighted in his Company. The King is reported to have ſaid, that to converſe with the Conquerors, is only to haſten being overcome, and make the Change of Fortune Habitual. The Governour was glad he could afford him that Satisfaction; and ſending immediately for Captain *Villagra*, deſir'd he would go divert the King, and make much of, and entertain him with Art, that he might be comforted. The Captain readily comply'd, and the King expreſs'd ſingular Satisfaction in his Company. He ſupp'd, and went to Bed, diſcourſing all the while with the Captain concerning Martial and Religious Affairs.

Two Days after the Governour directed Colonel *Gallinato* and Captain *Villagra*, together with *Paul de Lima*, to propoſe to the King to enter into Treaty with him, in his Majeſty's Name, for ſettling Things in a State of Security, and Safety; and to perſwade him, that was the Way to deſerve well, and put himſelf into a better Condition. They three went to him, attended by other Perſons of Note, and among them ſome religious Men of the Orders of *S. Auguſtin*, and *S. Dominick*, and the Society of *Jeſus*, who all behav'd themſelves commendably in their Stations. The King did not refuſe to capitulate, and after ſettling the Form, by the Interpoſition of *Paul de Lima*, and granting ſome Things he deſir'd of the King of *Spain*, the following Articles were drawn and ſign'd. *Treaty ſet afoot with the King.*

The firſt Thing requir'd of *Cachil Sultan Zayde*, King of *Ternate*, and of the reſt who are Priſoners with his Highneſs, is that he ſhall deliver up to his Majeſty King *Philip* our Sovereign, the Forts he is now poſſeſs'd of, being thoſe of *Gilolo, Sabubu, Gamocanora, Tacome*, thoſe of *Machian*, thoſe of *Sula*, and the Reſt. To this he anſwers, that he will deliver up to his Majeſty the aforeſaid Forts, and to that Effect, will ſend the Prince his Son, and his Kinſman *Cachil Amuxa*, with the Perſons appointed to take Poſſeſſion of them, and that they ſhall be deliver'd up, with all the Cannon, Ammunitions, Muſkets, and Fire-Arms there are in them. *Articles between the General and King of Ternate. The King to deliver up all Forts.*

Secondly, That he ſhall reſtore all the Priſoners he has, either Chriſtians, or Infidels, being our Subjects, as well of the Provinces of the *Pintados*, as of the Reſt that are ſubject to the *Spaniards* in the *Philippine* Iſlands. He anſwer'd, that all ſuch as can be found at preſent ſhall be deliver'd, and the Reſt hereafter as they are diſcover'd. *To releaſe Priſoners.*

Thirdly, That he ſhall deliver up the *Dutch* he has in his Power. He anſwer'd, That when he departed the Fort of *Ternate*, 13 or 14 that were with him fled; and he ſuppoſes they repair'd to the *Dutch* Ship, becauſe he has not ſeen them ſince; but if they ſhall be found, he will deliver them immediately. *To deliver up the Dutch.*

Fourthly, He ſhall deliver up the Renegado *Spaniards* that were in the Fort of *Ternate*. He anſwer'd, that there was but one, and he fled as well as the Reſt, the Day the Fort was taken; that he knows not where he is, but will cauſe Search to be made, and deliver him. *And Renegado Spaniards.*

Fifthly, That he ſhall deliver up all the Towns which are in *Batochina*, and is call'd *El Moro*, they having been formerly Chriſtians; as alſo the Iſlands of *Moratay*, and *Herrao*, which were alſo Chriſtian, with all the Artillery and Ammunition there is in them. He anſwer'd, he is ready to deliver up all, as he had done his Perſon. *Alſo Batochina, Moratay, & Herrao.* Theſe

These Articles *Don Pedro de Acunna*, Governour, and Captain General

The Form of tendering the Capitulation authentick

of the *Philippine* Islands, President of the Royal Court residing in them, and General of this Fleet in the *Moluccos*, committed to the General *John Xuarez Gallinato*, and to Captain *Christopher de Villagra*, who concluded them in the Form as above, by the Interposition of *Paul de Lima*, a *Portuguese* born in these Islands, who serv'd as Interpreter of the Languages. And the said King subscrib'd his Name, after his Manner. Given in the Fort of *Ternate*, on the tenth of *April*, 1606. The said General, and Captain also sign'd it, with the said *Paul de Lima*.

How it was sign'd.

The King sign'd in *Persian* Characters, with graceful Flourishes, and the *Spaniards* plainly ; and this Original Capitulation was brought into *Spain*, with the other authentick Instruments.

Commanders go to take Possession.

In Pursuance to this Agreement, the Commanders imbark'd to take Possession of the several Places, carrying along with them the King and Prince, and other Prisoners in two Galleys being the Admiral, and Vice-Admiral, with all *Villagra*'s Company, and Part of that of *Cervantes*. The first Place taken Possession of was the Fort of *Tacome*, next that of *Sula*, both in the Island of *Ternate*. Thence they sail'd to the great *Batochina*, where are

Gamocanora what it signifies.

those of *Gilolo*, formerly a flourishing Kingdom; of *Sabubu*, and *Gamocanora*, which we corruptly call *Gran Bocanora*; but in that Country Language, *Gamo* signifies Middle, and *Canora* Land, so that *Gamocanora*, altogether signifies, Mid-Land, because it lies in the midst of *Gilolo*, and *El Moro*. Possession was taken of all these Forts, none landing but *Villagra*, with *Cachil Amuxa*, *Antony de Sylva*, and *John de Vega*, who did the Part of a Notary, being appointed, and authoriz'd for that Time. The *Cachil* assembled the People at all the Forts, acquainted them with the Success of *Ternate*, and

Manner of taking Possession.

that all was now subject to the *Spaniards*, by whose Authority that Captain came to take Possession, that so all might pay their Obedience to his Majesty. The People having been attentive to what was propos'd to them, knelt down, and raising their Voices made the *Zumbaya*. Then the Captain display'd the Standard advancing it in his Majesty's Name, to denote Possession. Then he commanded the Natives to bring out the Cannon, and draw it down to the Shore, to be imbark'd aboard the Galleys. This was the Method observed at *Gilolo*, and in other Places of less Note.

K. of Tydore recovers his Towns

In the mean while, the King of *Tydore*, making his Advantage of the Victory, sent the Prince his Son with some Troops, to possess himself of the Towns the King of *Ternate* had taken for him, as he actually did. *Don Pedro* being inform'd of it, was offended that an Enterprize should be undertaken without his Order, and thinking the King of *Tydore* had therein given Tokens of Distrust, and Disrespect, had Thoughts of taking such Satisfaction, as he judg'd the Matter deserv'd ; but the King of *Tydore* reflecting on his Misbehaviour, and that the Governours Resentment swell'd up to absolute Indignation, he found Means to appease him, excusing himself, and saying, that Invasion had been carry'd on without his Order, or Knowledge, and desisting expected to be restor'd by *Don Pedro*, as we shall soon see.

The Method observ'd at other Forts, could not be followed at that of *Sabubu*, where Queen *Celycaya* was, because *Cachil Amuxa* fell sick, or pretended so to do *Villagra* had Regard to the Circumstances of Times. *Cachil Pete*, *Sangiack* of *Gamocanora*, the King's Nephew, and a brave Soldier, landed

landed inftead of the other. The People of that Town imagin'd, that *Villagra* brought confiderable Forces, and therefore to fecure the Queen, and themfelves, they gather'd above 2500 fighting Men, under Pretence they would not fuffer *Celycaya* to be taken away. They hid themfelves with their Arms, yet not fo but that the Captain knew of it. He took no Notice, but coming up to one of the Baftions of the Town, which were both next the River, drew oft the Cannon, fome few of the Natives, and thofe Boys helping him; the Reft waiting for more confiderable Action, in Arms. Then he difarm'd the other Baftion, affifted by *Francis Romanico*, and *John Rodriguez Bermejo*, Captains of the Galleys. The Town ftands on the Bank of a River, up which they had run in their Boats; but returning with the Men that row'd, the Guns were loaded, the *Sangiack Rete* forwarding of it. He finding the People in an Uproar, would not have had the Cannon carry'd away, at that Time. Poffeffion was not taken till afterwards, out of Refpect to the Queen, and by Reafon of the Mutiny of the People, who efcap'd not unchaftis'd. The Galleys return'd to *Gamocanora*, and not being able to get into the River, nor to ftay out, becaufe of the Flats, where an indifferent Wind may do much Harm, the leaft Part whereof was the Lofs of the Veffels; *Gallinato* therefore confidering, that if they fhould be caft away, the King was in his own Country, whence it would be impoffible to get him out again, tho' a greater Power fhould be gather'd for that End, than what came from the *Philippine* Iflands, and having confulted with him about the Method to be us'd to get in to *Gamocanora*, the *Sangiack* of that Place faid to him. *Sir, if you have fuch Confidence in me, as I know you may, and my Advice is of any Force with you, do not go thither with thefe Galleys, for you will expofe them to Shoals, and Winds. Since therefore here are two* Carcoas of *Tydore, let the Captain* Villagra, *the Notary, and the Interpreter go aboard them, and I will go along with them to my Country, where the fame fhall be done, as if the Galleys went in.*

Gallinato confulted with *Villagra*, and they approv'd of the Method, fetting out in the *Carcoas* on *Saturday* in the Afternoon, and on *Sunday* Morning a League fhort of the River, the *Sangiack* told the Captain, he well knew he had been long from his Country, attending the King, and that his Subjects had no certain Account of him, and therefore, they might then as they us'd to do at other Times, come out to the Mouth of the River with a Fleet, to guard the Entrance. That if it fhould fo happen, he muft not be difturb'd, for they fhould all ferve him. The Captain, told him, how much he confided in him, fince he had fo eafily follow'd his Advice, and was come to his Country almoft Naked; and that whatfoever happen'd he would not miftruft him. Being come near the Mouth of the River, they faw 13 Veffels come out, and when in the Sea, they drew up in a half Moon, and made up to enclofe the Captain's *Carcoa*. The *Sangiack* feeing them near at Hand, went foward, and calling out, commanded them to be peaceable. As foon as they knew him, they obey'd, drew together their Veffels, and came to fpeak to him. He enquir'd into the Pofture of his Affairs, and ask'd whether his Mother was there. They faid fhe was, and gave him a long Account of all Things. They went before to carry his Mother the News of his Coming, and he order'd them to affemble all the People of the Town, and that none fhould appear arm'd, for they never us'd to lay afide their
Campilanes.

The People of Sabubu *in Arms.*

Cachil Rete.

His Advice to the Spaniards.

Villagra trufts the Sangiack

He appeafes his Subjects.

Campilanes. Being come in, they found all, and even the Women got together, and imbarking again, met the *Sangiacks* Mother in the Middle of the River, she then coming down, to see her Son, in a Vessel all full of Women, clad in several Sorts of Silks, with high Feathers, and several of them arm'd. Some handed the Sails, others ply'd the Oares, and others attended about that Princesses Person, so that there was not one Man among them.

The Mother being impatient, advanc'd as soon as ever she came to her Son's *Carcoa*; but he more nimbly leap'd into that Vessel of Women, and after paying the due Respect to his Mother, there pass'd extraordinary Demonstrations of Love on both Sides, she imbracing, and kissing her Son. Thus they all went up the River, against the Stream, till they came to the Town. On both the Banks there appear'd People clad in gay Manner, with Feathers, but unarm'd, and the *Sangiack* having desir'd his Mother to go ashore, all the Prime Men to perswade her leap'd into the Water, and carryed her in their Arms. The *Sangiack* and *Villagra* came to the Market-Place, in the midst whereof they found an Arbour, or Hut made of Boughs, on Timbers, and in it two Chairs, on a Carpet. They set down with the usual Ceremonies, and the *Sangiack* declar'd to his Subjects, that all the Dominions of the King of *Ternate*, and their Persons, were then subject to the King of *Spain*, as he was himself. That hereupon follow'd the Obligation of delivering up the Forts to him, and he was possess'd of all the Rest, only that being wanting. That they should so order that Captain *Villagra* might take Possession of it and the Artillery. *Villagra* intreated the *Sangiack* to go see his Wife, and Children, and he would receive the Surrender of the Fort, and Arms, in the Afternoon; but he answer'd, that he came not to rejoyce with his Family, but to serve the King of *Spain*. Afterwards he added, If you will have me see them I will make Use of your Leave; and if you refuse it, will imbark without seeing them. *Villagra* would not allow of such rigid Nicety, pressing him to take the Satisfaction of his Family, before the Act of Possession, and in the mean while, stay'd himself with *John de Vega*, and *Antony de Sylva*.

As soon as the *Sangiack* came Home, he sent the Captain about 30 *Indians* loaded with Provisions, one after another, but first they brought Tables, Chairs; and Table-Linnen in their great Dishes, and Salvers, and on them the Salts, Knives, drinking Cups, and Ewres, Variety of Fruit, Pullets roasted and fry'd, Goats Flesh roasted and boil'd, and other Dishes, after the Fashion of their Country. A little before the Dinner was ended they brought a Bed, and Pillows of green Satin, which they laid upon Carpets, to take an Afternoons Nap on. It was not long before the *Sangiack* himself came, follow'd by all the People, leading his Mother, and with them many Men loaded with the Arms he was to deliver up, gather'd from private Men, as also Drakes, Muskets, and other Fire-Arms. *Indians* brought them on their Shoulders, adorn'd with Boughs, in Token of the Satisfaction they had in delivering them. The same was then done in the Fort, as had been in the others. The *Sangiack* that Night gave the Captain a Supper in the same Manner as the Dinner had been. The next Day they breakfasted, and imbarking, return'd where *Gallinato* waited for them

in

A Vessel sail'd by none but Women.

Meeting of the Sangiack and his Mother.

His great Submission to the Spaniards.

His noble Entertainment.

Arms deliver'd.

in the Galleys, at *Tacome*, with some *Indians* of *Sabubu*, who came with a Meſſage to *Villagra*, inviting him to go take Poſſeſſion of the Fort.

He ſuſpected they had a treacherous Deſign, which was, that when they came to *Sabubu*, they would endeavour to have the Galleys come into the River, the Bar being proper for them, and having 1500 Men in Ambuſh, on both Sides of it, they would at Night ſend down ſome Fire-Ships upon them, then thoſe that were in Ambuſh giving the Alarm, they might at leaſt reſcue their King, and the other Priſoners that were aboard; and in Caſe the *Spaniards* would not go in with their Galleys, they would ſeize Captain *Villagra*, when he landed, that the Governour might, in Exchange, for him deliver them the King of *Ternate*. A *Portugueſe* Woman, who retir'd to *Tacome*, flying from *Ternate* when it was taken, and marry'd to a Renegado, tho' ſhe was herſelf a Chriſtian, gave *Gallinato* Advice of this intended Treachery. He took no Notice, but privately adviſ'd *Villagra* to pretend he was ſick. The Natives of *Sabubu*, again preſſed for the Captain, that they might deliver him the Fort, and *Gallinato* deſiring him to make ready to go thither, he excuſ'd himſelf, alledging his Indiſpoſition. *Vega* and *Sylva*, and ſome other Officers, went without him, and did the ſame Thing he could have done, avoiding the Danger of the Treaſon.

Treacherous Deſign of the People of Sabubu.

A Portugueſe Woman diſcovers the Deſign.

They return'd with the Galleys to *Ternate*, where they found *Don Pedro*, who condeſcending to ſome juſt Requeſts, and to others which depended on Courteſy, being only Matter of Bounty, reſtor'd ſeveral Towns, wrongfully taken. Theſe were beſtow'd on the Kings of *Tydore*, of *Bachian*, and of *Sian*. The laſt of theſe, tho' he ought to have joyn'd the Governour before the Expedition, came late, by Reaſon of contrary Winds. He reſtor'd eight Towns to the King of *Tydore*, *Cachil Mole*, he having been before poſſeſs'd of them in the Iſland of *Machian*. On *Cachil Raxa Laudin*, King of *Bachian*, who was always faithful to the *Spaniards*, and wounded at the Siege *Andrew Furtado* lay'd to *Ternate*, he beſtow'd the Iſlands of *Cayoa*, *Adoba*, and *Bayloro*, which are near *Bachian*, as alſo *Lucabata*, *Palomata*, and other Towns. He gave *Ruy Pereyra*, the *Sangiack* of *Labua*, a notable Chriſtian, and the King of *Spain*'s Subject, the Iſland of *Gane* to hold as Governour; and others to *Paul de Lima*, which his Family had formerly been poſſeſs'd of.

Don Pedro reſtores Towns to the Owners.

Some Aſſemblies were held, to conſult, what was to be done with the King and his Son. Upon ſumming up the Votes, it was Reſolv'd, that neither the one, nor the other, or any of the Priſoners of Note, being his Kinſmen, *Cachiles* and *Sangiacks* of Repute, ſhould be left in the *Moluccos*; and that, for conſiderable Reaſons, then appearing, it was not convenient, at that Time, to depoſe the King, but to allow him to appoint ſuch peaceable Perſons as he thought fit, to Govern the Kingdom. *Don Pedro* had, during this Time, writ to the King of *Spain*, acquainting him with the Succeſs of the War, and approv'd of the Method of appointing Governours, and accordingly order'd the Captive King and Prince ſhould be told, that this Form of Government was pitch'd upon to ſecure us againſt their Confederacies, ſince it was certain that they expected the *Dutch*, and had ſent to invite them againſt the *Spaniards*. That the King was to underſtand, that his Liberty, and Reſtoration to his Kingdoms, depended on his good Behaviour for the future, and that of his Subjects; and their aſſiſting the *Spaniards*

Don Pedro reſolves to carry the Priſoners to Manila.

King of Ternate directed to appoint Governours.

L l   that

that were to be left at *Ternate*, and their friendly Entertainment of them. This Meffage was deliver'd to the King by *F. Lewis Fernandez*, of the Society of *Jefus*, *Gallinato*, and *Efquivel*. They did it with much Refpect, adding, that he was to go to *Manila*, and therefore he fhould appoint fuch Perfons, as he would have to Govern during his Abfence. The King complying, fubmitted to every Thing, and nam'd *Cachil Sugui*, and *Cachil Quipat*, both of them his Unkles, to be Governours, becaufe they were of a peaceable and honeft Difpofition.

Cachil Sugui, and Cachil Quipat Governours.

A Day was appointed for the folemn Act of doing Homage. The great Hall in the Fort was hung with Silk, rich Canopys fet up; the Governour took his Seat under the chiefeft of them, all the Forces being at Arms; and then he declar'd to the Kings the Occafion of affembling them together, which was to fwear Fealty to his Majefty, a Duty that had been fo long put off, and at the fame Time fo much labour'd for by War.

Solemnity for fwearing Fealty.

They fwore Fealty to our Sovereign Lord King *Philip*, in the Perfon of the Governour *Don Pedro*. The firft was *Cachil Sultan Zayde Buxey*, King of *Ternate*, and *Cachil Sulamp Gariolano*, the Prince, his Son. Then *Cachil Mole*, King of *Tydore*; *Cachil Raxa Laudin*, King of *Bachian*; *Cachil Dini*, King of *Sian*, who had never done it before, but only profefs'd Friendfhip. After them fwore the *Sangiacks* and *Cachiles*, *Tulo*, *Codate*, *Amuxa*, *Rete*, *Ale*, *Nayo*, *Quipate*, *Colambaboa*, *Dexebes*, *Pamuza*, *Babada*, *Barcat*, *Sugi*, *Gugu*, *Boleyfe*, *Gulila*, *Maleyto*, *Banaba*, all of them Princes, Kinfmen, and Subjects to the *Molucco* King. They promis'd not to admit of the *Dutch*, nor any other Nations, to the Trade of Clove, and to preferve it entirely for his Majefty, and his Subjects; and to be affifting with their Perfons, Forces, and Ships, whenfoever they fhould be call'd upon by the Commander of the Fort of *Ternate*, or of the *Philippines*. It was alfo agreed, that they fhould not any Way obftruct the Converfion of the Gentils that were inclin'd to embrace Chriftianity.

Perfons that fwore Fealty.

They were all fatisfy'd with this Beginning of their new Subjection, becaufe the King of *Ternate* opprefs'd them, as being the moft potent, and fupported by the *Dutch*; nor had they any Security againft his Tyranny; efpecially fince he caus'd the King of *Tydore*'s Father to be treacheroufly murder'd, the King of *Bachian*'s in War, and a Kinfman of his, which they both ftill refented. *Don Pedro* order'd another Fort to be erected at *Tydore*, and a Captain with 50 Men to Garrifon it; at the Requeft of the King, by whofe Affiftance it was finifh'd. It was refolv'd, that for the prefent, the third Part of the Duties the People of *Ternate* us'd to pay, fhould be taken off, fo to make them eafy, that they might reap fome Benefit of our Victory, and not be perfwaded it tended to increafe their Oppreffion. The old Fort being fmall, and unfit to make any confiderable Defence, it was thought fit to build one on a higher Ground, larger, and ftronger. The Plan was laid out, and Orders given for carrying on the Work. The faid old Fort was brought into a narrow Compafs, whilft the new one was raifing, which the Governour, before he departed *Ternate*, faw finifh'd, quite enclos'd, and ftrengthned with Ramparts. Six hundred Men, diftributed into fix Companies, were left in it, to defend the Ifland againft any Invafion. Six other Captains were reform'd. There were alfo twelve Gunners, 65 Pioneers, 35 Mafons, and two good Brigantines, which, in Cafe of Neceffity, might

Another Fort built at Tydore

Ternate eas'd of Duties.

Men left at Ternate.

might be mann'd with Pioneers. Colonel *John de Esquivel* was appointed Esquivel
Commander in chief, and Governour of all the *Moluccos*. Governour

Don *Pedro*, the Day before his Departure, gave the said Governour his Instructions, which had been maturely weighed, and debated, after several private Conferences with him, providing for all Accidents that might happen.

All the Prisoners, being the King and Prince of *Ternate*, and 24 *Sangiacks* and *Cachiles*, were put aboard the Admiral Galley, under the Care of Captain *Villagra*, with particular Orders to convey them to *Manila*. This done they set sail. Our Fleet being departed with the Booty, and Prisoners, the Colonel, *John de Esquivel*, apply'd himself diligently to the Affairs of his Charge, and to haftning on the Fortifications begun in several Parts. Whilst the Conquerors sail'd away, on the fourth of *May*, he order'd the King of *Tydore*, with his Fleet, and in it some *Spaniards*, commanded by the Captains *Pasqual de Aragon*, and *Martin de Esquivel*, to sail for *Sabubu*, to perswade the *Cachiles*, *Sugui* and *Quipati*, to return to the City; because by their Examples the Citizens and Multitude would do the like, they being fled to the Mountains on Account of the War; for so they would quit those Deserts, be encouraged to confide in the Conqueror, and settle in Peace. The King of *Tydore* arriv'd at *Sabubu*, with his Company; sent Messengers to them, who deliver'd what they were commission'd with, adding, that if they requir'd Hostages for their safe coming, they should have the *Spanish* Captains that were in the Fleet deliver'd to them. The Governours were so far from giving Ear to their Message, that they sent to conjure them to depart *Sabubu*. *Esquivel* was concern'd at this mistrustful and rough Behaviour, because the greatest Part of the People of the Island were in that strong Hold, and in *Gilolo*, and that Repulse in the Presence of the Natives that were fled, seem'd to threaten greater Opposition. Whilst he prepar'd to reduce them, he endeavour'd by fair Means to attract the Inhabitants of a Town, call'd *Tacome*, two Leagues from *Ternate*, whither also some of those that had fled were retir'd. He sent them a considerable Quantity of Plunder, plac'd Safeguards in *Tacome* and *Malayo*, to quiet, and defend them against the *Tydores*, their Enemies and Conquerors.

Prisoners shipp'd for Manila.

King of Tydore sent to Sabubu.

The Governours refuse to come.

The King of *Tydore*, and our Commanders, returning without any Effect from *Sabubu*, they sail'd with the Fleet to *Machian*, to recover peaceably that Part of the Island, which the Governour, *Don Pedro*, took from the King of *Ternate*, to restore it to him of *Tydore*. At the same Time two *Dutch* Ships arriv'd there; one of them was the same our Fleet found some Days before in the Fort *Talangame*; which having been a Witness to our Success, rejoyn'd the other, and both of them came together to the *Moluccos*, by Order of the *Dutch* Commander residing at *Amboyna*, to encourage the King of *Ternate* to persist in his Disobedience, and assist him against our Fleet. Our Men sent the Colonel Advice, who order'd our Galliots to set out, to find, and pursue those Ships, that so their Boats might not offer to move far from them, and to endeavour to obstruct their trading with the Natives. Tho' the Orders were obey'd, the said two Ships appear'd before *Ternate* the third Day after, and holding on their Course, anchor'd at *Gilolo*, where most of the Natives of the *Molucco* Islands, who were fled, had fortify'd themselves. These Guests, according to their Custome, call'd together all

Spanish Ships at Machian.

two Dutch Ships.

the

the Inhabitants, who were diſpers'd about in other Towns, and reſolv'd to go over to *Gilolo* and *Sabubu*. They gather'd all their Veſſels, and thought, with them, and the *Dutch* Ships, to obſtruct the Ravage our Galiots made, and to ſupport their Friends. This new Rebellion was carry-ed on in Sight of the *Dutch* Ships lying at Anchor before *Gilolo*, and they ſecur'd, and defended them againſt our Squadrons.

Rebellion at Gilolo

The Colonel intreated the King of *Tydore*, who was newly return'd from *Machian*, to gather a greater Number of arm'd *Carcoas*, that our Infantry might be carry'd in them, and the Galiots, to attack *Gilolo*, and *Sabubu*, in Order to ſuppreſs that Miſchief in its firſt Riſe, there being other Places for our Veſſels to put into, beſides the Harbour where the Enemies Ships lay at Anchor. The King of *Tydore* ſtarted ſo many Difficulties, that *Eſquivel* could not prevail upon him. Another more effectual Method was found. It being certain, that the Fugitives muſt bring their Proviſions, and parti-cularly Rice, from the Province *del Moro*, and Iſland of *Moratay*, where there is great Plenty; and that we having burnt the Ships of the *Moluccos*, during that War, they would ſupply the Want of them from thoſe ſame Places; the Governour therefore reſolv'd, that Major *Vergara*, and the King of *Tydore*, ſhould repair thither with 120 *Spaniards*, to diſappoint their Deſigns, that ſo Neceſſity might reduce them to ſubmit.

Methods for ſup-preſſing it

Our Forces arriv'd at the Iſland *Batochina*, which is the ſame as *Gilolo*, and where *Sabubu* ſtands. Leaving the Shore, they march'd over extraor-dinary wooded Mountains, along the Side of the River *Gabocanora*, to a great Town, the Receptacle of many of the Fugitives. They met with no Oppoſition, or other Obſtacle in the Way, but only thoſe ſharp pointed Stakes they uſe to drive into the Ground. The Enemy had plac'd their greateſt Defence upon the River; but abandon'd it upon the Approach of the *Spaniards*, running up into the Mountains, and leaving their Houſes and Veſſels. Our Men fell upon both, burnt them, and took ſuch as durſt ſtay behind. In fine, they all, diſmay'd at the Sight of the Flames and Deſtruction, embrac'd more ſubmiſſive methods. The City *Viſoa* un-derwent the ſame Fate, and the Remains of it ſued for Pardon, and com-ply'd.

120 Spa-niards ſent to Gilolo.

They burn Towns and reduce the Iſland.

The King of *Tydore* went away from this Place with eight *Carcoas*, lea-ving the reſt, and the Galleys, with the Major. The City *Mamuya*, having made Reſiſtance, was alſo burnt. Our Men went over in ſmall Veſſels to *Galela*, a Town built in a large Lake, which held out till reduc'd by Fire and Sword, the very Children ſwimming away. *Tolo, Chiava*, and *Ca-maſo*, which are three Leagues from *Galela*, and whoſe Inhabitants had been formerly Chriſtians, prevented Military Execution, by ſending Depu-ties from *Tolo*, the ſtrongeſt of them, with Boughs of *Bonanas* in Bloſſom, and Green, and White Cloves. They came unarm'd, and with Muſick, and expreſs'd much Sorrow for their late Rebellion, for which *Sultan Zay-de* was to blame, and for having forſaken the Chriſtian Religion, which they were there ready to imbrace. The *Spaniſh* Commander prais'd, and treated them Courteouſly. Our Men now ſickned a pace, for which Rea-ſon, as alſo becauſe the weſterly Winds began to grow boiſterous, he was oblig'd to defer the ſubduing of *Moratay*. However he left ſome Men at *Tolo*, with the ſmall Guns taken at *Gabocanora*, to ſecure the Towns that were

Galela de-ſtroy'd.

Tolo Chi-ava and Camaſo ſubmit.

were reduc'd, and defend them againft thofe of *Galela* and *Tabelo*, which are biger than they. This done he return'd to *Ternate*, but not without Storms, and Dangers, incurr'd by giving Credit to a *Molucco* Slave.

The Governour mann'd a Galliot, a Brigantine, and fome fmaller Veffels with Soldiers, and *Chinefes* to row, under the Command of the Enfign *Chriftopher Suarez*. He fail'd with a fair Wind for the Ifland *Mateo*, which we call *Celebes*, the neareft Part whereof is 30 Leagues Weft from *Ternate*, and its Length above 150 Leagues. The furtheft Part of it is fubject to the King of *Macaffar*, a *Mahometan* Prince, with whom the People of *Malaca* have Trade, as alfo with three other heathen Kings, of whom there was a Report, that they defired to be Chriftians; but they fell under the Tyranny of the King of *Ternate*, and fuffer'd by his Invafions and Burnings. *Efquivel* fent to acquaint them with the King of *Spain*'s Victories and Succefs; and exhorted them to come under his Dominion, but above all to be united to the Church. He made them Prefents of *European* Commodities, which are as good as Money with them, and offer'd the Protection of the *Spanifh* Power, which had pull'd down that Tyrant, to whom they were Tributary. He faid, he fent them Ships and Arms, and that for the Time to come, they might fafely repair to trade at the *Moluccos*. Thefe Princes were two Brothers, the one King of *Bool*, the other of *Totoli*. They rejoyc'd at the coming of the Embaffador *Chriftopher Suarez*, and he prefenting them fome Pieces of Velvet, in Token of Friendfhip, they return'd other Gifts, and Abundance of Provifions, and difmifs'd him, with a Letter to the Governour. Queen *Dongue* of *Caripa*, teftify'd to *Efquivel* no lefs Satisfaction, and Inclination to be united to the King of *Spain* by Vaffalage.

Meffage from Efquivel to the Heathen Kings of Bool, and Totoli.

The Garrifons of the Rebellious Towns were affaulted by the *Spaniards*, and compell'd to fubmit. The King of *Tydore* made Havock on the Coaft of *Batochina*, or *Gilolo*, where he recover'd for his Majefty, and for himfelf, the Towns and Forts that had been taken from him by the King of *Ternate*. He plunder'd the great Town of *Mira*, in *Moratay*, and made Captives of many that oppos'd him, who had alfo been Chriftians. Among the reft he took a *Guimala*, which fignifies, a Chief, or Head of a Quarter, or Ward, whom he again fet at Liberty, at the Requeft of our Men, fending him away with two other *Guimalas*, in the Company of Captain *John de la Torre*. The Iflands in thofe Parts were reducing by Degrees, with little Oppofition. Thofe of the *Meaos*, lying to the North-Weft, towards *Manila*, being among, and full of large Towns, defended themfelves, with tle Affiftance, and Induftry of the *Dutch*; but *B. Antony Flores*, a Lay-Brother, of the Order of S. *Auguftin*, who fought againft the *Sangleyes* of *Manila*, as has been faid above, coming thither with the Galleys, they fubmitted. The Enfign *Lewis de Zuazo* arriv'd after the Bufinefs was over, and they being now fuccefsful, and underftanding that the *Dutch* Ship was fail'd from *Gilolo*, made after her. She was fo good a Sailer, that they labour'd in vain; but carry'd on the War at *Gilolo* and *Sabubu*, which made the *Ternate* Governours put up their Complaints, and lay afide their Defigns. They writ to the Governour, and he anfwer'd them, fending a Copy of the Articles, upon which they offer'd to repair to *Ternate*, in peaceable Manner. All our Commanders were difpers'd in feve-

ral

King of Tydore's Actions.

Meaos Iflands fubdu'd.

Reduction of other Iflands.

ral Places, reducing the Iſlands of the *Moluccos* that had Rebell'd, either by Force of Arms, or other Methods; and particularly thoſe belonging to the *Sultan* of *Ternate*, which are few under an hundred; and thus Peace began to be eſtabliſh'd, which if not Wiſh'd for, was at leaſt Tolerated, and accepted of with ſuch Appearances as are becoming to make it honourable.

The King and Molucco Priſoners attempt to eſcape.

Whilſt the *Molucco* Iſlands ſubmitted by Force to receive the Yoke, the Governour, *Don Pedro de Acunna*, was ſailing for *Manila*. Captain *Villagra* was at a Diſtance from the Fleet, with the King, Prince, and *Sangiacks* that were Priſoners, aboard the Admiral Galley. This made them form a Deſign to attempt to make their Eſcape to *Mindanao*, and they had ſucceeded, if not prevented by the Soldiers that guarded them. Captain *Villagra* either Suſpected, or had Information of it, and therefore doubled the Guards, and put eight of the moſt daring into Chains. Among the moſt remarkable were *Cachil Amuxa*, the *Sangiack Rete*, and he of *Mofaquia*. They all arriv'd at *Manila*, but their Fetters were taken off before they came thither, after they had worn them ten Days, with much Regret of the King, whom they ſatisfy'd with Hopes, and acquainting him with ſome of the Grounds there were to ſuſpect, till the Danger of laying them aſide ceas'd. The Hazard at *Mindanao* was, that thoſe Iſlands are not Tributary, yet they value themſelves upon entertaining Friendſhip with the King of *Ternate*; and it is moſt certain, that had he attempted to fly, and ſucceeded in it, they would have ſupported him there; and *Villagra* had Intelligence given him, that the King either made, or approv'd of the Propoſal; tho' there was no want of Care and Vigilancy either in *Don Pedro*'s Ship, or the Admiral Galley.

Don Pedro de Acunna ſuppos'd to be poiſon'd.

During all this Time we have ſpoken of, the News of our Succeſs was not brought to the *Philippine* Iſlands. This long Silence, and Want of Intelligence, became an Argument in thoſe Parts, and particularly at *Manila*, that *Don Pedro* and the Fleet were loſt, or at leaſt had met with ſuch ill Succeſs as deſerv'd to be generally lamented. Virtue never fail'd of envious Perſons to perſecute it, and accordingly *Don Pedro* was not without them at *Manila*; but tho' they were well known, in ſo much that in the general Opinion of all Men, they are ſuppos'd to have given the Poiſon, whereof that great Man was thought to have dy'd 22 Days after his Return, we will nevertheleſs ſuppreſs their Names, ſince it is not the Part of an Author, whoſe Duty it is to obſerve an exact Neutrality, and not to be led any Way by Affection, to confirm that Depoſition, which, as yet, is no better grounded than on Suſpicion. They are all Dead long ſince,

Falſe Reports abroad.

and have been try'd before that great Tribunal, where the leaſt thought cannot paſs without being accounted for. Theſe Men gave out, That *Don Pedro* attacking *Ternate*, enter'd it ſucceſsfully; but that his Men had been too intent upon Plunder, the Enemy rallyed, and falling upon the *Spaniards*, beat them out again, killing moſt of them. And that the General being aſham'd of his ill Conduct, durſt not return to *Manila*.

Indians begin to Mutiny

This Report being ſpread abroad among the *Indians*, did ſo much Harm, that they began to Mutiny, eſpecially in the Provinces of *Camarines*, and *Pintados*; in ſo much that the Fryers who attended their Inſtruction, could not deal with them any longer, for they ſaid, That ſince the People

of

of the *Moluccos* were victorious, why should they be still subject to the *Spaniards*, who did not defend them against the *Moors*, and these would now plunder them daily with the Assistance of *Ternate*, and it would be worse for the Future. Nor were they satisfy'd with muttering, but proceeded to confer Notes together, and to contrive putting their Projects in Execution. But all this vanish'd at the Sight of Truth, and the News of it, brought in before the Arrival of the Conquerors, and the Preparations they saw made for their Reception, and triumphant Rejoycings. The Weather was seasonable, and favour'd them in all Respects, and they arriv'd at *Manila* on the ninth of *June*, loaded with Honour and Victory, after they had rested in the Port of *Cabite*, two Leagues distant.

The Captives diverted themselves with our Men, to put off the Remembrance of past Times, whilst rich Garments of several Sorts of Silks were provided for them at the publick Charge, which is the King's Treasury in the *Philippine* Islands. They look'd dejectedly, and with Admiration, on the Harbour, Walls, Forts, and Buildings of the City, the Sight whereof made them call to Mind the last Day on which they fell from their boasted State of Liberty. Our Commanders dropt some courteous Words of Comfort in their Discourse, telling them, that as soon as the News could come to *Spain* of their being reduc'd, and that good Order was taken against falling again into the former Dangers, the King would order them to be restor'd to their Liberty. All these Expressions were not of Force to satisfy those *Indians*, who on the contrary began to complain of the General, because they either suspected, or were told by some of our Men, that he would not observe the safe Conduct, and promise he had made them in the King's Name, and on which they had rely'd ; and that in Case *Sultan Zayde* were continu'd in the *Philippine* Islands, it was certain they would send his Son, Prince *Gartolano* into *Europe*, by the Way of *New Spain*. The general being acquainted with these melancholly Reflections of theirs, thought it concern'd the Reputation of the Christian Religion in general, and of the *Spanish* Nation in particular, to dispell those Jealousies, and therefore he writ to them, and directed the Captain, who carry'd the Letters, to perswade the King not to conceive the least Mistrust of the King's Word, and Security he had confided in. This compos'd their Thoughts, and they either did, or pretended to take Comfort.

The Prisoners came with the Forces to the City, which the Fleet saluted with its Cannon, and were answer'd by the Artillery and small Shot from the Walls and Forts. The King landed in a Garden the Governour had without the Walls, where he repos'd himself that Night, and when Lodgings were provided for him, with the greatest State that could be, and answerably for other Prisoners, according to their Qualities, *Don Pedro* enter'd *Manila* with the Forces, and Ostentation of Captives and Booty. There wanted not Triumphal Arches, with such Inscriptions as are Generally set on them in Honour of Conquerors. The Habit of the Prisoners, in rich Mantles, Turbants and Plumes, was not sutable to their Fortune; as making their Countenances look more haughty, and representing Arrogancy. That King was strong body'd, and his Limbs well Knit; his Neck, and great Part of his Arms he wore naked; his Skin being of the Colour of a Cloud, rather inclin'd to Black than Tawny. The Features of his Face were like

an

Prisoners disconsolate.

Don Pedro's Entry into Manila.

Description of the King of Ternate.

an *European*. His Eyes large, full, and sparkling, to which they add the Fiercenefs of long Eyebrows, thick Beards and Whifkers, and lank Hair. He always wore his *Campilane*, or Cimiter, and *Criz*, or Dagger; the Hilts of them both refembling the Heads of Snakes gilt. This is affirm'd by Officers that attended, and convers'd with him familiarly, to whom he was obligingly Courteous, and it appears by Relations, and by the Picture drawn to the Life, which the General fent into *Spain* for the King.

Rejoycings　　The Rejoycings for the Victory were continu'd with much Solemnity, the *Indians*, who were the principal Subject of them, being prefent. The King of *Ternate* underftanding that Meffengers were fending away to *Spain* to carry the News of the Succefs, and Account of the Prifoners, writ a fhort Letter to the King, intermixt with Commendations of *Don Pedro de Acunna* and fome other *Spanifh* Commanders. He reprefented the change of his Condition, with fomewhat of Submiffion, but not Humility, or rather Meannefs; and intreated his Majefty to extend his Royal Goodnefs towards the Conquer'd, for his own Magnanimity's fake, and on Account of the perpetual Fidelity, and Vaffalage they had fworn to him. This Letter was writ by another Hand, and in *Spanifh*. When it was given him to fign, the King turn'd the upfide down, and Writ his Name on the white half Page in *Perfian* Characters, thinking he had fign'd at the Beginning, or Top of the Letter, as is practis'd by the Princes of thofe Countries. The *Moluccos* being Reduc'd, our Minifters and Preachers went over thither, and the Voice of the Gofpel refounded again in the utmoft Borders of the Earth.

F I N I S.

THE

INDEX.

Barbofa

INDEX.

INDEX.

Directions for placing of the C U T S.

PLace the Map before Page 1. The Cut of the *Champan* and *Junk* before Page 5. The Melancholly Tree, and *Molucco* Habit, before Page 8. The *Carcoa* and *Almadia* before Page 61.

E R R A T A.

PAge 4, Line 7, *for* 1404, *read* 1494. p. 4, l. penult, *for* Nagalhaens, *r.* Magalhaens. p. 8, l. 28, *for* deferves *r.* deferve. p. 10, l. 13, *for* roving *r.* rowing. p. 11, l. 4, *for* Caeiz, *r.* Caciz. p. 17, l. 8, *for* Inlguez, *r.* Iniguez. p. 26, l. 3, in the Marginal Note, *for* mad *r.* made. p. 33, in the firft Marginal Note, *for* Portuguefe Poffeffion *r.* Portuguefes take Poffeffion. F. 42, in the third Marginal Note, *for* King of *Tydore*, *r.* King of Gilolo. p. 49, and ellewhere, *for Mindanos r.* Mindanao. p. 54, l. 30, *for Cachilas r.* Cachiles. Ibid. l. 44, *for Babie*, *r.* Babu. p. 49, l. 35, *for* Falcage *r.* Foliage. p. 60, l. 36, *for* Reparations *r.* Preparations. p. 62, l. 37, *for* did they not look, *r.* had they not look'd. p. 63, l. 4, *for* Advantages, *r.* Advantageou*r.* p. 77, l. 33, *for* cavil *r.* cavil. p. 97, in the fecond Marginal Note, *for* Duenas from, *r.* Duenas fent from. p. 118, in the third Marginal Note, *for Cachil Mandrata*, *r.* Cachil Mandraxa. p. 120, in Marginal Note, *for* Nuno *r.* Duarte. p. 140, in the third Marginal Note, *for* 820, *r.* and 20.